D1493867

ALSO BY DIETRICH FISCHER-DIESKAU

Wagner and Nietzsche
The Fischer-Dieskau Book of Lieder

SCHUBERT'S SONGS

SCHUBERT'S SONGS

A Biographical Study

by

DIETRICH
FISCHER-DIESKAU

Translated from the German by

Kenneth S. Whitton

Limelight Editions   New York   1991

Second Limelight Edition, September 1991
Translation Copyright © 1976 by Dietrich Fischer-Dieskau and
Kenneth S. Whitton

ISBN 0–87910–006–0

Manufactured in the United States of America

Library of Congress Cataloging in Publication Data
Fischer-Dieskau, Dietrich, 1925–
Schubert's songs.
Reprint. Originally published: New York : Knopf, 1977.
Translation of Auf den Spuren der Schubert-Lieder.
Bibliography: p.
Includes indexes.
1. Schubert, Franz, 1797–1828.
2. Schubert, Franz, 1797–1828. Songs.
3. Composers—Austria—Biography.
I. Title.
ML410.S3F573 1984   784.3′0092′4   84–790

To
Heinz Friedrich
in gratitude

CONTENTS

TRANSLATOR'S NOTE

For this edition, explanatory biographical and historical notes have been inserted where necessary to help the English-speaking reader, and the relevant number from Otto Erich Deutsch's *Thematic Catalogue* has been added to each song. There is every likelihood that Schubert's Lieder will eventually be known by these Deutsch numbers, which are given in the three books of texts issued with the author's three-volume recording of some five hundred Schubert Lieder, Deutsche Grammophon: Vol. I, DGG 2720006 (643547–643558); Vol. II, DGG 2720022 (2561013–2561025); and Vol. III, DGG 2720059 (2561235–2561238). The datings of the Lieder given here agree in the main with those in the books of texts, unless there were compelling reasons to alter them.

Except where it is essential for the sake of clarity the titles of the Lieder have not been translated, for the excellent reasons that were advanced by the late Maurice Brown in his Schubert biography: 'There are no generally accepted equivalents amongst the several English versions of these titles, and to give yet more, and still different, English titles seemed more likely to confuse, than to clarify the position.'

I am most grateful to Dietrich Fischer-Dieskau and his secretary, Diether Warneck, for their interest and assistance with problems of translation, to Miss Anne Carter, of Cassell & Co., for her patient and enthusiastic editorial contribution to this labour of love, and to my wife, for her help at all stages of the work.

KENNETH S. WHITTON

ONE

The Composer

Franz Schubert transformed a world of poetry into music. He raised the art song (*Kunstlied*) to hitherto unknown heights and laid bare the essence of all art: intensity, concentration, a distillation into the purest of forms. 'Nature and Art seem to shun one another, but before one realises it, they have found each other again.' Schubert's works confirm Goethe's wise *aperçu*.

We live in an age which rejoices in paradoxes. This is particularly obvious to those of us who perform Schubert's Lieder, either professionally or as amateurs. No matter how great our admiration for Schubert may be, we only realise later in life what it is that raises him so far above the level of other composers: Schubert is *authentic*. His 'style' should not really be called style, since his successors have accustomed us to think of 'style' as something affected, something attained by 'art', in a studio. Schubert writes as he thinks, feels and speaks, and his thoughts, feelings and words are faithfully reflected in the notes of his music. This must be called a 'natural style', although we should not wish to claim that such a natural style is the hall-mark of the great composer. There are far too many important exceptions. But we would repeat: The musician whose style is 'natural' is one of the miracles of music. That the public and the critics ever managed to consider Schubert as an intuitive creative artist *only* surely proves that they do not believe in miracles?

Almost all of his contemporaries, even the musicians, underestimated Schubert's greatness. It is true that, in his continual hungering after knowledge, he preferred the company of literary men and painters, and that, in his circle of friends, only a few composers are to be found—and they too had little enough to say about him later. Apart from Beethoven (whom he probably did not want to meet) and Hummel, whose sporadic praises pleased him, there was first and foremost Anselm Hüttenbrenner (1794–1868) who, however, even in Schubert's lifetime, lived mostly in Graz, as a landowner, composer and Director of Music. (The songs which he began to write in 1850, to poems already set by Schubert, betray a Schubertian influence.) Another friend from his student days under Antonio Salieri, and a fellow choir-boy from the years in the *Konvikt*—the Imperial and Royal City Seminary—was the composer and conductor Benedikt Randhartinger (1802–1893). Franz Lachner (1803–1890), who was far and away the best musician in the Schubert circle, was his closest friend. Like all the children of the Lachner family (the sisters included), this son of an unknown Bavarian village organist was an organist, too. Lachner came to Vienna in 1822 when he was twenty. A brilliant success in a music competition rescued the young man from penury and provided him with the position of organist in the Protestant church. Schubert and Lachner did not become closer friends until 1826, when Lachner, then Deputy Conductor at the Kärtnertor Theatre, began to hold musical evenings at his home at which some of Schubert's works were performed. Along with an extraordinary amount of chamber music, Franz Lachner, an extremely prolific composer, also wrote songs which betray a strong Schubertian influence and often set, quite independently, the same poems as Schubert. One might count Lachner and Randhartinger among the first to help the Lied on its triumphal progress round the world. After Schubert's death, however, both men held exaggerated opinions of their own importance and were therefore in some part responsible for those misleading judgements which damaged Schubert's reputation for so long. Randhartinger, for example, could write: 'I am truly sorry that he remained something of a dilettante to the end', and Lachner, speaking to the Schubert scholar, Max Friedländer, in 1884, said: 'It is a pity that Schubert didn't learn as much as I did, since, with his extraordinary talents, he could have become a master too.'

Yet it was only Schubert's work that survived. We should not forget nevertheless how shamefully few of his songs have actually become part and parcel of the general musical consciousness. His enormous output seems to have militated against this, and it is certainly to the credit of our much-maligned commercial music industry that it has managed to rescue hitherto unknown treasures from oblivion.

The speed of Schubert's way of working, the ease with which he composed, has led critics time and again to overstress the 'intuitive' side of his character and the 'unconscious' element in his composing. Yet this 'intuition' is always only a beginning, the raw material, as it were, nothing more. The anecdote that Schubert is supposed not to have recognised one of his own early songs is grist to the mill of those who claim that the creator of more than six hundred songs could not have achieved this as part of a conscious process. Such a point of view fails to recognise *a fortiori* an undeniable factor in Schubert's instrumental music—namely, the proof of his wrestling with structural and contextual problems.

Nor is the often-heard assertion that Schubert simply 'threw off' his compositions and was content to abide by his first version anywhere near the truth. Schubert's way of working was different from Haydn's, Mozart's or Beethoven's. It is strange that he rarely made sketches, a fact which contributed substantially to the 'throwing off' legend. It is true that the musical 'polishing', which makes Beethoven's sketch-books look like battlefields, was not Schubert's method. Since the work was already clearly conceived in his head, he was able to write down a composition from beginning to end and corrections were only rarely necessary. If, after the last revision, the work did not satisfy his intentions, it would be begun again after three days, a few weeks, six months or even several years. Thus, he frequently made different versions of the same texts after varying periods of time—which led to confusion, since it was not always the final version which found its way into the printed editions.

Because Schubert often composed a series of songs in one day —five on 19th August 1815, six on the 25th of the same month and as many as eight on 19th October 1815—many people have felt able to deduce that such productivity could only be the result of instinctive inspiration. One glance at the concise accuracy with which he put his intentions down on paper should give the lie to such fantasies. It is true that Schubert supplied only a few indications of dynamics in his songs, yet, where they do exist, the surest way to the best interpretation is to follow them to the letter. If the strophic songs, in particular, lack detailed notations, it is clear that the treatment of words and emotions varies from stanza to stanza.

In all of Schubert's works, in the largely instrumental as well as in the vocal works, *piano* and *pianissimo* play a very important rôle in the resolution of contrasts as well as in the introduction of the main themes. The additional dynamic significance of the *crescendo* —and *diminuendo*—signs should also be noted. These dynamics are never merely externals—they obey an internal logic.

Can genius, the most sublime manifestation of intellectuality, *really* work passively to the dictates of hypnosis? Shortly before his death, Schubert considered resuming the study of counterpoint with Simon Sechter, a leading exponent of the theory of music, a proof, surely, of his awareness of the need for ordering and structuring his first inspirations?

In his *Kulturgeschichte der Neuzeit* (A Cultural History of Modern Times), Egon Friedell describes the gauche, bespectacled, obstinate suburban schoolmaster whose private world and greatest joy were the conversations at the *Heurigen*—the Viennese festival of the new wine—and who was the first to show mankind what a Lied really was: 'Just as the German *Märchen* was created by the Grimm Brothers, not invented but raised to a work of art', wrote Friedell, 'so Schubert ennobled the folk-song and gave it a place alongside the highest forms of art.' But this remark should not lead us to believe that Schubert was a 'folksy' artist. This was made abundantly clear when, in his later years, Schubert gradually abandoned the strophic form.

He was torn between two worlds. Music as a tonal, dynamic form, the beautiful illusion of aesthetics, the dominating element in many of his early songs, found its essence endangered. Schubert's love of the ingenuous clashes with his love of expression. Nowhere more than in music does the ingenuous seem to be nurtured and developed by technical ability. But its very marriage to verse compels music to reassert itself.

To achieve this, Franz Schubert orientated himself on Goethe. The titanic lyrics of *Prometheus* or *An Schwager Kronos* became the medium (and, at that time, certainly not the obvious medium) for plumbing the unknown depths of the soul. Schubert, the Lieder composer, a child of the new age in his surprising major–minor modulations, fertilises Schubert, the instrumental composer, even beyond the five actual cases in which Lieder were the direct models for instrumental works.

These authentic song-variations offer to the miniature art-form an inexhaustible supply of new material. Probably heading the list are the variations on the theme of *Der Tod und das Mädchen* from the D minor String Quartet, probably one of Schubert's most impressive movements; then the use of the C sharp minor cantilena from *Der Wanderer* in the C major Fantasia for piano as a basis for ingenious variations which illuminate the musical idea from all sides. The difficult but joyous Variations for flute and piano on *Trockene Blumen* should also be mentioned here, as well as the very demanding A flat major Variations on *Sei mir gegrüßt* which form the slow movement of the C major Fantasia for violin and piano. Finally, the timeless charm of the *Trout* theme with its metamorphoses in the Pianoforte Quintet in A major. Schubert's creative sensibility has coloured the tone, and colour and tone acknowledge their relationship in a musician from whom flow never-ending riches. The art of transition, which was to become the glory of modern music, is hinted at early in Schubert's works.

The narrow view of Schubert based on the falsely sentimental picture of a 'Schwammerl' ['Tubby'—Schubert's nickname—Ed.] has been replaced for a large section of the public by an appreciation of the true radiant force of his work—particularly for the most recent generations, unencumbered by old-fashioned notions. It has taken long enough for the general public to accord him the independent position which is his by right—and not to place him in the shadow of Haydn, Mozart and Beethoven. Those who deny him the rôle of innovator must be deaf to the futuristic chords which can be heard in the piano sonatas, the quartets, the String Quintet, and in *Die Winterreise*; one is astonished at every turn. Perhaps the pedants have seen him in such a light because he is so difficult to categorise? Nomenclatures such as 'classical predecessor of Romanticism', 'the Romantic outsider of Classicism', mean little to those truly bewitched by him.

Our concentration on the relationship of the songs to Schubert's life is justified not only by his acknowledged reputation as the 'Prince of Song', a title granted to him during his lifetime and enjoyed by none more than he. The first truly comprehensive publication of his Lieder on LP records gave me the stimulus to collect material, and the idea of offering my own contribution to the truly vast literature on Schubert. Much to my surprise, and in much greater compass than intended, my work on the Lieder produced a literary portrait which, in broad outlines and with the help of typical examples, covered a century of German lyric poetry, from the German Anacreontics by way of the Classics to the Romantics. Poems set to music by Schubert from the older world literatures, those of Aeschylus, Anacreon, Petrarch, Shakespeare, Ossian and Scott, for example, without exception exercised a considerable influence on Schubert's century; he knew them through the translations of his friends or of distinguished poets of his age.

There is really little to tell about Schubert's life; he lived it from within, under the compulsion of composition which was his attempt to impose a form on his life. He needed to imagine what he could not experience. That is why he loved poets above all others. They gave him inspiration and stimulus, they offered him pictures and shapes, a reality which he would otherwise never have known. Led by them, he could enter the realm of the word, and could enjoy such an intimate relationship with them because he so rarely thought of himself.

The literature on Schubert, now swollen to about four thousand titles, is based on a very limited number of documents mostly unearthed by the Austrian scholar, Professor Otto Erich Deutsch.[1] All who write on Schubert are indebted to his labours. Faced with these documents, we must in many cases resort to vague speculation; in others, we must strive to reach the median of probability in the reminiscences of Schubert's friends, culled from their fading memories after Schubert's death and which are therefore often contradictory. Fortunately, Schubert's letters and sketches offer a more reliable gloss on these events. But the enormous gaps in our knowledge are made visible when one thinks of Beethoven's fifteen hundred or so letters and Mozart's three hundred. The few Schubert documents that we do possess are all the more important because not many of his actual conversations have been handed down. I have not hesitated to make use of certain works and song-texts—even when they are of dubious literary value—to fill in some of these gaps. Above all, they fill in *psychological* gaps. The fact that Schubert's creativity is uniquely related to his life is of great value.

[1] Deutsch, D. E.: *Schubert: A Documentary Biography* (trs. Eric Blom), London, 1946 and *Schubert: Memoirs by his Friends* (trs. Ley and Nowell), London, 1958. It can be seen from this collection that much of our information on Schubert's life is taken from recollections made late in life by sometimes unreliable witnesses.

Schubert's music was truly his life's work. His life is a mere shadow and it is not surprising that the world around him was of little significance. The texts of his songs hint at the bitterness within him, and these texts can perhaps explain how complete a representation of and for his age he was, without presenting us simply with sentimental pictures of the romantic *Biedermeier*[1]. Perhaps he was interpreting in music the day-dreams of his friends.

It is typical of our age that it has no such protoartist—not among musicians at least. The food for the intellect that Schubert offered his contemporaries and their grandchildren is still enjoyed by young people today because the power of his art transcends the mediocrity or evanescence of many of the poems that he chose. Sorrow and happiness, humility and arrogance, modesty and pride, contemplation and passion speak to us out of Schubert's music, now as then. We know that Schubert did not command such immediacy of musical language at all times in his short career. If we examine his songs from the first to the last, we can see how he developed into a musical poet. At the beginning, he simply supplied a background to the poem. As he developed, his work took on the character of a translation into the language of music, and, in that process, the music frequently defines the poetic thought more precisely—or develops it further.

There are three basic Lied-types: In the *strophic* song, the melody and the accompaniment do not change from stanza to stanza. In the *scenic* song, several contrasting sections are combined in different keys and tempi. In the '*through-composed*' (*durchkomponiert*) song, a single accompaniment unites thoughts and moods which are independent of the stanzas of the poem. There is also the *modified strophic* song where the original melody is slightly altered in the reprise. When we examine the songs, we see that Schubert did not develop from the 'elementary' strophic song to the 'advanced' through-composed song, as it were. He remains faithful to the strophic song to the end, as *Am Meer* or *Die Taubenpost* (D 957, nos. 12 and 14) prove.

When we think of the high regard and the love which Schubert's Lieder evoked from his friends and his first listeners, then we can scarcely doubt that, despite all the faith he had in himself and in the

[1] The name given to an art style in Germany between 1815 and 1848. A sober domesticity. (Ed.)

sureness of his technique, he did not abide rigidly by his principles of composition in all cases. Popular taste was certainly the deciding factor in many of his light pieces, without however damaging the song in question. It is evident from his songs that Schubert was well aware that his music was expressing something that no one before him had been able to convey.

Schubert always manages to surprise us. Within a relatively narrow technical compass lie inexhaustible riches. And always, when he leaves a beloved poetical territory, such as 'birds' or 'wandering' or 'childhood' or 'death' to turn to another, *he* changes too. His material reveals itself to him through the love he brings to it. Art is no different from other spheres of life; without love, the secrets remain hidden for ever.

TWO

Beginnings

'Music' was hardly an esoteric term in the Imperial Vienna of Schubert's day. There were not only the catchy tunes of the ballad-singers, harpists and the street musicians, and the music of the inns and dance-halls. But serious music was also the daily bread of the population. Vienna was the rendezvous of the musical world —albeit not for very long. Of its three deities, Mozart was still a living memory for countless people; Haydn was to live for another twelve years to become a contemporary of Schubert, while Beethoven's titanic presence dominated the city until his death in 1827 at the age of fifty-seven. Vienna's serious musical history was to all intents and purposes only a generation old. The symphony, the sonata and the quartet were the most popular musical forms, since opera was largely an Italian preserve.

Gluck, Mozart and Weber had, of course, some success as composers of songs, although not on the same scale as their other compositions. There were, however, no local precursors of Schubert's style, apart from one or two minor Austrian song-composers whose influence can be traced here and there in his works. But, even in the wider German-speaking area, there were no forerunners of this most personal style, if one excepts the models for the early ballads which came from the pen of Johann Rudolf Zumsteeg (1760–1802) and which are to be found in the Supplement to the first *Gesamtausgabe* (Collected Edition) published by Breitkopf & Härtel—but these were more teach-yourself exercises for young Schubert. Nor can one find a precursor in Mozart, whose *Das Veilchen* was the first of a new type of Kunstlied and from whom one could certainly have expected an important contribution in this field had he lived longer.

Beethoven, too, with his quite different, idiosyncratic song-style demonstrates at the most what potential expressiveness there was in the Lied at that period.

Songs, dance music and piano pieces were widely distributed by the publishing houses. The pre-eminence of the piano popularised the weekly *soirées musicales* which took place before a goodly number of guests in the houses of rich merchants, lawyers or civil servants, and where all types of chamber music and naturally also solo and part songs were performed. All this served as a stimulus for Schubert, and his deeply felt songs replaced the trivialities accepted hitherto and made him the centre of a circle of friends whose love and admiration can best be appreciated in the memoirs of the painter Moritz von Schwind (1804–1871). Many years after Schubert's death, he returned to Vienna, not to see the town, but to recall those places where his friend Franz's piano-playing and old Michael Vogl's singing had so won the hearts of the 'Schubertianer' at the houses of Josef von Spaun, Franz von Bruchmann or Karl Hönig.

But we have anticipated our story. Franz Theodor Florian Schubert (1763–1830) and his family played music together as did most teachers' families. Besides the easy duets, trios and quartets, they also played the more difficult Beethoven quartets (opus 18, for example). It was not surprising that the young Franz, after listening fascinated, should soon be included in the quartet. Such amateur music-making developed his feeling for musical form and beauty. Painful memories, such as the picture of his dead brother in his coffin and his usually stern father weeping, are paired with happy ones, such as his delight in playing with his little sister, Maria Theresia. Franz could not spoil 'Reserl' enough; he cradled the child when she was asleep and composed a lullaby which was hummed in chorus with his brothers to get the little one to go to sleep. Fate's major and minor modes are revealed from the beginning in that tense relationship which was to reappear so fascinatingly in his music. This could also serve as the beginning to our story.

It was Schubert's eldest brother, Ignaz (1785–1844), twelve years his senior and a teaching assistant with their father, who gave Franz, the fourth son, born on 31st January 1797, his first piano lesson. His sister Maria Theresia (1801–1878) recounted later how Franz approached an apprentice carpenter to let him see the inside of a piano workshop. The second of the five surviving children,

Ferdinand Lukas Schubert (1794–1859), wrote in 1839, when he was the director of a teachers' training college in Vienna:

Franz was now receiving piano lessons from Ignaz. Piano, violin and voice instruction were given later by the *regens chori*, Michael Holzer, who often asserted, with tears in his eyes, that he had never had such a pupil 'for', he said, 'whenever I wanted to teach him something fresh, he knew it already; often I just sat there admiring him, speechless'.

Ignaz recalled later:

I was very surprised when, after only a few months, he informed me that he would not need my tuition any more and that from now on he wanted to manage on his own. And I must admit that, in a short time, I had to recognise him as a master, far superior to, and far beyond me.

Even today, anyone who wants to become a school teacher in Austria must be able to sing and to play an instrument. Franz Theodor Schubert took it for granted that all his sons would follow him into the teaching profession. After some beginners' instruction on the violin, it was time for the musical training which was always given to amateurs. Schubert's father, a stern, serious, energetic man, sent Franz to have singing lessons from Michael Holzer, the organist in the parish church of the Vier Heiligen Nothelfer in Liechtenthal, Schubert's birthplace and a suburb of Vienna. Schubert had to learn the music of the church services. His brother Ferdinand wrote in 1839:

At eleven, he was first soprano in the Liechtenthal church. Even at that age he performed everything with just the right expression.

A friend from Schubert's schooldays in the *Stadtkonvikt*, Anton Holzapfel (1792–1868) called Holzer 'a rather drunken but thorough contrapuntalist who taught all the Schubert brothers'. Josef von Spaun (1788–1865), later Schubert's most faithful friend, had this to say about Holzer: 'Schubert remained grateful to the end of his days to this fine old teacher who had the pleasure of having a Mass dedicated to him by his gifted pupil.' One can say of Holzer—at that time still in his mid-thirties—that he was the first true friend that Schubert had had outside the family. Ferdinand Schubert continues:

Franz also played a violin solo in the choir at that time and composed little songs, string quartets and piano pieces. His father was amazed by his rapid progress and was therefore determined to give him the opportunity of further training by getting him into the *Stadtkonvikt*.

There appeared in the official *Wiener Zeitung* of 3rd August 1808 an advertisement of a vacancy for a soprano voice in the Chapel Royal Choir. Schubert's father, convinced of his son's outstanding gifts and his beautiful voice, presented himself and his son without delay before the examiners. The President, Antonio Salieri (1750–1825), the all-powerful figure in Vienna's musical life—mainly because he had found favour with the Emperor—and Joseph Eybler agreed to admit Schubert; indeed they praised him highly.

The *Konvikt* had been re-founded by Emperor Franz II in 1803 to ensure that the clergy could supervise the teaching. The stern Principal, Innocenz Lang, who terrified his pupils, later became the Rector of the University and a *Hofrat* (Court Councillor). In order to preserve social distinctions the worthy fathers had created two schools, one for the scions of the nobility and one for the sons of officials and the lower officer ranks. (Both schools were closed in 1848.)

Ferdinand, a ready reporter of interesting details, writes of the entrance examination:

The boy [Schubert] wore a light-blue, almost white coat, so that the other people, and the other children who were to be admitted to the *Konvikt* made fun of him, saying things like 'he must be a miller's son, there's always got to be one of them' etc, etc.

But it was not the white coat alone that made the schoolmaster's son stand out—the Court *Kapellmeister* Salieri and Eybler, and the choral director, Phillip Korner, were impressed by his sure renderings of the vocal test pieces.

In autumn 1808, Schubert entered the *Konvikt* on the Universitätsplatz in Vienna as an Imperial choir-boy. The successful singers wore a handsome uniform, received a general secondary education and, apart from singing, also learned the violin and the piano. The parting from his family had probably been tearful, but this was soon forgotten when he quickly made new friends. Among these were Josef von Spaun, who played second violin in the school orchestra and who was to become Schubert's most faithful benefactor; then the cellist, Anton Holzapfel, the two violinists, Anton Hauer and Johann Leopold Ebner. The latter made many copies of Schubert's Lieder which were later to become invaluable substitutes for lost manuscripts.

Then there was Joseph Kenner (1794–1868), whose ballad *Der Liedler* (1815) Schubert comically, and at great length, set to music (D 209), the poet Johann Senn (1795–1857) and finally Albert Stadler (1794–1888), who, through his collection of Schubert's manuscripts and copies of his Lieder, became an important research source. With his friends, Schubert used to make music every day in the practice-rooms of the *Konvikt*—chamber-music, Lieder singing and four-handed piano music. The choir sang in the fifteenth-century Court Chapel and were accompanied in the Mass by its orchestra.

These rich opportunities for singing had a fateful significance for Schubert and the development of the Lied. Schubert's father was naturally thinking of the University course to which these school studies gave the *entrée*. His son was to have 'something better' than he had had.

On 17th April 1809, Schubert completed his first Semester successfully, which was not always to be the case in later years. His report says, *inter alia*:

> Report on the moral behaviour, the progress in studies and in music of the Court Chapel Choir boys of the k.k. [Imperial] *Konvikt* in the 1. Semester 1809 in Vienna.
>
> Schubert, Franz: Conduct: Very good, Studies: Good, Singing: very good, Piano: good, Violin: very good. Comment: A musical talent.
>
> LANG n.p. Principal

Franz von Schober, who was at a similar institution in Kremsmünster, received a confidential note from young Franz von Schlechta at the *Konvikt*. 'I particularly dislike the nasty faces that the prefects make at us. I feel so constricted and tearful.'

Spaun said that Schubert found the school 'uncongenial'. When Spaun then left in September, Schubert cried out: 'You're escaping from a prison, you lucky fellow. I am sorry that you are leaving.'

Shortly before this, however, they had all been upset by political events. On 13th May 1809, Napoleon had been defeated by the Austrians at Aspern, after two days of bloody fighting. The victors failed to press home the final attack however and gave Napoleon a much-needed respite, which he used on 6th July for the final defeat of the Austrians at Wagram. The provisions of the peace treaty signed at Schönbrunn destroyed the last remnants of Austrian patriotism. Spaun tells of the excitement among the pupils:

A student corps was formed as the French approached Vienna. Our pupils were forbidden to enlist; but when we heard the appeals to patriotism from Field Marshal Koller in the University Hall opposite and noted the enthusiasm with which the students were enlisting, we couldn't help enlisting too, and we returned jubilantly to the *Konvikt* with the red and white ribbons, the symbol of enlistment. The Principal received us with bitter reproaches, but we took no notice of them, for we were so enthusiastic—and we marched off in the next day or two. On the third day, there appeared a command from on high, from Archduke Rainer, ordering us to dismiss and, as we were then locked up in the *Konvikt* for several days, our playing at soldiers was over. We saw a howitzer grenade land in front of us on the University Square and burst in one of the lovely fountains. Suddenly there was an explosion in the house itself; a grenade had fallen on the *Konvikt* building. It went through all the floors right down to the first, where it exploded in the room of Walch, a prefect who was just turning the key to go into the room.

Johann Senn and Michael Rueskäfer, both *Konvikt* pupils, were sons of Tyrolese leaders who had continued to fight after the Armistice. Senn became a lifelong friend of Schubert. Kenner gives this description of him: 'A wonderfully friendly boy, an obstinate philosopher, open to his friends, but secretive to others, a generous, violent boy who hated discipline. His fate provoked my deepest sympathy.'

This fate was prepared for by the miniature revolt which broke out among the Tyrolese in the *Konvikt*. One pupil received a draconian punishment. Kenner continues:

The punishment caused a revolt among his friends who wanted to rescue him from his secretly imposed incarceration. Senn took part, as did Rueskäfer. The latter indeed left the *Konvikt* voluntarily. Senn lost his scholarship place because, although he was poor, he could not humiliate himself by accepting the justice of that punishment. His independent spirit became notorious; his indomitability was considered dangerous. He seemed to have known Schubert prior to this.

So it can be seen that the word 'prison' was justifiably used by Schubert. Distance certainly did not lessen the friendship with Johann Senn—it only intensified it. It also bore artistic fruit when, in 1822, Schubert set two of Senn's poems for which he felt an affinity.

The statutes of the *Konvikt* prescribed regular musical studies and the pupils certainly did not neglect them. Schubert's fellow-pupil Anton Holzapfel tells us:

The then Principal, the Reverend Innocenz Lang, of the Order of Pious Schools, had the happy idea of assembling an orchestra composed exclusively of *Konvikt* pupils of differing ages and he trained these not very accomplished young people to perform a whole symphony every evening and then to finish with a rousing overture. Lang paid for the stringed instruments and the rest himself, and even for the teacher of wind instruments. The Assistant Principal Schönberger donated the tympani. Since the Principal himself knew nothing about music, he put one of the oldest pupils in charge, and one of the younger, reliable choir-boys had to perform the onerous function of what could be described as 'orchestral attendant'. This duty, the very difficult one of lighting the tallow candles, stringing and tuning the instruments and keeping them and the scores in order, was carried out by Franz Schubert for a few years, while he performed as a violinist at the same time. Apart from the daily practice and religious duties, the Principal allowed the pupils to form small groups for the performance of string- and vocal-quartets; songs with piano accompaniments, especially Zumsteeg's ballads and songs, became very popular. Altogether, there was a good deal of hard music-making going on at this time in which Schubert (who was not yet the pianist he was later to become) took his active share.

Schubert was soon promoted from second violin and 'orchestral attendant' to assistant conductor to Wenzel Ruzicka (1752–1823), an indispensable figure in the life of the *Konvikt*. Born in Moravia, Ruzicka was Court organist and violist at the Burgtheater in Vienna; almost all the instrumental instruction at the *Konvikt* was under his supervision. Franz Eckel, a flautist in the *Konvikt* orchestra, says this about Schubert, the most gifted of his school friends:

> Even as a boy, Schubert lived an introspective intellectual life which never expressed itself in words, but almost always only in music. Even with his nearest friends, like Holzapfel and myself who were the first to read and sing these early Lieder when the ink was still wet on the paper, he was taciturn and uncommunicative, except in matters which concerned the divinity to which he dedicated his entire, though brief life. An inborn tactful balance of calm, seriousness, friendliness and good nature, allowed neither the friendships nor the enmities so common among young schoolboys. The less so since Schubert spent all his free time in the music room, usually alone; Holzapfel and I joined him only when he had written a song. Even if only a few of us knew of the songs he had composed in the *Konvikt*, all knew him as the first soprano of the Court Chapel, and first violinist and assistant conductor of the superb small orchestra.

Josef von Spaun, whom Schubert had met in the *Konvikt* in 1808, writes:

> Even as young as ten or eleven, Schubert was trying his hand at little songs, quartets and little piano pieces. He told me that he often put his thoughts down in music, but that his father must not know about it since he was against Schubert's becoming a musician. So I slipped him manuscript paper from time to time.

Throughout his life, Spaun introduced Schubert to new friends and encouraged him in his art. Spaun studied law later with Heinrich Watteroth at the University of Vienna and was friendly with the law students Johann Mayrhofer (1787–1836), Franz von Schober (1796–1882) and Joseph Witteczek (1787–1859), all of whom he introduced to Schubert.

The earliest surviving song by Schubert was composed on 30th March 1811: *Hagars Klage in der Wüste* (D 5), to a text by the Münster poet Levin Schücking, owes much to Zumsteeg's setting of the same poem. Wenzel Ruzicka showed the song to Antonio Salieri, and, in the course of time, Schubert, encouraged by Salieri's benevolent interest in him, became his pupil. Schubert had already composed some songs (now lost) before *Hagars Klage*. It is understandable why the influence of the veteran composer Zumsteeg (a friend of Schiller's, incidentally) on all the early ballad-like compositions was so strong. After all, Zumsteeg was considered to be the most important song-composer of his day and, to give him his due, he must be regarded as the first to give a stimulus to the Romantic German Lied. He was the first to challenge the rather dominant domestic strophic songs of the North German school, which was at that time the only vocal music available for solo voice, with his *Lieder und kleine Balladen* ('Songs and Short Ballads'), too full perhaps of dramatic effects, but the first to attempt to portray the atmosphere and the mood of a poem. He sometimes loosens the structure of a poem so much that the music simply perambulates *under* the text, illustrating it.

It was probably the music of Friedrich Schiller's fellow-pupil, then, which led Schubert to the works of that great poet and which certainly opened up to him the literature of that circle: Klopstock, Bürger, Matthisson and Goethe. One of the marginal fascinations of a study of Schubert is the journey that we make with him through contemporary German literature, which he also enriched in his own way.

The sense of improvisation and uninhibited dramatisation raises *Hagars Klage* well above the model of the more experienced, older composer. The fourteen-year-old Schubert was still influenced by what he had experienced as a three-year-old. At that time the Schubert house consisted of a room and kitchen. Schubert's mother, Maria Elisabeth Katharina Vietz, formerly a cook, it was said, had twelve of her fourteen children there between 1786 and 1801. Five survived. In the age of Emperor Franz ('The Good'), child mortality was accepted as inevitable, so that Schubert's father would simply record the births and deaths, faithfully but laconically, in the family Bible.

Schücking's poem begins: 'Here I sit on a hot, sandy hill, and there lies my dying child, longing for a drop of water, fighting off Death, weeping, and staring at its distraught mother. You must die, my little one! I have not a tear in these dry eyes to still your thirst.'

It is astonishing how Schubert, still a child himself, was able to share the agony of Hagar, whose child was doomed to die in the desert, and how he was able to end the song in a mood of consolation. All the immaturity and clumsiness are as nothing beside such clarity and such exciting creative power.

Schubert has left us a few compositions in the style of *Hagars Klage*, not really Lieder, but rather a type of cantata then in vogue. Since these are no longer being written, it is difficult to assess what rôle they played in the musical life of the period. They are like miniature domestic operas without scenery or orchestral accompaniments.

Whatever their function, Zumsteeg's models encouraged Schubert to employ a wide range of dramatic expression and introduced him to poems which were not really suitable for musical treatment—a superb exercise! In addition, Schubert could range over many keys, something Salieri would certainly not have permitted.

Schubert begins *Hagars Klage* in C minor and finishes in A flat major, after a closing *adagio*, incidentally, whose beauty quite eclipses its forerunner. (Schubert displays his love for wandering unconcernedly through the various keys again in *Orest auf Tauris* (1817, D 548) when he begins in C minor and ends in D major.)

Just as Grand Opera now replaced Zumsteeg as Schubert's model, so later (in 1815) the ballad opera and the Singspiel became the models for the shorter Lieder. The titles of the few songs that survive from this period—*Hagars Klage*, *Des Mädchens Klage* (D 6) and *Klaglied* (D 23)—betray the morbid attraction for most young people of lachrymose literature. From Schubert's prentice treatment of the text of *Klaglied*, it is plain that the poem, at this stage, is a mere excuse for the composition. He had no compunction about altering the text, repeating or juxtaposing single lines and sections to serve his purpose. It is rather curious that it should have been this very song which circulated as a satire, with new words, among the pupils in the *Konvikt*.

Of the two surviving versions of *Klaglied*, only the first is an autograph. Schubert's first extant song in simple strophic form so disregards the second, third and fourth stanzas of the poem that the final product is rather unsatisfactory. Friedrich Rochlitz's Goethe-like opening lines: 'Meine Ruh' ist dahin, meine Freud ist entflohen' ('My peace has gone, my joy has flown') might be said to be, at the most, a preparation for *Gretchen am Spinnrade*. *Klaglied* is the only strophic song from this period. It became the best-known of Schubert's early songs because of its similarity to folk-song, as the many copies of it show. It is also the earliest song to be printed by Czerny prior to the publication of the old Collected Edition of 1830.

In the autumn of 1810, Schubert had had a serious quarrel with his father. While Schubert longed to live the independent life of a musician, his father was still determined to make him a teacher and an organist. For a time, he even forbade the boy to visit the house. Spaun speaks of a 'storm'. There was no chance of either the deeply religious atmosphere of the family house or the father's subservient attitude to the police state of Metternich bringing about a reconciliation. Spaun speaks of Schubert at this time as being 'always serious and not very friendly'. His inborn sensitivity, heightened by the approach of puberty, had been expressed for a year or so in his choice of texts.

In *Eine Leichenphantasie* (D 7) we read: 'Take joy, O father, in your fine son, once the slumbering seeds have ripened'. After the mention of the word 'Valhalla', the song astonishingly foreshadows notes from Wagner's *Siegfried*. (The final version of the manuscript is undated, but Walther Dürr claims that the manuscript notations point to the same period of composition as *Hagars Klage*.) This Schiller poem of 1780 is dedicated to the father of his deceased friend, August von Hoven. Schiller's *Des Mädchens Klage* contains the lines: 'My heart is dead, my world is empty; Life has no more to offer me.'

Schubert was not dismayed by the task of setting Schiller's highly philosophical poems to music. He set forty-two of them in all, some several times. It is remarkable how he managed to blend these long and reflective poems with music. On the other hand it can be seen that the dramatic aspects, particularly the recitatives, of his operas are less penetratingly, less decisively handled than the epic songs. Perhaps this is not so surprising, however, when one considers the weak libretti that he had at his disposal. Nevertheless, the monstrous *Der Taucher* (D 77), all twenty-three pages of it, does display a loving submersion in Schiller's difficult theme. There is no lack of descriptions of nature, of dramatic action or of emotional scenes in this poem. After the diver's second attempt to retrieve the cup, an orchestral interlude follows the sighing melody which mourns the young man's death. Schubert's naïve marking is 'bedauernd' ('with regret').

The later *Die Bürgschaft* (D 246), composed in 1815, is more compact and more intense. The listener is almost overwhelmed by the fullness of nature imagery: torrential rain, forest streams and sunsets. The declamatory sections are musically so effective that one is not surprised that contemporary singers like Hans Hotter and Hermann Prey have restored this song to the concert repertoire. Schubert certainly solved the difficult problem of setting this enormously long poem to music, although one must add that the tyrant's closing speech has too much Viennese *Gemütlichkeit* in it to be wholly effective. Even Carl Loewe, soon to be hailed as the country's leading ballad poet, never wrote anything better than this; indeed, his own lapses into sentimentality took the genre *ad absurdum*.

These two Schubertian ballads are among the longest and the most expressive in the entire literature of the Lied. They also show that Schubert did not concentrate on shorter poems because of his inability to handle the longer forms; he wanted to fill a Lied with the whole gamut of emotions. It is therefore a misunderstanding *a priori* to see in a Lied only a musical miniature with a poetic base. A Schubert Lied contains within itself the essence of all drama and the emotional depth of a cosmic experience. The extensive, illustrative treatment of Schiller's ballads makes us hazard the guess that, had he lived for another twenty or thirty years, Schubert would certainly have composed music-dramas. As it is, he gave lovers of musical declamation *Der Taucher* (D 77), begun in September 1813 and finished in August 1814. (Mandyczewski in the first Schubert *Gesamtausgabe* (Collected Edition) gives two versions which differ particularly in the recitatives. Max Friedländer skilfully combined the two (D 77 and D 111) for the Peters Edition. I should recommend the latter version; even though it is not entirely faithful to the original, it is very effective.)

The agony caused by the unbearable conflict between his vocation and his father's wishes was heightened by his mother's serious illness. On 28th May 1812, while Schubert was still forbidden the house, she died of typhoid fever, the disease to which Schubert himself was later to succumb. The father and the son are supposed to have been reconciled over the grave. The picture of Schubert standing with his father and family at the graveside was to reappear many times in the poems which he chose to set. But a true reconciliation was only reached when the indefatigable Spaun had collected glowing critiques of Schubert's compositions. Later, in his memoirs, he wrote: 'Now the barriers were down; the father recognised Schubert's great talents and let him go his own way.'

'Began counterpoint on June 18th 1812', Schubert noted on a sheet of manuscript paper. Ruzicka was no longer capable of meeting Schubert's demands in this subject, and Salieri, the teacher of Beethoven, Hummel and later of Liszt as well, proved to be the right man for the task. Salieri's feud with Mozart will be recalled, a feud which gave rise to speculation about the cause of the latter's death. The pair were deeply divided. There were fundamental differences of opinion on the aesthetics of dramatic music. Mozart, on the side of the older *opera buffa*, was opposed to Gluck's new 'reformed' opera, with whose claims for sole validity Schubert, too, had to contend.

Like the other students, Schubert received Salieri's tuition *gratis*. Much envied by his classmates, he was allowed to leave the *Konvikt* for these private lessons. Although he was disappointed at the beginning with the boring discussion of his homework (part songs), Schubert became very enthusiastic when he was introduced to the works of Gluck. In the school, he performed whole scenes from *Orfeo ed Euridice* and *Iphigénie en Tauride*. Soon, however, there arose a disagreement between teacher and pupil. Spaun explains:

It came about because Salieri disapproved of the one art form that irresistibly attracted his pupil, namely, the German Lied. The poems of Goethe, Schiller and the others which filled the young composer with enthusiasm and the irresistible desire to set them to music were distasteful to the Italian. He saw only barbarous words, not worth the trouble of setting to music. Salieri implored Schubert in all earnestness not to bother with such compositions just now, but to wait until he was older and more mature.

In addition to chamber music, a few occasional cantatas, string quartets, a Salve Regina, Kyrie and symphonic overtures, Schubert also wrote some songs at this period, among them Schiller's *Der Jüngling am Bache* (D 30), dated 24th September 1812. This can be regarded as Schubert's first true Lied, and only *Gretchen am Spinnrade* emulates it.

On no other work of this period is Schubert's personal style so clearly stamped. The four stanzas are to be found in Schiller's comedy *Der Parasit* (based on the French of L. B. Picard), and they attracted Schubert to write two further settings in later years. Even in this early version, the treatment of each stanza is effectively varied, particularly in the passionate transition from the initial F major to D minor when the lover laments that nature's thousand voices can find no echo in him. It must be said, however, that the piano part is rather dull. The 1815 revision of the song (D 192), simplified and transposed into the minor mode, hardly competes with the better-known third version of 1819 (D 638).

Accompanied by Spaun, Schubert frequented the balcony of the Kärtnertor Theatre where he saw operas by Boieldieu and Isouard, Gluck's *Iphigénie*, Cherubini's *Medea* and Mozart's *Zauberflöte*. He was thrilled by the art of the soprano Frau Anna Milder and of the baritone Michael Vogl, destined to become his enthusiastic apostle. 'I should love to meet Vogl and fall at his feet for the way he played Orestes', Schubert said.

The Court Choir boys regularly took part in public concerts and became familiar with Haydn's choral works. This music opened up new worlds to Schubert. After his voice had broken he gave up choral singing and, in 1813, at the age of sixteen, not without a feeling of relief he left the *Konvikt*. He sang as an alto in the Mass by Peter Winter for the last time, and we can read on his score: 'Schubert, Franz, screeched for the last time, June 26th 1812'.

He now accompanied his three brothers on the guitar. For the rest of his life, he had to make do with a modest, light baritone voice, singing in the vocal quartets so popular in the Vienna of that time.

We can see, with the benefit of hindsight, that the years in the *Konvikt* had an immense and mainly positive effect on Schubert. Not many other composers of his day were privileged to enjoy such a purposeful, concentrated and disciplined musical training before the age of fifteen.

Late in the autumn of 1812, Salieri had given his pupil three arias and a chorus to Italian texts of Pietro Metastasio as a composition exercise. These were problems which Schubert, quite differently orientated, was unable to solve at a stroke, yet the technicalities of his solutions betray a degree of concentration that could only come from a thorough and exacting musical grounding. In the early songs, and, in particular, in the Italian arias, Schubert is still a learner; this can even be seen in the notation marks which separate the piano hands, each of which has its own distinctive system. This explains the frequent key-changes in these settings. The best of them is probably *Pensa, che questo istante* ('Consider that this moment') (D 76), written for the Italian bass, Luigi Lablache. Schubert makes a conscious effort to keep a dignified vocal line and reduces the accompaniment to a minimum. To suit the Italian vocal style, he abandons all picturesque descriptive detail, a feature of almost all Italian vocal music.

The librettist Pietro Metastasio (1698–1782) had spent his last years in Vienna. By chance, he had once found a room on the third storey of that house in which the young Haydn had his miserable garret. He had been once an Abbé, but had apparently given up his vocation for women and alcohol. Everyone took him to be a poet of genius, whereas he was, in fact, only a very good librettist. He had been an Imperial Court poet, although he had always considered the organising of Court entertainments to be his main task.

Further compositions of this sort followed in 1820 and 1827. Spaun comments: 'He [Salieri] gave him short Italian poems to set to music but they left the impetuous composer cold; he barely understood the language, and had to struggle with these things without any real success.'

But neither disapproval nor prohibitions could force Schubert to withstand the temptation of working from the very beginning in his own language. Albert Stadler, the author of two Romances and a name-day poem which Schubert set to music, and a newcomer to the *Konvikt*, wrote in his memoirs:

> Spaun, Holzapfel and I and anyone else interested kept him supplied with ideas, and we rummaged through as many lyric and epic poets as we could get our hands on. He hardly ever turned down our choice. The genius was awakened and we watched with growing wonder as its mighty pinions rapidly unfurled. Yet Schubert was far from vain; I should say that he was the last to realise the high level of artistic excellence that he had already reached.

Schubert was soon to be more selective in his choice of texts. His early experimentation has often been interpreted, wrongly, as a lack of literary discrimination. The literary value of a text was only of secondary importance to Schubert; he was mainly concerned with the poem's function as a begetter of music.

On 4th May 1813 Schubert wrote a song to a poem far removed from the contemporary literature of sentimentality: Alexander Pope's *The Dying Christian to his Soul*, translated by J. G. Herder as *Verklärung* (D 59). This Lied marks the beginning of Schubert's conscious attempt to make an intellectual unity out of the manifold elements of form and expression.

Johann Gottfried Herder (1744–1803) studied theology under J. G. Hamann and Immanuel Kant in Königsberg. Later, in Strasbourg, he met the young Goethe, who was to be greatly influenced by the humanistic ideas of the older man. Herder became an important figure in the history of the German Lied through his translations of folk-songs; indeed, he coined the term Volkslied (now accepted as a German word) in his collection *Stimmen der Völker in Liedern* ('Voices of the People in Songs'), which appeared in 1778–1779. His scholarly essays, such as the *Abhandlung über den Ursprung der Sprache* ('Essay on the Origin of Language'), on Ossian and on Shakespeare, and also his *Ideen zur Philosophie der Menschheit* ('Thoughts on the Philosophy of the History of Mankind') continued to influence the intellectual development of Germany long after his death. Two of Herder's songs (*Verklärung* and *Eine altschottische Ballade*) stand at the beginning and end of Schubert's creative life.

Unlike many of their contemporaries, Herder and the Schubert of

1811–1813 had no sentimental feelings about, or longing for death. In the recitative to *Verklärung*, Schubert sings energetically: 'Grave, where is thy victory? Death, where is thy sting?'

The news that Theodor Körner had been killed at the battle of Gadebusch in Mecklenburg on 26th August 1813 greatly affected Schubert, for he had been an enthusiastic supporter of the Wars of Liberation. Spaun had introduced him to the 21-year-old 'Poet of Freedom' at the beginning of 1813 and Ferdinand Schubert reported the deep impression that the meeting had made on his brother. Körner had lived in Vienna since 1811 and his plays had been so successful there that there was the possibility of an attractive contract with the Burgtheater. In particular, his version of the legend of the Hungarian patriot *Zriny* had been received with noisy approval. The performance in the previous December had coincided with the news of Napoleon's crushing defeat in Russia.

It was in Vienna that Körner had decided to give up his studies in favour of writing plays and his decision encouraged Schubert to devote himself exclusively to music. The political developments drove Körner, eager to join the fray, from Vienna: 'Should I be writing comedies', he lamented, 'when I know that I have the courage and the strength to take part in a serious play?' Within five months of volunteering for the Lützow Freikorps, he was dead.

In 1815, Schubert set thirteen of Körner's poems, as well as the libretto of *Der vierjährige Posten* (D 190). Körner's battle-poems are hardly likely to appeal to a world sickened by war. The setting of the *Schwertlied* (D 170) is particularly comical; sixteen times at the end of the refrain, the chorus has to bellow 'Hurrah'! And underneath, Schubert writes: 'Clanking of swords at the Hurrah's', which one might just take as irony.

Nevertheless, some of the charming love poems should be performed more often. In these, Schubert is as far removed from heroics as he is from aestheticism. The hesitant lament of *Gebet während der Schlacht* (D 171) is reminiscent of the moment of paralysing nostalgia in *Kriegers Ahnung* without approaching the latter's musical impact, or the pathos of the leavetaking in *Schiffers Scheidelied*. Schubert prefers to imagine himself triumphant in love, like the hero in *Das war ich* (D 174). He notes proudly on the manuscript of *Amphiaraos* (D 166), the ballad of the death of the visionary hero in the Theban War, that the song was composed in five hours. This dramatic *tour de force* confirms the composer's feeling for the potentialities of the voice, even though the text somewhat reduces our enjoyment of the song.

There are two settings of *Sängers Morgenlied*, the first (D 163) teasing, the second (D 165), pensive; the latter's beautiful melody makes it the more persuasive. A rare treatment of a vaguely humorous poem is *Das gestörte Glück* of 1815 (D 309), where the young hero is always interrupted on the point of kissing his girl; as might be expected with Schubert, the joke is made so subtly that unless the singer stresses it, it will go unnoticed.

The little cantata *Auf der Riesenkoppe* (D 611) of March 1818 portrays Körner climbing the slopes of the Riesengebirge from his home town of Dresden. Schubert's similar love of the outdoors is depicted in the naturalistic yodel of the piano accompaniment, a device repeated only in the coloratura runs of *Der Hirt auf dem Felsen* or in *Am Erlafsee*.

A glance at one of Schubert's early poems—he wrote seven—which he also set to music as a vocal trio, attests to his early interest in the treatment of modified and unmodified vowels and of the diphthong. He seems never to have tired of reading the poems of Friedrich Schiller, and, in this poem, we can find a strong resemblance to the latter's *Elysium*, which Schubert made into a grandiose Lied five years later.

> Und im ewig schönen Flor
> Blühe seines Lebens Kranz.
>
> Wonnelachend umschwebe die Freude
> Seines grünenden Glückes Lauf.
> Immer getrennt vom trauernden Leide
> Nehm' ihn Elysiums Schatten auf.

(May his life blossom for ever. May joy garland with happiness the course of his burgeoning Fate, and, always free from travail, let the shades of Elysium bear him aloft.)

This occasional trifle for his father's name-day on 26th September 1813 is a splendid example of Schubert's love of vowel sounds—but the poverty of the music is certainly due to the speed at which it was written.

Schubert was always liberal in his use of exclamation marks, even in his own poems. Perhaps they express his relationship with his father whose one wish was to see his son attain higher social status and its concomitant privileges—but composing was the bread of life for the young man smarting under the confinements of military discipline in the *Konvikt*. The differences were to lead to many future conflicts with his father. Schubert's father has certainly not always been fairly judged. We should not close our eyes to his rectitude and his devotion to his ideals. He had taken over a poor school, transferred it to a larger house and there, underpaid and overworked, he had made himself into a respected leading figure of the community—no mean task.

In 1813 Schubert read the *Novellen* of the Count de la Motte Fouqué. The result, a group of three songs *Don Gayseros*, I, II and III (D 93) is of little musical interest. From a literary point of view we are reminded of the achievements of the Humboldt brothers, Karl Wilhelm (1767–1835) and Friedrich Heinrich Alexander (1769–1859). At the beginning of the nineteenth century, the Germans became aware of Spain; since the War of the Spanish Succession in the early years of the eighteenth century, Germans had neither wanted, nor been in a position to learn anything at all about Spain. The Romantic–Catholic wave brought with it an enthusiasm for Spain and Spanish culture, which is evidenced in the Calderón translations by August Wilhelm Schlegel between 1803 and 1809.

Since revolution was even more alien to Austria than to Germany, the short bursts of rebellion after the French successes were soon forgotten, and all liberal impulses were suppressed by the State, with its spies, uniforms, censors, and all the trappings of authoritarianism. Schubert's moral and intellectual conflicts at this time are mirrored in the choice of the curious poem *Der Vatermörder* (D 10), a massive ballad which he set to music one day in December 1813.[1]

The *Gesamtausgabe* at the end of the last century either did not know, or had forgotten, the author of the poem. There was argument as to whether this was a companion piece to Schiller's early *Kindsmörderin*, or if Schubert himself had written it. Only later was it established that the ballad was the work of Gottfried Konrad Pfeffel (1736–1809).

[1] Latest research suggests the date of composition was 26th December 1811.

The story of the patricide driven mad by guilt is set with exaggerated virility and is musically rather facile. Schubert struck such
pseudo-Italian chords only rarely.

Schiller, his idol, continued to attract him. *Thekla, eine Geisterstimme* (D 73) was to be Schiller's answer to questions about the fate
of Wallenstein's daughter in his trilogy *Wallenstein*. The phantom
voice tells us that she is now reunited with everything that she had
lost on earth, and that her father too is cleansed of the blood that
he had shed and is with his loved ones again. The alternating of
recitative and scraps of melody which characterises the first version
of 1813 is of little interest. (The second version is D 595 of 1817.)

Schubert tried to compose Schiller's *An Emma* three times
(D 113). He obviously found it difficult to interpret the poet's
sentimentality without a condescending smile. Nevertheless, apart
from a few songs which were published in journals, it was the first
Lied to appear (with two others) in print, as opus 58 in 1826.

Schubert had felt too restricted in the *Konvikt* and, after his
mother's death, and his father's re-marriage to Anna Kleyenböck,
a mill-owner's daughter twenty years his junior, there was no place
for Franz at home either. His brother Ferdinand wrote: 'After
Schubert had left the *Konvikt* because of his extraordinary devotion
to music, he was then called up three times to the colours. To avoid
such unpleasantnesses, he decided to become an assistant schoolmaster.'

After passing the examination with some difficulty, Schubert
was taken on as sixth assistant by his father, who now seemed to be
witnessing the realisation of his sole ambition for his son. The date
was 19th August 1814.

His creativity, the outpouring of Lieder, was in no way interrupted by these changes although, according to an anecdote
reported by Lachner, Schubert protected himself from any inter-
ference in his musical meditations by means of the teacher's
universal remedy—the cane—particularly when teaching his
youngest pupils: 'It is true that this little group annoyed me so
much when I was composing, that I regularly lost my train of
thought. Of course, I gave them all a good thrashing on those
occasions.'

The beginning of 1814 saw Schubert devoting himself, decisively
and entirely, to the Lied. In quick succession, and hardly inter-

rupted by work on other musical genres, there appeared songs which were mainly lyrical to begin with. These were the love poems of Friedrich von Matthisson. The first, Matthisson's *Lied, Die Schatten* (D 50), had been written a year earlier. The melodic line of the vocal part is only rarely interrupted by recitative, and the figuration of the piano accompaniment is therefore continuous. The initial key is the determining one, and the opening melody often reappears at the end. All these songs speak of love to come and premonitions of the impossibility of fulfilment.

Matthisson's *Adelaide* (D 95)—Schubert certainly knew and admired Beethoven's 1795 (opus 46) setting—was set in its entirety:

> Einst, O Wunder! entblüht auf meinem Grabe
> Eine Blume der Asche meines Herzens;
> Deutlich schimmert auf jedem Purpurblättchen:
> Adelaide!

(Once, O miracle, a flower from the ashes of my heart will blossom on my grave and, on each purple leaf, the name Adelaide will shimmer.)

Apart from producing poems which all the world could recite at that time Friedrich von Matthisson (1761–1831) had been a teacher, a theatre *Intendant*, a librarian in Magdeburg and Dessau, and he later became an economist. His rather pastel-like nature poetry, modelled on the eighteenth-century poems of Ludwig Hölty, was highly praised by Schiller. By this time, however, the Romantics, led by the Schlegel brothers, had lost interest in Matthisson's verses. His poems were set to music by most of the contemporary composers; Schubert alone set twenty-four.

Those of 1814 are perhaps the most interesting. They are simple, and very different from the longish and mostly sombre ballads of his early period. A different Schubert, lighter and more inclined to 'pure' music, speaks to us out of these songs. If we take Matthisson's *Der Abend* (D 108) as an example, it is difficult to understand why this song has been entirely and unjustly supplanted by the miracle of *Gretchen am Spinnrade*, composed three months later. The tone is graceful but serious at the same time; the recitative is introduced more skilfully than usual, and the nocturnal atmosphere is convincingly conjured up by the simplest possible means. The reputation which Matthisson enjoyed among his contemporaries should not blind us to the fact that he was a very poor poet—few of Schubert's Matthisson-Lieder from 1813–1816 are of the highest quality. However, they do make a cycle stylistically, and Bären-reiter treats them as such (and much to their advantage), in the new edition of the Complete Works edited by Walther Dürr.

Among these is *Andenken* (D 99), well-known in the Beethoven setting of 1809, but treated much more vigorously by Schubert. There are echoes of Goethe in the passage 'Ich denke dein', and the passage 'Denkst du mein' even relates musically to the descending fifths of the last verse of the Goethe song *Nähe des Geliebten*.

The semiquavers in *Lied der Liebe* (D 109) presage the accompaniment to *Gretchen am Spinnrade*, and though the last stanza may sound a cliché, it was a reality for Schubert.

> Die Freude sie schwindet, es dauert kein Leid;
> Die Jahre verrauschen im Strome der Zeit;
> Die Sonne wird sterben, die Erde vergeh'n:
> Doch Liebe muß ewig und ewig besteh'n.

(Joy is fleeting, pain does not last. Years flow away in the river of Time. The sun will die, the earth will disappear, yet Love will endure forever.)

An Laura, als sie Klopstocks Auferstehungslied sang (D 115) is a majestic song. Even if one cannot now do anything for the rather sentimental text, it expresses, in conjunction with the music—delicious and full of subtleties—a valid utterance. Schubert sets to music the meaning and not the Romantic preciosity. (*Die Betende*, D 102, receives a similar hymnic treatment.)

Adelaide brings us back to Beethoven again. Although Schubert's modest and intimate setting can hardly be compared with the magnificent range of his model, it nevertheless suits the style of the poem. The rich melody is not sustained throughout, however, while the details, if not the overall plan, owe much to Beethoven. It is clear that Schubert was well aware of this as a remark of Josef Hüttenbrenner's shows: 'The latter asked Schubert in 1817 for his *Adelaide* by Matthisson, "which I regard as Beethoven's best song". Schubert replied that he hadn't wanted to write it for he would have had to write it just like Beethoven.'

Der Geistertanz (D 116) must have given pleasure to the child that Schubert was, after all, at that time. The delightful C minor scherzo passage presages the Unfinished Symphony in the *rallentando* sections. The ghost story of *Romanze* (D 114), on the other hand, can hardly be rescued from the tower in which the ghost met its death. The cadences in the recitative to *Trost. An Elisa* (D 97) is an expressive example of pianistic independence.

Totenopfer (D 101) is an interesting exception to the usually formal recitatives of this collection of Lieder; here the song moves into declamation such as is often found in later Schubert. *Die Schatten* (D 50) refers to Matthisson's tribute to his friend, the Swiss philosopher, Charles de Bonnet. *Totenkranz für ein Kind* (D 275), a later Matthisson setting from 1815, has an unusual and, for the time, quite unprecedented harmonic structure. What would other composers of the period have made out of the text?

In August 1814 Johann Mayrhofer (1787–1836) was introduced into the Schubert circle by Josef von Spaun. Mayrhofer had studied for the priesthood in the Abbey of St Florian, near Linz—which was to be made famous later by Anton Bruckner, who was a chorister there. Mayrhofer soon gave up his theological studies, however, and went to Vienna where he became friendly with Schubert. After graduating as a lawyer he entered the State service. A poet *manqué*, languishing as a clerk in the Austrian censorship office, he became Schubert's closest friend, his fellow-lodger and supplier of texts. Mayrhofer wrote in 1829 about his friend:

> My friendship with Schubert began after one of his friends had given him my poem *Am See* to set to music. Schubert came with this friend into the room which we were to share five years later. It is in the Wipplingerstrasse. Both the house and the room had felt the weight of the years, the ceiling had sunk somewhat, the light was blocked by a large building opposite—there was a much-used piano and a tiny book-case. The room and the hours spent in it will never be erased from my memory.

There is a conflict of opinion about Mayrhofer's poems, more than forty of which were set to music by Schubert. Much of his poetry strikes us as rather peculiar nowadays, trite and dated, unacceptable to modern literary tastes. Sentimentality and veiled obscurities are among his weaknesses, as well as a penchant for the infelicitous expression. Yet the great intention strikes us every now and then, the exactly-observed image, and the diction. One cannot deny the inspiration which Schubert got from his poems, in the sense that he learned how to treat unsuitable material. But we must regard Mayrhofer as by far the best poet among Schubert's dilettante friends; he was the archetypal 'Romantic character'. Here is Grillparzer's charming characterisation of Mayrhofer, in which he correctly appreciates the latter's lyrical gifts:

> Mayrhofer's poems always resemble a text to a melody, either the anticipated melody of a composer who wanted to set the poem to music, or the melody of a poem that he has read shimmers through it and he reproduces it to a new text and a new emotion.

This is underlined by the testimony of friends, who wrote that Mayrhofer had often admitted that his poems only seemed really intelligible and readable after Schubert had set them to music.

Mayrhofer's *Am See* (D 124) which Schubert set in the style of the Matthisson songs, flows unwittingly from the poet's description of his own troubles—the conflict between his prosaic job and his artistic inclinations—into a hymn of praise to the 'Great German Leopold'. This was the Duke of Brunswick who, it is said, put his duty to his people before *his* artistic inclinations when he helped rescue some of his countrymen from the waters after a catastrophic flood in 1785 and was himself drowned in the process. Perhaps Schubert found the final eulogy too banal, for he repeated the modest opening stanza in place of a final verse:

> Das Schilfrohr neiget seufzend sich,
> Die Uferblumen grüßen mich,
> Der Vogel klagt, die Lüfte wehn,
> Vor Schmerzeslust möcht' ich vergehn.

(The reeds incline with a sigh, the flowers on the bank greet me. The birds mourn, the breezes waft, and I would fain die of sorrow.)

There followed further Mayrhofer settings in 1815 and the two libretti which Schubert wrote on Mayrhofer's themes: *Die beiden Freunde von Salamanka* (D 326) and the fragment of the opera *Adrast* (D 137).

One might mention here the lesser poems which Schubert accepted mainly from friends, and which he improved greatly by sublimating the core of the poem in music while remaining faithful to the text. The eternal question: Why did he bother with such rubbish when his own literary taste was unquestioned?—might be answered by pointing out that the poets of the day, geniuses apart, composed in a type of 'colloquial lyric' which kept to oft-repeated descriptions of Heaven, nature and the soul. The precision of modern poetry, with its contrived sentence-constructions and carefully chosen vocabulary, is a far cry from the carefree poetry of the *Biedermeier* era. The advantage of such poetry for the composer had been shown in the development of the Lied up to that time—the task of sublimation fell to the *music*. It could take wing unhindered by the 'pale cast of thought'. Schubert might well have been delighted at the chance to produce his own composition by, as it were, making a detour round the rhymester.

The first performance of the Mass in F major on 18th October 1814, in which Therese Grob (1798–1875) sang the soprano solo, was the occasion of Schubert's first, and probably only, passion. The enormous output of enthusiastic and joyful love-songs in 1815 was undoubtedly addressed to Therese. Yet the refuge which he sought with this simple girl with the lovely voice was not to be his, and even later in life, he refused to recognise the worlds which had separated them. Schubert never denied that Therese was no beauty. Holzapfel described her as rather plump, but with a good figure and a fresh round childish face on which smallpox had left its mark. Schubert hid his love from his friends. Anselm Hüttenbrenner related much later how Schubert used to talk about his girl-friend:

> There was one girl I loved very much—and she loved me too. She was a little younger than I was and sang the soprano solo in my Mass very beautifully and with deep emotion. She was not really very pretty and had a pockmarked face—but she was an angel. For three years, she hoped that I would marry her, but I could not find a post that could support us both. So she married another man at the wish of her parents—and I was deeply hurt. I still love her, and since then I have never met anyone who meant so much or more to me. She just wasn't meant for me, I suppose.

At this time of youthful love, Schubert began to compose warmer, more realistic and more personal music. His creative energy was boundless, the ease and certainty of his writing, exemplary.

1815 and 1816 can be regarded as the most creative period of his life. In 1815 150 Lieder were composed. Spaun wrote: 'Instead of becoming poorer by the waste of so many wonderful melodies, he only seemed to discover new and greater riches, and the spring of magical music gushed forth with ever-increasing abandon.'

The powers that were released in him by his love found their most immediate and most profound expression in the Lied. One should not consider only the numerous love-songs—the whole variety of human relationships with nature was included. Therese Grob was naturally their first exponent, with Schubert as accompanist. They went through them, song by song, and his guilty happiness spurred him on to ever greater heights. The night after the successful performance of the Mass, Schubert set Schiller's *Das Mädchen aus der Fremde* (D 117) for Therese. This fairy-tale ballad seems to be a compliment to Therese's simple naturalness set, as it is, like a folk-song. The song is accordingly written in an unpretentious 6/8 pastoral. Franz was seventeen, Therese a year younger. The pair were all the happier because the Mass had been warmly received and had been promised a second performance in the Augustinerkirche in Vienna. Schubert's father, delighted, made his son the present of a piano.

THREE

Goethe, or New Paths

It was fateful that Schubert's first encounter with Goethe's work should coincide with his first love. The lines of Goethe's *Gretchen am Spinnrade* 'Meine Ruh' ist hin, mein Herz ist schwer' (My peace has gone, my heart is heavy), herald the birth of the essential, the great Schubert Lied. After all the sickly rhymesters, one can feel the intellectual superiority which illuminates Goethe's poem. Yet this intellectuality does not detract from the beauty of the poetry. It is touching to see how independently and unslavishly Schubert comes to terms with these masterpieces. Sometimes his setting takes no account of single words in the sustained mood or rhythm, and yet no marriage of poetry and music has ever been so perfectly consummated. The intellectual experience that was Goethe was to shed its unchanging light over Schubert for the rest of his days. He set more than seventy Goethe poems, many in several versions.

That first masterpiece of 19th October 1814 (D 118) arrived unexpectedly. Music had never known anything like this before. The monotonous figure in the accompaniment, which personifies the spinning-wheel, pauses at the climax of the song and dramatically illustrates how despair has paralysed the girl's physical movements. Then the figure is resumed, fearfully and haltingly. We experience the painful return of sensuous perception. Yet such frightening details in no way militate against formal cohesion. Each of the three parts of the song end with Gretchen's cry 'Meine Ruh' ist hin', a division not found in Goethe. Schubert extracts from the poem itself the exciting sense of movement which pervades the whole, yet all this characteristic liveliness does not disturb the supreme genius of the melody-line—Schubert, the melody maker, is seen here at his best. Each stanza is given a different melody and harmonisation, while the semi-quavers in the right-hand of the piano accompaniment continue their steady hum.

The second stanza ends boldly on the G of the kiss ('Und ach! sein Kuß') extended to a *fermata*, then follow two diminished sevenths. The third stanza rises to the exciting and passionate 'Vergehen sollt' ('Should pass away'), and then dies away, while the opening words are softly repeated.

This is the first example of a uniform accompaniment being retained throughout—its success is a proof of Schubert's early maturity. Here is motion as well as hesitation, there are agonising heartbeats in the bass which are overlaid by the monotonous whirring of the spinning-wheel. After two climaxes, the music subsides as if exhausted, and Schubert again invokes the spinning-wheel as if apprehensive of the future. The song must be sung with an economical awareness of the two great climaxes, otherwise there is a danger of vocal exhaustion. Raimund von zur Muehlen's advice to his students is still valid today: 'All those bosoms on the concert platform which "long for him" ["nach ihm hindrängen"] on Gretchen's account are nothing but distortions and corruptions. We must remember that Gretchen is a young inexperienced girl, in love for the first time. You women, take care, lest the devil and your flesh lead you into unbelief, sin and shame! Gretchen is no lady of high society about to be divorced from her second husband in order to catch Faust!'

Sonnleithner printed *Gretchen am Spinnrade* privately on 30th April 1821, as opus 2. It was dedicated to Count Moritz von Fries (1777–1826), to whom Beethoven had once dedicated some early chamber works. Schubert received twenty ducats as a mark of the banker's respect and gratitude. It was difficult later to remember that Zelter, Loewe and Spohr had all set the poem, since Schubert's setting, although it took cavalier liberties with the stanza divisions, created a sensation far and wide. A 17-year-old had shown how form could be made the servant of emotion by opening up new dimensions of the language of music. Salieri's enthusiastic cry: 'Der ist ein Genie! Der kann alles!' (He's a genius! He can do anything!') was justified.

The second Goethe setting was composed on 30th November 1814. *Nachtgesang* (D 119) was made into the most delicate serenade —and the shortest strophic song. Each of the five quatrains is set to fourteen bars of playfulness, sleepiness and eroticism which never get trapped in detail.

Trost in Tränen (D 120) was written on the same day; the F major exhortations to the sentimental youth are answered, in F minor, by the moping lover and he has the last word. *Sehnsucht* (D 123), composed in the following month, so different from the heaven-storming Beethoven setting of 1810 and yet with so many delicate musical nuances, shows how Schubert could work in a traditional mould. But Goethe's anapaests lose all their vigour when alternated thus as recitatives and airs.

The first version of *Szene aus Faust* (D 126), which followed, was intended as a dramatic fragment for soprano (Gretchen) and alto (Mephisto), chorus and piano accompaniment. Markings such as 'tromboni' seem to point to plans for an original orchestral version, but in the two extant autograph copies (both 1814) Schubert had already decided on piano accompaniments. In the first, there is a note 'Sketch for a later version'. In the revised version, the registers of the Evil Spirit and Gretchen have been adjusted to one another, and a Lied-like dialogue has replaced the dramatic *scena*.

At the same time, around the turn of the year, Schubert sings of his love in a strophic song, *Das Bild* (D 155), by an unknown poet, which puts his feelings for Therese in terse and touching terms. It begins quietly. The natural phrasing of the words 'schwebet' ('hovers') and 'Himmelsreiz' ('Heaven's charms') offers us a glimpse of Heaven; the semiquavers of 'Ich seh's, wenn lieblich, wie das Bild', ('I see her when, sweetly, like the picture . . .') mirror an inner turmoil, for the word 'Bild' ('picture') is sustained by a *fermata*—the *Bild* is to stamp itself on our minds, and similar emphases on 'Gestalt' ('form') and 'Zier' ('delights') show us that the image will never disappear. Finally, 'Abendstern' ('evening star') and 'Altar' ('altar') ascend and hover for a whole bar on their own without the piano. The last syllable in A, the last note sung, returns as an open third in the F major piano postlude. This tiny, much-neglected Schubert song outdoes many a sentimental song or passionate operatic declamation.

Those friends, like Spaun, Holzapfel and Stadler, who had en-thusiastically encouraged Schubert's growing repertoire of Lieder, were now joined by Anselm Hüttenbrenner (1794–1868) and Franz von Schober (1796–1882), who was introduced by Spaun. Schubert's father was not pleased about their meetings in his house in the suburbs, because he was sure that they would interfere with his son's schoolwork, and, above all, with his private tuition. Even when they transferred their meetings to the Sunday tranquillity of the *Konvikt,* he was still unhappy. Stadler wrote:

Schubert's repeated appearances in the *Konvikt* displeased the directors, still more any longer stay. On Sundays, we had to attend the afternoon service in the neighbouring University church, and that always lasted a good half-hour. When Schubert was with us, we used to lock him up in a study while we were away, give him a few scraps of manuscript paper and any handy volume of poems, so that he could while away the time. When we returned from church, he had usually composed something —which he then gladly turned over to me.

Stadler used to accompany Holzapfel at the piano if Schubert did not want to. Stadler left this account of Schubert's playing: 'Lovely touch, steady hand, a nice clear playing, full of insight and emotion. He belonged to the old school of good pianists who didn't attack the keys like birds of prey', and Anselm Hüttenbrenner added:

He also played the violin and cello; he read all clefs with equal ease and never missed an important note, even in the mezzo-soprano and baritone clefs. His voice was weak but very pleasant. When he was 19, he sang baritone and tenor, and, in emergencies, if a lady did not turn up, for example, could also sing the contralto or soprano parts, since he possessed an extensive falsetto. He often had to do this when we were singing old scores from sight with Salieri in the Court Music Library.

Schubert's friends were true partners in his work, since they were interested in literature as well as in music, and kept supplying him with fresh material, not least with poems written by themselves, and sketches for operas. These were the germ of the later more institutionalised 'Schubertiaden', where the piano took the leading musical rôle. Merchants, lawyers and civil servants were to place their roomy comfortable houses at the disposal of Schubert and his friends, and songs, chamber music, piano duos and so on, were performed before their guests. Such musical evenings had long been a feature of Viennese life, but Schubert gave them the status and quality of a finished, more musicianly professionalism.

Most of the forty-two settings of Friedrich Schiller's poems were written between 1815 and 1818, poems which brought out so many characteristic beauties in Schubert's work, although it is true that some of the settings are rather superficial, and there is certainly hardly any comparison with the grandeur of the Goethe Lieder.

Almost all the Schiller Lieder pre-date 1818. Eighteen-fifteen brought fifteen Schiller Lieder, but twice as many to Goethe texts, as we have seen. After 1817, Schubert's interest in Schiller gradually diminished and his last Schiller song was written in 1823.

In *Hektors Abschied* (D 312), a dialogue for two voices (far removed from present-day tastes, but containing, as always, some beautiful passages, despite the aridity of the text), we meet that intoxication with things Greek so typical of the literature of the period, and which Schubert himself was naturally unable to resist, as many of his Lieder texts bear witness. Mayrhofer's and Schiller's poems, in particular, deal with the origins, effects and results of a movement which had such far-reaching consequences, especially for Germany. The view was that there existed an unbroken line from the earliest days of Ancient Greece to present-day western civilisation. Some philosophers of the second half of the nineteenth century questioned this assumption—or dismissed it altogether. Classical antiquity had resembled all other civilisations, with stages of growth, achievement and decline. The fevered fantasies of the German Romantics were centred on the Greece of the first two stages only, a Greece no longer remembered, even in the Hellenistic and Roman eras. The Greeks and the Romans acknowledged that they shared the same cultural heritage. One cannot regard the Germanic and Slav cultures of between 500 and 1000 AD as a continuation of Ancient Greece, despite the Roman and Byzantine elements contained within them. The culture of the Middle Ages appears as a self-contained phenomenon, an attempt to blend the now and the hereafter in Christ on Earth, in the Catholic Church. The exhaustion brought on by wars, by the destruction of national identities and by political pressures, doomed this attempt to failure. The Germans remembered a better, more harmonious antiquity, and felt themselves to be the spiritual and intellectual heirs of an imaginary idealised Greece to which they longed to return. They attempted to shape all aspects of their own lives in its image. They succeeded, yet their success was not a renascence, but seems to have been rather an expression of the decline of western civilisation.

Of those writers whose poems Schubert set to music, Goethe, Schiller, Schlegel and Mayrhofer wanted to measure their culture against that of Ancient Greece, or, rather, they believed that they were mirroring that culture—but their conception of Ancient Greece had never been a reality. None of them had ever visited Greece (if one excepts Lord Byron). Those who, like Goethe, Winckelmann or Wilhelm von Humboldt, travelled to Italy, disregarded early Christianity, the Renaissance and the Baroque, and were interested solely in the ruins of Ancient Rome or in replicas of late Greek sculptures. Schiller and Schlegel drew their knowledge of Ancient Greece more from literary works, and from those replicas and illustrations available to them. It is extraordinarily difficult for us to comprehend how they deduced so much from what, after all, they themselves had invented. They must have been tired of their own past, the past of western Europe, but also not quite honest with themselves. Hölderlin, Byron and Goethe made poetry out of their dreams of an ideal Greece, and thus these personal statements had a Grecian veneer, so to speak. Schiller translated some Greek literary relics, wrote the poem *Die Götter Griechenlands* (a fragment of which became a Schubert song), and some other similar works. Schlegel rediscovered the Roman Catholicism which inspired his later works.

But, of course, not all Schiller's work is marked by Hellenism. In 1815, the best-known of Schubert's three versions of *Des Mädchens Klage* (D 191) was composed. Schubert had treated it more or less as a dramatic *scena* in 1814, but now, and in the following year, he gave the poem a strophic setting.

It is unbelievable that on the day Schubert set Goethe's *Nähe des Geliebten* (D 162), namely, 27th February 1815, he could also sketch one of his longest songs, Schiller's *Erwartung* (D 159), along with some others. (Bertrand's *Adelwold und Emma*, twenty-six pages long, holds the record!) In the five long stanzas of *Erwartung* the poet five times mistakenly believes that his beloved has arrived. Charlotte von Lengefeld (later Schiller's fiancée) creeps in unnoticed at the end of the *scena*. Perhaps Schubert was interested in what at first sight seems an impossible task, simply because Zumsteeg had already attempted it. Like Zumsteeg, Schubert alternates recitative with *arioso*—but how inferior the older musician's setting is to Schubert's dewy-fresh music!

The *Klage der Ceres* (D 323) is likewise an attempt to outdo Zumsteeg. This work, begun in November 1815, stretched out into 1816. What finally emerged is like a five-finger exercise among the other strokes of genius. The heroine of Schiller's 1781 play *Die Räuber*, Amalia, also became the subject of a dramatic song (D 195).

The song was written a few days after the second version of *Des Mädchens Klage,* composed on 15th May 1815, and perhaps the most beautiful of the purely lyrical Schiller settings. The expansive melody hovers above pulsating C minor triplets. The delicate first version of *Das Geheimnis* (D 250) ignores the development inherent in the four stanzas; this lapse is corrected in the more elaborate version of 1823 (D 793), which however lacks the earlier versions special expression of shyness, and cannot entirely eclipse it. (This first setting's shadowy existence is probably due to its not being included in the Peters edition.)

Hoffnung (D 251) is not much more than a little folk-song, nor is *An den Frühling* (D 245), which has a charming Ländler-like prelude; Schubert set it again later in the same year (D 283), likewise in a 6/8 rhythm. He also set it for male chorus (D 338). Of some twenty settings of the poem by other composers, Schubert's second version is by far the loveliest.

To return to February 1815: Schubert set Goethe's *Nähe des Geliebten* twice on 27th February. The first version, in 6/8 time, accompanies the voice with semiquaver chords, while the second version is in a broad swinging 12/8 rhythm, which puts the song into restful balance, lending depth to the vocal part, and more transparency and warmth of expression to the whole. With a sensitivity and an emotional awareness which he possessed in unique measure, Schubert transformed otherwise identical versions, and, by an imperceptible rhythmical adjustment, he made a great song out of a beautiful one. I have ignored, however, one little note which was also changed in the second version: the singer's last note does not remain on D flat, but goes down to G flat. One can see from this tiny detail how Schubert possessed more than a merely musical intelligence. On first hearing, the sustained D flat on the word 'da' ('here'), seems to waft out soulfully enough. The descent from D flat to G flat, however, deepens the meaning of 'O wärst Du da' ('Oh, were you but here'). The expression of longing is turned

inwards by the tiny sigh. Thus, the circle closes: from the higher
G flat of the opening 'Ich denke Dein' ('I think of you') to the lower
octave of 'O wärst Du da'. Since Goethe's text does not fit the
melody in the third stanza, Schubert boldly inserts the word 'da'
in the line 'Im stillen Haine geh ich' ('I wander in the still
grove').

Such is the originality of the Goethe songs of 1815 (afterwards
to become so famous) that one feels tempted to place them at a
later date, but that would be forgetting the quite exceptional
Gretchen am Spinnrade of 1814. They do not all possess equal intensity, of course, but even in a comparatively conventional song,
such as the first Goethe setting of 1815, *Der Sänger* (D 149), the
Goethean model lifts Schubert's composition far above the level of
the normal contemporary Lied. The ballad is set in an idealised
Middle Ages, and Schubert gives it an 'old-fashioned' Haydnesque
treatment. The fact that the minstrel's actual song is omitted by
Goethe is probably why so many of the later settings (by Loewe,
Schumann and Wolf, for example) are so unsatisfactory. Schubert
certainly offers the most interesting interpretations. The poem,
from Goethe's *Wilhelm Meister* novel, is a pendant to Novalis's
Lied von der Wiederkehr eines goldenen Zeitalters (Song of the Return
of a Golden Age), and rests on the union of Spirit and Power, a
Romantic notion shared by Schubert, too, and which was meant to
usher in the 'poetic State', the 'harmonious society'. The Prince was
to appear as the 'artist of artists'. The Singer, the minstrel, the
messenger of Spirit and Poesy, was to play the mediator to effect the
metamorphosis of Man. Schubert's rather conventional, rococo-
like setting changes tempo frequently and mingles recitative with
arioso. Even if he nowhere reaches the spontaneity and formal
cohesion of *Erlkönig,* one senses nevertheless the challenge he had
to meet to bring to life the details of Goethe's poem.

The second book of Goethe's long novel *Wilhelm Meister* introduces the mysterious Harper. Goethe gives us very few of his songs,
but these were the poems which were to be the seed-bed of the art
of the German Lied. Schubert ignored Philine's song, but set those
of Mignon and the Harper many times. Mignon, the enigmatic
Italian child, is rescued by Wilhelm from a troupe of travelling
acrobats. Under his protection, and accompanied by the crazed
Harper, she joins his travelling players. Homesickness and a broken

heart sum up the life, love and death of the young girl. Only later are her secrets revealed and found to be closely linked to those of the Harper. He does not know that she is the child of that incestuous union, the memory of which has driven him to wander the earth, half-demented. Although the three famous 'Harper's Songs' were not written until 1816, the first attempt, *Wer sich der Einsamkeit ergibt* (D 325), appeared in 1815, but its naïve 6/8 rhythm is no match for the subtlety of the later settings.

The first of the six settings of *Nur wer die Sennsucht kennt* was also composed in 1815 (D 310). Two further attempts followed in the next year (D 359 and D 481). In 1819 it was set for five-part male voice choir (D 656), and in 1826 came the best-known version, in A minor (D 877, no. 1), and also at the same time a duet version (D 877, no. 4), which is perhaps closest to the Goethe poem, since this is not really *Mignons Lied,* as the 1827 publishers of opus 62 named it, but rather an 'irregular duet', sung at Wilhelm's bedside by Mignon and the Harper.

The Goethe song *Der Fischer* (D 225) written on 5th July 1815, is dedicated to Antonio Salieri. Schubert manages marvellously to capture the evocation of nature in the poem in a very simple setting with repeated stanzas. This music would be effective without any text. If these few bars are played as pure instrumental music and placed beside Zelter's version, for example, the inner beauty of Schubert's style becomes evident, even taking into consideration his complete ignoring of Goethe's indication that the poem was a 'Ballade'. (It was published in 1821 with other Goethe settings.)

Wanderers Nachtlied I (D 224) ('Der du von dem Himmel bist': 'Thou who art from Heaven), fuses three powerful *motifs* into a lyrical unity in a few short bars. Yet the deep meaning of the words does not find adequate expression in the music. Of all the many settings of this poem, Hugo Wolf's early 'psychological' version probably comes closest to the poet's intentions. Schubert's 'Ach, ich bin des Treibens müde' ('Oh, I am weary of wandering') is very unpessimistic. The singer's cry for peace is gentle, his goal here is mature resignation. Likewise at the words 'doppelt elend' ('doubly miserable'): *misery* is barely hinted at here, the first part of the song is matched to the second. The request for peace is made 'etwas geschwinder' ('rather faster') than the former very slow tempo. It has been rightly said: anyone asking for 'peace' in this fashion must already have found it. The quiet conclusion confirms this judgement. (Goethe wrote the poem for Charlotte von Stein on the Ettersberg in 1776.)

Erster Verlust (D 226), that naïve, eternally surprising setting of the famous poem, was written on the same day, but not published until 1821 as opus 5, no. 4. *Wonne der Wehmut* (D 260) can hardly be compared with Beethoven's 1810 setting; the words of the poem do not lend themselves to a simple strophic folk-song form.

In the month of July 1815 alone, Schubert composed eighteen Lieder, 150 in the whole year. He drew on divers poets, from Goethe down to his friends, who were the veriest amateurs. (The disparaging remark that Schubert could set a menu to music was proudly applied by Richard Strauss to himself!) Even if many of the poems hold little literary interest, it must be remembered that Schubert had to set mediocre poems *faute de mieux*, for his speed of composition meant that shortage of material was always a problem. There are sufficient indications that Schubert nevertheless selected fairly rigorously from the anthologies, annuals and individual poems that were brought to him.

For the wedding of a friend, he set Goethe's *Bundeslied* (D 258) on 19th August 1815, in the simplest singable form. The poem describes the spirit of good fellowship reigning among Schubert's like-minded friends. The best-known setting of this poem is Reichardt's. In his autobiography Goethe recommends his poem to posterity thus:

> Since this song has survived to the present day, and since hardly a festive meal is held without its being served up with joy, we recommend it to all those who come after us and wish all those who recite it or sing it the same inner joy and pleasure that we experienced when we wrote it, without any thought of the world outside, believing that our own small circle was a world in itself.

Zelter and Beethoven also set the poem to music.

August 19th saw Schubert completely obsessed with Goethe and with music. He set *Der Gott und die Bajadere, Der Rattenfänger, Der Schatzgräber, Heidenröslein, Bundeslied* and the first version of *An den Mond*, all with little effort, without complicated accompaniments, all the inspiration of the moment. Musically, *Heidenröslein* (D 257) comes off best. *Der Rattenfänger* (D 255) can be taken as a street-singer's song; the melody is folk-songish, the accompaniment does not go beyond a few chords, the modulations confine themselves to the related minor keys. Such simplicity certainly suits the character of the song, poles apart from Hugo Wolf's setting. Wolf saturates the music rather indulgently with a wealth of individual musical ideas, while Schubert sees the rat-catcher primarily as a good-natured braggart. There is nothing at all here of Wolf's grotesque caricature. Schubert's happy-go-lucky Pied Piper of Hamelin (to whom Goethe actually gives a violin instead of a pipe) is a harmless boaster.

Only the fever of work of that August day, or a complete misunderstanding of Goethe's poem, can explain Schubert's setting of *Der Gott und die Bajadere* (D 254) as a folk ballad in the manner of, say, Loewe's *Edward*—which it is decidedly not. When one studies the pedantic description of details—a fault of the Swiss composer Othmar Schoeck's modern setting, too—one might conclude that the theme is intractable.

The first version of *An den Mond* (D 259), on the other hand, is pretty, if insignificant; it hardly does the wonderful poem justice. Schubert did well to set the text again in 1816 (D 296).

On 21st August came *Wer kauft Liebesgötter?* (D 261), a couplet made complicated in the simplest manner. It never leaves the C–G–F keys, and yet causes the singer problems with its figurations and tongue-twisters. So as not to stem the oriental verbiage of the wily hawker, the singer is denied breathing-spaces. Goethe had written the song as part of his projected sequel to Mozart's *Zauberflöte,* giving the stanzas respectively to Papageno and Papagena, who bore 'golden cages with winged children'.

Gabriele von Baumberg (1796–1839), the lyric poetess whom the Viennese called their 'Sappho', had earned the praises of Goethe himself, but the Lieder which Schubert made out of her poems in 1815 are really only miniatures and of little significance.

The song *Furcht der Geliebten* (D 285), by Friedrich Gottlieb Klopstock (1724–1803), begins the series of thirteen settings of Klopstock's poems which were concentrated into the months of September and October 1815. With his masterpiece, the epic poem 'Der Messias' ('The Messiah'), which took him twenty-eight years to complete, Klopstock founded an entirely new style of German poetry in the eighteenth century by employing Greek metres and, later, free rhythms. Along with this revolution in poetic style he sought to bring about a new life-style which laid great emphasis on physical activity, on skating, walking and riding. His ideas had no little influence on Goethe. Klopstock greeted the American War of Independence with enthusiasm and, like Schiller, was made an honorary citizen of France for his celebration of the French Revolution in his Odes.

It is fairly safe to assume that Schubert found the meaning of *An Sie* (D 288) in the closing lines of this strophic song, for it is only at the third repetition of the music that the listener has any impression of unity of text and music. The Lied does justice to the peculiar syntax of the poem and, like the other Klopstock settings, has a style of its own.

The main work of the Klopstock series is undoubtedly the three versions of *Dem Unendlichen* (D 291), the second version being the superior one, though actually differing little from the third. This is obviously not a Lied but, rather, an aria with accompanying recitative. Given the sublimity of the text, no other form was possible. The pathos of the words could only be rendered musically like this—as if it were an aria from an oratorio.

The poem begins with sublime thought, so Schubert begins with declamation and not with melody. As if horrified by the temerity of even *thinking* of God, there is a *fortissimo* chord on 'denkt' ('thinks'). Consideration of his lowly self weighs down the heart deep into the C minor of 'Nacht und Tod' ('night and death'), but then the quicker passages raise it up again. Certainty of redemption is heard in the liberating modulations into F major, to be followed by a further optimistic ascent to B major. On the word 'Herrlicher' ('Majestic one'), glorification and dread are juxtaposed in a *fortissimo* C major and *pianissimo* A minor chords. The main tonality, not yet heard despite all the modulations, is reached only on the decisive word 'dankend' ('thankfully'). The jubilation which descends from the high A flat brings this wonderful recitative to a close. Now begins the *arioso* song of thanksgiving, with harps and trombones imitated on the piano. This is a 'classical style' which Schubert mastered with the same ease with which he composed his simple lyrics.

The Klopstock Lieder are in no wise respectful noddings in the direction of a great literary figure—one of their great charms lies in their infinite variety; the *Vaterlandslied* (D 287) could have come from a comic opera. It praises the blue eyes and sense of patriotism of a 'German girl', namely the girl Klopstock later married, Elisabeth von Winthen.

It is an interesting comment on the age that this 'German girl' poem evoked great enthusiasm. Matthias Claudius (1740–1815) wrote a companion poem:

> Ich bin ein deutscher Jüngling
> Mein Haar ist kraus, breit meine Brust . . .

(I am a German boy, my hair is curly, my chest is broad)

which was set to music as often as Klopstock's and became particularly popular in Christian Gottlob Neefe's version.

Shortly after Klopstock's poem appeared, the poet Christian Daniel Schubart published (in his *Deutsche Chronik*) an article by a Charlotte von Y . . . in which the noble lady took exception to the 'coarse and barbaric' subject-matter of the poem. She went on to assert that refined ladies and gentlemen could find little pleasure in vulgarities obviously meant for peasant girls. She therefore altered *Vaterlandslied* so that it could be sung in such refined society:

> Ich bin ein gnädigs Fräulein,
> Mein' Aug' ist schwarz und wild mein Blick.
> Ich hab' ein Herz voll Zärtlichkeit und Sentiment.

(I am a gracious lady; my eye is black, my glance is wild. My heart is full of gentleness and emotion.)

There followed another seven stanzas in a similar vein of parody which—to achieve the maximum effect—were placed in the journal alongside Klopstock's original. Observe, moreover, the date of the Schubert composition—1815. These inflammatory verses took on a more nationalistic meaning in the patriotic enthusiasm of the years of the Wars of Liberation. (Klopstock later produced a Low German dialect version of his poem.)

Hermann und Thusnelda (D 322) takes us into the world of heroic opera—but the pompous greeting offered by the hero's wife to the returned warrior sounds ludicrous today. The piano part of one section of this enormously long song seems to have pleased Schubert immensely, for it reappeared ten years later, almost note for note and in the same key (D flat major), in a song with similar sentiments—*Ellens Gesang I 'Raste, Krieger'* (D 837) from Scott's *Lady of the Lake.*

Das Rosenband (D 280) has been unjustly neglected. Richard Strauss's setting is the only one heard nowadays, but his late Romantic pastiche is much inferior to the immediacy and freshness of Schubert's version, which was one of the great glories of Elena Gerhardt's repertoire. The poem, written in 1753, attracted countless musicians. The first to set it, Rosenbaum, wrote in the preface to his ode of 1762:

> Furthermore, at the instigation of a friend I have called this unpublished song *Das schlafende Mädchen.* Its author does not need to be named, because the smallest detail calls to mind that original genius whose longer works have earned such admiration. Nor is there any need to indicate the unavoidable problems of such a composition. They will be readily apparent to all.

These problems are apparent, too, in the compositions of Corona Schröter, Johann Schenk and Carl Friedrich Zelter. Schubert's towers above them all.

Die frühen Gräber (D 290) hardly eclipses Gluck's masterpiece, but its musical simplicity can be effective.

Because it has usually been excluded from collections other than the *Gesamtausgabe,* the episodic *Die Sommernacht* (D 289) remains entirely unknown. If it can find a singer with the necessary breadth of interpretation, this series of melodic inventions will not disappoint the listener.

On 16th November 1815, Josef von Spaun witnessed the birth of *Erlkönig* (D 328):

> We found Schubert all aglow reading the *Erlkönig* aloud from a book. He walked to and fro several times with the book in his hand; suddenly he sat down, and in no time at all the wonderful ballad was on paper. We ran to the *Konvikt* with it as Schubert had no piano [Spaun is wrong here] and there, the same evening, the *Erlkönig* was sung and wildly acclaimed. Old Ruzicka then played through all the parts himself carefully, without a singer, and was deeply moved by the composition. When one or two of the company questioned a recurring dissonant note, Ruzicka

played it on the piano and showed them how it matched the text exactly, how beautiful it really was and how happily it was resolved.

The Schubert specialist Maurice J. E. Brown does not believe that the song was written so quickly, but it must be remembered that Schubert did not usually write out all the repeats in the accompaniment, so that given the very few key-changes and Schubert's speed of writing, he would hardly need four hours to write the song down.

It is not generally known that the poem comes from Goethe's ballad opera *Die Fischerin* (1782). The author's stage direction reads: 'Scattered under high alders at the edge of the river are several fishermen's huts. It is a quiet night. Round a small fire are pots, nets and fishing-tackle. Dortchen, busy, sings: "Wer reitet so spät ..."' Almost mechanically, the fisherwoman is singing an old familiar song as she works, just as Gretchen hums the 'König von Thule' to herself.

Erlkönig is one of those songs of which Goethe wrote: 'The singer has learned it somewhat by heart and recalls it from time to time. Therefore these songs can and must have their own, definite, well-rounded melodies which are attractive and easily remembered.'

Corona Schröter, who played the part of the fisherwoman at the first performance, had written a simple eight-bar melody for herself. The 18-year-old assistant schoolmaster, Franz Schubert, ignored the emphasis on simplicity in the poem and, in contrast to his musical precursors, Reichardt, Klein and Zelter, transferred the northern hobgoblin to the realms of seductive sensuality, disregarding all the aesthetic reservations of his contemporaries in the wake of the thrilling power of his *Sturm und Drang* song.[1]

Schubert seizes on the great rondo-form suggested by the text and interprets the three inveiglements of the *Erlkönig* as three subsidiary themes, whose wheedling tones interrupt the stormy onward drive. The final *stretto* with its *accelerando* (which must not be ignored) forms the coda. The ballad is built up on the principle of unified modulation. The rushing of the wind and the restlessness of the ride are in its basic rhythm. The triplets in the accompaniment never

[1] *Sturm und Drang*: The oddly translated *Storm and Stress* movement—*Drang* has more the meaning of urgency—united the young revolutionary writers in Germany between, say, 1767 and 1787. Herder, Goethe and Schiller were its intellectual leaders. It bears comparison with *Pre-Romanticism*. (Ed.)

stop, not even during the *Erlkönig*'s wheedlings. 'Ich liebe dich' ('I love you') causes such a change in the harmonics that it gives the impression that the boy has fainted. The minor ninths on the cry 'Mein Vater. mein Vater!' ('My father, my father!') are the notes which disturbed that first audience and led Ruzicka to demonstrate how appropriate they were. Despite the daemonic quality of the work, Schubert never goes beyond the bounds of what the critic Eduard Hanslick called the 'musically beautiful', notwithstanding the stark reality of the tempestuous riding-*motif* and the recitative at the very end. The heart of the song is not the cleverly managed descriptions and imagery, but the human despair of alienation and the depiction of burning passion. The difficulty of the accompaniment, a nightmare for many a pianist, was not the least of the reasons for *Erlkönig*'s fame—although it has been seen more as pianistic bravura rather than as an integral part of the song. Schubert himself used to play the right-hand octaves as quavers and not as triplets. The autograph manuscript, intended for Goethe, also, prudently perhaps, has quavers. It was a different matter when Franz Liszt, accompanying the French Schubert singer, Adolphe Nourrit, thundered out the left-hand runs in octaves!

After *Erlkönig*, the so-called 'piano accompaniment' had had its day. The piano part as a mere incidental, as an harmonic foundation which simply adorned the vocal part, was a thing of the past. It was now established as an independent composition, even when it is as simple and as concentrated as, say, in *Der Leiermann*, the last song of *Die Winterreise*.

An interesting detail is the original *ff* in the manuscript at 'Ich liebe dich, mich reizt deine schöne Gestalt' (I love you, your fair form attracts me). Schubert later altered this to a *pp,* in red pencil; he had realised how much more intense a *pianissimo* would be. Just how accurate Schubert's interpretation of the *Erlkönig*'s voice was, can be judged from a conversation with Goethe in 1827, reported by Friedrich Forster who was introducing his foster-son, Carl Eckert (later to win distinction as a conductor), to the great poet. The young lad had set *Erlkönig* when he was eight. When Goethe asked him which other settings of the ballad he liked, the boy answered that he knew only Klein's and Reichardt's, but didn't like them, because they made the *Erlkönig* sound so cruel. 'If the Erlking had gone on like that,' the boy said, 'the boy in the poem would have been afraid. The Erlking had to try to seduce the boy with his singing.' 'We have to agree that the lad is right,' remarked Goethe and gave him a friendly pat on the hand. 'After all, you must know best how a little chap riding through the night in his father's arms feels when the Erlking tempts him. Apart from that, we must also admit that the *Erlkönig*, a King of all the Spirits, can take on any singing voice he wishes: he can begin by being gentle and flattering, and then can turn to threats and rage.'

Carl Loewe's fine 1818 setting describes the spirits realistically, but it is musically more simple and never reaches the depths of tragedy of the Schubert version. Unlike Schubert, Loewe had the good fortune to meet Goethe, in 1820. Goethe's diary entry for September reads: 'Kandidat Loewe from Halle, very musical'. Loewe recounts in his autobiography:

Goethe was extremely kind. While we walked up and down in his drawing-room, he talked about the nature of the ballad form. I told him that I loved ballads above all other literary genres, and how the popular legend of his *Erlkönig*, clothed in the wonderfully Romantic garment of his poem, had quite swept me off my feet, so much so that I had had to set this *Erlkönig* to music. I considered the *Erlkönig* to be the best German ballad because all the characters are introduced in conversations. 'You are right in that', said Goethe. Then I asked to be allowed to sing my *Erlkönig* to him. 'Unfortunately I have no instrument here in Jena', he said. 'I regret this all the more because I always work better after having listened to music.'

Thus Loewe did not manage to extract a Goethean judgement on his music either, although the poet did allow his grandson, Walther, to study composition with Loewe. The archives of the *Gesellschaft der Musikfreunde* have a Beethoven draft of an *Erlkönig*-setting, whose 6/8 simplicity is more akin to Loewe's interpretation, and only emphasises the miracle that was Schubert's.

The most notable interpreters of the song have all been bass-baritones: Michael Vogl, Joseph Staudigl, Julius Stockhausen, Eugen Gura, Theodor Reichmann, Ludwig Wuellner and Hans Hotter. (If the ballad has also become a favourite with female singers, it must be said that, with very few exceptions, this has remained a one-sided love affair.)

No poet so fired Schubert's creative imagination as did Goethe. Everything that Schubert strove to express in music, clarity of thought and expression, deep emotion, imaginative language, all this he found in Goethe's poetry. Here he was confronted with that unity of Art and Nature which was part of his own personality. By the end of 1815 he had set thirty-four Goethe poems.

One of the most remarkable is *Meeresstille* (D 216). No other composer has ever managed to picture a windless, oppressive seascape with such convincing, yet obvious means. The graphic imagery of the uncertain broken chords, the gentle, almost apprehensive modulations, blend with the text to make a perfect unity. The score of the song looks like a drawing, with the vertical arpeggi illustrating 'Todesstille fürchterlich' ('a fearful deathly silence') and absolute immobility. At 'in der ungeheueren Weite' ('in the enormous expanse'), the heart of the poem, harmonic daring goes as far as it had ever gone. Schubert composed this marvellous song at about the same time as Beethoven's choral setting. The poem is from Goethe's collection of epigrams, and has a pendant in the lively *Glückliche Fahrt*.[1]

In every respect, the most important of the 40 published settings of *An den Mond* is Schubert's (D 296). Despite its charm, the first strophic setting of the same year (D 259) had not really been successful. But now the quite incomparable delicacy and longing contained in the poem, the alternation 'of joy and sorrow', find their most sublime expression. It was probably the death of the lovelorn Christel von Lassberg who drowned herself in the Ilm, not far from Goethe's garden-house in Weimar, which led Goethe to write the poem. In Schubert's first version, the third and fourth stanzas still mirror the daemonic, death-bringing powers of the water; there is little trace of 'lyricism' in the song, either classical or romantic. Such a miracle could be explained only perhaps by the purity of Schubert's artistic powers. We are shown the strength of music liberated, the essence of love made music.

The first three notes of the song exude such emotion that the anacrusis determines the pattern of the whole song. Words like 'art' or 'inspiration' fail for such immortal music. Reflection and

[1] *Meeresstille* was published in 1821 with other Goethe-Lieder as opus 3 no. 2. Reichardt's setting is also imaginative, and Mendelssohn's concert overture, *Meeresstille und Glückliche Fahrt*, of 1832, was inspired by the poem.

emotion interweave here as in few poems. What more could have been added?

The prelude begins with a chord which echoes the poet's feeling of unfulfilment, his inability to forget, his yearning for his friend. Schubert's ability to portray foreboding, the scope and certainty of his music, are beyond belief.

The first notes of the song direct our gaze upwards. Even the gesture of consolation in the spontaneous 'Nimmer werd' ich froh' ('I shall never be happy') points upward. Schubert has taught us to expect such musical intensity even in the most perfect poem, but music such as this beggars all the description, all the imagery, all the characterisation of the poem itself.

Schubert makes one song stanza out of each two stanzas of the poem, and recasts the sixth and seventh because of the odd number of stanzas. He introduces movement and harmonic variety in the form of a musical modulation to express 'Rausche, Fluß' ('Ripple along, river'), and so the last two stanzas can return to the tempo of the first two. Because they belong together, however, a two-bar interlude shortens the work, and the last line 'wandelt in der Nacht' ('wanders in the night'), is repeated as a coda an octave higher, as though raised up by hope.

But Schubert set a wide variety of Goethe poems. Because of the patchiness of the details, the version of *Am Flusse* of February 1815 (D 160) cannot be compared with that of 1822 (D 766), despite the turbulent D minor passages. The emotional climax on 'meiner Treue Hohn' ('scorn of my honour') is reminiscent of that in *Gretchen am Spinnrade*.

Die Spinnerin (D 247) tallies so closely with Goethe's own conception of the function of music in the Lied that one must agree with those who claim that he can never have looked at any of the Schubert settings sent to him, and that he would take advice from nobody about them. Had he looked at this composition he could not fail to be delighted with the obvious agreement with his own views.

Klärchens Lied (D 210), from Goethe's play *Egmont* (1788), is in two parts. The first part has eight bars of serene triplets in the treble, and a wonderfully declamatory vocal line above expressive harmonisation. 'Himmelhoch jauchzend, zu Tode betrübt' ('Rejoicing to Heaven, despairing unto death') leads, in mounting excitement, to the second part 'Glücklich allein ist die Seele, die liebt' ('Happy alone is she who loves'). After the victorious top B flat at the repeat, the song dies away in *pianissimo*. Beethoven, in his much-admired version for the stage performance, lengthened these brief lines by repeats, whereas Schubert was happy to leave well alone.

The version of *Kennst du das Land* of October 1815 (D 321) is rather weak, and one has to agree with Schumann's view about all settings of this poem prior to Hugo Wolf's: 'Beethoven's excepted, I know of no setting of this poem which could possibly compare with the effect of the poem itself, without music. Whether it should be through-composed or not matters little; ask Beethoven where he found his music.'[1]

Shortly before he composed the Goethe-Lieder of 1815, the 18-year-old Schubert set a poem by Bernhard Ehrlich, *Als ich sie erröten sah* (D 153). Although not comparable in terms of musical craftsmanship, it is a more subjective counterpart to the famous *Gretchen am Spinnrade*. It has the same rhythm and a similar line in the vocal part, as well as semiquavers in the accompaniment. This outpouring of youthful longing is to be sung 'mit Liebesaffekt' ('with loving emotion'); it looks simple enough, but it makes virtuoso demands on the singer, above all with respect to the lightness of intonation.

The Ossian-Lieder, most of which were composed in this year, 1815, are quite different. Regrettably, many valuable musical ideas are hidden in the Scotch mists of these at times incomprehensible texts. Behind the pseudonym 'Ossian' lurked the figure of James Macpherson (1736–1796), who launched a lyrical fashion in the late years of the eighteenth century with the publication of his *Fragments of Ancient Poetry collected in the Highlands of Scotland and translated from the Gaelic or Erse language* (Edinburgh 1760), which he ascribed to an old Scottish bard, Ossian. Other poems and several translations appeared, and Ossian became all the rage. The poems were later proved not to be genuine, but, along with Bishop Thomas Percy's *Reliques of Ancient English Poetry* (1765), they awakened an enthusiasm for folkloric simplicity in poetry. Goethe's Werther confessed that 'Ossian has replaced Homer in my heart'.

[1] The flood of settings encouraged many parodists too. Reichardt set one which began 'Kennst du das Land, wo stets die Veilchen blühn . . .' ('Do you know the land where the violets always bloom . . .')

It appears that Schubert encountered Ossian in a rather late and apparently poor translation by Baron Edmund de Harold. He must however have been quite captivated by these poems, else he would surely never have plunged with such vehemence into the adventure of setting to music these landscape pictures peopled by heroes. Nothing very important came out of it all, it must be said, excepting perhaps the artistry of the ballad *Lodas Gespenst* (D 150), with its virtuoso declamation and characterisation; the conclusion is reminiscent of Loewe's technique of suddenly returning to everyday banality, as in his *Prinz Eugen*. The autograph manuscript of 17th January 1816 was revised for publication in 1830. The text was refurbished, and, in the preface to the second edition, the publisher of the Harold translations felt obliged to apologise for the linguistic shortcomings of the Irish translator: 'In the meantime he has improved his knowledge of the German language.' In addition, the last bars of the ballad were replaced by a revision of Schubert's *Punsch-Lied* (D 277).

Leopold von Sonnleithner (1797–1873) gave the reason later:

Diabelli [the publisher] believed that a long vocal piece with such an indecisive conclusion was quite unsuitable for a public performance. In particular, he was of the opinion that at least one of the heroic songs should follow the recitative as the introductions seemed to promise, so that the work should come to a satisfactory conclusion. Soon he produced Schubert's setting of Schiller's *Punsch-Lied* ('many elements put together with feeling') and demanded that I compose another text to attach to *Lodas Geist* [*sic*] as a 'Heldengesang' ('heroic song'). In those days I used to amuse myself with all sorts of musical and poetical odd jobs, translations and the like, and in order to hasten the publication of the Ossian songs, I agreed to deliver the few verses demanded and to change the *Punsch-Lied* into a 'heroic song' . . .

It was clear that the task was undertaken with some reluctance, and Mandyczewski was right to restore the original concise ending in his edition of the ballad.

The fourteen pages of *Der Tod Oskars* (D 375), written in 1816, are proof of Schubert's great desire to write an Ossian-opera—if only he had managed to find a librettist.

Ossian's *Lied nach dem Falle Nathos* (D 278) will not be everyone's idea of *arioso,* but a certain formality and a few of the details betray Schubert's intentions, in particular the Gluck-like ending. But what was Schubert's purpose in giving the unstressed unimportant word 'in' half a note—and on a high F sharp?

Among the other extended ballads *Die Nacht* (D 534) deserves some attention, if only because, after Schubert's death, a finale was appended to it, taken from the *Jagd-Lied* (D 521) of Zacharias Werner, which was composed in the same year. It is significant that the shortest and most concentrated Ossian-Lied, *Das Mädchen von Inistore* (D 281), also has the most 'atmosphere'.

There are very few poems among the Schiller settings which possess those qualities so important to Schubert—a clearly defined emotion, a precisely located background, and, above all, a final stanza (or, at least, a final *line*) with an epic quality about it. Schubert usually found these desired qualities in the poems of lesser writers, whereas Schiller's high-flown effusions almost always let him down. It is therefore all the more ironical that *Lied* ('Es ist so angenehm, so süß') ('It is so pleasant, so sweet') (D 284), until lately ascribed to Schiller, is now believed to have been written by the patroness of his early years, Frau Caroline von Wolzogen. Schubert's genius is reflected in the flawlessness of this jewel.

The next poet to whom Schubert turned was the complete antithesis to Schiller. The pretentious style of the village priest on the Baltic island of Rügen, Ludwig Kosegarten (1758–1818), followed familiar paths. Yet, in the summer and autumn of 1815, Schubert was so fascinated by his poems that, on 19th October, he set seven of them to music.

An Rosa I (D 315) and *II* (D 316) are about the clergyman's beloved, and have little but technical competence to commend them. *Louisens Antwort* (D 319) offers much more, not least because it builds a spiritual bridge to Mozart. Kosegarten wrote the poem in answer to Kramer Schmidt's *Lied der Trennung,* which Mozart set in 1787. Schubert composed the music to the answer twenty years later.

Die Erscheinung (D 229) and *Die Täuschung* (D 230) both promise that love will be fulfilled 'Hochdroben, nicht hienieden' ('Not here but above'), in another world.

Schubert then began work on *Geist der Liebe* (D 233). He asks that the song be sung 'mit Kraft' ('powerfully') and in the piano part at the end he takes the broken E major seventh chord up through three octaves. The tension produced symbolises the moment of truth when the boy becomes a man.

> Nur der ist groß und göttlich,
> Den du zum Mann ermannst

(Only he whom You make a man is great and divine.)

Then the dissonance is resolved.

Schubert also finished the long, difficult dramatic *scena Hektors Abschied* (Schiller) on 19th October 1815, and he must have been longing to write some uncomplicated simple strophic songs. All seven Kosegarten songs are strophic—the day's work had been such that any other form would have been out of the question. Yet no singer should feel obliged to subject an audience to all seventeen verses of *Idens Schwanenlied* (D 317) or the seven of *Schwanengesang* (D 318) or even the nineteen of *Louisens Antwort*. There is just not enough substance in the poetry. One or two stanzas reflect a mood or inspire a musical thought, but a pedantic performance of them all would be a trying experience.

The typical Schubertian A minor of *Das Sehnen* (D 231) and the glorious harmonies of the long *Nachtgesang* (D 314) should be mentioned. Although the setting differs little from Zumsteeg's, its seriousness and the clever strophic divisions of the text just give it the edge.

At the head of a group of songs that could almost be regarded as a song-cycle stands *Die Mondnacht* (D 238), a poem which Schubert found especially challenging. It is in the harmonies and wealth of imaginative detail of such a song that one finds the essential Schubert. The following year he composed *An die untergehende Sonne* (D 457), which suffers both from excessive length and lack of inspiration.

For a long time Schubert was attracted by the poems of Ludwig Heinrich Christoph Hölty and he set nine of them as early as 1815. Hölty, the most important poet of the 'Göttinger Hain'[1] (of which Johann Friedrich Voss, translator of Greek and Latin poetry, the

---

[1] *Göttinger Hainbund*: lit. 'The grove league of Gottingen.' Poets who regarded themselves as the immediate heirs of Klopstock. The name suggests an affinity with Klopstock's 'bards' of northern poetry.

two Dukes of Stolberg and the lyric poet J. A. Leisewitz were also members), was the son of a pastor, who also educated his son for entrance to university. Even before Hölty went up to Göttingen University, he had shown poetic leanings. His delicate spring and love poems are still attractive today. He died in 1776, at the age of twenty-eight, younger even than Schubert was when he died. In addition to Schubert, Peter Cornelius and Brahms also set his poems to music.

Hölty's emotional range is narrow. His poems can be seen as forerunners of that strange mixture of melancholy and protest, so beloved of the Viennese *Biedermeier*. His name first appears in 1813 on Schubert's setting of *Totengräberlied* (D 44), which begins with a loud declamatory passage, followed by a good, solid, slightly ironical melody. The verses of this remarkable little song all begin in different keys, viz. G major, C major and A minor—and each time the melody changes slightly.

Die Mainacht (D 194) is structured even more rigidly. Schubert invents a flute-like melody to represent the poet's nightingale. Brahms's setting of *Mainacht* (opus 43 no. 2) made the *da capo* form famous. He did not set the second verse, but made the third into the middle verse and gave the fourth the same melody as the first. Beside this, Schubert's strophic version looks rather unadventurous but, when listened to carefully, the particular quality of his setting, stylistically much nearer the form of the original poem after all, will be recognised. It is really just a prejudice to claim that Brahms's setting is the more penetrating 'psychologically'. When Schubert considered a poem, he did not study its metrical form; indeed, he was rarely concerned with a slavish imitation of the poet's verse-forms, but was much more interested in his basic speech-rhythms. Hugo Wolf's scrupulous regard for formal verse-structures, which did not always redound to the advantage of the music, lay as yet in the far distant future.

On 17th May 1815 Schubert composed the poetic masterpiece of this series, *An den Mond* ('Geuß, lieber Mond') (D 193), exactly one year before he set Hölty's *Klage an den Mond* (D 436/437). The numerous modifications in these much-altered strophic songs will make difficulties for any pedant wishing to classify them. The beginning and end of *An den Mond* are related—and not by accident—to the first movement of Beethoven's *Moonlight Sonata,* both in their mood and in the 12/8 time. The two middle stanzas are in contrasting 4/4 time. How could the moon do other than console the forlorn wanderer when confronted with such a heart-rending supplication?

The second verse of *Klage an den Mond* is more firmly harmonised —it speaks of the bitter present day. Sorrow for what is past is expressed in the first verse by a gentle melody in 6/8 time. The third verse prophesies an early death; the new theme of this part shows how Schubert identifies himself with the poet.

Der Leidende (D 432) conceals the musical source of the Entr'acte in B minor from *Rosamunde* and bears a strong resemblance to Glinka's *A Life for the Czar*.

Both *An die Apfelbäume* (D 197) and *Seufzer* (D 198) were written shortly after *Die Mainacht* on 22nd May 1815.

Of similar intimacy and only for lovers of small-scale works are *Der Liebende* (D 207), *Der Traum* (D 213) and *Die Laube* (D 214). *Die Nonne* (D 208), a rather clumsy, typically Romantic ghost story, leaves us musically and textually cold, although Schubert did revise it two weeks later (D 212).

Winterlied (D 401) first appeared in the *Vossischen Musen-Almanach* in 1777 in a setting by J. F. Reichardt (1752–1814). It is astounding how often Reichardt first set poems which were then taken up later by Schubert.

The Hölty group of 1816 is again made up of short pieces. The title *Klage* appears twice—one, a Matthisson poem (D 415), the other by Hölty, and lines like:

> Stets in Glut und Beben,
> Schleicht mir hin das Leben

(Always a-fire and a-trembling, Life slips away from me)

certainly seemed to express Schubert's mood at that time.

Auf den Tod einer Nachtigall (D 201 and D 399) is slightly reminiscent of Telemann's *Kanarienvogel-Trauerkantate* (The Canary Cantata), but there is no trace here of Telemann's mocking tone, and the flood of remonstrations is replaced by unobtrusive sorrow.

The folk-song-like trio *Frühlingslied* (D 503), *Erntelied* (D 434) and *Winterlied* (D 401) could become a charming little song-cycle.

These were followed by a series of unpretentious love-songs, but the melodic power of *An den Mond* of 1815 is missing. (This, the most popular of the Hölty songs, was published in 1826 as opus 57, no. 3.)

During this period, Schubert had moved away from his parents' house for the first time and was living in the house of Professor Heinrich Watteroth, next door to the Pasqualet house on the Mölkerbastei where Beethoven met Bettina von Brentano[1] in 1810. There, too, lived his friend Josef Witteczek (1787–1859) who, over the years, acquired a vast collection of Schubert manuscripts and published works, which were to prove of priceless value in the documentation of Schubert's Lieder. The collection came ultimately into the possession of the *Gesellschaft der Musikfreunde* in Vienna.

To ensure that the Goethe-Lieder would be played and sung as Schubert would have wished, they were carefully copied and parcelled up on 17th April 1816 and sent to Goethe in Weimar with the following letter written by Spaun:

Your Excellency!

The undersigned ventures to rob Your Excellency of a moment of Your valuable time with these lines, and only the hope that the enclosed collection of songs might be a not altogether unpleasant gift can excuse him for taking so great a liberty. The works in the enclosed book are by a 19-year-old composer named Franz Schubert, whom Nature had endowed from his earliest years with the most remarkable talent for composition, which Salieri, the Nestor among composers, has brought to maturity, by means of his selfless devotion to his Art. The general approval accorded the young artist for these songs, as well as for his other, already numerous compositions, by strict judges of the art, as well as by laymen, men and women alike, and the general desire of his friends, finally persuaded this modest youth to set out on his musical career by publishing a few of his compositions. By this act, he will almost certainly soon raise himself to that place among German composers to which his exceptional talents entitle him. It commences with a selection of

[1] Famous for her correspondence with Goethe and Beethoven. The sister of Clemens von Brentano, she married the Romantic poet Achim von Arnim.

German songs which are to be followed by some longer instrumental works. This will comprise eight volumes. The first two (of which the first is enclosed as an example) contain poems by Your Excellency, the third contains poems by Schiller, the fourth and fifth by Klopstock, the sixth by Matthisson, Hölty, Salis etc, the seventh and eighth, songs of Ossian, which latter excel all others. The artist wishes humbly to dedicate this collection to Your Excellency to whose so magnificent poetry he is indebted, not only for the origin of a large part of them, but essentially also for his own maturing as a German composer. Yet, as he is too modest to consider his works worthy of the great honour of confronting a name so celebrated wherever the German language is spoken, he has not the courage to request this great favour of Your Excellency. I, therefore, one of his friends, and permeated with his music, venture to ask Your Excellency for this favour on his behalf; care will be taken to prepare an edition worthy of this favour. I refrain from any further praise of these songs—they may speak for themselves. I must only add that the volumes to follow are in no way inferior in their melodies to the present, but might even be superior, and, further, that the pianist, who is to perform them for Your Excellency, must not be lacking in facility and expression. Should the young artist be so fortunate as to gain the approval of one whose approval would honour him more than that of any man in the whole wide world, then I may venture to be informed of such permission in two words. In boundless admiration, I remain, Your Excellency's most obedient servant, Josef Edler von Spaun.

The servile tone of this letter may have exaggerated Goethe's vanity and may also have contributed to the absence of a reply. A convincing explanation of Goethe's silence has not yet been offered. The approach to Goethe, which Schubert undertook only with reluctance, was brought about by the efforts of his friends to publish a series of music books in which the songs would be arranged according to the poets of the texts. The first two volumes would contain Goethe settings: *Gretchen am Spinnrade, Schäfers Klagelied, Rastlose Liebe, Geistesgruß, An Mignon, Nähe des Geliebten, Meeresstille, Der Fischer, Wanderer Nachtlied* (Der du von dem

Himmel bist), *Erster Verlust, Die Spinnerin, Heidenröslein, Wonne der Wehmut, Erlkönig, Der König in Thule, Jägers Abendlied.*

Schubert's fair copies of these songs can be seen in the Deutsche Staatsbibliothek in East Berlin. Scholars have not yet been able to establish whether this is the complete collection.

The second volume contains: *Nachtgesang, Der Gott und die Bajadere, Sehnsucht, Mignon, Trost in Tränen, Der Sänger, Der Rattenfänger, An den Mond* (first version), *Bundeslied, Wer kauft Liebesgötter?, Tischlied.*

One section of this second group, which is dated May 1816, is in the library of the Paris Conservatoire, the other in the Stadtbibliothek in Vienna.

Goethe, who either rejected these songs or treated them with indifference, could never have suspected that, in many parts of the world, his name would achieve immortality solely through the music of this poor Viennese schoolmaster. The first volume was returned to Spaun, the second was not even sent off to him. The expectations were not fulfilled. Schubert had been sure that one should not enter so lightly into correspondence with such a world-famous figure— and he had been proved right. And Spaun's worldly-wise approach had not done much good, either.

The claim that Goethe did not even *look* at the settings seems difficult to sustain; it might well have been the case that the gifted pianist suggested by Spaun in his letter was actually not available. In addition, Goethe relied entirely on the judgement of the very conservative director of the Berlin *Singakademie*, Carl Friedrich Zelter, who would dismiss Schubert's works with a wave of the hand, since they were hardly known, after all, outside Schubert's very limited circle of friends. One can also understand that the utterly novel musical language, particularly of the accompaniments, would mean nothing to Goethe, who knew only the old-style Lied. But what about *Heidenröslein* (D 257)? This famous setting combines the merits of the *Volkslied* (folk-song) and the *Kunstlied* (art song) and must be close to the Goethean ideal. It was a stroke of inspired genius that made Schubert leave the poem and its lovely melody to stand on its own, as it were. Thus, once the wonderful articulation has been found, nothing can detract from its simple rural charm. Herder, five years older than Goethe, had suggested that the latter should collect folk-songs from Alsace. Had Goethe not followed this advice so willingly, *Heidenröslein* could never have been written. But who was there to help Goethe appreciate the frightening magnificence of *Gretchen am Spinnrade* at the beginning of the collection?

The later masterpiece, *An Schwager Kronos* of 1816 (D 369), a setting of the poem written on a post-chaise journey in 1774 during Goethe's *Sturm und Drang* period, was probably also beyond the old man's comprehension, since it contains everything that was 'new' in Schubert's concept of the Lied. The former 'pretty tune' is replaced by a true interpretation of the poem. In Goethe's day, the postilion was called *Schwager* and the poet retains the image, as *Chronos* ('Time') rushes him through Life in an imaginary post-chaise bound for the Underworld. The piano accompaniment vividly conveys the 'rasselnden Trott' ('rattling trot'), boldly in the introduction, and then, in the vocal part, it is concentrated on three notes, which are now and then emphasised by accented chords. 'Ekles Schwindeln' ('an unpleasant giddiness') transposes the musical figures of bass and treble which become thirds in the interlude. 'Eratmender Schritt' ('exhausting march') is characterised by sighs in the bass. At 'weit, hoch, herrlich' ('far, high, magnificent') the bass ascends in octaves. The middle section, 'seitwärts des Überdachs Schatten' ("To one side the shade of the overhanging roof'), is given a dancing quality which becomes an idyllic passage in the accompaniment. Then it descends ('ab denn, rascher hinab') ('down, down') on a simple theme and without any acceleration. The frightening *subito piano* on 'ergreift im Moore Nebelduft' ('I am caught on the moor by a rising mist') is usually overlooked by singers, and yet it is so expressive, since it allows a renewal of the relentless dynamic surge.

This is an astonishing song; only Schubert's music reveals the sheer power of the poem, and some extra dimensions too. As in *Erlkönig,* a galloping *motif* is sustained over long passages although, in this song, it is treated more contrapuntally, and the 6/8 tempo is never abandoned throughout the entire bumpy ride. The motion of the journey is relentless, even when there are invitations to tarry by the way. At the end, the tempo must be sustained enough to suggest the notes of a post-horn, and the piano volume has to be so adapted to the low vocal register that only the accentuations remain to suggest the development of power. (The famous Bayreuth

Wotan, Anton van Rooy, was one of the first singers to give a concert performance of *An Schwager Kronos*.)

The song was published with two other Goethe settings as opus 19 in 1825 and dedicated to Goethe, whose youthful ardour had long since given way to a serene and contemplative old age.

FOUR

Lieder of 1816 – 1817

Most of the songs to poems by Johann Gaudenz von Salis-Seewis (1762–1834) belong to the year 1816. Salis was an officer in French service and a captain in the Royal Swiss Guard at Versailles. During a journey through Germany shortly before the outbreak of the French Revolution he met Goethe, Schiller, Herder and Wieland (a writer of 'romances' and epic poetry) in Weimar and also became friendly with Matthisson, who later published his poems. On his return, he left military service, but lived in Paris during the Revolution and then returned to Switzerland to take an active part in Swiss political affairs.

The eleven poems set to music by Schubert are of varied musical interest. *Lied* (Ins stille Land) (D 403) has an impressive gravity about it. It is interesting to note that the melodic structure of the song is not unlike that of the final version of *Nur wer die Sehnsucht kennt,* one of the *Mignon-Lieder.* It took ten years for the melody to find a suitable text. The relating of words to melody reveals the one-ness of Schubert's emotions, but he was also immediately attracted by the earnest and reserved nature of the poem. This little gem deserves to be better known.

Der Herbstabend (D 405) is a song for lovers of *bel canto. Das Grab* (D 330), a poem written in 1783, was a great favourite in Schubertian circles in Vienna. Schubert's friends, Hüttenbrenner and Randhartinger, also set it to music.

Die Einsiedelei (D 393 and D 563) was set twice as a solo Lied, but there is also a setting for male chorus of unknown date (D 337). In the two solo versions, a spring babbles merrily away in the triplets of the accompaniment under an independent melody.

Der Entfernten is best known in the version for male voices (D 331). *Pflügerlied* (D 392) and *Fischerlied* (D 351) are rather slight, but their charm, borrowed somewhat from folk-lore, is seductive.

The last Salis setting came five years after the first, in 1821; the captivatingly beautiful *Der Jüngling an der Quelle* (D 300). Schubert added the melodious name 'Luise' to the last line. (Friedländer wanted to alter this to 'Geliebte' ('beloved') for his edition, but the original is preferable.)

The official *Wiener Zeitung* of 17th February 1816 announced a vacancy for a post as music teacher at the Deutsche Normal-schulanstalt in Laibach: 'The applicant must have had a thorough training as singer and organist and must be an equally good violin-ist. He must possess not only the necessary knowledge of all the usual wind instruments, but also the ability to instruct others in them.'

The announcement was like manna from heaven for Schubert, for now at last he wanted a position as a music teacher to enable him to compose in peace. He was also vaguely thinking of getting married, but he could never live off the pittance which he earned from his father. Thus, in order to get something at all costs, he self-consciously stressed his good points in his application: '2. He has acquired such knowledge and skill in all fields of composition in organ and violin playing and in singing, that, in accordance with the enclosed references, he will be declared the most able and qualified of all the applicants for this position.'

In addition to Salieri, who supplied a half-hearted letter of recommendation, Canon Josef Spendou supported Schubert's application with a warm appreciation of the aspirant's capabilities. But Schubert was unsuccessful—the position was given to one Sokol, a music teacher from Laibach. In the following September, however, Schubert repaid Spendou's kindness by dedicating to him a new cantata (D 472, September 1816).

Great names from a new generation now appear among the poets of Schubert's song-texts. August Wilhelm von Schlegel (1767–1845), and his younger brother Friedrich (1772–1829), came from a literary family. They were the leaders of that literary movement known as the 'Romantic School of Jena'. August Wilhelm's forte lay less in his own creative work than in his wonderfully sensitive and formally perfect translations. He made the first complete German translation of seventeen of Shakespeare's dramas and also trans-lated numerous plays of Calderón and a good deal of the poetry of the Latin races. His lectures on dramatic art and literature in

Vienna, one of which Schubert is said to have attended, and his seminal works of literary criticism had a powerful influence on contemporary German literature. Schubert set ten of his poems to music.

Shortly before Schubert began work on these settings, Schlegel was living in Rome as travelling companion to Madame de Staël; there he engaged the sympathies of the Prussian Envoy to the Holy See, Wilhelm von Humboldt, who wrote about him: 'Schlegel was much less aggressive than I had known him to be; through his relations with the Staël woman, he has perhaps gained less in versatility than he has lost in activity. He has an undeniable, but, so far as I can judge, undoubtedly minor talent, and his true métier will always be that of the translator.'

This judgement is immediately confirmed by the interminable dialogue between the swan and the eagle in *Lebensmelodien* (D 395). Schubert does not seem to have read the poem very carefully; after a brief musical interlude, the absurd stanzas roll on and on. *Die verfehlte Stunde* (D 409) lives up to its name ('The missed hour'), in as far as the promising tension of the beginning suddenly dies away with the quick change of metre in the refrain.

Schlegel's *Sprache der Liebe* (D 410) is harmonically very interesting; after an artless beginning, tumultuous variations culminate in the semiquaver chord of G; then the music slips smoothly back into the original E major of this passionate serenade.

At the end of 1818 Schubert clothed the reflective poetry of Schlegel's *Lob der Tränen* (D 711) in a veil of melodic intimacy. The melody, once one of Schubert's most popular airs, gently descends in restless triplets. There are characteristic variations in the repeat section and then, despite all the sentimentality, it soars up triumphantly to the final section. The poet's view is that whatever delights the senses cannot refresh the spirit. Tears are our lot, inherited from the creative agony of a Prometheus. Pain alone can liberate and ennoble.

1816 was also the year of the last Matthisson settings—seven altogether. Severe though the demands on the singer are, it cannot be said that these songs contribute much to the development of Schubert's art. *Entzückung* (D 413) or *Julius an Theone* (D 419) may be vocally rewarding, but the shorter songs, because of their emphasis on intimacy, are more effective.

The eroticism of Count Stolberg's *Stimme der Liebe* (D 412) is like an intensification of Matthisson's *Adelaide*; its series of modulations, through almost the entire tonal range, compel attention. Like Platen's *Du liebst mich nicht* it received scant praise from its first reviewers.

Count Friedrich Leopold zu Stolberg (1750–1819) was a friend of Goethe. He translated Homer, Plato and Ossian and wrote poems as well, seven of which Schubert set to music. Two of these, *Morgenlied* (D 266) and *Abendlied* (D 276), were composed in 1815. *Daphne am Bach* (D 411) is one of the rare instances of a too nonchalant treatment of a text by Schubert. The features which in the poetry of Claudius, Hölty, Matthisson, Jacobi, Kosegarten or Salis seemed formal and old-fashioned and which therefore called for strictly strophic settings, cannot really be taken seriously in the present case, where the name Daphne seems to be too self-conscious and pretentious for the composer's simple tastes. Even if Daphne's opening phrase 'Ich hab' ein Bächlein funden' ('I have found a little brook') recalls the second song of the *Schöne Müllerin* cycle, *Wohin?* (namely the line 'Ich hört' ein Bächlein rauschen' ('I heard the babbling of a brook'), Daphne's stream cannot compare with the untroubled freshness of the miller-lad's; but even though Daphne's tears are turned into sickly sugar-icing, there is still some musical pleasure to be had from the song.

The musically naïve *An die Natur* (1816) (D 372) is based on a poem by Stolberg, who was inspired by the sight of the Rhine Falls ('by the banks of that river rushing down from Heaven') on a journey through Switzerland.

Schubert's setting of Goethe's *Rastlose Liebe* (D 138) had an astonishingly successful first performance on 13th June 1816 at the elegant house of Count Erdödy. The uninhibited drive of the song expresses more vividly than Goethe's words what the poet was trying to tell us.

In his diary for 14th June 1816, of which there is unfortunately only a fragment extant, Schubert tells us:

I too had to perform on this occasion. I played variations by Beethoven, sang Goethe's *Rastlose Liebe* and Schiller's *Amalia*. The first was enthusiastically received, the second less so. Although I myself thought that my *Rastlose Liebe* was more successful than *Amalia*, one cannot deny that Göthe's [*sic*] musical and poetical genius was largely responsible for the applause.

This would seem to have been one of the first of Schubert's semi-public performances. Earlier in the programme Martin Schlesinger, a leading violinist, had excited Schubert with a performance of music from Mozart's *Zauberflöte*. Both songs were composed in May 1815.

It was discovered some years ago in Linz that this diary-entry was part of the original manuscript of *Rastlose Liebe* which bore the date 19th May 1815. It is therefore certain that it was composed on the same day as *Amalia*. Schubert perhaps sang these two songs on that June day from the same volume, together with other songs written in May 1815.

The ingeniously formal construction of *Rastlose Liebe* is an excellent example of the three-part rondo form which, at the appropriate place in the poem, suggests the possibility of a *rallentando,* but then the music drives on with renewed *élan* to the victorious conclusion. This was meant to discourage a singer from holding the top note on 'Liebe' ('love'), as had been the custom hitherto. With Schubert's uncanny instinct for penetrating to the basic meaning of a poem, the words 'Glück ohne Ruh' ('restless happiness') became the core of the composition. The song races past us, concise, sharply accentuated, rhythmically compulsive, really conceived in orchestral terms. Yet Schubert manages to present the sense of disquiet in a series of climaxes; when for example 'immerzu, immerzu' ('on, on') has to be sung on a penetrating single note, or when the final jubilant 'Liebe, bist du!' ('Love, that is what you are!') is given an unexpected stress.

The poem was written in May 1776 (in a snowstorm), and belongs to the early days of Goethe's love-affair with Charlotte von Stein. The story goes that the 18-year-old Schubert was so excited by it that it took him only a few ecstatic moments to write the music down. Reichardt's setting is the only one comparable to Schubert's. Zelter and Hummel produced dull, insignificant melodies. There is a draft of a Beethoven version which he had mentioned to Goethe, but nothing came of it. It must have been difficult for Salieri to believe that Schubert's stormy and audacious setting was the work of one of his pupils, and yet it was to his old teacher that Schubert dedicated the song, as the first number of opus 5, when it was eventually published in 1821.

Here, as on other occasions, Schubert's pleasant voice was an attractive though, for the larger public, hardly effective enough medium of propaganda for his songs. For them to gain wider acceptance, a singer with a trained voice and interpretative skills had to be found. It was Schubert who created the so-called 'Kammersänger' [A singer of more intimate music. Ed.], who would specialise in the performance of Lieder, accompanied at the piano. Even today, singers usually feel more at home on the opera stage—so who in Schubert's day would have chosen this art form, so fundamentally different from the traditional operatic fare with all its opportunities for bravura performances? True: technique, vocal range, volume, all these were occasionally demanded in these new songs too, but, in the last analysis, what mattered were simplicity and lyrical restraint. Their aim was to reveal all the subtleties of the text through the poetry of music—*and* in German! Was Salieri then to be proved right after all? Had Schubert's teacher not warned him that there was little opportunity of public acclaim with these songs, and also that they might even prevent an *entrée* into the world of grand opera. Beethoven had just created the form of the 'song-cycle' with his best songs, *An die ferne Geliebte* (opus 98) ('To the distant beloved'), the first group of songs with a central *motif*. The publication of these songs, which corresponded so closely to Schubert's own musical ideas, came as a revelation to Schubert and gave him strength to continue his own struggle. Yet even the songs of a musician as famous as Beethoven received little attention from the world of music.

It was Schubert's setting of Schiller's *Laura am Klavier* (D 388) in March 1816, with its Mozartian flavour, which offended Salieri —Mozart's bitterest opponent—so much, and which finally led to the estrangement between Schubert and his old teacher. Laura is not presented as 'mastering the keyboard' or with 'voluptuous impetuosity', as is described in the text, but rather as the coy dilettante heard playing next door.

> Mädchen, sprich! Ich frage, gib mir Kunde:
> Stehst mit höhern Geistern du im Bunde?

> Ist's die Sprache, lüg' mir nicht,
> die man in Elysien spricht?

(Speak to me, girl, I ask, so tell me: Are you in league with higher powers? Is this the language (don't lie to me), that they speak in Elysium?)

With unprecedented audacity Schubert allowed the piano an independent rôle in the prelude and the postlude. (The name 'Philadelphia' in the text may well puzzle some singers, incidentally —it refers to a conjuror who used to entertain Frederick the Great!)

Let us remain for a while with the Schiller songs of 1816. Schiller's *forte* had been the epic- or ballad-like poem and it is plain that the extensive works which Schubert bravely tackled, often with great gusto, could not always succeed in musical terms. The music for *Ritter Toggenburg* (D 397) is entirely unconvincing. There are certainly occasional truly dramatic passages in the first section; there are fine lyrical sections, the recitative is not completely unsuccessful—but the poem just does not suit the music, and it is noticeable that Schubert's invention (or interest?) wanes in the second part. A tearful A flat minor dominates for four stanzas, and not even the transition to A flat major before the conclusion can enliven our interest. The regression to a slavish imitation of Zumsteeg had a paralysing effect on Schubert, who had little interest in the contemporary German interpretation of the Middle Ages.

Since they carelessly disregard the emphases in the poem, the twelve stanzas of Schubert's literary history in verse, *Die vier Weltalter* (D 391), make it difficult for any singer to carve out a singable version for himself. It looks as if he is left to find what tasty morsels he can out of this drinking song in 6/8 time. There is no middle way between never-ending narrative recitatives and brief lyrical interludes. And no one will blame the tenor who transposes the tiresomely high tessitura of *Die Entzückung an Laura* (D 390).

Only an obsequious admirer of Schiller could ever have undertaken to set *Der Flüchtling* (D 402) to music. Here again, Schubert relapsed into Zumsteeg's style, but his complete identification with the wanderer whose home is not on this earth, enabled him to find the dream-like march-*motif* for the introduction. A simpler poem might possibly have become a companion for *Der Wanderer* composed in the following year.

After some months I went out again one evening for a stroll. There is probably nothing more pleasant than to walk about outside in the evening after a hot summer's day, and the fields between Währing and Döbling [suburbs of Vienna. Ed.] seem to have been fashioned for this purpose. I felt so contented there with my brother Carl in the mysterious twilight. 'How beautiful it all is!' I cried and stood still, quite delighted. The churchyard nearby reminded us of our dear mother.

The same joy in, and deep feelings for natural things as expressed in the above diary entry for 14th June 1816 are contained in *Gott im Frühlinge* (D 448), a poem by Johann Peter Uz (1720–1796). Uz, the son of a goldsmith in Ansbach, was a lawyer in his native city, and was considered one of the leading figures of the German Anacreontics, an eighteenth-century group of German poets who attempted to write in the style of the sixth-century BC Greek lyric poet, Anacreon:

> Mit eurer Lieder süßem Klang,
> Ihr Vögel, soll auch mein Gesang
>   Zum Vater der Natur sich schwingen.
> Entzückung reißt mich hin!
> Ich will dem Herrn lobsingen,
> Durch den ich wurde, was ich bin!

(With the sweet sound of your song, O birds, my song too shall rise to the father of all nature. Delight transports me. I shall praise the Lord who made me what I am!)

Schubert's melody is totally convincing. Unfortunately only portions of the text are extant of what was probably his best Uz setting: *An Chloen* (D 363), the introduction to which was cut off by his half-brother Andreas (1823–1893). Uz wrote rococo poetry in imitation of the Italian and French poets in whom Schubert was interested during 1816.

Schubert's setting of the Twenty-third Psalm *Der gute Hirte* (D 449) is of interest mainly for its expressive harmonies. The picturesque expressiveness of *Die Nacht* (D 358), on the other hand, should not be weakened by a monotonous repetition of all its verses.

The day after the celebrations of Salieri's fiftieth birthday on 17th June, Schubert wrote in his diary: 'Today I composed for money for the first time, namely, a cantata by Dräxler for the name-day of Professor Watteroth. The fee is 100 florins.'[1]

That such a sum was more than double his annual salary gave Schubert cause for reflection. A group of students, Spaun among them, were planning an offering for their professor, Heinrich Watteroth, a freethinking teacher of Law at the University of Vienna. Philipp Dräxler, one of the students, hinting at Watteroth's brave stand against Metternich's police, chose the legend of Prometheus as the subject. To suit the festive circumstances, the cantata was to combine jovial playfulness with a more serious element. Schubert conducted the performance himself. During the rehearsals he became friendly with young Leopold Sonnleithner, who from then on was one of his most ardent supporters. This is Sonnleithner's glowing description of the impression made on him by the cantata:

> The work, full of expression and emotion and brilliantly orchestrated, nevertheless did not receive a public performance. I proposed it repeatedly for performance at the concerts of the *Musikverein*, but nobody would risk presenting the work of a young, as yet unrecognised composer. Alas, the work has taken its own revenge for this insult: it is lost.

Like Beethoven, Schubert was perpetually fascinated by the Prometheus legend, as can be seen from his bold and thought-provoking 1819 setting of the Goethe poem (D 674). The prejudice against the composer's youthfulness or lack of distinction could not prevent at least the news of the cantata's performance from leaking out.

A law student, Franz von Schlechta, who had been a fellow-pupil (on the aristocratic side) in the *Konvikt* shortly before Schubert's departure, composed a poem for the *Allgemeine Theaterzeitung* in Vienna entitled 'An Franz Schubert—als seine Kantate Prometheus aufgeführt wurde' ('To Franz Schubert—when his cantata Prometheus was performed'):

[1] The cantata was *Prometheus* (D 451), 'for the name-day of Heinrich Josef Watteroth'. The manuscript was lost. (Ed.).

In der Töne tiefem Weben,
Wie die Saiten jubelnd klangen,
Ist ein unbekanntes Leben
In der Brust mir aufgegangen.

(As the strings joyfully resounded through the deep web of the music, an unsuspected pulse of life suddenly surged through my breast.)

Both Schlechta and Schubert had sung in the *Prometheus* performance, which seems to have completely captured the passionate desire of these young men for freedom and human dignity. Franz Xaver Freiherr von Schlechta (1796–1875) later became a departmental head in the Austrian Finance Ministry and was granted the title of 'Wirklicher Geheimer Rat' (a high-ranking Privy Councillor). He had many stage successes, apart from his poetry.

Schubert had written the first of his Schlechta settings in the previous year, 1815. Its title was *Auf einen Kirchhof* (D 151), and it expresses very vividly the attraction that a churchyard, and the thoughts of the dead, held for a half-orphan (which Schubert was, too, of course). Recitative, *arioso* and aria all betray Italian influence. The young Schubert is identifying himself with the Baron's confession, and intensifies the answer to the dread question whether the spirit within him must also become 'eitel Staub' ('vain dust') like his mortal remains, to a euphoric *forte*:

Nein, was ich im Innern fühle,
Was entzückend mich erhebt,
Ist der Gottheit reine Hülle,
Ist der Hauch, der in mir lebt!

(No, what I feel within me, what raises me in rapture, is the pure spirit of the Godhead, the breath that lives within me!)

This is the third song of the year 1815. Unfortunately the fine expressive opening is swamped a little by the operatic drama of the conclusion.

The last setting of a Kosegarten text appeared in 1816. It demonstrates Schubert's ability to write a masterpiece, even when inspiration was either weak, or lacking altogether. *An die untergehende Sonne* (D 457) is in rondo form with two repetitions of the first address and two lengthy interludes. So as not to make an already extensive song even longer, the critical composer omitted half the poem. (It was published in 1827 as opus 44.)

There is an entry in Schubert's diary for 8th September 1816: 'There are only a few moments which enlighten Life's gloom; in the afterlife the blissful moments will become everlasting joy and more blissful ones will give us glimpses of more blissful worlds etc.'

At about the same time, Schubert wrote the piano cantata, *Lied des Orpheus, als er in die Hölle ging* (D 474), to a text of Johann Georg Jacobi (1740–1814):

> Götter, die für euch die Erde schufen,
> Werden aus der tiefen Nacht
> Euch in selige Gefilde rufen,
> Wo die Tugend unter Rosen lacht.

(Gods, who did create the earth for you, out of darkest night will call you to the Elysian fields, where virtue smiles under roses.)

Schubert's descending bass line is like a Goethean journey to the Mothers[1] and, even in this relatively early work, it follows the meaning of the poem serenely as well as passionately. Such rhythms and a few not very remarkable notes depict not only Orpheus' journey to the underworld, but also Schubert's continuing ability to pierce through the subconscious to the conscious. *Orpheus* is conceived as a large-scale dramatic cantata. Schubert must have had an extraordinary voice in mind, able to deal not only with the bass register at the beginning, but also the ecstatic tenor passages at the end. The high A's are avoided in the second version of the same date.

Jacobi was the publisher of *Iris,* a magazine for women, and was perhaps the most lyrical of the German Anacreontics. One of the closest of his many friends was Johann Gleim, whose poems were set so often by Haydn and Mozart.

The most significant of the Jacobi-Lieder is probably *Litanei auf das Fest Allerseelen* (D 343), the prayer-like intensity of which presents one of the greatest tests for a singer of Schubert, since he needs to spin out a seemingly endless legato. As the quality of the

---

[1] *The Mothers:* in Goethe's *Faust* (Part II), they stand for the 'primeval, still undifferentiated vitalistic principle of all things'. E. C. Mason, *Faust*: University of California Press, 1967, p. 320. (Ed.)

nine verses is very uneven the singer has to choose with care and should perhaps limit himself to two, since the solemnity of the slow melody would suffer from too many repetitions. The singer who can execute the long spun-out vocal line with a perfect legato and, at the same time, interpret each phrase meaningfully, probably knows everything that there is to know about the technique of singing *piano*. The impressive *ritornello* is one of those rare cases of a postlude which, by introducing a new musical idea, supplements the song, or expands it beyond its limits. (*An die Musik, Rastlose Liebe* and *Ganymed* are other examples.)

Like Uz, Jacobi furnished Schubert with eight Lieder texts, but only *Litanei* achieved immortality, and that only because of the music. (It has been ascribed to 1818 but was in fact set in 1816.)

With a few *pianissimo* notes, *In der Mitternacht* (D 464) captures the mood of nocturnal nature. *Die Perle* (D 466) is a delight in its chatty good humour, and demonstrates how, out of the opening two bars of a song, Schubert can develop a theme for voice and accompaniment. The piano part describes a nervous grasping motion—grasping not only for the lost pearl, but still more for the longed-for lover.

From the same diary entry mentioned above: 'Happy is he who finds a true friend. Happier still he who finds a true friend in his wife. . . . The husband bears misfortune without complaining, yet the pain is all the greater. Why did God endow us with compassion?'

The sentiments correspond exactly with those of the setting of Mayrhofer's *Abschied* (D 475), whose pre-Mahlerian sustained evocations of Nature's sounds were unlike anything else composed up to that time. The poem runs:

> Über die Berge zieht ihr fort,
> Kommt an manchen grünen Ort;
> Muß zurücke ganz allein,
> Lebet wohl! es muß so sein!
> Scheiden, meiden, was man liebt,
> Ach, wie wird das Herz betrübt!
> O Seenspiegel, Wald und Hügel schwinden all;
> Hör' verschwimmen eurer Stimmen Widerhall.

(You go over the mountain chains and come to many a green place, I have to return all alone, so let it be, Farewell! To part, to do without one's love, O how it saddens the heart! The glimmer of lakes, woods and hills disappear, your echoing voices fade into the distance.)

If the theme running through the poem reminds us of Gustav Mahler, the first three bars (which are repeated at the end of the song) and their similarity to the song of the prisoners in Beethoven's *Fidelio,* ('Schnell schwindest du uns wieder': 'You are leaving us again so quickly'), are one more proof of Schubert's veneration of Beethoven. Yet Schubert's question: 'Who can achieve anything after Beethoven?' did not stop him from trying. It was Beethoven's attitude of mind, rather than his abilities as a composer, that Schubert sought to emulate when Beethoven joined Haydn and Mozart as his exemplars.

The two most distinctive Mayrhofer settings of 1816, *Lied eines Schiffers an die Dioskuren* and *Fragment aus dem Äschylus,* show him to be the faithful disciple of Goethe who, having said farewell to his *Sturm und Drang* period, is now seeking a new 'classicism'. Both songs are in the Schubertian nocturnal key of A flat major, both enveloped in dark majesty.

The *Lied eines Schiffers an die Dioskuren* (D 360) is the noble and solemn song of the boatman to the stars watching over the sailors. There is a brief middle section which goes from F minor to F major and where the voice and piano in unison declare the boatman's faith in the spirits.

Schubert was intensely preoccupied with setting Mayrhofer's poems in 1816, beginning with ten songs which varied both musically and poetically. The first was *Fragment aus dem Äschylus* (D 450) which quotes a few lines of a chorus in Mayrhofer's translation of the *Eumenides,* and is given by Schubert to the solo voice.

Liedesend (D 473), a lengthy minstrel's ballad, is not particularly original.

Alte Liebe rostet nie (D 477) and *Zum Punsche* (D 492), a Ländler, both strive for a folk-song manner, the latter being the more successful. *Abendlied der Fürstin* (D 495), a pastoral in 6/8 time, anticipates the song from *Rosamunde.* The obligatory storm appears, even though it is quite unmotivated musically.

Goethe reappears in 1816. Mignon's song *Nur wer die Sehnsucht kennt* (D 359 and 481), set to music hundreds of times, attracted

Schubert six times in all and the various versions of the song span eleven years of his creative life. Who would now dare to support the banal theory of Anton Schindler, the Beethoven worshipper, '. . . that the extremely inventive Schubert should so lack what the literary world would call the art of polishing, which the connoisseur's eye so admires in all the works of the classics'?

Kennst du das Land was also written in 1815 (D 321) but has never been able to win the day over the many later rival versions, particularly that of Hugo Wolf. Mignon's third song *So laßt mich scheinen* (D 469) was left uncompleted in 1816.

The three *Gesänge des Harfners*, the Harper's Songs, also belong to September 1816. Schubert's desire to give the series an inner logic may have led him to alter the sequence of Goethe's poems.[1]

The first song introduces the Harper, the second gives us the reasons for his loneliness, and the third brings to an end what is really a small scale song-cycle, since it describes the old man's utter isolation on earth.

Wer sich der Einsamkeit ergibt, composed in a rather simple 6/8 form in 1815 (D 325), now received a worthier setting (D 478), and was published in 1822, as opus 12 no. 1. Schubert's broadly-conceived song does justice to the piercing sorrow of the poem, even though the music looks so simple and uncomplicated when compared with Schumann's and, in particular, with Wolf's setting. Each of these three composers poured his own self into his composition and has left us a self-portrait. Because he found his own circumstances mirrored there, Schubert loved *Wer nie sein Brot mit Tränen aß* best of the three poems. The three versions (D 480) written in 1816 grow one out of the other. (A definitive version was published as opus 12 no. 2 in 1822.)

All the arguments that Goethe's poems are psychologically more profound than Schubert's settings, and that this therefore proves Schubert's 'lack of understanding', have been influenced by Hugo Wolf's highly psychological treatment of these poems. Yet there are surely a sufficient number of passages containing tonal innovations which would prove Schubert's extraordinary comprehension of these particular poems. Goethe imagined the stanzas as being

[1] Goethe's No. 1 *Wer nie sein Brot mit Tränen aß*, is Schubert's No. 3; Goethe's No. 2 *Wer sich der Einsamkeit ergibt*, is Schubert's No. 1 and Goethe's No. 3. *An die Türen will ich schleichen*, is Schubert's No. 2. (Ed.)

sung and spoken in turn, and they are repeated more than once, while Wilhelm, the hero of the novel, listens to the old man. This gives Schubert a formal justification for repeating each quatrain of his opus 12. In the first repetition, the A minor melody is softened and muted by the major, and is then further modified by the F major cadence. The singer dare not avoid the extremely difficult *diminuendo* of this passage, since the composer is expressing the introspection of the lines. The voice is choked by tears, is forced to break off again and again, and the harp is left to play the interludes alone. Individual stanzas are repeated, thus creating the requisite 'mood of fantasy'. Schubert re-created every detail exactly, without giving the impression of having slavishly followed the text. Everything fits, freely and unforced. The two portions of the song present a complaint and an accusation. Each is repeated in a modified form, both are connected by a motivating middle section.

It goes without saying that a poem of high quality was needed to produce such a song. When the song finishes on the fifth and the piano postlude repeats the unanswered question, as if to say: none will find the answer, the listener is overwhelmed by a song in which Schubert has proved that he can probe the most intimate secrets of the heart. And the claim of the Hugo Wolf fanatics that, in these three songs, Schubert has come nowhere near the psychological interpretations of their idol, will in time be proved to be no more than their preference for the declamatory style of the younger composer over the more musical approach of the older.

The sustained bass line of Schubert's setting of the fragment *An die Türen will ich schleichen* (D 479) (which greatly resembles Beethoven's in his *Bitten*, opus 48) reflects the transitory, unstable mood of the poem while leaving the beginning and the end strangely vague. In the through-composed second stanza, too, the music merely nods to the text in passing.

Both versions of *Nur wer die Sehnsucht kennt* (1816) (D 359 and 481) are lyrically simple, above all when compared with the emotion-laden *arioso* of 1815 (D 310). The first setting, in 2/4 time, is marred by the threefold repetition of the opening lines at the end. The second clearly anticipates the famous version of 1826 (D 877).

Gretchen's Lied *Der König in Thule* (D 367) from Goethe's *Faust* Part I is not a great song, but its archaic simplicity, rather like an old wood-carving, probably does suggest Gretchen absentmindedly tra-la-ing the old air which keeps her thoughts far away from Thule and Norse mythology. Male singers might also make something out of the monotony of the old folk-song-like melody. Schubert has made *Der König in Thule* into a ballad by joining up three identical sections of two stanzas each; these capture the melody hummed at the spinning-wheel, just as the square harmonies capture the melancholy of the northern landscape, without however sacrificing anything of the wonderfully melodic vocal line.

The sliding sixths of *Jägers Abendlied* (D 368) with its restful cantilena conjure up a landscape, as well as the stalking ('schleichenden') gait of the hunter. Schubert does not follow the instructions which Goethe gave in 1814: 'The first and third verses have to be recited energetically, with some fire, while the second and fourth must be more gentle, because here a new emotion has appeared.'

Weber, Tomaschek, Zelter and Reichardt all set this poem, but all in the manner of the folk-song. Schubert omitted the more tempestuous third verse so as not to disturb the serenity of his even, dreamlike setting.

A disappointing fragment of a song also dates from 1816; it promised much but was never completed. The two and a quarter octave range of *Gesang der Geister über den Wassern* (D 484) was probably, if unfortunately, felt to be too ambitious for the bass singer Schubert had in mind, but what exists does suggest that a really great Lied has been lost. Schubert came back to the poem four years later and produced his most impressive choral work for male voices and low strings (D 704). [The final version (D 714) was written in February 1821 (Ed.).]

In October 1816 Schubert produced the archetypal Romantic Lied *Der Wanderer* (D 489), a setting of a poem by an amateur poet, Georg Philipp Schmidt (1766–1849), who called himself 'Schmidt von Lübeck' after his native town. After dabbling in many subjects, he took up medicine at Jena, where he came into contact with the literary circle at Weimar. Later, he travelled all over Europe, practised medicine for a time in Lübeck, worked in a bank, and finally entered the Danish administrative service in Holstein. Apart from his (at that time) very popular occasional poems, he also published historical studies. Now, however, he is remembered only through Schubert's *Wanderer*.

The *Erlkönig* alone surpassed the fame of *Der Wanderer* in the nineteenth century. Schubert had found the poem in an anthology of poems for public recitation published in Vienna in 1815, in which it was erroneously attributed to Zacharias Werner, and it appeared as such in the early Schubert editions. Cappi & Diabelli were the first to publish the song, in May 1821, in a second, only slightly revised version. Meanwhile the poet had altered his original title 'Der Unglückliche' to 'Der Fremdling' ('The Unhappy Man' to 'The Stranger'), whereupon Schubert re-titled his new version *Der Wanderer*. In 1818 he transposed the song into B minor (D 493) for his musical patron, Count Esterházy, and could not resist writing on the frontispiece: 'DER WANDERER: oder DER FREMDLING: oder DER UNGLÜCKLICHE'.

The poem is one of those emotionally charged pieces of doggerel representing the Romantics' reaction to the long dominance of the heroic mode and its strict metrical formality. The yearning for safety and security, neither of which was as widespread as the popular idea of the *Biedermeier* era would suggest, took shape in the characters of such young wanderers who, often in the guise of unhappy lovers, roamed the earth in search of an unattainable ideal. The most striking artistic prototype was to be found later in the songs of *Die schöne Müllerin* and *Die Winterreise*.

Johann Umlauff, a law student who met Schubert in 1818, argued with him about the correct emphasis on the line: 'O Land, wo bist du?' ('O land, where art thou?') Umlauff claimed that the stress should be on the 'du', and should therefore come on the first beat of the bar. Schubert, rightly, would not be moved.

The variations of the Pianoforte Fantasia in C major of 1822 are based on a much-altered extract from *Der Wanderer*. It has been suggested time and again that the piano work is a faithful echo of the sentiments of the song. But what have the words 'Die Sonne dünkt mich hier so kalt' ('I feel the sun so cold here'), uttered by the rootless wanderer, to do with the positive, joyful on-surge of the Fantasia? Liszt, who arranged the Fantasia for piano and orchestra, was certainly justified in calling it the 'Wanderer-Dithyramb', a description which, incidentally, suggested the exact tempo needed for the passage mentioned above, since in the Fantasia, the corresponding theme is marked 'adagio' while, in the song, perhaps by mistake, Schubert did not alter the minims which introduce this passage. Such an interpretation can, however, be challenged by the fact that, in the first version of the song, the composer requested the tempo here to be 'etwas geschwinder' ('rather faster').

It is rare for a song to begin with a pedal point as here. It is as if the wanderer had stopped to catch his breath before beginning to speak. After a passage of recitative, the voice goes into a tranquil cantilena in the major, followed by a passionate outburst, which sinks back after the climax into a mood of sad resignation. Finally, and truly as if with a dying breath, passages in unison lead into the last cadence which, notwithstanding all the melancholy, closes in the major. The most disparate elements have been fused into a convincing whole. (It is difficult to imagine that ambitious trombonists once claimed this piece as their own. This certainly made the song the comical victim of an optical illusion!)

Schubert finally left home and his teaching post in October 1816. At the end of 1815, Spaun introduced him to Franz von Schober, who quickly became one of Schubert's closest friends. Yet the others retained their concern, too, for their hapless companion, overwhelmed by his new independence. Mayrhofer voiced their general amazement at Schubert's never-ending creative activity in his *Geheimnis (an Franz Schubert)* which closes:

> So geht es auch dem Sänger,
> Er singt, er staunt in sich:
> Was still ein Gott bereitet,
> Befremdet ihn wie dich.

(This is what happens to the singer too, he marvels at himself and says: What God silently created, astounds him and you too.)

This was obviously an attempt, however clumsy, to express the friends' admiration for Schubert's genius. Quite unselfconsciously, Schubert set this paean of praise to music as well (D 491) but, because he was really much too modest to attempt an honest assessment of his own character, the music is rather naïve, as if inhibited by shyness. The phrase 'er staunt in sich' is given a sudden *forte* in the piano part. Did Schubert want to denigrate the 'marvelling' and put in 'thinking' and 'working' in its place? The conventional ending demonstrates quite clearly what little value he put on such self-advertisement.

Ritter Franz von Schober (1796–1882) was a versatile and wealthy dilettante idler who, after having toyed for a time with a career in the theatre, was still a student of literature when he met Schubert. Schubert's obvious preference for Schober was the cause of some jealousy on the part of his other friends. Nevertheless, Schober contributed twelve poems, all of importance, to the Schubert Lieder *oeuvre*.

His *Trost im Liede*, in particular, expresses Schubert's mood at that time as convincingly as *An die Musik* (D 547), the song which was for a long time the climax of every Schubert evening. Schober was quite unlike either Schubert or Mayrhofer. Volatile, extremely gifted and sophisticated, he could not be fitted into any traditional bourgeois mould, which is perhaps why he and Schubert were so attracted to one another. It is difficult to assess the truth of the prejudiced accounts circulated by Schubert's friends about the baneful influence which Schober was supposed to have exerted on Schubert. What *is* true is that, from first to last, Schober remained a reliable and faithful friend, ready to help materially when Schubert was hard pressed.

The first Schober poem to be treated was *Genügsamkeit* in 1815 (D 143). In this the effect of the simple Ländler-like setting was certainly rather marred by the sheer incomprehensibility of the text. *Trost im Liede* (D 546), composed in March 1817, is a typical Schubertian blend of intimate seriousness and relaxed musicianship. The remarkable declamatory music at the end of the song suggests a moment of carelessness on Schubert's part, all the more surprising since, only a little time previously, Schubert had been working on an improved version.

An die Musik immortalised the collaboration of the two friends. Of the numerous autograph copies which Schubert made from the original manuscript, one, now in the library of the Paris Conservatoire, is enclosed in an envelope inscribed: 'manuscrit très précieux'.

Schober's poem is derived from a stanza of 'Die bezauberte Rose' ('The enchanted rose'), by Ernst Schulze, which Schubert's friend and medical adviser, Dr J. Bernhardt, had proposed as a libretto for an opera, but which Schubert did not feel was dramatic enough. The following passage expresses the poem's close affinity to Schubert:

Du holde Kunst melodisch süßer Klagen,
Du tönend Lied aus sprachlos finstern Leid,
Du spielend Kind, das oft aus schönen Tagen
In unsere Nacht so duft'ge Blumen streut,
Ohne dich vermöcht' ich nie zu tragen,
Was feindlich längst mein böser Stern mir beut!
Wenn Wort und Sinn im Liede freundlich klingen,
Dann flattert leicht der schwere Gram auf Schwingen.

(O divine art of melodically sweet plaints, O song that is sung
out of a dark soundless agony, O playful child, who strews
scented flowers from happy days into our dark nights, without
you I could not bear what my evil star presages for me! When
word and meaning combine in song, then my worries take wing.)

The reproduction belongs as firmly to the *Biedermeier* as the model
from which it was taken, and even the musical setting, as perfect
an example of its type as one could wish for, cannot obscure that
fact. The vocal part and the piano bass conduct a symbolical dialogue. The simple repetition of chords is a familiar feature of Schubert's music; it allows the pianist a variety of dynamics and a greater
choice of tonal colours. Such repetitions allow a sonority which has
nothing to do with figuration. The Schubertian repetition of chords
has to be carefully distinguished from figurative content. This is
merely a pulsating emotion, there is no additional musical argument.

In 1816, Schubert set only one poem by Schober, the appealing
Am Bach im Frühling (D 361). It was rare for him to set an idyllic
poem so obviously for the baritone voice.

It is interesting to note how little we are moved by the setting
of a 'dogmatic' poem like Schober's *Pax vobiscum* (D 551); Schubert
obviously found the sickly piety of the poem too insubstantial.

In November 1816, Schubert read a collection of the poems of
Matthias Claudius (1740–1815), and chose a group to set to music.
Claudius began as a student of theology and then turned to political
science. From 1771 he published *Der Wandsbeker Bote* ('The Wandsbek Messenger'), a journal which had earned him popularity. The
conscious simplicity of his poetry set him apart from the academic
conceits and unnaturalness of many of his contemporaries, but also
soon earned him their hostility. Nevertheless, Claudius supported
his severest critic, Gotthold Ephraim Lessing (1729–1781), the

author of the plays *Minna von Barnhelm* and *Nathan der Weise*, and was a close friend of Klopstock, Voss and the Stolberg brothers.

The freshness and vividness of his poetry inspired many contemporary composers, including Beethoven, who set the humorous poem *Urians Reise um die Welt* (opus 52 no. 1). Because of its pre-eminence among the Claudius settings, *Der Tod und das Mädchen* D 531), composed in February 1817, must be mentioned first. The custom of performing the song as a dialogue between a youthful soprano and an answering bass has long since been disregarded. Nor is the drama of the dialogue the essence of the song; that is to be found in the sublimity of the D minor 'death' theme which treats death as a friend from the outset. The idea of death as 'Schlafes Bruder' ('The brother of sleep') had been with Schubert since his earliest days and it was now to run through all his works like a *Leitmotif*.

If Schubert's melodies could be called his breath, then his rhythms are surely his heartbeats. At times, the rhythm and the melody are as one; at other times, they reveal their own independent spiritual processes. There are several characteristic rhythms, all of which conjure up specific associations. Foremost among these is that secret heartbeat which accompanies the tread of death, and by means of which Schubert expresses that serenity which is death's alone. It is a rhythm based on three notes, one long and two short. Coursing through it is a secret argument as in the Chinese *Book of Changes,* in which one long dash signifies 'Yes' and two short 'No'. This is also to be found in twelfth-century Japanese Gagaku-music, whose pure abstract nature allows any and every interpretation.

In *Der Tod und das Mädchen,* and in the corresponding movement of the D minor String Quartet, rhythm and melody are indivisible. For Schubert, death was no biblical punishment, no merited chastisement for our sins, but rather a friend and comforter who opens the gates to another world. The skeleton which grimaces through the medieval Dance of Death, and again in those pre-Enlightenment poems which Schubert knew so well in his early years, gives way to the figure of Death from Greek cults, from the Eleusinian religion or that of Pythagoras. The beautiful youth of the Greeks, holding a downturned torch in his hand, is the *Doppelgänger* of that 'brother of sleep' who whispers his words of comfort into the young girl's ear.

Let us look now at some of the problems of performance of this great song. What does the singer do with the marking *mäßig*? Schubert provided his songs with German speed directions, which are neither as unambiguous nor as precise as the Italian, and one of the most ambiguous is *mäßig*—which would roughly correspond to the Italian *moderato*. If the *alla breve* sign is obeyed, then the singer will arrive at more or less the right tempo. But when comparisons are made with the second movement of the D minor String Quartet, whose theme is the piano introduction of the song, then we see that the half-bars are meant to be played rather faster than *mäßig*, since *alla breve* is marked for the strings as well. Schubert calls here in fact for *andante con moto*.

Without a preliminary investigation of the emotional content and the technical problems of the music, it is impossible to take Schubert's tempi for granted, since he continually qualifies his markings with *etwas* ('somewhat'), *nicht zu* ('not too'), *ziemlich* ('rather') and *mäßig* ('moderately').

By using this introductory theme in his famous String Quartet, Schubert ensured the continuing popularity of the song, both among his friends, and later. His half-brother Andreas could not restrain his joy of giving here either, and distributed separated sheets of the song among his friends.

The seven short Claudius songs of 1816 (whether idyllic or melancholy) are immediately appealing. *Am Grabe Anselmos* (D 504) and the other songs of this year prove, firstly, that much of Schubert's instrumental music could not measure up to the standard of his vocal works and, secondly, how much the Lied was the focal point of Schubert's creative activity. In the sphere of piano music, Beethoven still stood far beyond his reach, while Haydn and Mozart had clearly inspired his symphonic compositions. But who could have served Schubert as a model for song composition? The paths that Beethoven had opened up were really of more importance for Beethoven's own development.

A mood of deepest grief emanates from the very beginning of the prelude to *Am Grabe Anselmos,* then, in the middle section, remembrance moves the song into the related major mode.

Schubert's setting of the *Abendlied* (D 499) of the 'Wandsbek Messenger', as Claudius was playfully called, did not imitate the folk-song style of Reichardt's or Schulz's settings. (The latter is still popular today.) This is all the more surprising, since Herder had included this song in his folk-song collection of 1779 and had brought recognition to Claudius by terming it a model of its kind. The figures of the piano accompaniment in Schubert's version are so dense that the *pianissimo* demanded is hardly possible. Here again is a work of unrivalled simplicity; yet even where the text seems to ask for a 4/4 rhythm, Schubert can surprise us with a 3/4.

An eine Quelle (D 530) is a Mozartian pastel-drawing. The passage 'O wenn sie sich nochmal am Ufer sehen läßt' ('If she comes back to the river bank'), is pure Austrian in its modesty and good humour, a charming pendant to the North German flavour of the poem. It is a small masterpiece, particularly in the declamatory passages.

The rather too numerous stanzas of *Phidile* (D 500) startled by Cupid, can, however, be as entertaining as the joyous surge of *Lied* (Ich bin vergnügt) (D 362, 1816; D 501, November 1816). The miniature *An die Nachtigall* (D 497) makes a pretty musical point: although mainly in G major, it begins in C major. The performer must combine lightness of tone with precision of rhythm. It appeared as opus 98 in 1829 together with the most famous of Schubert's cradle-songs *Wiegenlied* (Schlafe, schlafe, holder, süßer Knabe) (D 498) which is all gracefulness. [Deutsch claims 'author unknown'. Ed.] It was no doubt a tribute from one master to another when Richard Strauss made no attempt to conceal the borrowed melody in his *Ariadne auf Naxos*.

According to his own note, Claudius intended *Täglich zu singen* (D 533) (1817) to be sung to the melody of the chorale *Mein erst Gefühl sei Preis und Dank* ('Let my first feelings be of praise and thanks'). The best-known of the many settings of this poem are those of Reichardt and Schulz.

The two autograph manuscripts of *Lebenslied* (D 508) (Matthisson) and *Leiden der Trennung* (D 509) (December 1816) are marked 'In H. von Schober's house'. In *Lebenslied,* Schubert cries with Matthisson:

> Fruchtlos hienieden
> Ringst du nach Frieden!
> Täuschende Schimmer
> Winken dir immer;

Doch, wie die Furchen des gleitenden Kahns,
Schwinden die Zaubergebilde des Wahns!

(In vain you strive here on earth for peace and are led astray by
will-o'-the-wisps. Yet the magic figments of your imagination
will vanish like the wake of the gliding boat.)

In *Leiden der Trennung*, Heinrich von Collin (1771–1811), the
author of the *Coriolan* for which Beethoven wrote his overture (*not*
for the Shakespeare play!), and which moved Schubert so much,
expressed what the composer doubtless felt:

> Es sehnt sich die Welle
> In lispelnder Quelle,
> Im murmelnden Bache,
> Im Brunnengemache,
> Zum Meer, zum Meer,
> Von dem sie kam,
> Von dem sie Leben nahm,
> Von dem, des Irrens matt und müde,
> Sie süße Ruh' verhofft und Friede.

(In the whispering stream, in the murmuring brook and in the
shaft of the fountains, the waters yearn again for the sea from
which they came, the sea which gave them life, and which
promised rest and peace from their exhausting wanderings.)

These two songs are characterised by a descending movement
from the beginning to the middle of each stanza, as if one were
speaking over a sigh of relief. *Leiden der Trennung,* one of the pieces
written for Schubert's narrow circle of friends in Vienna, occupies an
all too modest place in the Collected Edition, especially as it is not
even mentioned in Friedländer's edition published by Peters. The
poem, translated by Collin from the Italian of Metastasio, compares
the longing of the waves in rivers and fountains for the boundless
seas with the yearning of the young for a freer intellectual climate.
There are subtle hints of suppression in a song which awaits re-
discovery.

One of the few genuine duets in Schubert literature (i.e. for tenor
and soprano voices singing in unison at the same time) is *Licht und
Liebe* (D 352), based on a poem by the other Collin, Matthäus
(1779–1824).

In the spring of 1817 Schubert turned again to Goethe. The cheery *Der Goldschmiedsgesell* of 1817 (D 560) shows how a satisfyingly rounded picture can be drawn with a few deft strokes and made particularly charming by the conscious economy of the piano accompaniment. It is indeed sad that two of the fragments begun in that year were never completed, for *Gretchens Bitte* (D 564) might well have equalled *Gretchen am Spinnrade* in emotional intensity, while the difficulty of the poem *Mahomets Gesang* (D 549/D 721) must have accounted for Schubert's breaking off in the middle of some beautiful musical passages.

The second version of *Auf dem See* (D 543) was dedicated to Frau Josefine von Franck. The title of Goethe's poem, in Herder's valuable copy, is *Auf dem Zürcher See* ('On Lake Zürich'). Goethe did indeed spend the summer of 1775 in Switzerland with the Stolbergs, in order to put his feelings for Lili Schönemann, a rich banker's daughter in Frankfurt, to the test, and perhaps to escape from them as well:

> Goldene Träume, kommt ihr wieder?
> Weg, du Traum! so gold du bist;
> Hier auch Lieb' und Leben ist.

(Golden dreams, will you come back? Hence, dream, however golden you may look, love and life are to be found here too.)

These lines from the third stanza reflect Goethe's thoughts of Lili. To preserve a balance between the two parts of the song, Schubert repeats the penultimate verse; just before this the barcarolle tempo changes from 6/8 to 2/4, to match the change of mood in the poem. The rhythm of the oars in the first part, and the semiquavers of the lively morning breeze of the second part, do more than justice to Goethe's intentions in the poem. But the singer must never allow the tempo to drag along in a 4/8 time. Schubert handled such changes of rhythm as a poet in his own right. (Brahms's setting of Karl Simrock's imitation of Goethe's poem—with the same title—should be compared with Schubert's setting of Goethe.)

It was *Ganymed* (D 544), one of the great achievements of that year, which, not surprisingly, sealed the friendship between Michael Vogl and the young composer. In Goethe's literary estate were two dedicated copies of the song published in 1823 printed on heavy paper, which had been enclosed with Schubert's letter to

Goethe, and which are now preserved in the former Ducal Library in Weimar.

Reichardt's setting pre-dated Schubert's, but it had nothing of the independent creativity which was needed to match this pantheistic hymn. By beginning the song in A flat major and ending it in F major, Schubert showed how new forms of expression in poetry could challenge and then shatter even traditional moulds in music. The change in key transports us to a higher, purer sphere. One charming melody is superimposed almost vertically over another. The introductory *motif*, almost melodic enough in itself, is rivalled by a cantilena of Beethoven-ish provenance. The teasing triplets of the morning breeze are answered by the seductive trills of the nightingale. The climactic final phrase, blazing with high drama, makes the extended invocation 'Alliebender Vater' ('All-loving father') a searching examination of a singer's breathing technique. He would probably be wise to allow the phrase to die away with the *decrescendo*. Just as Goethe turns the legend of Zeus, who raises Ganymed up to the heights of Mount Olympus, into a more general representation of a beautiful summer morning, so too the singer must not concentrate on details, but rather see the song as a whole, so as not to lose the drive and colour of the poem. (The song was published in 1823 as opus 19 no. 3.)

Even surrounded by loving friends as he was, turning out one composition after another, and with a job as an assistant schoolmaster, Schubert's financial, social and artistic situation was still miserable. The Leipzig publisher Breitkopf had been sent a good copy of *Erlkönig*—to no avail. Nobody there had heard of a Schubert and thought that they were being hoodwinked. The firm directed its answer to a violinist in Dresden, also called Franz Schubert. This proud German music-master and composer of occasional church music wrote to the Leipzig firm on 18th April 1817:

> I wish to inform you that this cantata was never composed by me. I shall retain the same in my possession, so that I might learn who has sent you such rubbish in such an impolite manner, and also to discover the scoundrel who has so misused my name.

In despair in any case because of Goethe's failure to acknowledge the Lieder sent to him, this further contretemps left Schubert in a state of deep depression. In addition, the break with his father, who felt that Schubert's decision to leave school-teaching was both precipitate and ill-advised, contributed greatly to his spiritual malaise. He remained from that time on in debt to Schober for the rent as well—this was only collected from the sale of Schubert's compositions after his death. Schubert's father had always regarded music as too precarious a profession, and he suspected, too, that Franz would come into contact with people whose loose living-habits would be incompatible with the father's Catholic principles. He foresaw only too clearly what later actually took place.

It must be assumed that the availability of a piano in Schober's rooms in the Säulengasse led to the opening-up of a new area of creative activity for Schubert—the piano sonata—and therefore to a reduction in the number of Lieder composed in 1817. Nevertheless, Schubert set about fifty poems in that year, including eight by Mayrhofer, the largest single contribution, on Greek or Roman themes.

FIVE

Michael Vogl, Schubert's First Interpreter

Schubert's friends had decided to awaken curiosity and enthusiasm for his songs in a well-known singer. Johann Michael Vogl (1768–1840), who had impressed Schubert as an operatic baritone (see p. 22), was intending to retire from the theatre in order to concentrate on concert performances. Vogl was the son of a Styrian sea captain, who, after attending the Gymnasium in Kremsmünster, had attracted attention by his performances in short sacred plays and operas in the local monastery. Franz Süssmayr (1766–1803), well known for his close association with Mozart's *Requiem,* also made a name for himself there—but as a composer. The two hopefuls moved together to Vienna to try their luck. There, Vogl finished his law studies, while Süssmayr became *Kapellmeister* at the Hoftheater. On his suggestion, Vogl was engaged by the theatre in 1794 and sang there for twenty-eight years, for most of the time unaware of Schubert's existence. It is naturally pleasing that such a famous opera singer should show sympathy so late in life for a purely lyrical form of music—but not all that surprising, since it should not be forgotten that there were really no leading rôles for baritones in the early decades of the nineteenth century. Heinrich Marschner (1795–1861) was the first to supply these, with his operas *Der Vampir, Der Templer* and *Hans Heiling.* Prior to these, all main rôles were assigned to tenor or bass; even Mozart's Don Giovanni or Count Almaviva were thought of as bass rôles, and rightly, since a deep voice is needed to lead the ensembles. Marschner's operas were the first to place the baritone at the heart of the plot. Vogl, something of a 'literary' artiste, must have felt attracted by Schubert's new mode of expression, even if only as a substitute for his no longer being able to play the new heroic baritone rôles.

Vogl had a remarkable range and had sung Pizarro in the historic performance of Beethoven's *Fidelio* in May 1814. Nor had Schubert's friends forgotten his performance as Orestes in Gluck's *Iphigénie*. Spaun wrote:

> Once after having heard *Iphigénie* with Mayrhofer and Schubert, which, to the recurring shame of the Viennese, was again played before an empty house, we went full of enthusiasm to the 'Blumenstöckl' in the Balgassl for supper, and when we gave vent to our delight, one of the University professors present chose to make mock of us. He shouted out that Milder had crowed like a cock, that she couldn't sing at all, she didn't know how to do runs or trills, and that it was a positive disgrace to engage her as a prima donna, and that Orestes (Vogl) had feet like an elephant. Schubert and Mayrhofer jumped up enraged, whereby Schubert knocked over his full glass of wine: a loud argument ensued which, because of the obstinacy of our opponents, might well have led to blows, had not conciliatory voices quietened us all down. Schubert was in a blazing rage at this, something quite alien to his usual mild temperament.

Vogl was without doubt an unusual person. Although no longer young, he had actively supported the New German Opera and had even on occasion directed operas. His wide reading and broad general education set him apart from the general run of professional singers; in addition to his knowledge of classical and modern languages, he was an amateur composer and the author of a treatise on singing.

This enormous man, whose broad flat feet certainly did seem rather incongruous in the Greek heroes whom he portrayed, used to conquer his stage fright by engrossing himself in Latin authors backstage between his entrances. One would not expect this serious, autocratic artist to capitulate to the prevalent Rossini craze. Spaun documents how carefully Schubert's friends went about their task:

> Schubert, who had always had to sing his songs himself, often expressed the great desire to find a singer for them, and his long-standing wish to make the acquaintance of the Court opera singer

Vogl became even stronger. Our small circle therefore decided that Vogl had to be won over for Schubert, and his songs. Since Vogl was not an easy man to approach, the task was a difficult one. Schober's deceased sister had been married to the singer, Siboni, who was still connected in some way with the theatre and this enabled him to approach Vogl. Schober gave Vogl glowing accounts of Schubert's songs and asked him to try some of them out with him. Vogl answered that he had had more than enough of music, and that he was trying to get away from it rather than to learn new things. He had been told hundreds of times about young geniuses and had always been disappointed, and this would certainly be the case as well with Schubert; he wanted to be left in peace and to hear no more about it. We were all saddened by this rejection, with the exception of Schubert, who said that he had expected such an answer and found it quite natural. Meanwhile Vogl was repeatedly approached by Schober and others; at last he promised to come one evening to Schober's to see, as he put it, what it was all about.

So Franz von Schober arranged the meeting. Spaun says of the big day in March 1817:

Schubert was rather embarrassed at that first meeting. The first song he produced for Vogl's opinion was the newly-composed *Augenlied* [D 297, October 1815] by Mayrhofer. Vogl recognised Schubert's talent immediately, and examined with growing interest the other Lieder which the young composer, overjoyed by Vogl's approbation, laid before him.

In another passage, Spaun goes into greater detail:

Vogl, full of dignity, arrived at Schober's house on the agreed hour, and when the small insignificant figure of Schubert made rather a clumsy bow and, in his embarrassment, stammered a few disconnected phrases about the honour of meeting Vogl, the singer wrinkled his nose rather disdainfully and the meeting seemed to portend disaster. At last Vogl said, 'Now, then, what have you got there? Come with me.' Then taking up the first manuscript, Mayrhofer's *Augenlied*, a pretty, very singable but rather insignificant song, he hummed rather than sang it and then said non-committally, 'Not bad!' When, after that, he was accompanied in *Memnon* and *Ganymed*, both of which he sang only *mezzo-voce*, he became noticeably friendlier, although he left without promising to return.

The twenty-year-old composer's setting of *Memnon* (D 541), mentioned above, was Schubert's masterpiece to date. Mayrhofer treated the well-known legend in an utterly subjective manner, by endowing the speaking statue with human emotions. The tragedy arises from Man's failure to comprehend the depths of feeling contained in the note with which the statue greets the morning. So orchestral is the soaring prelude in D flat major that Brahms decided to orchestrate it for the baritone Julius Stockhausen. The recitative that follows this prelude grows as from nothing, darkens with the modulation from major to minor, and then ascends with painfully coiled dramatic power to the climactic 'mit dir, des Morgens Göttin, mich zu einen' ('To unite with you, O goddess of the morn'). In the final *arioso,* the subdued recitative is transfigured in the image of the ideal envisaged by the melancholy poet. The gently transfigured *Abgesang*[1] is allowed to die away in a glorious piano passage.

Spaun's account of the meeting with Vogl continues:

As he was leaving, he [Vogl] slapped Schubert on the shoulder and said to him, 'There is something in you, but you are not enough of an actor, not enough of a charlatan. You squander your fine ideas without taking them far enough . . .' To other people, he expressed a much more favourable opinion. When he saw Mayrhofer's *Lied eines Schiffers an die Dioskuren,* he said that it was almost incomprehensible that such profundity and maturity could come out of that tiny young man.

Let us stay for a while with the Mayrhofer poems of this period, which are of very variable quality.

The critics were unstinting with their praise of the rather conventional *Lied eines Schiffers an die Dioskuren* (D 360) which has already been touched on (p. 77). The *Allgemeine Musikalische Zeitung* in Frankfurt, which regularly reviewed the new Schubert works, usually rejected songs like these, since the prevalent German conception of the Lied was a strophic song, and anything

[1] *Abgesang*: 'afterstrain', a term used for the final lines of the poems of the thirteenth-century *Minnesänger,* the German form of the *troubadour.*

durchkomponiert ('through-composed') was criticised as violating the rules. The situation was even worse in Berlin.

Mayrhofer imitates Goethe and Schiller in *Der Alpenjäger* (D 524), (composed in January 1817), and here Schubert finds melodies which simplify, and therefore enrich, his friend's poem.

> Je eher Gefahr aus Schlünden,
> So freier schlägt die Brust.

(The more precipitous the abysses, the freer he feels.)

The banality of the music, coupled to the post-card-like verses, produces something like a coloured drawing.

In *Uraniens Flucht* (D 554), on the other hand, the pathos of the Uranian Aphrodite's 17-page-long plaint to Zeus after she has returned disillusioned to Mount Olympus from her visit to earth, is really too excessive to hold our attention.

Likewise very dramatic is the scenic fragment *Antigone und Oedip* (D 542) in which Antigone, on the way to Colonos, implores the gods to transfer their fury from the blind king Oedipus and bring it down on her own innocent head. Oedipus awakes and tells of having had a dream, a vision of his own death at Colonos; he then takes leave of his ill-starred life to a broad sweeping melody. The cantata was published in 1821 as opus 8 no. 2, and the Viennese *Allgemeine Musikalische Zeitung* of 19th January 1822 carried this critical reaction:

> It is regrettable that the poet's words 'Laßt einen milden Hauch des Trostes in Ödips große Seele wehn' ['Waft a gentle breath of consolation into Oedipus's great soul'] have been altered to the following which completely distort the sense. The composer has the poet say: 'In des Vaters Seele wehn' ['Into the father's soul'], which destroys the metre. The original words would not have disturbed the cantilena. The treatment of a text should show the same respect for the poet as we show for the composer's creation.

It is true that Schubert's reading does not respect the metre, but it does clarify the passage: the distancing technique which made Antigone refer to her father as 'Oedipus' seemed inappropriate to Schubert.

Because of its sombre grandeur, *Fahrt zum Hades* (D 526) deserves more attention than that of the small band of Schubert specialists. Its bass line plunges mysteriously, the recitatives are full of impressive power, and the closing section holds out the promise of salvation. Schubert inserts a contrasted section, full of nostalgic memories of all that has been lost, between the grave solemnity of the first section and its repetition in a different key. Only those totally unwilling to be seduced by the magic of Schubert could quibble about the justification for the closing recitative.

Freiwilliges Versinken (D 700) is an address to the allegorical sun god Helios; Helios's answer is Mayrhofer's own view of the rôle of the artist. Schubert's setting is a mixture of recitative and song. (It was possibly the interval leaps for the voice in this song that Alban Berg had in mind when, in the 1930's, in an interview on Austrian radio, he attempted to defend the disconnected nature of 'atonal' vocal music by quoting typical examples from past centuries.) It is doubtful whether the disappearing sun and the rising moon have ever been more beautifully depicted than in the interweaving of voices in the postlude of *Freiwilliges Versinken*. 'Ich nehme nicht, ich pflege nur zu geben' ('I do not take, am wont only to give')—how better could one describe Schubert's whole art? The modulations of the very first bars are striking and the trills on the second crotchet whet our anticipation. The *fermata* on the second 'Wohin?' ('Whither?') sends the question echoing out into the far distance. The words 'scheide' ('depart'), and 'herrlich' ('in glory'), twice bring the great leap of the descending diminished ninth, whereupon the major mode wonderfully depicts the nightfall and the departing sun. In the piano postlude, the left hand has to follow the right, mirroring the appearance of the pale morning stars.[1]

Rather exceptionally, Antiquity is not the theme of *Auf der Donau* (D 553), composed in April 1817. Mayrhofer's vision of the Danube valley landscape near Vienna is still accurate today. Schubert, who was always fascinated by the tragedy of transitoriness, poured all his art into this song. The coloration of the piano accompaniment anticipates Schumann and Brahms, and, notwithstanding the artificiality of Mayrhofer's middle stanza, the song makes a seamless garment of figuration and melody.

[1] Maurice Brown established that the composition date is 1817 and not September 1820, as was previously assumed. (Brown, M. J. E.: *Schubert*, Macmillan 1958, p. 75.)

The stormy accompanying figure of *Der Schiffer* (D 536) has more unity, and the song expresses an unparalleled defiant vitality. Schubert does not retain the still picture quality of the poem, instead, he seems to be letting a film run on. This strophic song for bass voice was dedicated to Mayrhofer when it was published at the end of 1823 as opus 21, with *Auf der Donau* and *Wie Ulfru fischt*.

The energetic marching figure of *Wie Ulfru fischt* (D 525) makes an astonishing journey through remote keys although the song never abandons the simple strophic form.

To return to Spaun:

After only a few weeks, Vogl sang Schubert's *Erlkönig, Ganymed, Der Kampf, Der Wanderer* etc. to a small but delighted audience and the enthusiasm with which this great artist performed these songs was the best proof of how moved he was himself by them. But this magnificent singer had the greatest effect on the young composer himself, who was overjoyed to see his long-nourished hopes fulfilled beyond all his expectations. As a result of their constant association, the two artists formed a bond which became ever tighter, and was broken only by death. Vogl supplied his young friend with well-meaning advice from his rich store of experience and cared for his wants like a father, whenever the income from Schubert's compositions was inadequate.

Der Kampf (D 594), mentioned above by Spaun and written by Schiller, was composed in November 1817. It is expressly scored for bass voice and deserves special mention since here the style of the operatic arias of Heinrich Marschner, Ludwig Spohr and Carl Maria von Weber intrudes unexpectedly into the intimacy of the Schubert-Lied. It must be said, however, that the pathos of the hero, unable to choose between love and duty, seems to invite this degree of expansiveness.

The operatic ending to the song gives some indication of this:

> Der einz'ge Lohn, der meine Tugend krönen sollte,
> Ist meiner Tugend letzter Augenblick!

(The only reward for my virtue is its last moment on earth.)

Schubert revered Schiller, the great man of the literary world, and it was this which enabled him to overcome the cold inhospitability of Schiller's poetry. The pulsating, sensuous power of *Der*

Kampf (Vogl's favourite song) is therefore all the more remarkable an achievement. It is Schubert who breathes life into that banal trio: love, duty and destructive passion. As we know, Schiller was one of the first poets to swim into Schubert's ken and, again and again, Schubert accepted the challenge of setting these poems to music, even when their unpoetical or unmusical aspects distressed him. When we listen to Schubert's settings, we realise how truly mediocre Schiller's lyrical gifts were. The setting of *Der Kampf* does become too rhetorical, but even the opening theme seems to be given symphonic stature.

Probably the most important Schiller setting of 1817 is *Gruppe aus dem Tartarus* which Schubert had worked on some years before (D 396, March 1816). The music of that fragment is likewise of high quality. Only in this 1817 setting (D 583), however, does Schubert manage to pierce through Schiller's dense wordiness to the heart of the poem, represented by that image of Saturn manifested in the final sustained arpeggio, played after a long pause. Before this, the setting is on a colossal scale, and Schubert's orchestral language tempted Brahms to score the song for full orchestra. Schubert's composition is full of unrest, drama and violent contrasts; the total effect is frightening; even today an interpreter will find that, if the song is placed at the end of a programme, the listener will be left stunned and terrified. The great C major chord on 'Ewigkeit!' ('Eternity!') before the opening theme dies away is part of the total effect of this eternally recurring tragedy. Its passionate representation of Tartarus's banishment in Schiller's *Sturm und Drang* poem points the way to Wagner and Wolf and is far removed from the conventional Lied, even from Schubert's own. The voice no longer has a 'song melody', the action is depicted more by the harmonic and rhythmical audacities of the piano than by the song. This does not mean that the vocal and instrumental parts are not in balance, but it *does* mean that Leopold von Sonnleithner's erroneous generalisation that Schubert placed the beauty of the song before the interpretation of the text, is refuted in its entirety—yet some still hold this view today. To attempt to pigeonhole Schubert's art into declamation, on the one hand, and lyrical beauty on the other, is an impossibility; in addition, the yardstick by which his German songs were measured by his contemporaries is no longer available. The word, and the manner in which it was treated for the voice,

were the *points de départ* for every vocal composition, and it was
from this basis that the composer sought to satisfy the demands of
the music. Interpretative singing is the end of a maturing process
which begins with the formation of vowels and consonants. It has
nothing to do with the distorted and toneless sounds which were
said to have emanated from Michael Vogl, whose voice was already
past its prime. In his notations, Schubert takes great pains to
indicate where he wants the melodic line to be pure and where he
wants a word to be either very subtly or very dramatically coloured.
Thus, if these notations are followed, the correct style for each of
his Lieder will be found; but *only* by identifying these accurately
will the singer be able faithfully to interpret what is happening in
the composition—the balancing of asymmetrical phrases by, for
example, harmonic regressions or shifts of emphases, or the inter-
ruption or restoration of metrical balance through variations in the
dynamics, the texture and the register, all of them, that is, seemingly
technical details of musical conception.

Schubert's *Elysium* (D 584), composed shortly after *Tartarus*,
proved what could be observed as early as Dante—that Paradise
offers substantially fewer artistic possibilities than Hell. Because of
its length, and the difficult phrases requiring great breath control,
it is rarely performed, but it presents a beautiful, subtly characterised vision of heavenly joy. Schubert never saw Death as harsh or
unyielding—he always attempts to illuminate this abyss with fresh
insights and he approaches Death as a man in love with Life. On
the closing words 'feiert sie ein ewig Hochzeitsfest' ('it celebrates
an eternal wedding feast') Schubert, by sustaining the word 'ewig'
over more than ten bars, demands inexhaustible supplies of energy
from the weary performer.

Schubert now turned once again to *Thekla* (sub-titled *Eine
Geisterstimme*) (D 595). It will be recalled that he set it for the first
time in 1813 (D 73, 22/23 August). The pure lyricism of this
1817 setting is encompassed within a fourth. The second version
of this setting is written half a tone lower and the stanzas receive
rather more individual attention. (This version was published as
opus 88 in 1827.) As Schubert first began to work on this poem
when he was sixteen, he must have been fascinated by Schiller's
grandiloquent notions of raising the barriers between the now and
the hereafter. Yet such notions did not tempt Schubert away from

simplicity. In the apparently simple major-minor modulation in the third line of the first, third and fifth stanzas, Schubert conceals the harmonic step that can bridge these two worlds, a step that can only be taken by those whose belief in innovative creativeness has remained intact. This is true also of the passage where Schiller says of the nightingales 'Nur solang' sie liebten, waren sie' ('Only as long as they loved did they exist'). The mysterious relationship between the living and the dead is the subject of many of Schubert's works, since he himself always believed in an afterlife. Schiller's eerie, phantom voice leads Schubert into familiar regions; he is not afraid to bridge the gulf with a smile.

That Schubert wrung music out of the uninspired poem *Der Alpenjäger* (D 588) is nothing short of a miracle. The two sections of the poem are treated strophically, with a closing summary by the mountain spirit who, alas, does not speak in the naïvely amiable accents of the Austrian writer Raimund.[1] The poem is dedicated to the painter Ludwig Schnorr von Carolsfeld whose stern, moralistic, biblical figures match Schiller's allegorical characters very well.

The impression that Schubert's songs made on Vogl can be culled from this entry in his diary:

Nothing has more clearly demonstrated our lack of a proper school of singing than Schubert's songs. But for that, what a tremendous universal effect would these truly divine inspirations, these products of a musical *clairvoyance,* have had in all those parts of the world where the German language is spoken. How many would have understood, perhaps for the first time, the meaning of language, poetry set to music, words in harmonies, thoughts clothed in music? They would have discovered how the most beautiful poems of our greatest poets when translated into such musical language, could be further enhanced and even improved upon. Countless examples are available: *Erlkönig, Gretchen am Spinnrade, Schwager Kronos, Mignon,* the *Harper's Songs,* Schiller's *Sehnsucht, Der Pilgrim, Die Bürgschaft.*

In Vogl, Schubert had found a highly critical artist whose interpretations brought to fruition Schubert's own creations. Nor was the influence purely impersonal; Vogl helped Schubert financially

[1] Ferdinand Raimund (1790–1836), Austria's leading writer of comedies in Schubert's lifetime. Raimund wrote *Der Alpenkönig* (1828). Schiller's poem is called *The Alpine Hunter*, Raimund's play *The Alpine King.* (Ed.)

wherever he could and counter-balanced the often undesirable influences of his friends.

Sonnleithner remarked:

He [Vogl] shunned vulgarity in life as in art and had in that respect a favourable influence on Schubert. His performances of many of Schubert's songs were thrilling and deeply moving, even if, particularly in later years, they were marked by an unmistakable affectation and wilfulness. Schubert was often forced to follow his dictates, and the complaint that many Schubert songs are not completely suited to any one range of voice is largely due to, and could be excused by, Vogl's influence. In performance, Vogl often achieved a momentary effect with a word spoken tonelessly, a shout or a falsetto note, none of which could be justified artistically, nor repeated by anyone else.

and in Spaun's memoirs we read:

In many of the homes in which regular musical evenings were held, particularly in Dr von Sonnleithner's and at the concerts of the *Kleine Musikverein* [a reference to the private *soirées* of the *Gesellschaft der Musikfreunde*], Schubert's compositions were now performed regularly and were always greeted with general applause. Schubert's songs, too, were frequently sung in the home of Matthäus von Collin, who had died young, but who had been an enthusiastic admirer of Schubert's compositions. They were performed before a distinguished group of people of talent and position, all of whom were delighted to welcome these new works at so sad a time, and who then individually did their best to make Schubert known to the world. Here, too, Schubert was introduced to Count Moritz von Dietrichstein, Hofrat von Hammer, Hofrat von Mosel, the future Patriarch of Venice, Frau Karoline von Pichler, and many other eminent persons, all of whom honoured and encouraged him by their approbation.

Anselm Hüttenbrenner gives us a brief description of Schubert the accompanist:

Schubert was not an elegant, but a sure and technically very proficient pianist who accompanied his singer excellently, always keeping strict time, and, like old Salieri, playing from scores with great facility.

Since the simple folk-song style was still regarded as too stark, Vogl ornamented the vocal line in the old-fashioned way, and many of these ornamentations found their way into the published editions. Spaun disapproved of this, but denied that Vogl had had any significant influence on Schubert's compositional methods:

> No one had the slightest influence on his way of composing, even though attempts were made from time to time. He did make concessions to Vogl's vocal range, but even there only rarely and reluctantly.

A deep admiration for his young protégé soon replaced Vogl's initial condescending attitude, and there is a touching reminiscence from a young student called Haller who came from Vogl's native town of Steyr and had stayed in Vogl's house while studying medicine in Vienna. Haller agreed that 'Vogl was brutal to most people, particularly to those who did not flatter him. Only Schubert, or rather his genius, possessed the magic to tame his coarse nature.'

And when Schubert, as was his wont, suddenly disappeared from functions, or perhaps did not even turn up, Vogl used to defend his friend and say, 'We must all bow to Schubert's genius and, if he does not arrive, then we must crawl after him on our knees.'

A month after finishing *Der Tod und das Mädchen* and two unimportant songs, *Täglich zu singen* and *Das Lied vom Reifen* (D 532), by Claudius, Schubert began work on a companion piece, *Der Jüngling und der Tod* (D 545), from a poem by Spaun:

> Die Sonne sinkt, o könnt ich mit ihr scheiden,
> Mit ihrem letzten Strahl entfliehn!
> Ach, diese namenlosen Qualen meiden
> Und weit in schön're Welten ziehn!

(The sun sinks. O could I go with it, flee with its departing rays, avoid these nameless sufferings and seek far fairer worlds!)

There are certainly many differing interpretations of *Weltschmerz* possible here; this is the same resignation that shattered Niklaus Lenau, the Hungarian lyric poet who studied in Vienna but emigrated to America in 1833 to avoid the 'flood of tyranny', reduced Franz Grillparzer to artistic silence and which certainly did not leave Schubert unscathed. This was no passing fad, but rather an agony caused by the contemporary feeling of passivity, the lack of will-power of Austrian youth facing the horrors of the restoration of the Hapsburg monarchy. The many suicides, and the still more numerous attempted suicides, in the Metternich era should not be forgotten.

In the second of the two extant versions of the song, Death's response is provided with a prelude and a postlude which borrow from *Der Tod und das Mädchen*. The later song may not be the equal of its companion, but *Der Jüngling und der Tod* is interesting, if only because the youth's plea for death forms the major section, while Death grants him his request in just a few bars—the exact opposite of the earlier situation. Death is chosen as the subject only when Schubert can feel that it is an exhorter, which, from its knowledge of the end of all human existence, can offer our lives that profundity and earnestness which makes for a total experience. In this context, the rhythmic symbol for Death has the force of a declaration.

In the summer of 1817, Schubert wrote *Der Strom* (D 565) for Albert Stadler, who was about to leave Vienna for his home in Upper Austria. Thus began a series of leave-takings, and Schubert's distress at these is clearly visible in his choice of texts, and in the despair of the music. *Der Strom* was probably written by Stadler himself. He had been one of Schubert's *Konvikt* friends, and also wrote the libretto for one of Schubert's least successful operettas, *Fernando* (1815) (D 220). *Der Strom* is marked by an incessant semi-quaver movement which vehemently sweeps the listener along from the very first bar.

More distressing than the separation from Stadler was the departure of Franz von Schober, who left to spend a year in Sweden. On 24th August 1817 Schubert wrote 'in the album of a friend' one of his own poems dedicated to Schober and to which he also provided a simple sensitive setting:

> Lebe wohl, du lieber Freund!
> Ziehe hin in fernes Land,
> Nimm der Freundschaft trautes Band,
> Und bewahre es in treuer Hand!
> Lebe wohl, du lieber Freund!

Lebe wohl, du lieber Freund!
Wenn dies Lied dein Herz ergreift,
Freundes Schatten näher schweift,
Meiner Seelen Saiten streift,
Lebe wohl, du lieber Freund!

(Farewell, dear friend, departing for a far-off land, take the intimate bond of friendship with you and preserve it for ever.
Farewell, dear friend, when this song seizes your heart and the
shadow of your friend hovers near you and touches my soul,
Farewell, dear friend.)

Abschied von einem Freunde (D 578) is neither polished nor particularly inspired—Schubert was simply expressing an emotion.

Schober brought his brother back from France with him, which
meant that Schubert had to move out of his lodgings and return to
teaching to earn some money. After having enjoyed months of
freedom, he was naturally depressed; for one longing to express
himself creatively, this seemed to be an additional, unnecessary
burden.

Die Blumensprache (D 519) was composed in early Autumn. I have
not been able to establish if the poem is really by Anton(?) Platner
(1787-1855), a well-known eccentric who had been a shepherd near
Innsbruck. He had taken Holy Orders after University, but then
turned eccentric, writing poems and diaries in his isolation. Both
his Christian name and the authorship of this poem remain a
mystery. The name could even be Eduard Plattner.

Die Blumensprache allows the bringer of the flowers, and not the
flowers themselves, to speak, and he does so in that whimsical
typically Viennese way which Schubert's music captures so accurately.

Although Schubert had composed *Die Forelle* (D 550), from the
poem by Christian Daniel Schubart (1739-1791) in the summer of
1817, eleven years were to pass before the *Wiener Zeitung* printed the
song. Schubert dedicated the fourth autograph copy of the song to
his faithful friend, Josef Hüttenbrenner, whom he normally treated
so roughly that his friends used to call his behaviour 'tyrannical'.
Schubert is reported to have said of Hüttenbrenner, 'That fellow
likes everything by me!' Hüttenbrenner, who later shared a lodging
with Schubert, was living in Graz at this time. At midnight on

21st February 1818, Schubert, with Josef's brother, Anselm, beside him, wrote to him from Vienna:

Dearest friend,

I am extraordinarily happy that you like my songs. As proof of my most sincere friendship, I am sending you a new one that I have just written here at midnight at Anselm Hüttenbrenner's. I wish that we could become even closer friends over a glass of punch—Just now, as I meant to sprinkle the thing with sand in something of a hurry, I was very drowsy, and, taking up the inkwell instead, calmly poured it all over the manuscript. What a calamity![1]

Schubart, a very talented poet, musician and orator, had founded the newspaper *Deutsche Kronik* in 1774, while he was still a student and working also as a private tutor and organist. The paper's advanced ideas influenced men like Schiller, who took the plot of his drama *Die Räuber* (1781) from a short story by Schubart. When his political satires drew the wrath of the Duke of Würtemberg down on him, Schubart was incarcerated without trial in the fortress of Hohenasperg, and was only released ten years later in response to the pressure of public opinion. He then became director of the Court Theatre in Stuttgart until his death in 1791. His *Ideen zur Ästhetik der Tonkunst* (Thoughts on the Aesthetics of Music) show him to have been a considerable musical theoretician.

Schubert set four of his poems to music, of which *An den Tod* and *Die Forelle* have gained much more popularity than the really more important settings of 1817. There are four extant copies of *Die Forelle*, but there were certainly others. When one realises how many identical copies Schubert made of his works, his work rate is almost frightening to consider.

The four well-known autographs of *Die Forelle* appeared as follows: 1817, in Franz Sales Kandler's album; 1818, in Hüttenbrenner's album; 1820, for the first published edition (handed over to Anselm Hüttenbrenner, and lost); and 1821, for the final published edition. Only the last one contains the six-bar introduction with the 'jumping trout' theme. *Die Forelle* gives us some indication of Schubert's literary taste, since he omits two verses from Schu-

[1] This famous manuscript with the ink-blot was photographed in 1870 and so we can at least see a facsimile, for the original soon disappeared [D. F-D.].

bart's original poem which appeared in the *Schwäbischen Musenal-manach* of 1783:

> Die ihr am goldenen Quelle
> Der sicheren Jugend weilt,
> Denkt doch an die Forelle;
> Seht ihr Gefahr, so eilt!
>
> Meist fehlt ihr nur aus Mangel
> Der Klugheit, Mädchen, seht
> Verführer mit der Angel!
> Sonst blutet ihr zu spät!

(You who wait at the golden source of happy youth, just think of the trout, if you see danger, then flee! It is only wanting in intelligence, so my girls, see the tempter with the rod—otherwise you'll bleed too late!)

The didactic poem with its Baroque moral is cleansed by the symbolically spilled blood and thus given its 'heavenly brevity'. *Die Forelle* is a classic example of the strophic song with *Abgesang*, the 'after-strain'; where the situation remains the same, the same melody is used—at the moment where the text describes the water being made 'tückisch trübe' ('stirred up maliciously'), the *Abgesang* begins. The main melody is taken up again at the end, the boundaries of the *da capo* song proving to be elastic.

Once again, there is a consistently maintained piano rhythm which ascends in triads in the treble and then plunges back into the bass. The vividness of the imagery, with the alternate troubling and smoothing of the surface of the water along with the exuberance of the melody itself, account for the song's universal appeal. This has led to countless piano transcriptions, of which Stephen Heller's pleasantly pianistic version enjoys the questionable distinction of having been performed most frequently.[1]

The setting of Schubart's *An den Tod* (D 518) never loses its basically serene character, even when the melody is subjected to fascinating modulations. There must be no sentimentality in the closing phrases; Schubert's naïve sincerity will then match the words of the poem all the more convincingly. Death is welcomed

---

[1] Stephen Heller (1814–1888) was a distinguished concert pianist who had known Beethoven, Schubert and Schumann. (Ed

as a liberator, but is warned to keep away from the budding flower. Schubart's poem had sixteen verses and the composer ran each two of the quatrains into one verse. When Mandyczewski, the editor of the *Gesamtausgabe,* printed only two verses of the setting, he had good reason for doing so.

The little titbit *An mein Clavier* (D 342) of 1816 might remind us of the hapless poet's love of music. Schubart gave the lines to a girl and entitled his poem *Seraphine an ihr Klavier.* Schubert's setting dispensed, however, with the girl and with two verses, which he obviously considered too 'seraphic'. His sole object here was to give thanks for the consolation that music had brought him in times of trouble, even if Schubart's word 'sanft' ('gentle') would refer rather to the clavichord, which had been so popular in middle-class families in Germany a generation before, than to the piano.

Finally, *Grablied auf einen Soldaten* 'Dirge for a Soldier' (D 454), which has not much to offer other than the traditional funereal C minor.

Teaching was always a burden to Schubert, even when the subject was music, and the elementary school post which he held up to 1816 was particularly burdensome. The one exception to the distasteful rule was the offer of Count Johann Karl Esterházy (1775–1834), in the summer of 1818, to accept the post of music teacher in his house. This was not Haydn's celebrated patron, nor his completely unmusical son, but a relative from another branch of the family. Schubert accepted the offer and went to Zseliz on the Gran, the family seat in Hungary, 'fourteen post-stations from Vienna'.

Schubert taught the daughters, Marie and Karoline, and the son, Johann Albert, although he was really a jack-of-all-trades, since no firm duties had been laid down. He wrote vocal exercises for the girls, and gave the mother, who had a fair contralto voice, a few singing lessons. He accompanied the Count, the possessor of a powerful bass voice, and wrote a few songs for him as well. While there, he also found time to write four-handed piano pieces for the girls, and some vocal music for the occasional improvised concerts in the evenings.

Schubert was naturally pleased that the family enjoyed music-making so much, particularly as one of Vogl's pupils, Freiherr Karl von Schönstein (1797–1876) used to take part in the evening concerts. This young man was not only one of the first Schubert interpreters, he was also destined to be the man to whom Schubert dedicated the *Schöne Müllerin* cycle.

On 3rd August 1818, Schubert wrote to his friends in Vienna:

Dearest, most precious friends!

How could I forget you, you who are everything to me! Spaun, Schober, Mayrhofer, Senn, how are you all? Are you well? I am keeping very well. I live and compose like a god, just as if it had to be this way.

Mayrhofer's *Einsamkeit* is finished, and I believe it is the best thing that I have done, for I was so carefree. I hope that you are all as healthy and as happy as I am. Now I am living at last, thank God, it was high time, for otherwise I would have become just another frustrated musician. Schober should pay my respects to Herr Vogl. I shall take the liberty of writing to him soon. If you can, ask him if he would be kind enough to sing one of my songs—any one he chooses—at the Kunz concert in November.[1]

Give my greetings to all the friends you can. My deepest respects to your mother and sister. Write to me soon, every single word from you is precious to me.

Your ever faithful friend, Franz Schubert.

Despite the cheerful tone of the letter the musical harvest of these months is comparatively meagre; about eight songs, the opus 10 variations for piano duet, and the fragment of a piano sonata in F minor. Schubert's high regard for his very interesting setting of Mayrhofer's *Einsamkeit* (D 620) might be explained by the fact that he had not used the cantata-form for some years. Above all, the song gives some proof of Schubert's close relationship with these friends, the poet Mayrhofer and others. Schober was really the ring-leader of the group, but Schubert felt himself just as attracted to the melancholy Mayrhofer, who was finally driven to suicide in 1836 by the conflict between his censorship work and his belief in freedom of thought and speech. The hint to Schober to play the middleman to Vogl emphasises Schubert's at times rather reserved relationship with the older singer.

Many have believed that Schubert's statement, that this song was

[1] This was a concert given by Babette Kunz on 3rd December 1818 in the Müllersche Saal. In the event, Vogl did not take part. (Ed.)

the best that he had composed to date, shows his lack of critical judgement about his own work. These critics fail to recognise, however, the new and exciting features of the song, which were not appreciated because of the work's rather diffuse form. It is one of the most extensive songs that Schubert has left us, almost a song-cycle in itself, made up of six philosophising stanzas. The unity of the musically disparate movements is maintained by the expression of longing and demanding. Mayrhofer describes the life of a dis-satisfied man who is driven from the monastery into a life of wild activity, then to rural idylls and happy friends, who experiences the bliss of love and the horrors of battle, until he finally finds the fulfilment of his youthful longings in the serenity of nature. Loneli-ness, action, friendship, bliss, sadness—all these moods are evoked in the poem, and Schubert utilises them all as a sort of *résumé* of his own creative potential, and, quite legitimately, incorporates the recitatory declamation in the expressive *arioso* cantata movements.

But, of course, Mayrhofer's extremely abstract hero can relate to Schubert's identification with portions of the text only in a cir-cuitous way. It is interesting that the climax is reached in the last pages of the song, where the poem speaks of the hero's retreat into the arboreal calm:

> Und ein Leben rauh und steil
> Führte doch zur Seligkeit.

> (And a life's way, rough and steep, led at last to bliss.)

In content, this composition is not unlike a rather unusual Schubert 'song', which possibly dates back to March 1816,[1] and is from a poem by Adolf Pratobevera, Freiherr von Wiesborn (1806–?). He also published political epigrams and a few articles on legal matters. The fragment entitled *Abschied von der Erde* (D 829) is taken from Pratobevera's play *Der Falke* (The Falcon). It is in the style of many of Raimund's poems; the voice speaks softly over a simple, restful piano accompaniment. What is it that makes this effect—now long since exploited to saturation point by film and television—always so moving? If we compare other celebrated examples, the dialogue of Leonora and Rocco in *Fidelio*, Violetta's letter scene in *La Traviata*, or those portions of the text in Marschner's *Vampir* which are spoken against a background of

---

[1] Deutsch dates the song 1825–1826. (Ed.)

gusty nocturnal showers, we see that it is the unique departure from the usual composition for the singing voice. Schuman, Liszt and Richard Strauss made much use later of the melodramatic recitative. But none of them achieved the musical intensity of this brief contemplation of the power of love to turn sorrow into joy.

During this Hungarian summer in Zseliz, Schubert felt powerfully but secretly attracted to the beautiful young Countess, although this did not hold him back from an affair with her maid, Pepi. Yet he finishes a letter to his brother Ferdinand with these words:

> However happy I am, however healthy I am, however many good people there are here, nevertheless I am looking forward to the moment when I can say: To Vienna! To Vienna! Yes, my beloved Vienna, in your narrow confines, you hold everything that is precious and dear to me and nothing but the sight of you, the heavenly sight of you, can still my yearning.

Among the many interpretations of the conclusion to this letter is Heinrich Werlé's, who believes that Schubert had his prematurely deceased mother in mind here. That June, he had paid tribute to her in a setting of a poem which, Arnold Schering claims, he wrote himself. The last two stanzas of *Grablied für die Mutter* (D 616) anticipate Schubert's allegorical tale *Mein Traum* (My Dream):

> Bleich und stumm, am düstern Rand,
> Steht der Vater mit dem Sohne,
> Denen ihres Lebens schönste Krone
> Schnell, schnell mit ihr verschwand.

> Und sie weinen in die Gruft,
> Aber ihrer Liebe Zähren
> Werden sich zum Perlenkranz verklären,
> Wenn der Engel ruft.

(Pale and silent, the father and son stand at the graveside bereft of life's fairest crown. They weep, but their tears will be transfigured into a wreath of pearls when the angel calls.)

It is just possible, too, that the yearning note at the end of the letter could have been caused by boredom, since the Esterházys had prolonged their holidays. Schubert was missing his friends as well as the theatres and cafés of Vienna.

Thus, in a letter to his friends on 8th September 1818, he wrote:

That the opera folk in Vienna are so stupid as to perform all these lovely operas without me makes me mad, for in Zseliz I have to be everything rolled into one: composer, editor, audience and goodness knows what else. Not a soul here has any true feeling for Art except (if I am not mistaken) the Countess now and then. So I am all alone with my beloved and have to conceal her in my room, in my piano, in my breast. Although this often saddens me, on the other hand, it often inspires me all the more. Do not fear that I shall stay away any longer than is strictly necessary. I have composed several songs, some really good ones, during this period. I am not surprised that the Greek bird [i.e. Vogl = Vogel Ed.] is fluttering about in Upper Austria, that is his homeland, after all, and he is on holiday. I only wish I were with him. Then I would certainly make good use of my time.

Among the songs mentioned in that letter was the virtuoso piece for high bass voice *Das Abendrot* (D 627), technically very demanding because of the enormous intervals over which the voice has to leap. The poet was Aloys Wilhelm Schreiber, a literary historian at Heidelberg University. The noble seriousness of the main part of the song is, alas, replaced by a Carl Loewe-like rhetorical device when the low E's of the last pages are reached. (When the song was published in 1867, it was designated 'for bass', which confirms the suspicion that it was specially written for Count Esterházy.)

Aloys Schreiber (1763–1841) was a prolific author as well as a Professor of Literary Aesthetics and a theatre critic. He published literary magazines, books on travel, and works on the Rhine legends, as well as numerous plays.

Schubert set four of his poems in 1818. His *Das Marienbild* (D 623) bears similarities to Schlegel's *Vom Mitleiden Mariä* or to Jacobi's *Litanei*. Its delicate 6/8 time reflects the emotions that Schubert said he always experienced when he came across an image of the Virgin Mary at wayside shrines on his walks in the country. Beauty, he believed, was that element of Art which affected the beholder, and Schubert found an allegory here for his own work.

An den Mond in einer Herbstnacht (D 614), written in these unhappy spring days of 1818, turned out to be one of Schubert's most intimate confessions. Schreiber's words must have struck a chord in Schubert's heart, for the music seems to come direct from the very centre of his creative being, and only the length of the song can explain its failure to be included in the standard Lieder repertoire.

The 'soft steps' suggested by the poet become the somnambulistic march-theme which runs through the work, giving the effect of its being played by brass instruments. The second piano sonata in A minor of 1823 repeats almost note for note the theme of peaceful resignation that follows the last words of the song, 'die schöne Erde' ('the beautiful earth').

When Schubert's brother, Ignaz, wrote to him (on 12th October 1818) complaining about how misused he was as a schoolmaster, how 'freedom' was only a word to him, and how he envied his brother for having been released from this chore, Franz answered on 29th October:

Anyway, I shall never make political capital out of my most intimate feelings. I say what I think and there's an end to it. My longing for Vienna grows daily. We shall set off in November when the weather is good.

Longing for Vienna meant also longing for Therese Grob. The few 'nice girls' that Schubert had met in the meantime could not make him forget her, and, in September, he composed a song full of such homesickness, *Blondel zu Marien* (D 626). The poet is unknown, although Friedländer ascribes it erroneously to Franz Grillparzer. There are so many *fioriture* of the quasi-Italian sort in the vocal part that Mandyczewski considered them to be 'embellishments' added by Michael Vogl. Elaborate Italianisms of this sort are reminiscent of Beethoven's writing, and appear again later in Carl Loewe's cavatinas.

If we compare this song with the little Baroque pastiche setting of Goldoni's *La Pastorella* (D 513) of 1817 we can see how, for Schubert, such embellishments were synonymous with a strained artificiality of expression.

On his return to Vienna in November 1818 Schubert opposed his father's wish that he should take up his assistant schoolmaster's post again and, as a consequence of this new breach, he went for a time to share Mayrhofer's tiny lodgings in the Wipplingerstrasse. Mayrhofer's theoretical passion for freedom was strained, as his memoirs show:

> During our time together, idiosyncrasies inevitably came to light. Since both of us were well endowed in this respect, there were bound to be repercussions. We teased each other in all manner of ways, revealing our sharp edges to our own amusement and pleasure. His happy, relaxed sensuousness and my introspective nature became more sharply delineated, and led us to give each other suitable names, as if we were playing defined rôles. Alas, the rôle I played was my own.

In November and December Schubert set three Petrarch sonnets in translations by A. W. Schlegel.

Francesco Petrarch (1304–1374), the Italian Renaissance master of the sonnet-form, was returning to Italy from his law studies in France when he caught sight of 'Madonna Laura' in the church of St Clare in Avignon. From that moment on he worshipped her in song like a troubadour. Unattainable, idealised, she shone through his poetry until her death ten years later. Petrarch created the sonnet form, and Schubert's musical interpretations suffer only from the disadvantage of not being based on the original language. In addition, they stand practically on their own in the literature of music, if one excepts the three important Petrarch settings which Franz Liszt composed as a young man in Italy, and which he revised twice more in his lifetime. Where Liszt was primarily concerned with a 'beautiful sound', Schubert strove to do justice to the formal features of the poetry.

Apollo, lebet noch dein hold Verlangen ('Apollo, s'ancor vive il bel desio') (Sonnet I, D 628), alternates between recitative and *arioso*. Petrarch frequently uses the laurel tree ('lauro') as a symbol for Laura's name. The allegory of the planting of a tender laurel tree can be understood as a request to Apollo for good weather to speed Laura's recovery. Schubert's treatment of the poem's abstractions is stiff and remote.

The G minor opening of *Allein nachdenklich* ('Solo e pensoso') (Sonnet II, D 629) is immediately attractive; 'wie gelähmt vom Krampfe' ('as if lame with cramp') is syncopated to mark the dragging footsteps of the poet shunning the paths of man, an effect rivalled only by Schumann in his setting of Heine's 'Schöne Wiege meiner Leiden'.

Mandyczewski adopted Schubert's and Schlegel's error of attributing *Nunmehr, da die Erde schweigt* ('Or che'l ciel e la terra e'l vento tace') (Sonnet III, D 630) to Dante, which is why Dante's name has figured for so long in lists of Schubert's poets. This lengthy song, brimming over with musical ideas, compares the serenity of a sunset with the war in the poet's breast. As in his setting of Novalis's *Nachthymne* (D 687), only here much more consciously, Schubert makes extravagant use of triads to conjure up the air of mystery.

On 28th February 1819, a Schubert song was performed in public for the first time. As was noted in the press, Goethe's *Schäfers Klagelied* was sung 'with feeling' by Herr Franz Jäger, the principal tenor of the Theater an der Wien. Soon after that, the same pretty, but not very important song (composed in 1814) was heard again. At that time, only very few knew of the existence of Schubert's songs. Now even foreign papers began to take notice. We read in the *Berliner Gesellschafter* for 22nd March 1819:

> *Des Schäfers Klage,* by the young Franz Schubert, gave most pleasure. Indeed, we look forward to hearing a larger work by this promising artist.

On 23rd March 1822 the following analysis of the song appeared in the *Wiener Zeitschrift für Kunst etc.*

> The sound, unique to the pastorale, is superbly sustained and given full melodic expression. The accompaniment is appropriate and binds together the melodies separated by his characteristic modifications. . . . The characterisation is so deeply moving that no explanation is required for it to be felt by everyone.

Schubert does indeed raise the words of a well-known folk-song, paraphrased by Goethe, far above their intrinsic worth and clothes them in a seamless musical garment. This song, from the same period as *Gretchen am Spinnräde*, is an impressive work of uneasy warmth, in which the emotional climax on 'wem ich sie geben soll' ('To whom should I give them') or the tired resignation after the thunder, ('die Türe dort bleibt verschlossen') ('the door there remains closed to me'), are most moving. The intensified vivacity of the middle section reverts to melancholy on 'alles ist leider ein

Traum' ('all is, alas, but a dream'). The repetition is significantly different; the two parts of the first section are reversed, resulting in an extended *da capo*, which proves again how malleable form can be in the hands of a master. A good poet need never be afraid of using the same metres again and again. The same is true of Schubert's favourite pastoral rhythms, which, moving from 6/8 into 3/4, are introduced here to great effect. One never tires of meeting this Sicilian movement in both his early and his later works, for Schubert always invests it with a particular interest. *Schäfers Klagelied* is an impressive proof of how sure his command was of the form of the modified strophic song, even as early as 1814.

The second version in C minor (of the same year) differs from the first in E minor only in the omission of the four-bar prelude. (It was published with three other short Goethe settings as opus 3 in the summer of 1821, and was dedicated to the deputy director of the Hoftheater, Ignaz von Mosel. Mosel used to compose in the style of Handel—which earned him the ridicule of Beethoven—and was the first conductor to use a baton.)

SIX

Lieder of 1819 – 1820

Schubert was introduced to Franz Grillparzer (1791–1872) by Katharina Fröhlich (see p. 147). Grillparzer was an important Austrian writer of the nineteenth century. A civil servant, he gained fame with his drama *Die Ahnfrau* (1818), and his most important works were all dramas, while his poetry rarely rises above the level of occasional verse. Embittered by the public's lack of understanding of his work and by the continual pressure of the censorship, Grillparzer withdrew at a comparatively early age from the public gaze and hid his works. He really belonged more to the circle around Beethoven and he helped the latter's works to just recognition. He also supplied Beethoven with the libretto for an opera entitled *Melusine*, but it was never used.

Schubert's universally known *Ständchen* ('Zögernd leise') (D 920) for contralto solo and chorus (of 1827) is undoubtedly more significant than *Bertha's Lied in der Nacht* (D 653) which Schubert set for the heroine of *Die Ahnfrau*, and which, despite its inspired music, can really make no sense whatsoever out of context. For a proper appreciation of the song, one would have to be more familiar with this 'Fate Tragedy', and realise that the 'Ahnfrau' ('the ancestress'), a symbol of ancient inherited guilt and the personification of 'Fate' in the house of the Counts of Borotin, continually enters the plot in the guise of Bertha, the Count's young daughter. The metre, unrhymed Spanish trochaics, suits the eerie background to this improbable ballad, and only in the case of this nocturnal song does it rise to rhymes. Despite the efforts of the Fröhlich family, Schubert never came very close to Grillparzer, possibly because he felt that the poet belonged more to Beethoven's circle of friends. This probably also explains why he only set three rather poor poems by him, although many poems by Austrian authors are represented in his corpus of Lieder. Perhaps he did not know Grillparzer's true convictions about the age in which they lived, for it is difficult to believe that they would not have become friends had there been a true meeting of minds. A Grillparzer poem of 1826/27 makes clear that he well understood who this Schubert really was, although there is no mention of Schubert in the books recording Grillparzer's conversations with Beethoven:

Schubert heiß' ich, Schubert bin ich,
Und als solcher geb' ich mich.
Was die Besten je geleistet,
Ich erkenn' es, ich verehr' es,
Immer doch bleibt's außer mir.

Selbst die Kunst, die Kränze windet,
Blumen sammelt, wählt und bindet,
Ich kann ihr nur Blumen bieten,
Dichte sie und—wählet ihr.

Lobt ihr mich, es soll mich freuen,
Schmäht ihr mich, ich muß es dulden,
Schubert heiß' ich, Schubert bin ich,
Mag nicht hindern, kann nicht klagen,
Geht ihr gern auf meinen Pfaden,
Nun wohlan, so folget mir!

(I am called Schubert and I am Schubert, and that's how I present myself. I recognise and respect what the best have done, yet that has nothing to do with me. I can only offer my contribution to that art which chooses and collects flowers and binds them into wreaths. You must choose the ones you want. If you praise me, I'll be happy; if you scorn me, I'll just have to put up with it. Schubert I am called, and Schubert I am, I can't prevent it, I can't complain. If you want to walk along my ways, fine then, follow me!)

Here, possibly by chance, Schubert's artistic credo vis-à-vis Beethoven is skilfully and accurately portrayed. His brave independence, of which he never said much, is underlined.

The evening sky is praised in two Lieder to poems by Johann Peter Silbert (1772–1844) of February 1819; Silbert was a teacher at the Gymnasium and later a Professor of French who worked mainly as a translator.

The dreamy *Abendbilder* (D 650) demonstrates Schubert's gift for never stressing illustrative moments in the accompaniment at the expense of the musical substance. The song of birds, the sound of distant bells, the shimmer of moonlight on the church roof, all these are unobtrusively incorporated into the musical pattern. Metrical problems, the alternation of longer with shorter lines, always held a fascination for Schubert. The unified *motif* of the accompaniment, and the artistically varied melody of the vocal part, combine to give an intense emotional experience. If in some other songs, the frequently-heard water-*motifs* lie particularly well under the hands, pianists will be attracted no less by the figure of branches moving in the wind in this song, a figure which recurs of course in the later *Lindenbaum* in *Die Winterreise*. But the form of this song is too loose, and it is too reserved in expression, for it to be suitable for public performance. In cases like this, the gramophone offers us a means of getting to know the work.

Himmelsfunken (D 651) seeks to bring the stars, the symbols of divinity, nearer to devout mankind. The lively modulations do more to retain one's interest than do the words of this simple, strophic song.

Schubert was staying with Johann Mayrhofer in a stuffy room in the house of the 'widow Sanssouci'. They presented a strange picture to their friends; Mayrhofer's introspective anti-social behaviour did not seem to be compatible with Schubert's open-heartedness, but poets understood Schubert best and he was deeply attracted to Mayrhofer, who always encouraged him in his work. Seventeen years later, Eduard von Bauernfeld, who was too young at the time to belong to Schubert's circle of friends, wrote a satirical poem on Mayrhofer, in which he claimed that the only thing that would bring Mayrhofer out of himself was a Schubert Lied.

Spaun gave the real reason for Mayrhofer's unapproachableness:

Mayrhofer was renowned above all for his profound knowledge of Latin, Greek and the classical authors. He was often very badly off, but, apart from his pipe, he had few wants. Since his superior literary background was well known in certain circles, he was given a minor, though reasonably well-paid post in the office of the book censor, and was later promoted to the post of book censor. Since he had extreme liberal, indeed democratic sentiments, and was keenly in favour of a free press, only necessity could have driven him into the office of the book censor. What is surprising, when one considers his views, is that he was feared by all book-sellers, because of his strictness.

Schubert responded to this Dioscuri-like friendship by fulfilling Mayrhofer's hopes that his poetry might describe for posterity the struggle to find the meaning of existence. Just what effect Mayrhofer hoped to have on Schubert is made particularly clear in *Heliopolis II* (D 754), composed in 1822, where Mayrhofer speaks directly to his younger friend. In his setting, Schubert, in keeping with the text, opposes the serene progression into light (which marks its linear companion-piece *Heliopolis I* (D 753)) with quick, powerful, energetic strokes. This energy emanates from the C minor theme which dominates the whole work. The closing section proceeds chromatically through F minor to D minor. By frequently supporting the voice in triple octaves, the piano accompaniment gives an impression of rock-like security. The aligning of the three seventh chords on E, B and C let the 'Leidenschaften sausen und brausen' ('passions rage and swell'), and lead on to the thunderously repeated 'rechtes Wort' (right word'), which Schubert has certainly found here! Beethoven is not far away when we listen to the defiant, jagged rhythms which charge through several keys, until the right word finds the right sound in a blazing C minor. (*Heliopolis I* used to bear the mysterious heading 'Number 12'; the explanation is that the two texts were taken from the twelfth poem of Mayrhofer's collection *Heliopolis*.)

Mayrhofer's poem *An die Freunde* (D 654) reflects in stark terms the poet's frequently expressed intention to kill himself. Schubert translated this sentiment into his own personal premonition of death, which is treated with the same measure of humble piety as is his polyphonic study *Vom Mitleiden Mariä* (D 632) by Friedrich Schlegel. Both songs express suppliance in an abstractly linear form, reminiscent of the masters of the Baroque, and rarely found elsewhere in Schubert's work.

An die Freunde is built up on arid quavers, separated from each other by rests, and which are then combined into crotchets to represent the friends' conversations. Schubert's empathy with his friend overcomes the poet's self-destructive impulses, since Schubert does not share Mayrhofer's attitude towards death.

An die Freunde is one of five Mayrhofer songs composed in 1819, among which was also *Die Sternennächte* (D 670). For once not warring with the powers of Fate, but rather calmed by the prospect of the starry heavens, the poet inspires the composer to a 6/8 melody which flows gently over transparent accompanying chords, mostly in the treble.

The choice of a poem by Friedrich Schlegel, *Der Wanderer* (D 649), set in February 1819, appears as an imaginary disengagement from the confines of his life with Mayrhofer, and affirmation of the need for creative solitude.

The poet, the younger Schlegel, had been an apprentice in commercial life for only a short time, before embracing a career in the arts. His Romantic predilections led him to studies of Greek philosophy and sculpture, of the older periods of German, Spanish and Italian literatures, and also of oriental languages and Indian philosophy. Like his brother, August Wilhelm, he lectured on philosophy and aesthetics, and contributed frequently to art and literary periodicals.

Schubert must have felt Schlegel's patriotic support for Austria against Napoleon to have been as heartfelt as his own enthusiasm for freedom, for he set sixteen of Schlegel's poems.

Friedrich Schlegel was certainly no great poet, but rather a critic of genius (in Romantic terminology), whose views on art, history and philosophy are still of value today. His theory of 'progressive Universalpoesie' (progressive universal poetry), whose irony should burst through traditional boundaries, is scarcely visible in the poems which Schubert chose to set. These have the effect rather of being more gifted pendants to his brother's poetic miniatures. (Both brothers lectured on drama and world literature in Vienna in 1816.)

The song, *Der Wanderer* (D 649) is a miracle of concentration and conciseness; yet, because of the fame of its namesake (Schmidt's *Der Wanderer* (D 489)), it was doomed to oblivion. In it, Schubert expressed his *Weltfrömmigkeit* ('universal piety'), to use Eduard Spranger's term, his close relationship to the world about him, which he experienced precisely because he was compelled to go his own way, alone. A careful reading of the unusual text will reveal the obstacles in the way of a simple musical setting:

> Wie deutlich des Mondes Licht
> zu mir spricht,
> Mich beseelend zu der Reise:
> 'Folge treu dem alten Gleise,
> Wähle keine Heimat nicht.
> Ew'ge Plage
> bringen sonst die schweren Tage.
> Fort zu andern,
> Sollst du wechseln, sollst du wandern,
> Leicht entfliehend jeder Klage.'
> Sanfte Ebb' und hohe Flut,
> tief im Mut,
> Wandr' ich so im Dunkeln weiter,
> Steige mutig, singe heiter,
> Und die Welt erscheint mir gut.
> Alles Reine
> seh' ich mild im Widerscheine,
> nichts verworren,
> in des Tages Glut verdorren:
> Froh umgeben, doch alleine.

(How clearly the moon's light speaks to me, encouraging me on my journey: 'Follow the old path, do not choose a homeland yet, lest the hard days bring constant worries. Go forth to others if you want to change or wander, fleeing from every lament.' Gentle ebb, high tide, low in spirits, I wander on in the darkness, climb with courage, sing with joy and the world seems to be so good. I see all that is pure in the moon's reflection, nothing confused or dried up in the fierce glow of daytime, surrounded by friends, but alone.)

Nevertheless, the music makes mock of any suspicion of difficulty and moves along, ethereal and featherlight. (It was published as opus 65 no. 2 in 1826.)

The *motif* of the charming trifle *Das Mädchen* (D 652) of February, 1819, whose lover attempts to kiss away her complaint that he does not truly love her, is heard first in the major and then in the minor mode. A piece of pure Schubert.

The idea behind *Der Schiffer* (D 694), the boatman who is lazy to the point of yawning, is a brilliant one. The waves splash against the boat, the summer afternoon is full of sultry drowsiness, the phlegmatic boatman is hardly moved even by the thoughts of his beloved. The opening *motif* spreads itself like the azure-blue sky over this idyll and is repeated in a manner often imitated later by Hugo Wolf. At the conclusion, the singer is allowed, exceptionally, to hum, a realistic effect used only this once in Schubert's songs. The music is as teasing and as playful as the words, and, since only wishes and hopes are expressed, it is only natural that the opening should be repeated, but with the omission of the four bars with the startling drop of an octave.

In *Die Sterne* (D 684), Schubert is seeking to reproduce the oscillation of the stars in the heavens as an echo of his own mood. It was the first stanza which moved him particularly:

> Du staunest, O Mensch, was heilig wir strahlen?
> O folgtest du nur den himmlischen Winken,
> Vernähmest du besser, was freundlich wir blinken,
> Wie wären verschwunden die irdischen Qualen!

(You wonder, O man, how sacred are our beams? Oh were you to follow the heavenly signs, you would understand better how friendly these beams are, and how all earthly sufferings would vanish.)

It is revealing how frequently Schubert was controlled by extra-musical influences. We are often made aware of textual nuances even when the thoughts are inadequately expressed by the poet himself. This then becomes a greater challenge to Schubert's musical technique. If a song like *Die Sterne* sounds impressive, that is not the merit of the trivial poem. The superb vocal line, particularly on 'ewigen' ('eternal'), and 'reinen' ('pure'), has a counter-melody in the piano (C–A flat–F against F–A flat–C), which is later reversed. Because of a rather truncated return to the original key, the conclusion seems strangely abrupt.

There are hardly any Schubert songs in the major mode which do not contain at least passing references to the minor, even in naïve settings like *Der Schmetterling* (D 633), a nature study of unbelievable delicacy, and godfather to Hugo Wolf's *Zitronenfalter im April*.

The colossal dimensions of Schlegel's *Im Walde* (D 708) are no obstacle to the dense thematic content of Schubert's setting. This is perhaps his most extensive through-composed work. The listener marvels at his ability to depict in music every tiny detail. By repeating the first section at the end, he imposes form on the poem's rambling fantasies. To avoid monotony, the pianist must take care to colour the unchanging semiquavers' movement of the rustling of the leaves and branches.

The twice-repeated 'wie zu Gott hinaufgefodert' ('as if God had called it upward') moves from E major to B major like a flash of lightning. Immediately afterwards, in the C major section, there is a modulation to D flat major on 'lockend' ('luring'). The 'Liebesfülle' ('love's fulfilment') is given ever new variations. The 'schöpferische Lüfte wehen' ('winds which inspire creation') are repeated in chromatic melodic and harmonic sequences back to D major and, within a few bars, Schubert has returned to the original key of E major and thence to the conclusion.

Die Vögel (D 691) (1820) is the counterpart to such longwindedness. Schlegel's birds mock at men as did those of Aristophanes, only here, all is transferred to the world of German folk-song, which inspires Schubert to compose the most delicate of Ländler, whose chirping and fluttering seems made to order for a lyric soprano. Deeper voices can, however, also demonstrate the delicacy of Schubert's treatment of final syllables. (On the very next page of the *Gesamtausgabe* is a similar song *Der Knabe* (D 692), in which the boy wishes he were a bird.)

'Everything seems to be speaking to the poet', says Schlegel in *Abendröte* (D 690), which is demonstrated by a detailed description of pictures and sounds. As dusk falls, the poet surveys the harmony of all natural phenomena. As if painting with dark colours, Schubert outlines the sweep of the mountains in a broad bass line, while the silvery stream winds its way through the often-interrupted figures of the piano.

Schubert's modulations between major and minor make of *Blanka* (D 631) a charming portrait of a young girl, half-awake, whose feelings are clothed in the most delicate of musical garments. Soaring triplets enhance the charm of this genre-painting.

It is no great step from Schlegel to the friend who was closest to him and who emulated him: Friedrich von Hardenberg (1772–1801), known as Novalis, studied philosophy under Fichte in Jena, law in Leipzig and Wittenberg and geology in Freiberg. He is one of the most important figures in German Romanticism. Although Novalis, as an opponent of the French Revolution, was certainly involved in ideological arguments, his renown rests on the sensitivity with which he described the anguish of his conflict with the social realities of his day, and in particular, on his defence of that questionable new Catholicism, proclaimed in his glorification of the feudal Christian Middle Ages.

Schubert has the distinction of having been the only composer to set texts of Novalis. In 1819 he set five Hymns and a poem to the Virgin Mary. Once again, he finds appropriate music. The unique simplicity of the musical structure of these settings matches the strangeness of the poems. It is possible that an Italian influence could be found here, perhaps Rossini's, whose *Otello* impressed Schubert greatly during the Italian's stay in Vienna. The intellectual stimuli provoked by Novalis, before his death in 1801, originated in Friedrich Schleiermacher's *Reden über die Religion* (Speeches on Religion) (1799) which inspired Novalis to write his *Geistliche Lieder* ('Spiritual Songs'). Schleiermacher's writings on Christianity anticipated Novalis's political praise of a unified Christendom in the 'genuinely Catholic ages'. However, the poets who were later to be called 'Romantic', and who had moved away from Novalis to gather round the Schlegel brothers, sought to undo much of the work of the French Revolution. What Novalis wrote at this time could have come from the pen of a disillusioned critic of today's society:

> True anarchy is the conceptive element of religion. Out of the destruction of everything positive, anarchy raises its illustrious head as the founder of a new world, a new Jerusalem, a new golden age of eternal peace, a new and lasting Church. . . .
>
> Blood will continue to flow over Europe, until the nations become aware of the fearful madness which is driving them on and, moved and pacified by sacred music, they all come together at their former altars, ready to undertake works of peace, and, shedding hot tears, celebrate a great love feast, a festival of peace at the incense-laden holy places.

The highly unorthodox religious enthusiasm of the early Romantics fired Schubert too, but, apart from that, the composition of religious songs was a much more popular and natural exercise than it is today. There are the settings of Gellert's religious poetry by C. P. E. Bach and Beethoven, as well as Schubert's settings of the poems of Klopstock, Claudius and Pyrker (which can scarcely be termed 'Lieder').

The hymn set to Klopstock's *Das große Halleluja* (D 442) was obviously conceived as a choral work—whether for a female chorus, as the Breitkopf edition assumes, is, however, doubtful. Schubert employs Mendelssohnian Baroque elements, anticipating, as it were, the latter's reversions to earlier styles. The second song from this 1816 Klopstock group, *Schlachtgesang* (D 443), might also have originally been written for a chorus. Klopstock's *Die Gestirne* (D 444) can only be compared with *Die vier Weltalter* in the length and complexity of its stanzas. It is difficult to relate the disparate textual emphases to the standard set by the first stanza. If, on the other hand, repetitions are minimised to avoid monotony, the effect is necessarily incomplete. The carefully-constructed conciseness and the beautiful melody of *Edone* (D 445), in which a young girl pines for her absent lover, is much more attractive.

Matthias Claudius's less pathos-laden, more domestic way of expressing religious emotions is given appropriate musical form in *Bei dem Grabe meines Vaters* (D 496) (1816) which, though seemingly undemanding, has still a good deal of art in its simplicity. It cannot be a coincidence that Schubert had set Aloys Schreiber's *Marienbild* and Friedrich Schlegel's *Vom Mitleiden Mariä* (both late 1818) shortly before his work on the Novalis Hymns.

The first hearing of *Vom Mitleiden Mariä* (D 632) is an unforgettable experience. The accompaniment, a polyphonic study for three voices, demonstrates that mastery of line which a superficial consideration of Schubert's work might not detect. The song is a partner to that four-handed fugue which suffers near-oblivion at the end of the volumes of piano works (D 952).

But to return to Novalis: he could combine the maternal and the virginal aspects of the Mother of God into manifestations of love. Thus, these lines come from the most celebrated of the *Geistliche Lieder, Marie* (D 658) set by Schubert:

> Ich sehe dich in tausend Bildern,
> Maria, lieblich ausgedrückt,

Doch keins von allen kann dich schildern,
Wie meine Seele dich erblickt.

(I can see you portrayed, Mary, in a thousand images, yet none
can picture you as my soul sees you.)

Victory over death is the main theme of all the Schubert Novalis
settings. Schubert's struggle with this phenomenon is manifested
here as the personal experience of an act of faith. His subjective
shaping of this experience demonstrates his ability to penetrate to
the depths of human emotions—and beyond. From Novalis's
gospel of the omnipresence of the golden age, the central theme of
his poetry, Schubert extracts the concept of victory over death, one
of his major preoccupations.

The first of the short cycle of Novalis Hymns to be set contains
lines which mark Schubert's attitude to life. The entreaties are to
be repeated, an unusual departure for Schubert:

Hätten die Nüchternen
Einmal nur gekostet,
Alles verließen sie,
Und setzten sich zu uns
An den Tisch der Sehnsucht,
Der nie leer wird.

(Had those who are hungry tasted only once, they would have
left everything to sit down with us at the table of longing that is
never bare.)

Unlike the other short and lapidary hymns, *Hymne I* (D 659) and
Nachthymne (D 687) (see pp. 131–2) are somewhat extensive. In their
manner, *Hymne II* (D 660) and *Hymne III* (D 661) ('Wenn ich ihn
nur habe' and 'Wenn alle untreu werden'), both strophic and both
in the key of B flat major and minor, differ hardly at all from
Schubert's little secular love-songs.

The musical, conscious return to the stylistic naïvety of the fourth
Hymne (D 662) ('Ich sage es jedem, daß er lebt'), likewise strophic,
is unmatched. Schubert's Lieder are like a melting-pot, in which
are blended the multiplicity of intellectual movements of contemporary German-speaking society. His music immortalises not
only the great writers, but also those weary of the world and
longing for death.

Schubert had found in Michael Vogl the interpreter who could make these songs a moving experience for all men and women. Spaun wrote:

> The interest which Vogl showed in Schubert's songs suddenly enlarged the circle in which the young composer had moved up to then, and Vogl's superb performance of these songs soon won Schubert loud and friendly acclamation. Accomplished dilettantes now began to acquaint themselves with the spirit of Schubert's compositions and perform the wonderful songs with enthusiasm and happiness.

Schubert was now able to enjoy other comforts. Schober and Vogl were supporting him and he accepted their help without demur. The assistance was indeed less humiliating than his father's demands that he should give up his independent artistic work. He would no longer teach with his father. He even gave up his summer teaching post with the Esterházys, who had to travel to Zseliz without him. Perhaps Schubert sensed that the growing recognition of his work by the Viennese made a lengthy absence from the city inadvisable. However, when the hoped-for première of his operetta *Die Zwillingsbrüder* did not materialise, he decided to join Vogl on a short holiday trip which unexpectedly turned into a concert tour.

Vogl took his young friend with him to Upper Austria. Their goals were Linz and Steyr, the planned journey to Salzburg having to be abandoned. They took their meals in Steyr at the home of Josef von Koller, a merchant. Franz wrote to Ferdinand Schubert on 13th July:

> In the house in which I am living there are 8 girls, almost all pretty. You can see that there is plenty to do. The daughter of Herr von Koller, in whose house Vogl and I take our meals, is very pretty, plays the piano very nicely and is going to sing several of my songs.

Josepha, nicknamed Pepi, von Koller was the most musical of the five Koller children. In gratitude for her performance of his songs, Schubert dedicated the newly-composed Sonata in A major (opus 120) to her. Schubert also conceived the 'Trout' Quintet in Steyr, an example of how his songs influenced the other areas of his music.

Schubert and an enthusiastic cellist, Sylvester Paumgartner, planned the Quintet together. Paumgartner, a deputy director of the local mines and a bachelor, lived in an imposing house in the market square in Steyr. Vogl was, of course, a native of Steyr, and Spaun, Holzapfel, Stadler and Mayrhofer all came from this region. They were singing Schubert's songs in Steyr before they were even published. Copies made by Viennese friends were circulated among Schubert's admirers in a district of whose existence Schubert knew nothing. In the second storey of Paumgartner's house, in the little music room, Stadler heard Vogl and Schubert perform:

> In these rooms in 1819 we enjoyed most of all Vogl's and Schubert's music; but as Vogl was not always in good humour and disposed to sing, good old Paumgartner had to beg for it, as it were. Then you could have heard a pin drop. Paumgartner would not permit any disturbance during the music. But, after the concert, the guests for the evening were generously compensated for this in every respect.

Die Forelle was so often requested at these evenings that Schubert was asked to compose a piano quintet for the same group of instruments as in Johann Hummel's Quintet in E flat, opus 87. In the fifth movement, Paumgartner's favourite song is treated in five sets of variations, until it finally appears in the form with the 'jumping trout' accompaniment.

It was also in the Koller house that Vogl received a birthday surprise. He always used to celebrate his birthday during his holiday in Upper Austria. The surprise was a cantata composed by Stadler and Schubert. (*Kantate zum Geburtstag des Sängers Johann Michael Vogl: Der Frühlingsmorgen* (D 666) ('Spring morning'.) The text contains a number of references to Vogl's most famous operatic rôles. Pepi Koller sang the soprano part and Bernhart Benedict and Schubert the others. Vogl was immensely pleased with both the work and the performance, and tears filled his eyes at the passages about Steyr.

On the way back, the two friends passed through Linz, Spaun's birthplace. Schubert wrote to Mayrhofer on 19th August 1819:

> I am in Linz at the moment; I went to the Spauns and met Kenner, Kreil and Forstmayer as well as Spaun's mother and

Ottenwald [Ottenwalt—Ed.], to whom I sang his *Wiegenlied* which I have set to music.

This Dr Anton Ottenwalt (1789–1854) was Spaun's brother-in-law, a lawyer and an Adjunctor in the law department in Vienna. He bore the title of *Hofrat* (Court Councillor). This *Wiegenlied* (D 579), which Schubert had set in 1817, has a pretty, if not particularly distinguished flowing melody in C major.

Schubert composed only two Goethe songs in October 1819. In the sonnet, *Die Liebende schreibt* (D 673), the girl pleads for a letter from her lover. For a long time, Goethe had no interest in the sonnet-form, but, in 1807, presumably during his passionate involvement with Minna Herzlieb, he did write a group of sonnets. This setting is in pastel tones, and only at the modulation from B flat major to G flat major do the colours become stronger. The piano suggests tears which do not fall, but dry on the cheeks. The first section is separated from the second by a change of tempo, with a noteworthy final modulation to G flat major on the word 'weinen' ('to weep'). 'Gib mir ein Zeichen' ('Give me a sign') could not be more passionate. (Mendelssohn also set the poem as his opus 86.)

The *Prometheus*-monologue (D 674) towers over miniatures like *Die Liebende schreibt*. The autograph manuscript calls for a bass voice. The difficulties for a composer are even greater here than in *Ganymed*, as there are so few lyrical passages in the poem. Schubert manages to find them nevertheless, and develops his melodic themes out of them. Grandeur and dignity speak out of this music, and nowhere is its clarity or its transparency sacrificed for the sake of expressiveness. The models here are the 'recitativi accompagnati' of Mozart or Beethoven, and one can also trace a line leading to Verdi, who developed a similarly pure, 'classical' style from the same sources, enriched in his case by the brilliance of his own orchestration. As in the case of Verdi, Schubert's instrumental part essentially underpins and extends the dramatic action, the recitation of the act of heroic defiance.

Prometheus points to the future and blazes a new trail. Not only Hugo Wolf, who later set the poem in a Lisztian manner, learned from Schubert; dramatic music of coming generations owed much to songs such as this. The varied tempi, tonalities, and dynamics match the different moods of the individual stanzas. Not until Wagner's *Tristan* do we meet another composition with such daring harmonies and fascinating progressions.

If we read the three scenes which Goethe sketched for a Prometheus-drama (which was never completed) we can see how accurate an interpreter of the words Schubert was. He has no need to apologise to Hugo Wolf, who accused him of failing fully to understand the text. Schubert's defiant neo-creator of man as the prototype of the artist is nearer Goethe's conception than the Wolfian reflective Prometheus, which is fashioned more on Aeschylus's figure. *Prometheus* is not the only work to make us regret that Schubert never found a satisfactory opera librettist. It is not idle speculation to wonder what would have become of opera had he done so. To judge from his first encounter with a Goethe poem, it is possible that he would have revolutionised opera long before Wagner. The mystery that there was not even a collaboration with Ferdinand Raimund, who had been a successful author of folk- and fairy-tales since 1807, has still to be solved by scholars.

Prometheus is one of the many incomprehensibles about Schubert. The manifold and differing potentialities dwelling within him were incalculable. His friends, who saw their happy Franz principally as a kind-hearted, innocent, modest man, inclined to laziness, must have been astounded by these glimpses of territory as yet untrodden. That is why, for all their affection, they were never entirely happy with the uncompromising Schubert of the *Winterreise* or of the great Goethe-Lieder. The complexities of the *Schöne Müllerin* were just within the general public's grasp. It is no wonder, therefore, that this complex-ridden man often entertained doubts about himself and his work.

Reichardt's *Prometheus* is a puny thing beside Schubert's, but Schubert probably knew it, since he copies some of the formal features of the older man's setting. Reichardt, Zelter and Mendelssohn, incidentally, do not show themselves at their most inspired in their *Prometheus* settings, and only after the baritone Eugen Gura had performed Schubert's in public did it gain a regular place in the concert repertoire.

Since 1820 was to be a particularly unhappy year for Schubert, it is not surprising to find him setting Novalis's *Nachthymne* (D 687) at the beginning of that year—and to the 'death-rhythm', which had become so familiar since 1817:

> Hinüber wall' ich,
> Und jede Pein
> Wird einst ein Stachel
> Der Wollust sein.

(I wander into the beyond and all pain becomes a stab of delight.)

The song is conceived on a large scale, but the effect is marred by the repetitions used to pad out the text. In addition, the wealth of splendid musical ideas is squandered on the banality of the closing theme. Nevertheless, the true Schubertian will find this collaboration with Novalis, and its undertones of private confidences, a rich experience.

Spaun's fiancée, Franziska von Roner, was the recipient of four Italian songs to texts of Vittorelli and Metastasio, all composed in January 1820 (*Vier Canzonen* (D 688) Ed.).

When Schubert was working with a foreign text, he always felt obliged to swamp the ideas and images conjured up by the words with music—this accorded with his ideas of Italian style—so too here, and the music emerges slightly frustrated, if still inspired.

That his contacts with Pepi von Koller and Albert Stadler in Upper Austria were still retained can be seen from the note in Schubert's hand on the autograph manuscript of *Morgenlied*: 'N.B. To the singer P. and the pianist St. I particularly recommend this song! ! ! 1820.'

Morgenlied (D 685) is dedicated to the Patriarch of Venice, Johann Ladislaus Pyrker von Felsö-Eör, and takes up a recurrent theme in Schubert's songs: birds. The poet, Zacharias Werner (1768–1823), born in Königsberg, studied jurisprudence there and also attended Kant's philosophy lectures. Schiller championed him, and Goethe took a keen interest in his published work. Encouraged by the actress Frau Bethmann-Unzelmann, Werner wrote dramas, of which the 'Fate-tragedy', *Der 24. Februar*, is the best-known for its influence on contemporary German drama. But it is difficult to find any interest today in Schubert's harmless little song and its naïve dialogue with the birds.

In the spring of 1820, Schubert fell foul of 'authority': he was arrested on suspicion of subversive activities. The previous year in

Mannheim, a student had murdered August von Kotzebue, the poet and alleged Russian spy. Schubert's friend, Senn, would not allow the police to search his papers, and since Schubert happened to be in the lodgings at the time, and had not spared the police his verbal comments, he, too, was arrested, though soon released. (Senn will be remembered from the *Konvikt* days where he wrote the famous song *Der rote Adler von Tirol* (The Red Eagle of the Tyrol). He was deeply hurt when the Hapsburgs simply ceded his 'beautiful Tyrol'). Senn was sentenced to fourteen months' imprisonment and then deported back to the Tyrol, after cross-questioning had proved fruitless. Schubert never saw his friend again. He did, however, manage to keep in touch, as the songs *Selige Welt* and *Schwanengesang* prove. We shall return to them later.

The continued lack of success of his operas did not discourage Schubert, but, in his determination to conquer the operatic stage, he made the repeated mistake of setting libretti in which he had no interest—a mistake which he had early overcome in his song composing. He was not downcast by the dismal failures of his operas; if one did not please the audiences perhaps the next one would. Yet not everybody could bear disappointment as stoically as Schubert. His modesty often puzzled his friends. Spaun writes:

> It knew no bounds. The loudest jubilation of his friends and the greatest acclamation of countless people could not turn his head. Even the most respectful recognition paid to him by artists like Weber, Hummel, Lablache etc., etc., did not affect his quiet modesty. When the performer of his songs was overwhelmed by enthusiastic applause, and no thought was given to the little man sitting at the piano accompanying the songs so feelingly, this modest artist did not feel in the least insulted by such neglect.

The première of *Die Zwillingsbrüder* (The Twin Brothers) (D 647) took place in the Kärntnertor Theater on 14th June 1820. On 27th August, the *Wiener Konversationsblatt* carried some cutting comments by Baron von Schlechta—only one voice in the critical chorus. Nevertheless, von Schlechta drew attention to a composer who, up to then, had been unjustifiably known solely as the 'Liederfürst' ('The Prince of Songs'). Von Schlechta went on:

> In his beautiful songs, alas too little known, we meet a spirit which is as simple and profound as it is poetically pure. Perhaps

he was too anxious to find something in this material which would help him to show his *forte*. He *will* achieve something, great and beautiful things. In that hope, let us extend a friendly welcome to this modest artist.

Liebeslauschen (D 698), by von Schlechta, is a genre-painting like the subject of the poem, a picture by the Romantic illustrator of the Bible, Ludwig Schnorr von Carolsfeld, and has a charming simplicity. There is a delightful surprise at the end, when the tempo changes from 3/4 to 2/4. The poem scatters trochaic and iambic rhythms about with gay abandon, but Schubert, capable of dealing with any metrical problem, turns the poem into an ironical, charming little serenade, making its own delightful impact through its surprising conclusion. Carolsfeld's picture shows a cavalier playing his zither under his beloved's window in the moonlight. The piano interludes foreshadow the serenade-music to the Rellstab *Ständchen* (D 957 no. 4) of 1828.

SEVEN

After the Separation
from Therese

On 21st November 1820, after a series of quarrels, Schubert had to give up all hope of marrying Therese Grob. If Hüttenbrenner is to be believed, he had given up hope as early as the end of 1817, since, in addition to the opposition of the Grob family, Schubert's differences with his father also played their part. The latter forbade Franz the house as long as he refused to be tied down to teaching.

On that fateful day in 1820, Therese Grob married Johann Bergmann, a master baker, in the Liechtenthal Parish Church. In 1858, Ferdinand Luib, who was collecting material for a biography of Schubert, spoke to Hüttenbrenner, who told him: 'From the moment I met Schubert, he had no affairs of the heart.'

This might well be a slight exaggeration, even if it is true that Schubert only had had the one great love. Hüttenbrenner continued:

He was rather a boor in his dealings with the fair sex, although nothing less than *galant*. He neglected his appearance, particularly his teeth, smelt strongly of tobacco and was not at all qualified to play the suitor—hardly suitable, as they say, for polite company. Yet, according to his own account, before we met he had had his eye on a teacher's daughter from the country, and she had been quite fond of him too. [Therese Grob was actually the daughter of a silk-worker. D. F-D.] She won his heart when she sang the soprano solo from one of his Masses so beautifully. What her father was called and where he lived, I cannot remember. [The father was already dead. D. F-D.] The girl could not marry Schubert, since, at that time, he was too young, with neither money nor a post. Apparently against her will, she obeyed her father and married another who could provide for her— From that moment on, when he saw that he had lost his beloved, he had a strong antipathy to the daughters of Eve. [Other reports make this hard to believe. D. F-D.]

Therese's name is important for another reason; the descendants of her brother Heinrich, a family called Meangya of Mödling near Vienna, owned a volume entitled 'Therese Grob's album' containing three Schubert songs not included in the *Gesamtausgabe*: *Am ersten Maimorgen* (D 344), by Claudius, *Mailied* (D 503), by Hölty, and *Der Leidende* (D 512) (anon.), all composed in 1816. Thanks to the tireless and dedicated efforts of the Belgian scholar, Pater Reinhard van Hoorickx, the reluctant owner was persuaded to let him publish these songs some little time ago.

To help him over his loneliness, Schubert threw himself into the social whirl. Watteroth, Collin and Karoline Pichler introduced him to the Sonnleithners. Leopold von Sonnleithner, it will be recalled, had taken a part in Schubert's *Prometheus* cantata when still a student. Since then, he had been an enthusiastic supporter of Schubert's music and, in 1819, had the cantata performed again, this time in the house of his father, Ignaz Sonnleithner, a barrister and professor of commercial law. Leopold's uncle, Joseph von Sonnleithner, a secretary at the Burgtheater, was a playwright and had edited *inter alia* the libretto of Beethoven's *Leonora*. The Sonn-leithner residence, the famous 'Gundelhof' on the Bauernmarkt, was the scene of the regular musical soirées, at first weekly, then fortnightly, attended by up to 120 guests; out of these soirées developed the celebrated *Gesellschaft der Musikfreunde* (The Phil-harmonic Society of Vienna), of which the Sonnleithner brothers were co-founders. At these gatherings, a young civil servant, August von Gymnich, who had a beautiful, well-trained tenor voice, per-formed, with Schubert at the piano, those songs previously known only to the composer's intimate circle of friends. Unfortunately, Gymnich died quite young in 1821.

Sonnleithner's private concerts soon found imitators in middle-class circles. These 'Schubertiads' included Lieder, dances, piano and other music in their programmes; Vogl's contribution was always one of the great attractions. The Bruchmann family, the Spauns, Karl Hönig or Johann Umlauff, and many, many others acted as hosts. Leopold von Sonnleithner ('Poldi') introduced

Schubert to Matthias Fröhlich, a retired businessman, who liked to have interesting people around him—and who also had four pretty, good-natured daughters. One of them, Anna, was studying the piano with Beethoven's celebrated friend, Johann Nepomuk Hummel. (She later became a singing teacher who taught for a time at the Konservatorium attached to the *Gesellschaft der Musikfreunde*.) She left us this account of Schubert's introduction to the family:

Dr Leopold Sonnleithner brought us some songs by a young man which, as he told us, were supposed to be good. Sister Kathi [Grillparzer's great love.Ed.] sat down at the piano and tried the accompaniment. Suddenly Gymnich, a civil servant with a good voice, looked up and said, 'What's that you are playing? That's wonderful, something quite extraordinary', and we sang the songs the whole evening long. A few days later, Sonnleithner brought Schubert along. That was when we were still in Singerstraße 18, and, after that, he came by often. Sonnleithner asked him why he had not had the songs published, and when Schubert answered that no publisher would accept them and that he had no money to have them published himself, Sonnleithner, Grillparzer, the university proctor, Schönauer, Baron Schönstein (later the supreme Schubert singer) and Schönpichler got together and had the songs engraved in a series of brochures. [Actually Grillparzer and Schönstein took no part in this, whereas Josef Hüttenbrenner did. D. F-D.]

At one of the next Friday soirées at Kiesewetters [in fact it was at Ignaz Sonnleithner's. D. F-D.] Sonnleithner appeared with the whole bundle of engraved songs, and, after they had been sung to general admiration, Leopold laid the bundle on the table and announced that if anyone wanted to possess these songs, he could buy them in these books. 100 copies had been printed by Diabelli and, to prevent fraud, Sonnleithner wrote an 's' on the back of every copy. [The mark is, in fact, either 'Sch.' or 'Schbt.', both in Schubert's own hand. One can see these on copies which still turn up in second-hand dealers. D. F-D.]

Anna continued:

Schubert was now a regular visitor and was always very happy to hear something good from another composer. Once, when many of his songs were sung one after the other at a gathering, he called out, just as they were going to continue with them: 'Now now, that's just about enough, I'm getting bored.'

Naturally, the great success, *Erlkönig*, was made opus 1 of the series, with *Gretchen am Spinnrade*, opus 2.

The name Hüttenbrenner also appears among the authors of song-texts, although only once. This was Heinrich Hüttenbrenner (1778–1830), a poet *manqué*, who was a lawyer and a professor at the University of Graz. He was also an occasional critic for the *Allgemeine Wiener Theaterzeitung*.

The Hüttenbrenner brothers, Anselm, Josef (1796–1873) and Heinrich, came from a well-to-do Graz family. Anselm got to know Schubert through Salieri, who made him (Anselm) into a very competent musician. All three brothers were friends of Beethoven —who died in Anselm's arms.

Heinrich Hüttenbrenner's *Der Jüngling auf dem Hügel* (D 702) does not seem to have interested Schubert very much—as a poem. He treats it rather mechanically, following his friend's text word for word, so that the poet's platitudes become musical banalities as well, although one should except the middle section from that stricture. The air of melancholy is retained throughout. (The impressive funeral procession in the middle section reminds us of Loewe, even, maybe, of Schumann.)

Frühlingsglaube (D 686) by Ludwig Uhland (1787–1862) has become a perennial favourite with audiences. Schubert set only this one of Uhland's poems (in November 1820), but the result promised immortality. The richly melodic introduction contains all the qualities of an independent song. A typical change of rhythm symbolises the feverish expectation of the birth of new hope: instead of having the third and fourth bars simply follow the example of the first two, the second beat of the third bar is surprisingly repeated instead. By the time the intensified cantilena begins which prepares us for the climax with a recitative-like *rubato* in the penultimate phrase, the listener has simply surrendered to an onslaught of voluptuous sound.

On 1st December, August von Gymnich sang *Erlkönig* at Ignaz von Sonnleithner's house, an artistic ray of sunshine after dark months of disappointment and resignation. There was an enthusiastic reception for the singer as well as for the accompanist, Anna Fröhlich. One would hope that Schubert managed to see the December issue of the *Dresdner Abendzeitung* which carried this review:

> He knows how to paint in sound, and these songs surpass in the truthfulness of their characterisation anything else in the world of Lieder. To the best of my knowledge, they have not yet been engraved, but pass from hand to hand in manuscript copies.

The latter comment still applied of course to the majority of Schubert's songs. It was therefore a minor miracle when the *Wiener Zeitschrift für Kunst, Theater und Musik* printed *Die Forelle* as a supplement [on 9th December 1820—Ed.].

Schubert's emotional crisis was accompanied by an extraordinary burst of creative activity, although it is doubtful whether one could normally trace any causal connection between the two.

1820 had proved to be another year of astonishing experimentation which left his friends marvelling. In December two songs were printed as supplements in periodicals. Schubert had come across Baron von Schlechta's *Widerschein* (D 639) in a *Tagebuch zum geselligen Vergnügen* (Diary for sociable pleasures), published by the Göschen Verlag in Leipzig. The poem lent itself to a gently ironical treatment. The opening rather hesitantly sustained piano passage asks half-humorously how long one will have to wait. 'Ein Fischer harrt auf der Brücke' ('A fisherlad is waiting on the bridge'), but 'Die Geliebte säumt' ('The loved one takes her time'). In his annoyance, the lad contemplates the brook dreamily, and, at the repetition, the melody is raised a fourth. 'Die Geliebte säumt' is repeated *pianissimo*, and, as though preparing us for a surprise, the opening bars reply. A lively G minor movement announces the girl's arrival—she had hidden herself in order to watch her lover—but she was quite unaware that her face, beautifully drawn in the F major middle section, had been reflected in the water. The theme of the boy's annoyance now returns, happily transformed into a representation of long kisses. The reasons for the staccato are obvious. (Both songs were published later by Diabelli, *Die Forelle* in 1825 as opus 32, and *Widerschein* as part of the *Nachlaß* (Schubert's unprinted papers), in 1832 in B flat major, instead of the original D major, and in a text slightly revised by von Schlechta. Maurice

Brown has established that this is not a second version of the music, but a copy, probably prepared by Schubert for the publisher.)[1]

Among the many new friends which Schubert's connections with operatic celebrities brought him was Karoline Pichler, whose exaggerated enthusiasm for Schubert and his songs caused him no small displeasure. Anselm Hüttenbrenner paints a fine picture of Schubert's reactions:

> When Schubert sang his songs at musical gatherings, he normally accompanied himself as well. If others sang, I accompanied them, and Schubert used to sit listening in a corner of the salon, or even in an adjoining room. One evening he whispered to me: 'You know, I cannot stand these women with their compliments. They know nothing about music and they don't really mean what they say. Go on, Anselm, slip in and get me a little glass of wine.'

Nevertheless, Schubert used one of Frau Pichler's poems as the basis for a moving summation of all the agonies of that past year. *Der Unglückliche* (D 713) starts with a gentle cradling movement and builds up to syncopated disquiet and a cry of pain. That Schubert should take the, for him, unusual step of making a sketch of the song, shows how much this soliloquy meant to him. There are even two versions of the final manuscript copy extant. There is a strange mixture of styles in this passionate, exciting song; the very lyrical beginning is reminiscent of the Andante of the A major Sonata (opus 120). Then it goes *etwas geschwinder* ('somewhat more quickly'), building up in emotional intensity into the quick B major section. Suddenly comes a piece of pure recitative, far removed from the song, followed by the wistful sorrow of the 'schönes Traumbild' ('the beautiful dream-image') in G major, and all ends in resignation in B minor, just like an afterthought, unsatisfactory, but faithful to the text.

The final Andante reminds us of other unconvincing conclusions to other excessively long compositions: *Die Erwartung,* for example, where the genuine emotion of the beginning becomes more and more abstract as the song progresses. But we should not allow these weaknesses to affect our appreciation of passages of pure genius.

Karoline Pichler, née von Greiner (1769–1843), was a close friend

[1] *Schubert,* p. 102.

of Grillparzer, and had presided over the most famous literary salon in Vienna. Her dramas and stories are collected in innumerable volumes. There are two further Schubert settings of 1816, *Der Sänger am Felsen* (D 482) and *Lied* (D 483), to texts by Frau Pichler, but neither, it must be admitted, is of much significance.

On 10th February 1821 Schiller's *Sehnsucht* was on the programme of the tenth evening concert of the *Gesellschaft der Musikfreunde*, to be sung by Josef Götz. This was the second version (D 636), composed in 1819, a year in which Schubert also revised two of his earlier Schiller settings.

In this second version, Schiller's *Sehnsucht* appears rather less vague than the first version of April 1813 (D 52), although the individual parts still hang together only somewhat loosely. The composer experiences difficulty in raising this multisectional song, approaching an operatic *scena* here and there, above Schiller's didactic verses. The poet's own remark, 'the master of style is revealed in what he wisely conceals', can hardly be applied to this song. Still, there are many admirable examples of Schubert's illuminating genius here, both in the illustrative and in the transitional passages. The effect of the quick decision 'Frisch hinein!' ('Take new heart!'), which, within the space of a bar, hurls *fortissimo* octaves into the key of the closing section, is overwhelming. It is the musician again, and not the poet, who makes the decisive transition of mood and emotion. Faith is allowed its easy triumph over reality, but the victorious finale (the only section to be taken over from the first version) is really rather artificial. There are only minor differences between the two versions in the *Gesamtausgabe*.

Amusingly enough, the voice part in the second version is for bass, whereas the first version goes even lower, for example, on the words 'goldenen Früchten' ('golden fruits'). (This version appeared as opus 39 in 1836.)

The annual Ash-Wednesday 'Große Musikalische Akademie' (Music Festival) took place in the Kärntnertor Theater on 7th March 1821, this time as a charity concert organised by the 'Gesellschaft adeliger Frauen zur Beförderung des Guten und Nützlichen' (The Society of Noble Ladies for the furthering of good and useful causes.) Vogl sang the *Erlkönig* for the first time in public, and the dramatic soprano Wilhelmine Schröder-Devrient (she was the first Leonore in *Fidelio* in 1822) and the dancer, Fanny Elssler (then only ten years of age), appeared in the programme as well. Other works of Schubert which were performed were: the male quartet *Das Dörfchen* (D 641) and the first performance of *Der Gesang der Geister über den Wassern* (D 714) for male chorus and bass strings—which turned out to be an abysmal failure. Vogl, on the other hand, had to repeat the *Erlkönig*, possibly a tribute to his fame and his charismatic appearance. Of Vogl's relationship with Schubert it could be said that, at the beginning, the composer needed Vogl and treated him with great respect. As they got to know each other better, their opposing natures clashed, particularly on matters of interpretation. Vogl believed that certain songs should be revised. Schubert gave way more than once, but less to the singer of Lieder than to the 'k.k.Hofoperisten' ('The Imperial Court Opera singer'). Despite the occasional disagreements between Schubert and the ageing singer, Vogl's unique importance for the Schubert-Lied cannot be gainsaid.

Schubert was well aware of the value of their inner rapport—and that was what ultimately mattered in the interpretation of his Lieder. But it is clear that the *Wiener Allgemeine Musikalische Zeitung* was exaggerating when it claimed on 17th June 1820: 'We owe the existence of this young composer in large part to Vogl's care and protection.'

Spaun attended this concert as usual and reported later:

After Schubert's Lieder had been enthusiastically received at many public concerts, and, in particular, at those of the small *Musikverein* [the 'Gundelhof'], a larger audience was won over to the young composer at the beginning of 1821, through Vogl's magnificent performance of *Erlkönig*, in the Hoftheater near the Kärntnertor. The most careful attention and the tumultuous applause of the large audience rewarded the composer and the singer who, having just finished this demanding song, had to repeat it immediately. The same applause greeted the first performance of *Das Dörfchen* for four voices.

To compensate for the failure of *Der Gesang der Geister über den Wassern*, a few of Schubert's friends in high places agreed to have songs dedicated to them. Count Dietrichstein accepted *Erlkönig*, Count Moritz von Fries *Gretchen am Spinnrade*, and the Patriarch of Venice, Archbishop Pyrker, *Der Wanderer*.

Behind all these dealings, one can detect the helping hand of

Josef Hüttenbrenner, who was also responsible for diverse publications of Schubert's works. (His brother Anselm intended to write a setting of *Der Wanderer*.) The dedication of *Erlkönig* to Count Dietrichstein (who had just become Director of the Court Opera) was obviously made with an eye to Schubert's operatic ambitions. The Deputy Director, Mosel, dealt with the matter and wrote to Hüttenbrenner on 17th April: 'Being aware of the friendly disposition of His Excellency, Count von Dietrichstein, towards the talented composer, Franz Schubert, I have no doubt at all that His Excellency will approve the dedication.'

It was eighteen months since Schubert had written his magnificent *Prometheus* and now, in March 1821, he composed its pendant, *Grenzen der Menschheit* (D 716). Goethe wrote the poem in Weimar about 1780. The presumptuousness of the rebel is followed by the humility of the more prudent man. This song is also set for bass voice, and here too, the conception of the piano accompaniment goes far beyond the instrument's capabilities. *Grenzen der Menschheit* is one of those through-composed, philosophical and reflective songs which resists classification, and which can only be treated in a complicated song-structure. This means, of course, that such compositions can never gain the popularity of the pure strophic song.

Once again, Schubert's genius finds solutions to both the musical and the dramaturgical problems. A contrast to the basic mood of the poem is effortlessly shaped into a subsidiary theme which, at the appropriate moment, finds its way back to the initial mood. Thus, Schubert has built up an architectonic, but by no means formally rigid structure. With its dreamy mood of solitude here transfigured by the concentrated musical form which anticipates the Richard Wagner of the *Ring* cycle, this song demands a singer with an extraordinary range and powers of expression. (Curiously enough, Hugo Wolf's setting of the same text makes him look like a simple imitator of Wagnerian techniques.)

Setting this poem to music must have been an unbelievably daring undertaking for Schubert; not only because it appears doubtful whether music can ever really reach the deeper springs of philosophical poetry but, above all, because this poem treats ideas rather than emotions. But Schubert was able to share the emotions of the poet lost in these contemplations, and, miraculously, he remained naïve, where another might have been tempted to appear profound. Once again, Schubert demonstrates his ability to shape a monumental song. Is this song heard so rarely because the long-drawn-out chords of the piano part sound so thin? Or is it, quite simply, the rarity of extraordinary voices with the requisite sonorous low E? The song is still awaiting the recognition of the general musical public.

All four of Schubert's settings of Goethe's 'Westöstlicher Divan' poems were composed in 1821.

For the inspiration for the poems, Goethe was indebted to the orientalist, Joseph von Hammer-Purgstall (1774–1856), who had published a translation of Hafiz's *Divan* in 1813–1814. Originally, 'divan' meant a collection of a poet's works in alphabetical order; Goethe had no wish to imitate the Persian poet by observing this definition, and created rather a cycle which combined ideas of universal love, wisdom and polarity from East and West, in one work.

On 25th July 1814 Goethe set out on a visit to the Rhineland. The first poems were written in the stagecoach and are paeans to a *joie de vivre*. After meeting Marianne Jung, the 'half-gypsy', in Wiesbaden, he wrote the poem 'Geheimnisse', and then, on 18th September, he visited her in the Willemers' house in the Gerber-mühle. When they met again in October, she had become Frau Geheimrat Willemer after a hasty marriage. Goethe took his leave on 20th October and returned to Weimar, a changed man. There, he continued to work on the cycle, but the central section, the Suleika songs, only ripened after the second Rhine journey, begun on 24th May 1815. Marianne's lyrical answers to Goethe's letter-poems now gained equal status as part of the cycle. Goethe went on to Heidelberg and returned to Weimar without seeing Marianne again. The rest of the *Divan*, which was finished in Weimar, is the echo of that brief encounter.

The last poem in the *Divan*, the humorous 'Abglanz', drew one final contribution from Marianne: 'Suleika' (all her poems are in the *Buch Suleika*). Many of the 200 poems of the twelve books of the *Divan* have been set to music, by Mendelssohn, Schumann, Wolf, Schoeck or Reutter. Schubert was the first with *Versunken* (D 715), one of the very few erotic texts to be set by him. Listening to the music, one can see the girl's hair being loosened, and the accompaniment brilliantly captures the eroticism and the barely suppressed sexual excitement. Schubert wallows in realistic details, and yet manages to keep the song moving forward, mastering on the way the most daring, but most effective modulations. The setting, written in February 1821, omits two stanzas.

This song, with *Geheimes*, was enclosed with Schubert's letter (not extant) to Frau von Milder. *Geheimes* (D 719), dedicated to Franz von Schober in 1822, stands unique in its personal interpretation of the text. The whispering piano part is wonderfully lightened by the rests, and just before the climax, the music retreats into a *pianissimo,* as if it had already said too much. The coquettish twirl at the end of each stanza takes away the directness of the rather candid utterance. The short, graceful trochees make the friendly impudence disarming. There is a slight resemblance to Rückert's *Daß sie hier gewesen,* only this is a mood of happier intimacy, and the declamation seems more successful. The happy idea of repeating the lines, 'Weiß recht gut, was das bedeute' ('I know only too well what that means'), and 'ihm die nächste süße Stunde' ('to tell him about the next happy meeting'), and to give them a graceful coloratura must not be misunderstood as an empty musical gesture. The prelude and postlude show the same daring which the piano quickly retracts and glosses over. After the hesitant breathing pauses in the accompaniment, which the voice follows at first, the soaring sustained notes are all the more effective. The similarity of the closing section to the passage 'Ist das Glück von mir gefloh'n' ('Happiness has fled') from Florestan's aria in *Fidelio,* is curiously moving, since Schubert is expressing the prospect of future bliss, while Beethoven is mourning a happiness apparently lost for ever.

It is of some interest that Goethe learned of the composition through Marianne Willemer, although he was not told the name of the composer. Marianne's letter to Goethe on 26th April 1825 contains the following lines: 'Early this morning I sent to a music shop for Beethoven's wonderful song "Herz, mein Herz" ("Heart, my heart")[1] and they sent me a really lovely song on the East wind "Was bedeutet die Bewegung" and *Geheimes* from the Divan.'[2]

The music of the other Suleika poem, *Suleika I,* which pleased the authoress so much, is filled with vibrant life, desire and passion.

[1] 'Herz, mein Herz' is Beethoven's 1800 setting of Goethe's *Neue Liebe, neues Leben* (New love, new life). (Ed.)
[2] 'Was bedeutet die Bewegung' is Schubert's *Suleika I* (D 720). (Ed.)

The even rhythms of the soughing semiquavers of the east wind bring a refreshing coolness. This song continues the Romantics' musical representation of Nature first met with in Beethoven's *Adelaide*, *An die ferne Geliebte* and the Sixth Symphony. The urgent, passionate syncopations, and the exultation of joy, are followed by the calming influence of the unchanging, endlessly struck F sharp that runs through the closing melody. 'Ach, die wahre Herzenskunde' ('Oh, the true knowledge from the heart').

Robert Franz, the composer, wrote once in a letter: 'I, for my part, would find fault with even the greatest genius who wanted to emulate Schubert's setting of Suleika's song, for he has extracted every ounce of musical marrow from the poem.'

Only rarely do we come across the form of two or three co-ordinated main themes as in *Suleika I* and *II*. Each of the songs is divided into equally important halves, and seems to consist therefore of two parts, held together by the continuity of the inner tension. In the first song, calm contemplation above an even accompaniment is followed by a romantically lyrical meditation. Conversely, in *Suleika II*, the second half is an emotional intensification of expression. There is a hint of oriental colouring in the little G minor interlude. The few bars of introduction to *Suleika I* represent the movement of the wind which, coming from Goethe's town in the east [i.e. Weimar], touches Marianne's sensibilities and creates the atmosphere in which the song can develop. The words 'die Bewegung' ('the movement') are, in Schubert's interpretation, the breath of Marianne's love. He subsumes the ascending semiquavers into two arpeggio chords, the first of which opens as a sigh and merges into the second, into the smile of those whose love transcends all insufficiencies.

In *Suleika II*, the broken octaves in the right hand go beyond the usual range of Schubert's piano accompaniments, and the voice is carried up to the high B flat. (*Suleika II*, with the dedication to Frau Milder-Hauptmann, was published in 1825 as opus 31.)

About the same time in 1821, Schubert began work on the heroic ballad *Johanna Sebus* (D 728). The poem was based on an event still fresh in the minds of Schubert's contemporaries. A seventeen-year-old girl had drowned in the flood-waters of the Rhine in 1809. After saving her mother, she had gone back to help some children to safety, but was drowned. A tempestuous D minor dominates the six completed pages, after which the song suddenly breaks off. Perhaps Schubert shied away from the length of the project, which, like the *Mahomet* of 1817 (D 549) had already threatened to become another *Erlkönig*.

The Viennese public was made even more aware of the 'talented young composer' when, shortly after the *Erlkönig* performance, a Schubert song was sung for the first time at the fourteenth musical *soirée* at the Sonnleithners'. Josef Preisinger sang Schiller's *Gruppe aus dem Tartarus*. Grillparzer was in the audience and his poem, 'Als sie Schubert zuhörend, am Klavier saß' ('When she, listening to Schubert, sat at her piano'), rather fulsome in the contemporary manner, gives a picture of his 'ewigen Braut', Kathi Fröhlich, during the performance. This is the last verse:

> Da trieb's mich auf: Nun soll sie's hören,
> Was mich schon längst bewegt, nun werd' ihr's kund;
> Doch sie blickt her, den Künstler nicht zu stören,
> Befiehlt ihr Finger, schlicht'gend an den Mund;
> Und wieder seh' ich horchend sie sich neigen,
> Und wieder muß ich sitzen, wieder schweigen.

(Suddenly I thought: now she will hear it, now she will know what has been troubling me. Yet she looks at me, so as not to disturb the artist, she puts her finger to her lips; again, I see her bending forward, listening, and I must keep silent.)

The poem follows accurately the emotions of the Schiller work.

On 31st March 1821 *Erlkönig* appeared in print at last; Josef Hüttenbrenner, who was largely responsible for the publication, wrote in the *Wiener Sammler* on 31st March:

The ballad performed by the renowned Court Opera singer, Herr Vogl, pleased so much with its music, that, by general request, it had to be repeated. The same composition earned its merited, that is to say, tumultuous applause. Those concerned with the promotion of music in Vienna can only welcome the greater publicity given to this composition.

His remark, 'In Schubert there has arisen a second Mozart of the *Lied*', earned poor Hüttenbrenner the epithet 'mad' from the rival publishing firm of Steiner & Haslinger. The *Wiener Allgemeine*

Musikalische Zeitung greeted the appearance of *Erlkönig* with en-thusiasm, and found that 'the triplets accompaniment enlivens the entire song', and that 'the bass cadence enhances the charm of this wonderful song. . . . By ending the song with a recitative, the composer proves that he truly understood Goethe's poem. We congratulate the young composer heartily on this first, so successful effort which, through Herr Vogl's unsurpassable performances at various private and public gatherings, has been rewarded by loud applause.'

(In April 1821, Schubert began to write out a duet, *Linde Lüfte wehen*, for soprano and tenor, to the text of an unknown poet, but this was abandoned, just where 'Balsamdüfte' ('balsam airs') was given a gentle 2/4 rhythm.)

On 1st May 1821 *Gretchen am Spinnrade* was finally printed as well, although the dedicatee, Count Moritz von Fries, showed his devotion to music more by championing Anselm Hüttenbrenner than Schubert. Anselm's brother Josef ignored Haslinger's previous reaction, and wasted no time in praising the newly printed song:

This song was performed to great applause in several private concerts and every lover of song must look forward eagerly to the public appearance of a composition which does such honour to the pupil of the great masters, Salieri and Vogl. The impression left by this musical portrait could not be more moving. The pianoforte part which brings out so felicitously the movement of the spinning wheel, and the masterly working-out of the main *motif*, are also particularly noteworthy. Indeed, this little song must be granted as much originality and uniqueness as Beeth-oven's *Adelaide*, and Mozart's *Chloe* and *Abendempfindung*.

The printing of the songs should not be thought of as publishing ventures; Sonnleithner met all the expenses. The elegant music firm on the Graben in Vienna, Cappi & Diabelli, acted as agents and kept half of the receipts. A Schubert song sold for one florin. Only *Erlkönig* reached two florins. Since the music was soon sold out, not only did the dealer run no risks, but Schubert also, at long last, came by some more money, which enabled him to pay off a few longstanding debts.

To begin with, 600 copies of *Erlkönig* were sold. *Gretchen am Spinnrade* had caused a furore in private and semi-public concerts, and, within a short space of time, between 500 and 600 copies of that were sold. The first seven opus numbers, which Schubert put together for sale between 1821 and 1822, reached similar figures. They included most of the great Goethe songs, and *Der Tod und das Mädchen*, as well as some less important works.

On 22nd May, *Heidenröslein* was published by Cappi. That very year, it was being played on a musical clock, which had been installed in the hotel, 'Zur ungarischen Krone'. It is certain that Schubert did not receive a penny of the profits made by the publisher and the clock-maker, and yet the song soon became so popular that the music sold like hot cakes.

In May 1821, Schubert moved out of the lodgings he had shared with Johann Mayrhofer, who wrote in his memoirs: 'Circumstances and society, illness and our changed views on life, had kept us apart later; but what had once been could not be taken away . . .'

Much ink has been spent on the mystery of this relationship; one finds even the unproved assertion that Schubert had brusquely rebuffed the homosexual advances of the older man. But the differences in their characters proved to be irreconcilable. Schober told Ludwig August Frankl in 1868: 'They respected each other enormously, but when they were together, they didn't get on, and teased each other mercilessly.'

Mayrhofer, a manic-depressive, made a quarrel out of every tiny difference of opinion. Holzapfel wrote:

In view of the elated, but, from time to time, melancholic and depressed state of mind, which drove Mayrhofer to suicide in 1836, it was no wonder that he attached himself to the gifted Schubert and that they lived together; but it is also no wonder if that daily life together, the little economic difficulties, for example, for which Schubert was possibly more often to blame, made a continuance of it impossible.

The separation did not affect the friendship in the long run. Schubert took up lodgings nearby, and, although he may have been disgusted with Mayrhofer's temperament, he did not dismiss him as an artist, and confirmed this by continuing to set his poems. One of these was *Nachtviolen* (April 1822) (D 752) which sorrowfully recalls their friendship. It is certainly not just the musicality of the name translated into the musical theme, which produces from

Schubert a masterpiece of individuality and innovation such as to make it possibly the most beautiful of his many 'flower songs'. It is unique, from its dense scoring to the echoing of the main theme in the piano part after the voice has died away.

The other flower song of this period, Schlegel's *Die Rose* (D 745) portrays once again the delicacy of the flower in high close har monies. A modulation into the minor and some agitation in the piano part during the middle section introduces a contemplative mood which prevails until the return into the original major just before the end.[1]

Schubert's first question about a newcomer to his circle of friends was 'Kann er was?' ('Is he any good?'), and the 'Kanevas'-evenings derived their title from this question. After Mayrhofer had left the group, a young painter, Moritz von Schwind, was invited to take his place. The seventeen-year-old Schwind (1804-1871), an unusually gifted amateur singer and lutenist, had been attracted to Schubert's songs while still a talented art student looking for an artistic base, and he was amazed by what he found in this circle. All that had attracted him previously to Romanticism, a yearning for simplicity, the reconciling of the poetic world of fairy tales with the demands of Art, had been of no great moment, but now he found all this inimitably embodied in Schubert. He became the illustrator of the volumes of Schubert's Lieder and was particularly moved and inspired by the Goethe settings (*Erlkönig, Schwager Kronos, Schatzgräber*). Eduard von Bauernfeld wrote this about the growing friendship between the two artistes:

> The relationship between Schubert and Schwind was special and unique. Moritz Schwind, an artist through and through, was as much made for music as for painting. The romantic element in his nature was for the first time convincingly and compellingly satisfied by the compositions of his older friend—this was the music that his soul had longed for. And so he moved closer to the master with all his youthful passion and gentleness. He loved him dearly, and Schubert, who jokingly called him his beloved,

[1] In 1827, Diabelli reprinted some musical supplements from periodicals, among them *Die Rose*. This publication is worth a mention, since it is the first list of Schubert works published up to that date. Opp. 1 to 74 also contained works not published by Diabelli. What opus 74 was remains a mystery. *Die Rose* was published twice in Schubert's lifetime in G major, while both extant manuscripts are in F major.

took the young painter to his heart. He thought a great deal too of Schwind's understanding of music, and every new song or piano piece was first played to his young friend, to whom it always sounded like a fresh revelation of his own soul.

Thus the year 1821, with success after success, passed comparatively happily, although there were grotesque interludes: On 13th August, Anselm Hüttenbrenner published his *Erlkönig*-Waltz. The title alone ensured its success. The publisher probably imagined that, by combining the arts of dance and song in which Schubert was now well established, he could not go wrong, even if Schubert had not composed the work himself. And it was one of Schubert's oldest friends, of all people, who had this bowdlerisation published by Cappi & Diabelli. Although Hüttenbrenner received his just deserts from a critic of the *Allegemeine Musikalische Zeitung*, Friedrich August Kanne, in a sequence of savage couplets, it did not prevent Diabelli from publishing the *Erlkönig- und Wanderer-Galoppe* only six weeks after Schubert's death—*and* under Schubert's name. Since Schubert, of course, never wrote these special dance arrangements, they were presumably Diabelli's own work and directed towards increasing his sales.

Josef von Spaun, who had turned his back on Vienna for five years, received the following letter from Schubert on 2nd November 1821:

Dear friend,
    Your letter gave me great pleasure and I wish you all joy in the future. Now I must tell you that my dedications have done their job, for the Patriarch [of Venice Ed.] has come up with 12 ducats, and Fries, through Vogl's intercession, with 20, which pleases me very much. So please be so kind as to close your correspondence with the Patriarch with appropriate expressions of my gratitude.

On 18th May, the Patriarch of Venice, a faithful follower of the Habsburgs, who also wrote poems in German, had thanked Schubert for the dedication:

Sir! I accept your kind offer to dedicate to me the fourth volume of your incomparable songs with all the greater pleasure, since it will recall all the more often to me that evening when I was so moved by the profundity of your emotions, shown particularly in the music of *Der Wanderer*. I remain, with the greatest respect, Your most devoted servant, Johann L. Pyrker, Patriarch, Venice.

In 1821, Schubert wrote the last and best of his settings of poems by the poet, Salis: *Der Jüngling an der Quelle* (D 300). This is a more delicate, and rhythmically slower, example of Schubert's 'water music'. It is a genre-painting over a murmuring accompaniment that wanders up and down the triad of the fifth, while the boy's sighs rise up to a high A, until he finally whispers, above the sustained dominant, the musical name which Schubert added to the end of the poem: 'Luise'.

The sentimentality of the lyrics of *Der Blumen Schmerz* (D 731) by Count Johann Maylath (1768–1855) is hard to bear. This lawyer was a civil servant who worked later as a free-lance author. For political reasons, he lived in Munich after the 1848 revolution, and, after getting into financial difficulties, finally committed suicide, in Lake Starnberg, the last refuge of so many of the world-weary of that generation.

Schubert's music redeems the poet's unnatural blooms; he listens to the breeze and the least quiver of the leaves, as if he understood their thoughts and had translated them into music. Musically indeed, the song is not inferior to some of the *Schöne Müllerin* settings.

Cappi had published four songs as opus 8 at his own expense. In December 1821, Schubert sent another three songs for engraving. The *Harper's Songs* and *Suleika I* received the opus numbers 12, 13 and 14 respectively. There was really no risk for anyone with these songs. Nevertheless the *Wiener Allgemeine Musikalische Zeitung* reviewer called Schubert a 'composer of genius' when discussing the songs, even though the review regretted his apparently arbitrary alterations to some of the texts.

Anton Diabelli, the owner of the Diabelli firm, had overcome his initial misgivings, and had accepted these and other Schubert songs. He looked after the orders and shared the profits with Schubert, who, on 19th January 1822, wrote to Josef Hüttenbrenner, his faithful factotum: 'I wish that you would look into my accounts with Diabelli to date since I need money.'

Did Schubert really drink all his profits as has frequently been asserted? Perhaps we should trust Josef von Spaun, who was, after all, a not uncritical observer of Schubert's life from beginning to end, and who wrote on the appearance in 1864 of the first Schubert biography by Count Heinrich von Kreissle-Hellborn:

> Schubert was always a moderate man, and, had he not been so by nature, his finances would have forced him to it. For many years, I ate with him every day in an inn, and spent many evenings with him and our friends at the superb suppers which followed the *Liederabende*—and never once did Schubert over-indulge himself. In summer time, when it was very hot, he loved to go for long walks, not because of the wine, but because he loved beautiful scenery, as the descriptions in his letters of the wonderful land-scapes of Upper Austria demonstrate. There was one occasion only, I believe, when he, his brother and their friends, after a long walk on a very hot day, went into an inn in Grinzing, and he had rather too much to drink—but there was really no trace of immoderation in him.

On 22nd January 1822, Schubert appeared once again as a singer of his own songs. Eduard von Bauernfeld reported an evening when Schubert was used, to the point of exhaustion, as accompanist to one of the frequent dance functions. Schubert really preferred less merry, more intellectually stimulating companions:

> Spent the evening with [Josef] Fick at [Vincentius] Weintridt's. Schubert the composer was there and sang several of his songs. Also my old friend Schwind, who brought Schubert along, the painter Kupelwieser, Professor Stein, Count Lanckoroński, Stadion, etc., were there. We stayed till after midnight.

The music-connoisseurs were becoming more and more unanimous in their respect for Schubert, and to them was due the growing attention paid to him by the newspapers. Friedrich von Hentl wrote in the March number of the *Wiener Zeitschrift für Kunst etc.*:

> Schubert's songs, through their undisputed excellence, have raised themselves to the rank of masterpieces of genius, calculated to restore a debased taste. He is a genius who, in all his rich profusion, can endow the masterpieces of German poetry with the finest musical interpretations in these exhaustive, unfailingly characteristic songs.

One should add about these 'characteristic songs' that, despite the relatively light technical demands of the music, they are nevertheless unpredictable and full of surprises, so that the student of Schubert is never certain whether he is going to be confronted with completely new styles or forms of expression.

Schubert's friends would often find him in bed in the mornings, busily scribbling away on the piles of manuscript paper heaped up in front of him. He would sometimes even keep his spectacles on at night, so that he could start composing as soon as he woke up. He could even forget to wash, to dress or to eat—but tobacco was the one thing that he would not go without. Schubert was particularly careless about the safe-keeping of his own compositions. Anselm Hüttenbrenner wrote:

> Schubert paid little attention to his numerous compositions. If good friends came to see him to whom he played his new songs, they would often take the manuscripts away with them, promising to return them soon—which they rarely did. Often Schubert did not even know who had asked for this song or that one, so Josef, my brother, who was living in the same house, decided to round up the stray lambs, which he managed to do after much searching. I noticed one day for myself that my brother had over a hundred Schubert songs stored and properly arranged in a drawer. This pleased our friend Schubert so much that, while we were living together, he gave all his subsequent works into my brother's safekeeping.

Hardly any of his friends were aware of Schubert's mental anguish during these months. The banishment from his parents' house grieved him all the more after his separation from Therese, particularly since his relationship with his father had recently deteriorated. The latter simply refused to understand Franz's need for freedom to compose. Schubert's sorrows are reflected in the allegorical tale *Mein Traum* written on 3rd July 1822, in the style of Novalis and rightly attributed to Schubert:

> For years I felt torn between the most intense pain and the most intense love. Then I was informed of my mother's death. I hurried to see her, and my father, softened by grief, did not prevent my entering. When I saw her corpse, tears flowed down

my cheeks. I saw her lying there, just as she had been in those good old days of yore in the spirit of which we were to live on, according to the wishes of our dear-departed. And we followed her remains, grief-stricken, and the coffin was lowered. From that time on, I remained at home. My father took me into his favourite garden again. He asked me if I liked it. But I found the garden repulsive and did not trust myself to say anything. So he asked me a second time, angrily, if I liked the garden? I said, 'No', trembling. So he struck me and I fled. And for the second time, I turned away and, with my heart full of unending love for those who scorned it, I wandered away again afar. For many long years I sang my songs. Whenever I wanted to sing of my love, it turned to pain. And when I wanted only to sing of pain, it turned to love. Thus love and pain tore me asunder.

Towards the end of June 1822, Schubert read poems expressing similar painful sentiments by Count August von Platen (1796–1835), which are impressive not least because of their high degree of formal perfection. The unobtrusive way in which Platen fused form and content produced from Schubert feats of astonishing harmonic daring.

Du liebst mich nicht (D 756) foreshadows all the refinements of modern psychiatry. Schubert's restless modulations suggest aimless wandering. A feeling of unrest dominates this lovely song, which should be sung without fear of the dynamic contrasts called for. The lines

> Wiewohl ich dir flehend und werbend erschien,
> Und liebebeflissen, du liebst mich nicht!

(Though I came to you begging, pleading and full of love, you do not love me!)

might almost refer to his argument with his father.

Something of the same planned aimlessness informs the middle section of the other Platen setting *Die Liebe hat gelogen* (D 751), even if the beginning and the end display a more resigned despair, which is therefore perhaps all the more effective. Platen is often referred to as the master of the German sonnet, too preoccupied with formal qualities, a detached 'Parnassian' poet. Perhaps his handling of the difficult Persian 'ghazal' form, in which the two halves of the first line rhyme and the remaining couplets must follow the same rhyme-scheme, is rather too nonchalantly elegant. However, the extraordinary intensity of Schubert's setting banishes all thoughts of rhyme-play. Thus, the effect of the modulation into the minor in the fifth bar of *Die Liebe hat gelogen* is almost painfully direct. Schubert increasingly employs this duality to express contrasting moods. In the middle section, 'heiße Tropfen fließen', the 'hot tears' do flow in chromatic ascent. The *da capo* of the first part compresses the musical utterance without truncating it, particularly in the last modulation on 'betrogen' ('betrayed'). The lament becomes the remorseless, comfortless truth, there is no ray of hope here. Schubert's sorrow, which the introductory death-rhythm proclaims like a *leitmotif*, is laid bare.

The reasons for the many divergencies in tonality between Schubert's manuscripts and the first published editions lie in the publishers' fears of extreme ranges. That is why *Du liebst mich nicht* was published in A minor, although the manuscript stipulates G sharp minor. (The song was published with three Rückert settings as opus 59 in 1826. Its companion, *Die Liebe hat gelogen*, became separated and appeared as opus 23 no. 1 in 1823.)

In the same year, Goethe, in a conversation with his schoolfriend Löwenthal on 20th October, said that he could not recall the arrival of a packet from Vienna some time before. It is likely that he had not been able to study the many other Schubert settings of his poems either. In his 'defence', however, it might be noted that, not long before his death in 1832 (when Schubert was no longer alive), Goethe heard his *Erlkönig* sung by the young soprano, Wilhelmine Schröder-Devrient. He kissed her on the forehead, saying, 'I heard the composition once before and did not particularly like it, but, when sung like that, the whole work becomes a visible picture.' The singer was the daughter of the Burgtheater actress, Sophie Schröder. Weber admired her as Agathe, Wagner worshipped her as Norma, and Beethoven was so carried away by her performance as Leonore in *Fidelio* that he promised to compose a new opera for her. And now her artistry almost converted Goethe to Schubert's Lieder. . . .

On 8th September 1822, we meet the name Johann Senn again. Under police surveillance, despised as an atheist, and with a fourteen months' prison sentence behind him, he was ekeing out his livelihood as a clerk in Innsbruck, copying out lawyer's briefs. One of Schubert's closest friends, Franz von Bruchmann (1798–1867), visited Senn in exile and wrote to Franz von Schober:

> I spoke to Senn yesterday and spent the half-day with him in the mountains. We got on well and had a happy and affectionate meeting. He is still the same unchanged eternal. . . .
>
> So he went on about it, even although my visit undertaken on behalf of you all and all of us, proved that we were not put off by what had happened. It is the turbulence of a great excited heart which has been denied information. As far as his external circumstances and his present, far from ideal situation and his plans for release from the Austrian claws are concerned, I shall report when I see you, since the expected change in his situation in a few months' time will afford us an opportunity to act, but here, too, there is not much explicit news. You will, I hope, be satisfied with these few lines, since it is difficult to write with Senn so near. Farewell. My regards to Schwind and Schubert, Your Bruchmann.

Schubert set only two poems by Senn, both in 1822; *when* in 1822 is not known, but Bruchmann's journey gives a clue. It is more than likely that he gave Schubert Senn's poems as a token of friendship on his return. *Schwanengesang* (D 744) and *Selige Welt* (D 743) seem to be preliminary studies for *Die Winterreise*. The powerful setting of *Selige Welt* derives its musical character from Schubert's feelings about his brave friend. On New Year's Eve 1849, Senn wrote:

> My poems, too, some of which Schubert set to music, were written partly in this group, or may be seen as echoes of it, even though the ever-changing present claimed its rights too. However unworthy they may be to take their place beside the abovementioned works of others, they mostly do not deny their origins, in either the literal or the broader sense of that word, and the setting often proves this.

Like *Mut* in *Die Winterreise*, the musical exuberance of the setting of *Selige Welt* proves to be only a mask hiding a profound inner sorrow. (*Selige Welt*, along with the highly emotional, more lyrical miniature *Schwanengesang*, was published the next year as opus 23.)

Franz von Bruchmann probably found some parallel traits to his own fate in Senn's, for, depressed and in fear of the police, he withdrew to rural isolation to translate Spinoza and study mathematical philosophy. Then he attended the lectures of the philosopher Schelling at Erlangen University, before finally returning to Vienna to take Holy Orders, as his wife had died in the meantime and he was barred from study for political reasons. Schubert recorded his impressions of this frightened, yet worldly-wise friend on 30th November 1823:

Bruchmann now back from his journey is no longer the man he was. He has apparently reconciled himself to the demands of the world, but, just because of that, he has lost his charisma which, in my opinion, came entirely from his obstinate disregard of all worldly matters.

Perhaps Schubert was disturbed by Bruchmann's all too pronounced political commitment, but it is certain that Bruchmann was revolted by the unproblematical, easy-going ways of Schober which so attracted Schubert. There were two groups: Schubert, Schober and Schwind on the one side, Bruchmann and Josef von Streinsberg, on the other. When Schober became secretly engaged to Bruchmann's sister, Justina, it came to an open breach between the two groups. Moreover, the political pressures on all aspects of intellectual life had taken their toll and had broken up the circle of friends. Bruchmann described later the sense of intimidation: '. . . because we were all too weak to carry on the fight against this secular authority and because we deserved to be punished for our exuberances, our fiery opposition and for our headstrong, yet impotent defiance.'

Schubert expressed Bruchmann's defiance in music with his powerful, tumultuous setting of Der zürnende Barde (D 785) of 1823. The bard of the poem is enraged to think that someone might dare to destroy his lyre. The twice-repeated 'Wer wagt's' ('Who dares'), and 'noch tagt's' ('it is daybreak'), are perfectly captured in Schubert's rapid G minor passages, spoken here like a declamation. The E sharp major melody, with the piano accompanying the voice in thirds, comes close to triviality. Yet the lack of intellectuality, and the sprightly originality of the song, compensate for any lack of individuality on the artist's part.

Immediately after *Der zürnende Barde*, Schubert relaxed with Bruchmann's *Am See* (D 746). This song, with its long sustained cantilena line, makes heavy demands on a singer's breath-control. The poem itself is no lyrical masterpiece, and only the music lends it a meaning. The poet's far-fetched comparison of the soul with the surface of the water into which stars fall 'flammend-leuchtend' ('flaming and glittering') is translated by Schubert into a gentle rocking motion, which dominates the two outer sections of the song. The agitation of the C minor middle section then forms a natural contrast to them. Typically, and beautifully, Schubert extends the nine-bar initial line to one of twenty bars at the repetition of the words 'Ach, gar viele' ('Oh, too many'). Finally, a semi-quaver passage dreamily flows into the words 'Viele, viele' ('Many, many').

In the autumn, Schubert began to look for a more enterprising publisher. On 31st October 1822, the day of the last stroke of the pen on the so-called Unfinished Symphony, he wrote to Josef Hüttenbrenner:

Dear Hüttenbrenner!
    Since I have some important corrections to make to the songs I have entrusted to you, please do not give them yet to Herr Leidesdorf, but bring them out to me. Should they have been sent off, they must be fetched back straightaway. Franz Schubert.

He had therefore already been in touch with the Viennese publisher, Max Josef Leidesdorf (1787–1841), without Diabelli's knowledge. The correctness of his decision showed itself in the spring of 1823.

On 7th December 1822, he wrote from Vienna:

Dear Spaun!
    I hope that the dedication of these three songs will give you a little pleasure which you have so truly earned, that I should really, and ex officio, make it an enormous one, and should do so, if I were in a position to. You will also be happy with the choice of songs, for I chose the ones which you yourself indicated. Along with this volume, there appear at the same time two more, one of which is already engraved, and I enclose a copy, and the other is now being engraved. The first of these contains, as you will see,

the three Harper's Songs, of which the second *Wer nie sein Brot mit Tränen aß*, is new and dedicated to the Bishop of St Pölten.

Bishop Johann Nepomuk von Dankesreither thanked Schubert for the dedication of the songs, a token of gratitude for the hospitality extended to Schubert during a visit to St Pölten in Upper Austria in 1821:

Sir!

Please accept my deep gratitude and the confession that I regard myself as being greatly indebted to you.

As is so often the case, the new version of Goethe's second Harper's Song (see pp. 78–9) appears in several authentic readings, all of which are in the Breitkopf *Gesamtausgabe*. Vogl's attempts to produce more effective interpretations have resulted in the addition of many 'embellishments' to this song, as to many others. Even in the first printing, Schubert bowed to the will and fame of his somewhat overbearing, but well-meaning friend, and admitted some of the mordents, slurred notes and similar ornamentations, which still appear in the popular editions. The autograph is more powerful, simpler—and consequently, more effective.

What favours had Spaun done for Schubert? During the late summer, Spaun, with boundless patience, had managed to bring about a reconciliation of father and son. The father, finally and reluctantly, realised that Franz could be measured by no ordinary yardstick, and that one could not expect his creative powers to be fettered for ever to the routine job of schoolmastering.

The songs dedicated to Spaun were *Der Schäfer und der Reiter* (D 517), *Lob der Tränen* (D 711), and *Der Alpenjäger* (D 524) by Mayrhofer.

The first setting is the best of the three. It is of a poem by Friedrich de la Motte-Fouqué, the librettist of the opera *Undine* by E. T. A. Hoffmann. *Der Schäfer und der Reiter* (1817) attempts to cross the narrow dividing-line between the Lied and the Ballade. The surprising changes in tempo and key suggest a lack of musical discipline. The dramaticism, that looks forward to Hugo Wolf, and the biographical note at the end of the song, are of some interest.

The author, Friedrich de la Motte-Fouqué (1777–1843), came from a French Huguenot family. Born in Brandenburg, he served as an officer in the 1813 Wars of Liberation against Napoleon, but, as a poet, he belonged to the conservative Prussian wing of the Romantic movement. His novels, dramas, epics and poems show a genuine feeling for folk poetry, but he never attained the stature of Clemens von Brentano (best-known for *Des Knaben Wunderhorn* ('The Boy's Magic Horn'), a collection of folk-songs written with Achim von Arnim) or Josef von Eichendorff, the leaders of the Heidelberg group of Romantic writers. Only the opera *Undine* —a theme used by Hoffmann (rediscovered by Pfitzner), Albert Lortzing, Dvořák and Tchaikowsky brought him fame.

Schubert continued in that letter to Spaun:

I have also composed some new Goethe songs: *Der Musensohn, An die Entfernte, Am Flusse* and *Willkommen und Abschied.*

Zelter's setting of *Der Musensohn* is like a Volkslied; Schubert's (D 764) raises it to the rank of a Kunstlied. Zelter's allows the voice to sing out unaccompanied here and there; Schubert's blends voice and instrument, giving equal status to both. The lovely, whirling accompaniment, with its bouncy quick-waltz tempo, should not be hurried. If it is, the *commodo* (leisurely) expression which, if played with restraint, makes the rhythm particularly lively, turns into mere virtuosity. Schubert must have felt a certain kinship with this 'son of the Muses', above all, when he 'excited the young folk' by playing his waltzes, German dances and Ländler for hours on end, although *he* only rarely managed to be driven 'weit vom Haus' ('far from home') and leave the narrow confines of Vienna.

The superb *An die Entfernte* (D 765) does not yet enjoy the popularity it richly merits. Goethe's poem is based on an earlier work by Schwabe which begins:

> So hab' ich dich gewiß verloren,
> Dich, meine Doris, meine Ruh'?
> Nein, noch glaub' ich's nicht meinen Ohren;
> Die Falschheit trau ich dir nicht zu.

(So I have lost you, Doris, and my peace of mind? No, I cannot believe my ears, I cannot believe you to be false.)

Charlotte von Stein is probably the 'ferne Geliebte' ('the distant beloved') for whom Goethe laments. The poem was written in 1789. Schubert masters every nuance of detail, and his setting was to determine the style of musical declamation for a century.

His setting of *Willkommen und Abschied* (D 767) is more successful than that of his rival, Reichardt, even though the turbulent romantic music (apart from the triplet accompaniment), is not at all typical Schubert. However, the throbbing life in the song, and its opera-like conclusion, are very attractive, especially to singers with powerful voices. The key of C major, in which the song was first published as opus 56, is to be recommended. This 1826 edition was dedicated to Carl Pinterics, one of those rescuers of manuscripts to whom we owe the existence of the major portion of surviving Schubert works. (Pinterics, a civil servant, pianist and singer, bequeathed 505 manuscripts when he died in 1831.)

The poem *Willkommen und Abschied* dates back to Goethe's time in Strasbourg in 1771—the girl who is waiting impatiently for the horseman was his young love, Friederike Brion.

To return to Schubert's letter to Spaun:

> I would be quite well, were it not that the disgraceful business with the opera sickens me so much. Now that Vogl is away from the theatre and I am no longer embarrassed in that connection, I have joined up with him again. I even think that I might come up with him, or after him, this summer, to which I am greatly looking forward, since I shall see you and your friends again.

The remark about the opera refers to Domenico Barbaja (1778–1841), the new lessee of the Kärntnertor Theater, who, Schubert believed, was not well-disposed towards his plans to compose an opera. In fact, Barbaja's representative, Louis Antoine Duport, showed more interest in Schubert's operas than had his German predecessors. Vogl avoided the new director (who also appeared as a singer), and retired from the theatre, a move which, of course, allowed him more time to devote himself to Schubert's songs. Vogl, the protagonist of the new German Opera, was most directly affected by its decline in Vienna. Schubert, as opera composer, thus lost an important ally; Schubert, as Lied-composer, could not have had a greater stroke of fortune. That Vogl could now make Lieder-singing his life's work helped to give birth to a new type of singer, one that could certainly not survive for long in this form: the pure

Lieder-singer. All too frequently, opera singers had made a virtue out of necessity (ageing, or failing voice-production), and had taken refuge on the concert platform. Our new era of large concert halls and the public's demand for perfection put an end to that.

In the summer of 1822, Vogl and Schubert had a disagreement, for which the former was by no means solely responsible. When Vogl arrived in Steyr without his friend, there were many disappointed faces and many questions asked. Vogl had expressed the opinion in no uncertain manner that Schubert was not going about his opera commitment in the best way. Anton von Spaun wrote from Steyr to his wife, Henriette, on 20th July 1822:

> Vogl is extremely friendly towards me. He told me with great candour all about his relationship with Schubert, and, unfortunately, I cannot excuse the latter at all. Vogl is very annoyed with Schober, on whose account Schubert behaved so ungratefully towards Vogl, and who misused Schubert, in order to get himself out of money difficulties and to pay expenses which have already exhausted the larger part of his mother's capital. I wish there were someone here to defend Schubert, at least against the more obvious reproaches. Vogl also says that Schober's opera is very bad, a complete failure, and that Schubert is altogether on the wrong path.

There may have been a little jealousy behind Vogl's bitterness towards Schober, but there is also no doubt at all that Schober had wanted to use Schubert's reputation to procure private funds for himself. In any case, the intellectuals were uneasy about Schober's frivolity and lack of seriousness.

A year older than Schubert, Schober had returned with his Viennese mother to his home-town after his father, a German estate manager, died in Sweden. There was something of the charlatan in Schober, whose lack of stability only became evident on closer acquaintance. Schubert concerned himself little with the hatred which his friends gradually evinced towards Schober, and even the fact that his illness was possibly a consequence of Schober's influence over him, did not deter him from regarding the 'göttlichen Kerl' ('the divine fellow') as a friend to the end of his days. He never forgot how friendly Schober had been to him in the difficult times of his disputes with his father. The so-called 'Atzenbrugger

Gesellschaften' ('Meetings at Atzenbrugg'),[1] and the reading-circles were also Schober's idea. Many of his poems, too, show a deep insight into Schubert's character and wants.

Just at that time, deeply hurt by Vogl's anger over Schober's disastrous opera libretto for *Alfonso und Estrella*, Schubert set Schober's poem *Schatzgräbers Begehr* (D 761). As in *Totengräbers Heimwehe* (D 842), the *ostinato* chromatic figure in the bass suggests the innerplay between thought and action. The soliloquies remain in the minor mode, but as soon as the author turns to speak to the bystanders the music, after resting briefly on the dominant, goes over into the major. *Schatzgräbers Begehr*, in its various modifications, is a good example of the rhythm Schubert employed whenever he wanted to depict wandering and wanderers, even if only symbolically. The impression left, that the song is merely 'interesting', does no justice at all to its extraordinary musical power. (It appeared as opus 23, no. 4 in 1823.)

The setting of Schober's *Todesmusik* (D 758), which is interspersed with recitatives meditating on death, is an extensive work in several movements. The concluding passages fall below the standard of the concentrated beginning. (The *Kamöne* of the first part is not a flower, but the German form of Camena, the Muse who helps her votary in his dying hour.)

In addition to his prose letters, Schubert wrote in music to his friend Spaun. Those seeking curiosities among the Lieder of Schubert will not be disappointed by *Epistel* (D 749) from a text by Matthäus von Collin (1779–1824)—Spaun's cousin and brother of Heinrich von Collin. Based on a C minor aria in the style of Gluck, the thundering recitatives contain many successful parodies of heroic opera. The finales are repeated *ad nauseam*, but there is a good deal of interesting music in this occasional composition.

Josef von Spaun was not the only one to whom Schubert dedicated songs in 1822; opus 7, including *Der Tod und das Mädchen*, was sent with a dedication to the author of the other two poems in that volume, Count Louis Széchényi von Sárvár-Felsö-Vidék (1781–1855), the brother of the eminent Hungarian statesman, Stephan Széchényi. *Der Flug der Zeit* (D 515) (1817), which, with its surprising major–minor modulations, expresses very forcefully

[1] Meetings of Schubert's friends held in Atzenbrugg, *c.* 20 miles from Vienna, from 1817–1822. Schober's uncle managed the estate. (Ed.)

the paradoxical nature of all experience, is well worthy of mention. *Die abgeblühte Linde* (D 514) (also 1817), with its recitatives and *arioso,* and its adjuration to cherish lovingly all true friendships, must have lain close to Schubert's heart, so personal and detailed is the attention given to the music.

A critic in the *Wiener Allgemeine Musikalische Zeitung* wrote on the publication of opus 7:

> This volume provides a welcome opportunity to recommend to the public these, and even more so the earlier published works of this richly talented composer of lyrical songs, and to express openly our regard for his outstanding talents.

At the end of 1822, in a strange parallel to Beethoven reminiscent of the earlier parallel to *Adelaide* (see p. 30), Schubert, twenty-five years old, began work on *Der Wachtelschlag* (D 742). He did not stray very far from Beethoven's version of twenty years earlier, for, in both versions, the call of the tiny bird (*Wachtel,* a quail) sets the musical scene. In Schubert's version, the strophic song moves into the minor when the text speaks of tempests and wars, while Beethoven addresses the listener rather more didactically and colourfully. The poet, Samuel Friedrich Sauter (1766–1846) was a schoolmaster from Baden and was caricatured by Ludwig Eichrodt (1827–1892) as the prototype of the *Biedermeier. (Der Wachtelschlag* appeared as a supplement to the *Wiener Zeitschrift für Kunst etc.* on 30th July 1822, and was published by Diabelli in 1827, with an Italian text, as Schubert's op. 68.)

EIGHT

The Background to
His Illness

January 1823 saw the beginning of a very difficult year for Schubert. It is true that the two earliest Schubert biographers, Heinrich Kreissle von Hellborn and August Reissmann, both place the onset of his illness in 1824, but, in fact, Schubert had contracted venereal disease towards the end of 1822, and the symptoms became obvious in January 1823. Apart from Spaun, who was kept in ignorance, all of Schubert's close friends were aware of his condition. It may well have been Schubert's depression and illness which accounted for the irritable tone of this letter to Leopold von Sonnleithner:

Dear Herr von Sonnleithner!
You yourself know how my later quartets have been received; people have had enough of them. I suppose I could invent a new form, but one cannot count on something like that. Since, however, my future is a matter of some concern to me, you, who flatter me by your interest in my affairs, must probably also agree that I will have to proceed with caution, and that I am therefore unable to accept the invitation, honoured though I am, unless your esteemed society would agree to a performance of the Romance from the *Zauberharfe* by Jäger which would then satisfy Your most obedient servant, Franz Schubert.

The theme of the letter was the form that the part-songs for male chorus should take. (Whether indeed the composition was to be performed by a group of solo voices or by a male-voice chorus had up till then been dependent on the voices available at the time of performance.) Schubert had already developed this art-form far beyond all previous attempts at the genre, and his innovations were to be the yardstick for the coming century. Strangely enough, the substitute he offered was a quite uninteresting piece, still unpublished today.

Wilhelm von Chézy, son of the authoress of *Rosamunde* and an elegant member of the 'jeunesse dorée', wrote in 1863:

> Unfortunately, Schubert's thirst for life had lured him into byways from which there is usually no return, at least, no healthy return. The charming Müller-songs were composed under sufferings of a quite different kind from those immortalised in the music which he put into the mouth of the poor lovelorn miller-lad.

This malicious comment takes little note of the mental agony into which Schubert's disease had plunged him. Schober provided him with a doctor, and the embarrassment caused by the whole situation prevented Schober from joining the others, when they later published their reminiscences. After two broken engagements, things became too hot for Schober, and he left Vienna suddenly in the middle of July, in order to train as an 'actor' in Breslau, and stayed for two years.

Schubert's illness had an appalling effect on him, but it also spurred him on to an unprecedented intensification and concentration of his creative powers. The six years of creativity left to him included, it is true, periods of depression and recurring mental stagnation, but the products of his bouts of creativity were staggering. At the end of 1822 he composed the second version of Goethe's *Am Flusse* (D 766). The organ-like drone of the accompaniment is a lament of isolation. There is a mood of finality here:

> Verfließet, vielgeliebte Lieder,
> Zum Meere der Vergessenheit!
> Kein Knabe sing' entzückt euch wieder,
> Kein Mädchen in der Blütenzeit.

(Flow along, beloved songs, to the ocean of oblivion. No lad will ever again sing them, nor a maiden at blossom-time.)

After the merely melancholy mood of the first version (D 160 of 1815) Schubert now shares the resigned smile of the poet. *Am Flusse* is probably one of the simplest of Schubert's mature songs. Under the even flow of the quavers in the right hand, the bass provides a steady, droning background, which becomes more pronounced as the song progresses. Perhaps the earlier version, in which Schubert had sought greater clarity of expression, was long since forgotten. Here we have twenty-five bars of pure flowing melody; but no one should disparage this typically Schubertian stream of sound, even if, at first hearing, it seems to offer nothing spectacular.

As his health deteriorated, Schubert left Schober's house and was drawn back to his family, and, in particular, to his brother Ferdinand, whose schoolhouse in the suburb of Rossau now became Schubert's home during the following year. In 1823, Schubert had broken off relations with Diabelli, mainly because of the intransigence of Peter Cappi, who had learned of Schubert's contacts with Sauer & Leidesdorf, and also with the Steiner firm. Schubert's letter to Cappi on 10th April closes thus:

> You will discover that my demands are not only the greater, but also the more just, although I would nevertheless not have made them, had you not so disagreeably reminded me of them. Since the debt has therefore long since been settled, I beg you to acknowledge that there can be no question either of the publication of songs, which in the past you could not value cheaply enough and for which I am now receiving 200 florins per volume, and Herr von Steiner has repeatedly offered to publish my works. To close, I must beg you to return, if you will, all my manuscripts, the engraved works as well as those not yet engraved. Respectfully, Franz Schubert, Composer.

Schubert must have been in desperate financial straits to have written so provocative a letter. A short while afterwards, Hüttenbrenner acknowledged receipt of a Piano Sonata in A minor (opus 143) (D 784), two volumes of songs, and two songs on a separate sheet. Yet, even after the break with Cappi, Schubert's compositions continued to be published by 'Diabelli et Comp.' Leidesdorf soon proved to be just as unsatisfactory a business associate, since he lacked both capital and business experience. In addition, his eternal pessimism got on Schubert's nerves, and the latter became more and more of a recluse, finding little interest even in his friends. Only Josef Hüttenbrenner, his unpaid secretary, remained close to him.

Nevertheless, public recognition was growing steadily. The *Steiermärkische Musikverein* in Graz made him an honorary member, in return for which Schubert presented them with the still unfinished B minor Symphony. Then the new publishers, Sauer & Leidesdorf, brought out some male choruses and five volumes of songs, among them *Der Zwerg* (opus 22) (D 771), from a poem by Matthäus von Collin. These volumes show that Schubert had made alterations in the plates after the delivery of the first printing and had added dynamic notations. This refutes suggestions that Schubert had no say in the publication of his works. He generally revised his manuscripts thoroughly before they were engraved, and hardly a single one went unrevised to print. He made revisions to the music and to the dynamics, as well as to the text.

Like his brother Heinrich, Matthäus von Collin was originally a lawyer, who, in 1810, became professor of aesthetics and philosophy in the University of Cracow (which at that time belonged to Austria). In 1812, he took over a similar post at Vienna. His fame as a scholar, poet and editor was such that he was entrusted with the education of the Duke of Reichstadt, the son of Marie Louise, who was brought to Vienna and spent all his adult life there, being proclaimed Napoleon II in 1815. Collin wrote an enormous number of historical dramas, but Schubert immortalised him with five songs. One of his printed volumes of songs (opus 22) is also dedicated to Collin. There is a story of Randhartinger's that Schubert quickly scribbled down the music to *Der Zwerg* just before they were setting out for a stroll. Whether one believes that or not, *Der Zwerg* is an extraordinary piece of futuristic music, which, apart from the fascinating descriptions of human passions, introduces a new way of using brief *motifs*. This technique appears later in Wagner, where it is employed as an end in itself for extra-musical purposes.

Beethoven's 'Fate'-theme, represented mainly in the Fifth Symphony, stalks through the accompaniment, but Schubert makes it his own property here. The *tremolandi* in the piano so common in Schubert (in, for example, *Die junge Nonne, Einsamkeit, Am Meer*) must be kept rigidly to the beat and never played *ad libitum*, particularly in this song. Because of the rather abstruse text, the dramatic power of *Der Zwerg* is often not appreciated. It must be repeated here that Schubert should not be censured for using his friends' poems 'to make music'—rather than just those of the great writers; 'this' Schubert deserves just as much credit as the composer of more worthwhile literary texts. Just like Bach faced with those cantata-libretti, or Beethoven with his scissors-and-paste *Leonore*, Schubert too remains the same great, overpowering musician.

Collin's poem follows the contemporary fashion of horror stories begun by Victor Hugo's *Han d'Islande* in 1822, which would confirm the singer and painter Franz Stohl's assertion that he had seen *Der Zwerg* along with *Schatzgräbers Begehr* as early as 1822. The song dates probably from the turn of the year, 1822/1823.

Here is a paraphrase of a famous singing teacher's version of the events leading up to the song:

Death has taken away a king's wife, and nothing can bring him peace. In the ladies' chambers, his young daughter is being instructed in the duties of being a princess. At great expense, the king has sent for a jester from abroad to amuse him at the court festivities. But the jester has seen the world, is witty and learned, and, before long, the king recognises his virtues. He therefore takes the hunchback to the ladies and appoints him tutor to the princess. The summer afternoons are spent on walks in the beech woods, while the jester tells the girl stories of his homeland in the south. The two lonely people are joined by a close bond. But the princess has never seen the jester in his cap and bells answering crude riddles. Then there comes a king from the barren isles and asks for the girl's hand in marriage. The father accepts, the girl obeys him. The king leads his daughter to the ship, the jester accompanies him. After a long journey, they sight the rocks of the island kingdom. The king summons his child, two of her ladies and the jester: Take these three as a wedding gift, they will bind you to your homeland. The jester trembles like a faithful dog, he senses a great change coming. His features betray signs of a terrible decision. Then come the arrival, festivities, feasting. The father departs, but the festivities continue. The young queen sees the jester for the first time in his servile rôle, the one who had been all to her, who had taught her everything, whom she had chosen in her heart as her lord and master. She rises and leaves the hall. The guests rise too, all is silent. Early next morning, the queen unbars the gate with her own hand and enters the castle yard. She is not surprised to find the jester, she had expected him. They walk slowly through a side-door into the fields. A few of the servants mutter together. Steps lead steeply down to the sea. With a wave of his hand, the jester points to the rock, the queen bows her head in agreement. An hour later she comes back to the castle and retires. As the sun sets, she reappears in gorgeous attire. The jester, who has waited for her, offers her his hand. Slowly they descend the slope. The queen is missed. They send to the look-out, who spies a boat far out to sea. It takes time to float another. They find the boat, upturned and dashed to pieces, on a little rocky island. The next morning, the waves wash up a thread of red silk at the foot of the cliffs under the castle.

This is roughly how Raimund von zur Muehlen (1854–1931) used to explain to his students that the events related in the story were to be brought to life as the result of an act of the imagination, since everything leading up to the tragedy has taken place before the song begins: 'You must not let yourself become lazy', he used to say to those who were not prepared to follow the composer's instructions, and who, by allowing the text to remain obscure, failed to do justice to Schubert's musical intentions. The singer has to find three voices: narrator, queen and jester. The tempo is 'nicht zu geschwind', which certainly means fast—but not too fast. There must be an atmosphere of gruesome tension from the beginning. The queen's words are to be sung softly and gently. Despite all his passion, the dwarf's voice must keep in strict tempo. 'Ihm brennt nach ihr das Herz so voll Verlangen' ('His heart burns for her so full of passionate desire') becomes more and more intense, until the climax is reached at the major. The closing words ('an keiner Küste wird er je mehr landen') ('He will land no more on any coast'), on the other hand, are to be sung as if the singer were quite numb. (The bass Josef von Preisinger gave the first public performance at a *soirée musicale* on 13th November 1823.)

Schubert was a welcome guest in the freethinking atmosphere of the Collins' home. Here he played with Anselm Hüttenbrenner the four-handed variations which he had dedicated to his idol, Beethoven. Here too, to his own accompaniment, he sang *Der Wanderer*. Spaun, who was related to the Collin family, wrote:

Schubert's songs, too, were frequently sung in the home of Matthäus von Collin, who had died young, but who had been an enthusiastic admirer of Schubert's compositions. They were performed before a distinguished group of people of talent and position, all of whom were delighted to welcome these new works at so sad a time, and who then, individually, did their best to make Schubert known to the world.

Schubert was to be still more indebted to Collin later. He made an intermezzo out of Collin's poem *Wehmut* (D 772). The major and minor mode clash at 'so wohl, so weh' ('so happy, so sad'). The double chord on 'Frühlingslust' ('Spring's joy') is very noticeable, since it is missing in the musically parallel 'Fülle' ('fullness'), a Schubertian invention. In the second section, the piano *tremolo* tightens the tension of 'Schönheit, die er schaut' ('the beauty that he sees'), but the song ends in a breathtaking stillness. Fading and perishing are reflected in the halting vocal•part, the chromatic descent of the bass, and the soft closing cadence of the piano postlude.

The key to the understanding of these 'nature hymns' lies in the understanding of that serious-minded Schubert who wrote to his father on 25th (28th?) July 1825:

If he [Schubert's brother Ferdinand] could but see these heavenly lakes and mountains, the sight of which threatens to devour or crush us, he would not love this puny earthly existence so, nor would he consider it anything but good fortune to be entrusted to the indescribable power of the earth to create new life.

Such a man had looked deep into the soul of nature and was as receptive to her as Goethe had been. Thus, even a second-rate poem like *Wehmut* could inspire him to paint landscapes which contain the most powerful and profound of lyrical images. (*Wehmut* and *Der Zwerg* were published in 1823 as opus 22.)

Schubert must have loved flowers greatly to have been able to trouble himself with the flower ballads of his friend Schober. It is true, there are some delightful details buried under the terribly manneristic and boring Schubertian passages of *Vergißmeinnicht* (D 792) and its pendant *Viola* (D 786), but they could not bring these over-ambitious musical geegaws to life. The nineteen stanzas of *Viola* tend to become a comical biology-lesson, and one can only admire Schubert's politeness *vis-à-vis* his friend. However, the out-and-out Schubertian might be able to enthuse over the lovely E major section in *Vergißmeinnicht* as an independent piece of music. One should see the two songs as a preliminary exercise to the writing of song-cycles.

In Schober's *Pilgerweise* (D 789), every dotted crotchet is coupled to three quavers. The melody moves forward in the steady 'wandering rhythm', then ascends and slips almost imperceptibly into a dance rhythm which relieves the song of any heaviness. Did Schober write *Pilgerweise* for his friend Schubert?

> Doch freilich ihr, ihr könnt nicht wissen,
> Was den beseligt, der entbehrt.

(Yet you can hardly guess what makes him happy, who resigns himself to his lot.)

Schubert's harmonic inventiveness and adventurousness which shows itself even in the prelude, with a shift from F sharp to G major, compares well with Mendelssohn's very similar *Lied ohne Worte* (Song without Words) in the same key, written in 1833. Yet most impressive of all is the way in which Schubert keeps injecting life into his friend's terrible poem.

NINE

Die schöne Müllerin, 1823

What is known today of Wilhelm Müller (1794–1827), the poet from Dessau in Saxony, who now comes into Schubert's life? His name would have been long forgotten had it not been for Schubert. Although contemporaries, the two men never met. Yet no Schubertian can simply dismiss Müller out of hand. The anti-Müller camp claim that his situations and emotions are as cheap as nasty coloured postcards, but judgements such as these do Müller an injustice. His poems have form, imagination and, above all, they are singable. One must remember, too, that he lived in an age when it was not considered ridiculous to be tender of heart and to dissolve easily into tears. A mixture of unadulterated emotion and dawning scepticism, Müller was a child of his times.

He was the son of a master cobbler, and died a year before Schubert did, in 1827. Müller entered the University of Berlin at eighteen to study philology and history. After serving as a volunteer in the Wars of Liberation, he continued his studies. He made his Italian Journey, and then, in 1819, was appointed a teacher of classics at the Gymnasium in Dessau, where he later became librarian at the Ducal Court. His poems, 'Lieder der Griechen' ('Songs of the Greeks') (1821–1826), became so famous that he was called simply 'Griechen-Müller' ('Greek-Müller'), in recognition of his enthusiasm for the Greek freedom fighters.

Die schöne Müllerin is the first part of a collection *Gedichte aus den hinterlassenen Papieren eines reisenden Waldhornisten* ('Poems from the posthumous papers of a travelling horn player'), with the sub-title 'Im Winter zu lesen' ('To be read in winter'), which appeared in 1820.

The poems arose out of a kind of party game played as an intellectual joke by the young men and women of a Berlin literary circle; they each took reading parts, which were performed, without music, in the presence of the poet. It was meant as a parody on the simple virtuous *Biedermeier* folk poetry, which was already beginning to be ridiculed by the 'educated' classes.

Müller used to read a prologue which Schubert did not set—nor did he set the epilogue and some other poems which lifted the ironic mask a little. Müller was clearly attacking those literary people who had failed to recognise the change that had come over their world since the Congress of Vienna in 1814–1815. 'Gehabt Euch wohl und amüsiert Euch viel' ('Fare ye well and enjoy yourselves greatly'), he says at the conclusion of the prologue and hands over to the simple miller-lad. At the end of the cycle, Müller adds:

> Doch pfuschte mir der Bach ins Handwerk schon
> Mit seiner Leichenred' im nassen Ton.
> Aus solchem hohlem Wasserorgelschwall,
> Zieht jeder selbst sich besser die Moral.

(The brook has spoiled all my good work with its wet funeral address. You must draw your own moral out of such elevated music from a watery organ.)

Of course, the irony is still gentle and fairly unobtrusive. Heinrich Heine (1797–1856) was to attack the same quarter much more viciously later. However, Heine approved of Müller's intentions and showed this by dedicating to him a copy of his *Lyrischen Intermezzi*.

Every now and then, and contrary to Schubert's intentions, someone tries to include in a concert performance those parts of the *Schöne Müllerin* which Schubert did not set. Hans Joachim Moser did this in a radio broadcast in the 30's, when Julius Patzak and Mathias Wiemann shared the singing and the speaking rôles. I must admit that, in one of my three recordings of the cycle, I too included the spoken prologue and epilogue as a sort of curiosity. Now, however, they do seem to me to be extraneous to the cycle, for Schubert took the poems seriously and used them to realise a serious musical purpose. Generations of singers and audiences since then have likewise taken them seriously—and rightly so.

That does not imply, of course, that Schubert was not aware of the poet's ideas. He was far too critically alive and frequented literary circles too regularly to be so naïve. He proved the point by omitting three poems from the cycle: *Das Mühlenleben* has ten stanzas and is neither dramatic enough nor varied enough to be through-composed while, if it were to be set strophically, the same melody for ten stanzas would soon evoke boredom. The lines

> Seh' ich sie am Bache sitzen,
> Wenn sie Fliegennetze strickt,
> (I see her sitting by the brook, making fly-nets)

or

> Keiner fühlt sich recht getroffen,
> Und doch schießt sie nimmer fehl,
> Jeder muß von Schonung sagen,
> Und doch hat sie keinen Hehl.

(No one feels hit and yet she never misses; each one speaks of being spared, yet she spares no one.)

are not only clumsy, but lay themselves so clearly open to parody that Schubert decided not to set them.

Erster Schmerz—letzter Scherz ('First pain—last joke') is not only a terrible title, but, once again, is ten stanzas long. The opening lines: 'Nun sitz' am Bache nieder / mit Deinem hellen Rohr / Und blas' den lieben Kindern / Die schönen Lieder vor' ('Sit down with your pipe by the brook and play the children lovely tunes'), is a repetition of the closing lines of *Eifersucht und Stolz* (No. 15 of the cycle). So too with *Blümlein Vergißmein*.

There may be no single song in *Schöne Müllerin* (D 795) to equal the greatest of the Goethe or Rückert settings, but this was not Schubert's intention. The simplicity of the inter-related songs, none of which was meant to stand on its own, is what gives the twenty songs their cyclical character.

Walther Dürr quite properly recognises some authority in Vogl's alterations which, here as elsewhere, Friedländer rejects as 'falsifications'; they are no less important than Schubert's own variants, particularly those he made for the mannerisms of individual singers, as for example in *Rastlose Liebe* for Schönstein, or in *Der Wanderer* for Esterházy. With these examples in mind, Dürr is of the opinion that Vogl's alterations should find a place beside Schubert's own variants in any published edition.

Every Schubert edition comes up against two major problems: firstly to make itself comprehensible to the contemporary interpreter, and, secondly, to do justice to all the source material which has been handed down. This makes evident the need for, and the justification of, a 'critical' edition such as the Bärenreiter Verlag's.

The occasional necessity for transpositions also creates great problems in the case of *Die schöne Müllerin*. Schubert scarcely ever strays outside the two middle octaves of the piano in this cycle; only the brook murmurs all too frequently in the bass clef. This creates a problem when the songs are transposed downwards; in all events, they should never be transposed by more than a minor third. Naturally, the songs are heard to best advantage in the tenor register for which they were written. Moreover, Schubert avoided the upper range of the piano in principle in his songs, using that almost exclusively for virtuoso passages, partly because of the thinness of tone of the contemporary instrument in that range. Had Schubert had available the full-bodied tones of today's keyboard instruments, he would certainly have composed differently.

Müller called his first poem *Wanderschaft*. Here, as in many other less conspicuous instances, Schubert altered the text for greater musical effect. *Das Wandern* (No. 1) introduces us to the miller-lad setting out on his journey and singing of his love of 'wandering'. The first and last of the five stanzas give us the nub of the poem. The utter simplicity of melody and accompaniment make this the strophic song *par excellence*. If, as an experiment, the accompanist were to improvise a different rhythm, he would see just how inevitable Schubert's figure is. The opening of the cycle is masterfully controlled and allows a later intensification of emotion.

'Wandering' and 'distant places' never lost their attraction for Schubert. We have *Der Wanderer* (Schlegel) of 1819, Seidl's *Der Wanderer an den Mond*, *Wanderers Nachtlied I* and *II* of Goethe, and the first song of *Die Winterreise* ('Fremd bin ich eingezogen') ('I came as a stranger'). It has often (too often) been underlined that Schubert's family came from the Silesian-Bohemian-Moravian region, which is of interest, but should not lead to the false conclusion that Schubert belonged in any way to Silesia. Nevertheless, this 'Drang in die Ferne' ('Longing for far-off places') is always present as an undercurrent in his work.

Wohin? (No. 2) is marked by the transparent clarity of the rippling brook. The feathery lightness of the melody with its typically Austrian repetition of notes, is so irresistible that few could fail to succumb to its magic. Yet here already, the naïvety of the opening song seems disturbed, there are hints of the minor mode. The tinges of sadness soon vanish, however, and the wanderer resolutely follows the course of the brook.

Halt! (No. 3) shows us that the youth has arrived at the mill. He asks the stream if this has all been planned!

In *Danksagung an den Bach* (No. 4), in which the lad thanks the brook for leading him to the mill, a delicate figure in the bass responds to the melody in G major. When the lad asks if the miller's daughter sent the brook for him, the latter replies in the minor, but the boy ignores this, and finds his own way back to his G major. The brook lets the monologue die away in melody.

In *Am Feierabend* (No. 5), two subsidiary movements merge into a rondo form: the initial energy which expresses the lad's fanatical desire for work is contrasted with the companion theme of the peace of the leisure hours. The return to the first section shows Schubert's desire to structure the whole and to give it more psychological depth—which clearly goes far beyond the poet's intentions.

> Und das liebe Mädchen sagt
> Allen eine gute Nacht.

> (And the girl says good-night to them all.)

is particularly stressed. Where Wilhelm Müller speaks the words without any special emotion, Schubert's setting stresses 'allen' ('to all'), not to the lad alone. The minor ninth of the lad's final sigh,

> daß die schöne Müllerin
> merkte meinen treuen Sinn!

> (if only the girl would see how faithful I am!)

expresses not only weariness, but also a deep yearning.

In the delicate four-bar prelude to *Der Neugierige* (No. 6), the miller-lad seems to be accompanying his question on a lute. The brook is added to the accompaniment later. The song gathers in intensity, until it becomes a forceful recitative on the question of life and death for the lad. The transition to the chord of the seventh from the G, at the word 'Nein!', makes clear that there is no thought of rejection in the lad's mind. The calm reprise in B major which must be played as a true *adagio* is filled with quiet confidence.

Ungeduld (No. 7), with its thrilling prelude based on a three-bar model which alternates between major and minor, its exciting attack, which builds up to a twice-repeated climax on the A, and then the smooth descent to the final cadence, is one of the most popular songs for tenors. The tempo must be such as to allow the clear enunciation of the dotted semiquavers and avoid their being diluted into triplets.

The effect of the question in *Morgengruß* (No. 8) is underlined by the extended sequence in the accompaniment: G minor–A major–F minor–G major, descending shyly, pose the question: 'Verdrießt dich denn mein Gruß so sehr?' ('Does my greeting disturb you so much?') Only gradually, accompanying voices awaken, bring about a 'minor' darkening in the middle section, and even dare a tiny canon in the final third of the song. Because of the possibilities of varying the expression in each stanza, the habit of omitting stanzas should be discouraged. The breathing indications in the last phrase would have to be transposed accordingly.

An imaginary cello appears in the prelude to *Des Müllers Blumen* (No. 9) and accompanies the outpourings of the lad's heart with its quiet figurations. The tempo should be such as to allow a clear differentiation to be made with that of the next song *Tränenregen* (No. 10), which is also in 6/8 time. Here, three voices are woven together and are joined later by a fourth. In the brief interludes, the brook reflects what has already been depicted, and its semiquavers disturb the quaver rhythm of the scene. (These should be played with ever-changing pedalling and colourations.) The delineation of the final stanza, with its modulation into the minor where the surface becomes blurred ('im Spiegel so kraus'), and we get the most astonishing modulations, makes this one of the most significant of the cycle; indeed, it is one of the strangest of all Schubert Lieder. It is a quite magical combination of sound-painting, visual immediacy, spontaneous emotion, and reflection. The decisive factor is, however, that the song remains completely lyrical, despite the story, the imagery, and the lovers' conversation. The melody does not seem to be dependent on the emotion which may have evoked it.

Mein (No. 11) is nature intoxicated, but the brook, the wheels, the forest birds, the spring, and the sun, should not perhaps be celebrated at the customary over-enthusiastic speed which makes the singing of the little slurred notes impossible and contradicts the 4/4 marking. The triumph of the confirmation of his love is still not enough for the young lad; he flees from D major into B flat and then into the lonely key of G minor to get his breath back. Thanks to Schubert, he then regains his former state of bliss, something not envisaged by the poet. But the inevitable must happen. The contemplative *Pause* (No. 12) wanders from B flat major over G minor down to F major. Fearful apprehension takes the melody into remote harmonies and accentuates the rhythm. Peace reigns again, but then anxious tremors run over the strings of the lute in strange keys, symbolising confusion, uncertainty and unease. Finally, however, everything turns out for the best, despite all the passages in the minor.

One should not be misled by the carefree, cheeky tone of *Mit dem grünen Lautenbande* (No. 13). The pearly chain of laughing notes which introduce each stanza, and the girl's banal melody warbled in the lad's face, leave him with only half-hopes, indeed almost in tears, as he begins to have premonitions of disaster.

A stamping scherzo tells us that *Der Jäger* (No. 14) ('The Huntsman') is the cause. The initially shy indignation of the miller-lad mounts up until the voice almost breaks on the high G. This can be prevented by a carefully sustained *forte*—the music has all the *brio* necessary. The singer should also avoid too rapid a tempo, the phrase endings require minimal breathing, the pauses between the staccato notes are just as important as the notes themselves.

A flare-up in *Eifersucht und Stolz* (No. 15) sends the brook splashing hither and thither, and, at the words 'Kehr' um' ('Turn round'), it then actually descends. The irony of the middle section is more than a lesson in decorum and does not last very long. The lad's pride is broken, and it gives way, first to sadness, then to sentimentality, which cannot establish itself, however, in this emotional chaos. Apart from the sensitive transition to the bitter self-irony of the conclusion, the tempo and the rhythm are kept taut throughout. (The manuscript of *Eifersucht und Stolz* has survived, and we know from its dating, October 1823, that Schubert continued his work on it after his return from Upper Austria.)

Die liebe Farbe (No. 16) shows how it is possible to sing each stanza of a song differently. The basic emotion does not change, it is established in the first stanza; it is mixed with irony and passion in the second and echoes away in the third. The repeated refrain, 'Mein Schatz hat's Grün so gern' ('My beloved likes green so much'), demands great subtlety of interpretation. Resignation has followed the stormy passions. Sadness clothes the disappointed lover, who has discovered the reason for the girl's preference for green, 'the darling colour' ('die liebe Farbe'). That is why the penetrating F sharp of the huntsman's horn reverberates so uncannily through the lover's plaint. The customary slowing-down of the tempo of this song fails to take account of the minims specified in the score.

The resentment of unrequited love, softened again and again by passages in the minor, resounds passionately once again in the B major of *Die böse Farbe* (No. 17). The horn triplets are almost unbearably intense. The girl is lost forever, but the lad bears the blow with fortitude, heartbroken though he may be. These passages require both vocal and dramatic skill. The unbroken tempo of the accompaniment demands lightness of touch and virtuoso sound colouring from the pianist.

The melody of *Trockene Blumen* (No. 18) is characterised by a series of descending notes which express sadness and despair. Only in the section in the minor is there any sign of optimism, but this optimism is soon shown to be not of this world, like the touching helplessness of the alienated wanderer. When he finishes speaking, the descending bass figure turns into dull, hopeless renunciation. The tempo and the volume should gradually diminish, and the pianist must observe this in the postlude, too. (Schubert used the theme of *Trockene Blumen* for a set of 7 Variations in E minor for flute and pianoforte in January 1824. The variations were written for a friend, the flautist Ferdinand Bogner, who participated in many performances of Schubert's work and probably heard the song shortly after it was written in December 1823.)

Unbearable pain marks the opening of *Der Müller und der Bach* (No. 19). Unearthly waves ripple round the brook's consoling answer to the miller-lad's questions; the gentle rocking motion lightens the answer a little, until the lad, as if hypnotised, lets himself be drawn down into the cool peace ('die kühle Ruh'') of the brook. A sweet sense of secrecy lies over the final monologue, *Des Baches Wiegenlied* (No. 20), the epilogue which sings the miller-lad to sleep.

The essence of *Die schöne Müllerin* lies in the subtlety, in the supple phrasing and the empathy with the various stages of a mental experience, rather than in strong accentuation. The cycle is much more colourfully structured than *Winterreise*, which tends more towards through-composed songs. The formal structures differentiate the two song-cycles from one another, as much as do their themes and their moods, and one might, albeit with care, trace a line of development in Schubert's song-writing technique between the two cycles. No value-judgement is implied here, since Schubert, of course, wrote unsuccessful through-composed songs, as well as superb strophic songs. Nevertheless, there is a progression shown here from broad descriptive songs to a more concentrated musical utterance; all in all, a conscious striving for a more compact, more formal musical structure. From the eighteenth-century influences in his early works through many intermediary stages, Schubert developed a completely new symphonic style, characterised by its emphasis on modulations, which was to become the most important single influence on the musicians of the latter half of the nineteenth century, right up to the Impressionists, who also took Schubert as a model.

The cycle was dedicated to Karl Freiherr von Schönstein, a very pleasant amateur singer, though not quite in the same class as Vogl. Whatever Schönstein lacked in class, and in the way of culture and superior intellect—and the ageing Vogl possessed these in rich measure—he made up for in confidence and presence of mind.

TEN

Lieder of 1823 - 1825

In May 1823 Schubert's critical state of health forced him to spend some time in the care of two doctors in the Allgemeine Kranken- haus in Vienna. There are so many firmly dated compositions from this period that he could hardly have been working on the *Schöne Müllerin* songs as well, as has been asserted. In any case, the songs from this period offer nothing extraordinary, unless one were to number Schober's *Pilgerweise* among the confessional songs and therefore assign it a special place.

Despite his poor health, Schubert again spent the summer with Vogl in Upper Austria. They made new friends in Linz and Steyr and performed before enthusiastic audiences. Spaun introduced them to the Hartmann family in Linz, whose sons, Franz and Fritz, will appear later as conscientious diarists and chroniclers. The almost daily activities of the Schubert circle were faithfully recorded by them from the time of their move to Vienna in 1825.

From Steyr, Schubert wrote (on 14th August 1823) to the much-maligned Franz von Schober, whom many of the Schubert circle, especially Joseph Kenner, held to be mainly responsible for Schubert's condition. Although Schober was now working as an actor in Breslau, the letter shows Schubert's deep affection for him, especially in his time of illness:

Dear Schober!

Although I write rather belatedly, I hope that this letter will find you still in Vienna. I am corresponding regularly with Schaeffer [Schubert's doctor in Vienna] and am keeping fairly well, although I doubt if I shall ever recover completely. I am living here very simply in every respect, go for regular walks, do a good deal of work on my opera and read Walter Scott. I am getting on well with Vogl. We were together in Linz, where he sang a good deal and very beautifully. Bruchmann, Sturm and Streinsberg visited us a few days ago, and they too were sent off with a load of songs. Since I shall hardly see you before I return, I wish you all success again with your enterprise and assure you of my constant affection, and will miss you deeply. Wherever you may be, write now and then to your friend, Franz Schubert.

The opera mentioned above was *Rosamunde* to a libretto by the 'hapless Frau von Chézy', as the nineteen-year-old Schwind called her. The popular *Romanze* ('Der Vollmond strahlt auf Bergeshöhen') ('The full moon shines over the mountains') comes from this 'magic-play with music'. Helmina von Chézy (1783–1816) was the daughter of Karoline Louise Klencke, one of whose poems, 'Heimliches Lieben', Schubert set to music (D 922), and the granddaughter of the Berlin poetess, Anna Luise Karsch, much praised by Lessing and others in the latter years of the eighteenth century.

Frau von Chézy wrote the terrible libretto for Weber's opera *Euryanthe,* based on her grandmother's *Geschichte der schönen und tugendhaften Euryanthe* ('Story of the beautiful and virtuous Euryanthe'), which appeared in 1804. Schubert met the ladies in Vienna and composed the stage music for the romantic play *Rosamunde von Cypern* (which had its première on 20th December 1823) whose libretto was in all honesty just as dreadful.

Among the 'loads of songs' mentioned in the letter to Schober above was the wonderful Rückert setting *Greisengesang* (D 778).

Johann Michael Friedrich Rückert (1788–1866), Professor of Oriental Languages at Erlangen and Berlin, had strengthened the oriental strain in German literature introduced by Goethe in his 'Westöstlicher Divan' (see pp. 144–6), and he soon became a specialist in this lyric genre. He translated many important oriental literary works into German. His work on the older languages was reflected in his marked feeling for form, to which German literature owes some of its most beautiful poems, five of which Schubert set to music.

Dignified resignation is the theme of *Greisengesang,* a sustained piece in the minor mode. Strength and suppleness are the true musical equivalents to this brilliant poem from Rückert's 'Östliche Rosen' which had just been published, in 1823. Its key, B minor, is serious and austere and seems to suggest that there is no self-deception in the singer. The piano prelude is surprisingly severe and rather loud for the text. The contrast there, between the worlds of inner emotions and outward experiences, is brought home in the music by the juxtaposition of B major and the minor mode. Yet Schubert does not allow himself to be seduced into mere 'tone-painting'. At the most, at 'all gegangen einander nach' ('all are gone, one by one'), the piano repeats the descending vocal line. At the question: 'Wo sind sie hingegangen?' ('Where have they all gone to?'), the left hand descends mysteriously in octaves under the voice. The false ending takes 'Ins Herz hinab' ('Down into my heart') into G sharp minor. In the phrase 'Nach Verlangen, wie vor so nach' ('As one wishes, after as before'), the 'wie' and the 'so' are stressed as though to underline that no diminution is possible here. The quavers are not meant to be grace notes, the cadence is full of expression. The *forte* chords on which the song surprisingly closes after so transfiguring an experience are like the firm shutting of a door guarding its possessions within against any attack.

Although still young in years, Schubert demonstrated here a deep sympathy for, and understanding of the poetry of old age. The slight alterations to the second half of the poem, which is on the whole a repetition of the first half, underline, as it were, that there are now questions to be put, where before only statements were made. At the end of the questioning melody, the composer raises the vocal line. The last verse of the poem, omitted by Schubert, was included by Richard Strauss, when he set the poem in his later years.

On 30th November 1823 Schubert wrote to Schober about the first interpreter of the song:

Vogl is here and has sung once at Bruchmann's and once at Witzeck's [Witteczek]. He devotes himself almost exclusively to my songs. He copies down the vocal part himself and lives on it, so to speak. He is therefore very polite and obedient to me. And now let me hear from you. How are you? Have you already appeared before the eyes of the world?

There is great harmonic subtlety in *Schwestergruß* (D 762), which is conceived on a grand and earnest scale. The incessant triplets of the accompaniment remind us of *Erlkönig*. When the ghost of the deceased sister, in whose memory Bruchmann wrote the poem, appears, a fascinating *leitmotif* figure arises in the bass. But the fashionable graveyard romanticism, whose manneristic traits often detract from the greatness of a Schubert song, is again a stumbling-block, which his artistic intentions cannot overcome. If the first Bruchmann setting remained unknown, *An die Leier* (D 737), based on a poem by Anacreon, amply compensated in popularity.

The joyous songs of Anacreon (sixth century BC) were imitated in many later centuries (see p. 72). In eighteenth-century German literature, Uz, Gleim and Hagedorn became known as the German 'Anacreontics', and Anacreon's hedonistic poetry reverberates through the work of Klopstock, Hölty and Goethe. *An die Leier* ('To the Lyre') is divided into rhythmic-dramatic and hymn-like *arioso* passages, which are purposely not homogeneous, so as to make clear Anacreon's humorous accentuation of the reversion to the lyrical state from the strongly dramatic. This version of the Greek original actually gains from such a structural change, which, after two dramatic surges, allows the lyrical tone to reassert itself —it was also typical of Schubert's own state of mind at this time. After periods of excitement, he liked to subside again into a state of calm. In songs like this, it becomes very evident that a good Schubert singer must be able to command both harshness and softness of tone. This is meant to be a heroic song, and the listener's experience is to be both a poetical and a musical one. The song begins with great energy, the piano strews chords energetically about, quavers scuttle around, the second time in octaves, and there are defiant dotted diminished sevenths, above which the singer proudly proclaims his 'ich will' ('I will') for the whole world to hear. The piano is just beginning to develop its *motif* when the musical idea eludes us and wanders off in a different direction—and the tense pause following reveals that this is 'only' a love song, after all. Schubert's show of strength is not equal to his original idea. However beautiful the E flat major melody is, it disappoints our hero, who, after all, wants to *be* heroic and to be driven to his limits. So, it is understandable that, after failing with the first attempt, he should try again. His mistake is to believe that he has only chosen the wrong mode of expression—so he calls for a different instrument, more energy, a more powerful representation, the most sublime themes. He seems to be succeeding. 'Alcides Sieges-schreiten' sounds indeed like a 'triumphal march'. But, once again, the music slides over into a love-song. The singer is not resigned, however. He looks into his heart, renounces the heroic song, and returns to the love song he sings so well. As the trill on the low G on 'drohen' ('to threaten') proves, he still feels some resentment, but it cannot dampen his optimism. (*An die Leier* was published in 1826 as opus 56 with *Im Haine*, D 738, whose joyous 9/8 rhythm gives no indication of the composer's woes. The little strophic song breathes relaxation. All the Bruchmann settings are from 1822.)

Schubert's letter to Schober (30th November 1823) goes on:

> Since the opera I have composed nothing but a few Müller-Lieder. The Müller-Lieder will appear in four parts with vignettes by Schwind. For the rest, I hope to regain my health, and this regained treasure will make me forget many sorrows—only you, my dear Schober, you I shall never forget, for what you were to me, no one else, alas, can ever be. Now keep well and do not forget your eternally loving friend, Franz Schubert.

'A few Müller-Lieder'—how typical of Schubert's ever-modest understatements! He had composed three dozen songs in 1823. Among these was Goethe's *Wanderers Nachtlied II* (D 768), which demonstrates once more what little relationship there is between the length of a musical composition and its expressive power. Alfred Einstein rightly calls this 'the loveliest setting of this hackneyed song',[1] and the Munich scholar Thrasybulos Georgiades supplies a convincing and detailed analysis showing how the scene is married to the interpretation of the emotions.[2]

We need only add here that the introductory bars hint at Schubert's 'death-rhythm', in this case, a yearning for peace. It is noteworthy that composers have approached this nocturnal poem in a variety of different ways: it has been set for solo voice, as a duet, a vocal trio, a quartet, a choral quartet, a male chorus and so on.

Goethe wrote the eight short lines of poetry on 6th September 1780, on the wall of a mountain hut on the Kickelhahn in Thuringia. Thirty-three years later, by then an old man, he wept as he renewed the inscription. There is nothing in music to equal Schubert's concentrated 14-bar epigram. (Friedländer justified his omission of the

[1] Einstein, A.: *Schubert*, Cassell 1951, p. 254.
[2] Georgiades, T.: *Schubert, Musik und Lyrik*, Göttingen, 1967, a study of the relationship of words and music in Schubert, is highly recommended.

turn on the word 'balde' ('soon') as a later 'embellishment', but Mandyczewski gives it in his Collected Edition.)

The poem is called 'Ein Gleiches' ('A similar one') in Goethe's works, since it followed *Wanderers Nachtlied I*. It was printed twice in Schubert's lifetime, firstly as a supplement to the *Wiener Zeitschrift für Kunst etc* on 23rd June 1827, and then with three other songs and dedicated to Princess Karoline von Kinsky, in 1828. A month before Schubert's death, it was reprinted by a Leipzig firm (H. A. Probst). Curiously enough, Schumann's setting of the same poem is his opus 96 as well. Loewe and Liszt are only two of the many other composers inspired to set Goethe's poem to music.

In 1823, Count Friedrich Leopold zu Stolberg's name appears for the first time among the authors whose poems have been set to music by Schubert. Stolberg (1750–1819) and his brother, Christian, studied classical and modern literature in Göttingen. Both became members of the 'Göttinger Hain' (see footnote, p. 57), who were in sympathy with the free-thinking ideas which brought about the French Revolution.

Stolberg's *Lied* (D 788) ('Des Lebens Tag ist schwer': 'Life's day is heavy') (April 1823) suffers from an artificial *Weltschmerz* and from a certain musical detachment on Schubert's part. Perhaps the text lacked the imaginative power it was striving for. The song is a loving embrace of the idea of death, which is shown in the musical structure as well. The broad sustained melody of the opening lines passes through innovative harmonic progressions, handled here with great technical skill.

The next Stolberg setting, *Auf dem Wasser zu singen* (D 774), is, however, pure Schubert. His genius is shown in the conception of the song; a semiquaver figure runs under the melody throughout, and, after the sudden introduction of an octave or a minor ninth, it trickles gently downwards. This is perhaps the most telling of all Schubertian water-studies; he was probably challenged by the unique nature of the poem, which is composed of similar, but not identical, couplets, and the repetition conjures up a dreamlike mood. The song reveals all the charms of a Schubert Lied, a blend of the Austrian love of a voluptuous melody and the instrumental brilliance found in his piano works, the Impromptus and the *Moments Musicaux* of the same period. The A flat minor of the beginning is held long enough for the sun to set, then Schubert lightens the scene with a transition to A flat major. No musical composition could equal this Schubertian blending of intimacy and gaiety, warmth and relaxation. (The song was published, again as a supplement to the *Wiener Zeitschrift für Kunst etc*, on 30th December 1823, and was incorporated in opus 72 in 1827.)

Schubert turned to Schiller for the last time in 1823; *Der Pilgrim* (D 794) describes the fruitless journey to the Golden Gates. The song moves along steadily, even monotonously, for seven verses, until, suddenly, unexpected modulations announce the pilgrim's complete collapse, the severance of his links with reality. Schubert makes no attempt to reproduce faithfully the allegorical images of the famous poem. The opening chorale-like melody is altered only fractionally to form additional links in a chain of inter-related melodies. The eighth stanza brings a change in the firm, steady rhythm which is loosened at the resigned words:

> Hin zu einem großen Meere
> Trieb mich seiner Wellen Spiel;
> Vor mir liegt's in weiter Leere,
> Näher bin ich nicht dem Ziel.

(The river carried me down to the mighty ocean. Now it lies boundless before me, but my goal is still far distant.)

The song (opus 37) was appropriately dedicated to the allegorical painter, Ludwig Schnorr von Carolsfeld. Because of Schubert's difficulties with the problem of the poem, this cannot be ranked among the greatest of his songs.

Immediately before this last tribute to his idol Schiller, Schubert set *Das Geheimnis* (D 793), Schiller's own tribute to his fiancée, Charlotte von Lengefeld. Schubert had composed an early, purely strophic version in 1815 (D 250). The simplicity of that melody apparently did not satisfy him now, probably because it failed to do justice to the second stanza in particular. Nevertheless, the high-flown vocal line of the new setting cannot quite erase the memory of the more economical first version. Schubert takes his leave of the idol of his youth with a gay, energetic dance or student song of undeniable Viennese provenance.

The powerful piano part of *Dithyrambe* (D 801) sweeps along in such a way that even powerful bass voices find it difficult to be heard above the torrents of sound with which each stanza closes.

Whether the Schillerian rhetoric is mercifully drowned by the rapid, strophic treatment of the text—or whether Schubert has failed to interpret the text—is a moot point. The singer should observe that Zeus is supposed to be speaking in the third stanza, which can therefore be performed with more tone and expression. (The Friedländer family possessed a manuscript draft of a further Schubert setting of the poem for chorus, solo voice and orchestra. Schiller's poem, alternatively titled 'Der Besuch', has been set by Zelter, Reichardt, Kreutzer, David, Taubert, Ritz, Dorn and Max Bruch.)

Schubert's state of mind at the beginning of 1824 was certainly much less joyous and self-confident than this song would suggest. On 20th February, Sonnleithner's *soirées musicales* were discontinued on the thin grounds that there was illness in the family. The real reason was Schubert's poor health and his financial difficulties. In addition, Ignaz von Sonnleithner found himself faced with a *fait accompli*; for Schubert ('in a moment of weakness', as his biographer Kreißle put it) had sold Diabelli the plates and rights of all the published volumes (opp. 1–7 and opp. 12–14) to date, for a lump sum of 800 florins, and thus effectively ruined any chances of financial security. *Erlkönig* alone had brought in 800 florins in 1821; *Der Wanderer* is said to have earned 27,000 florins by 1827. Sonnleithner, the instigator of all the publications, must have felt betrayed.

Even if an annoying rash, which forced Schubert to wear a ('very comfortable') wig from time to time, had cleared up, there was still discord among his friends, as Leopold Kupelwieser's fiancée, Johanna Lutz, reported to him on 25th January 1824. It was therefore not by chance that Schubert returned to his setting of a fragment of Schiller's poem *Die Götter Griechenlands* (D 677) (November 1819) for the opening theme of the minuet of his A minor String Quartet (opus 29) (D 804), composed at the end of February or the beginning of March 1824. The four-times repeated lament 'Schöne Welt, wo bist du?' ('Beautiful world, where art thou?') contributed to the permeation of the cyclical chamber music by poetic ideas from the songs, as so often happened. Schubert missed beauty around him—beauty, that is, as he understood it, the simple and the natural. He had complained to Schober (on 30th November 1823) that the 'Kanevas'–evenings were threatening to come to an end:

For hours on end, under Mohn's supreme command [Ludwig Mohn, a painter] we get nothing but riding and fencing, horses and dogs. If it goes on like this, I shall not be able to put up with them for much longer.

Schwind added to this complaint of Schubert's:

Our life is so taken up with money matters and pranks, that even an undisturbed meeting is an impossibility. If you or Senn were to come in suddenly, we should be truly ashamed of this crowd! Schubert would agree with me.

The twelfth stanza of Schiller's ode to the gods of Greece mentions no god by name, which underlines its personal meaning for Schubert:

> Schöne Welt, wo bist du? Kehre wieder,
> Holdes Blütenalter der Natur!
> Ach, nur in dem Feenland der Lieder
> Lebt noch deine fabelhafte Spur.
> Ausgestorben trauert das Gefilde,
> Keine Gottheit zeigt sich meinem Blick,
> Ach, von jenem lebenwarmen Bilde
> Blieb der Schatten nur zurück.

(Beautiful world, where art thou? O return to us, divine golden age of Nature. But, alas, your fabled beauty is only to be found in the magical land of song. The fields lie barren, my eye sees no god, only the shadow of that life-giving image remains.)

Had he set the whole poem, he would not have been able to leave the open question at the end, which, in the first of the two copies printed by Mandyczewski, does not even allow the A to resolve the 6/4 chord.

Schubert's diaries also reflect the pain of his isolation. We read on 27th March 1824:

No one understands another's pain and no one understands another's joy! We always imagine that we are approaching one another and in fact we are only going alongside each other. O what pain for him who realises this! My works exist because of my understanding of music and through my pain! Those which were produced by my pain alone seem to please the world least of all.

Behind this confession lies the question of death, which Schubert never avoided. Many of his songs take death as their theme, especially in the later years of his life. In addition, he was becoming increasingly reserved and contemptuous of people and the world, in complete contrast to the frequent descriptions given by his friends, to whom he only rarely revealed his true feelings or state of health.

Lied (D 788), to the poem by Count von Stolberg, was composed the year before. The song expresses Schubert's mental travail. Even if the crisis stage in his illness was past, he knew that he would never completely recover.

Also in March 1824 came the artistic separation from Mayrhofer. The poem was *Auflösung* (D 807):

> Verbirg dich, Sonne,
> Denn die Gluten der Wonne
> Versengen mein Gebein;
> Verstummet, Töne,
> Frühlings Schöne,
> Flüchte dich und laß mich allein.

(Hide, O Sun, for the fire of your bliss burns my bones. Be silent, fair sounds of spring, flee and leave me alone.)

The mood of parting is intensified to the point of ecstasy. The 'ätherischen Chöre' ('ethereal choirs') sing out in swelling figurations and great arcs of melody. The hesitant conclusion 'Geh' unter, Welt' ('Depart, O world'), gives a picture of utter exaltation. One has the feeling that Schubert is not thinking of the world which Mayrhofer would like to see disappear, but that, in this emotional outburst, he is seeking his own world, which is certainly not the world of a man looking for death at any price. There is a good deal in this song characteristic of the contemporary concept of Art; the unchanging sequence of broken chords, shaping themselves into figures, obscures the individual formal outlines. False endings, and frequent excursions into triad-related keys, oscillate playfully around the central tonality. 'Geh' unter, Welt' forms a new theme, conditioned by the words, and interrupted by the ascending and diminishing 'ätherischen Chöre', until finally only one chord remains, through which the dying voice continues to speak.

Der Sieg (D 805) is a clear premonition of the 'better' world that Mayrhofer was to seek through his suicide. ('O unbewölktes Leben') ('O unclouded life'), in Schubert's relaxed melody, is neither uncanny nor uncertain, but points to that inner world which will reshape our material existence; no matter how hard Schubert tries to interpret his friend's mood, however, there is rather too much theatricality in the middle section. Certainly the four bars after 'und meine Hand, sie traf' ('and my hand dealt the blow') which lead back into the peaceful F major do bring a harmonic transformation that allows the melody to ascend, and the harmony to find its way from the tension of inclement weather into the cloudless security which Schubert would wish for his friend.

On 31st March 1824 Schubert wrote a distraught despairing letter to Leopold Kupelwieser in Rome:

> In a word, I feel that I am the unhappiest, most miserable person in the entire world. Imagine someone whose health will never improve, and who, in despair over this, makes things worse instead of better, whose brightest hopes have come to naught, to whom the joy of love and friendship can offer nothing but pain at the most, who is in danger of losing his enthusiasm (at least the sort which inspires) for beauty, and ask yourself if that is not a miserable unhappy wretch? . . . I spend my days joyless and friendless, and only Schwind visits me sometimes and brings a ray of those sweet days long gone. Our reading circle has died a voluntary death, because of the increase in the rough choir of beer-drinkers and sausage-eaters.

The reading-circles had been introduced and entertained by Schubert's old *Konvikt* friend, Franz von Bruchmann. They had read aloud, and discussed, Homer and the classics as well as modern literature. For Schubert, who had always been an avid reader, they had seemed like food and drink. Indeed, he was one of the first musicians to be what we nowadays would call 'educated'. Even among friends, he preferred a serious conversation, free from intellectual 'nit-picking', to the usual empty gossip. And now this stimulation too was gone and its absence made him feel his isolation all the more.

Mayrhofer's *Abendstern* (D 806) summed up perfectly his withdrawal and his isolation:

Was weilst du einsam an dem Himmel,
O schöner Stern? und bist so mild;
Warum entfernt das funkelnde Gewimmel
Der Brüder sich vor deinem Bild?

(Why are you so lonely and so gentle up there in the sky, my beautiful star? Why do all your twinkling brothers desert you?)

Within a small compass, with only a few notes, and, apart from a tentative leap to the larger third of the A major/minor scale, harmonically simple, one of the loveliest of the Mayrhofer-Lieder unfolds before us. Like the star to which it is addressed, it stands on a lonely spot, waiting to be discovered.

Mayrhofer's *Gondelfahrer* (D 808) (not to be confused, incidentally, with the choral setting of the same poem, opus 28, 1814, D 809) is in several parts. The passage

Vom Markusturme tönte
Der Spruch der Mitternacht!
(From St Mark's Tower echoed the voice of midnight!)

with the sound of distant bells, is particularly fascinating. With the ghostly reflection of moon and stars in the water, Schubert takes his farewell of this remarkable poet; it was the last Mayrhofer poem to be ennobled by Schubert's music.

Five weeks after Schubert had written that letter to Kupelwieser, the saddest of his life, and written out of the same feeling of despair as Beethoven's *Heiligenstädter Testament*, there took place (on 7th May 1824) the first performance of the Ninth Symphony of that other lonely man. Even if we cannot be absolutely certain that Schubert attended the performance, it is likely that he did so, since he had expressly mentioned the coming performance in that letter to Kupelwieser. In addition, two of his friends, Josef Hüttenbrenner and Fritz von Hartmann, were members of the chorus. Schubert must have been moved by the proclamation of the brotherhood of Man, and his frustrated enthusiasm for beauty must have been refreshed. He would certainly have recalled with some sadness that May of 1815, when he set the same poem as a gay, carefree song for male chorus with piano accompaniment (*An die Freude*, D 189). Beethoven wanted 'to free all mankind from all the misery that besets them', and, in fact, Schubert's suffering had strengthened his belief in beauty and humanity. Schiller's hymn is obviously meant to be sung chorally by a solo singer with an accompanying chorus; this is made clear by the changes in the metre. As always, Schubert followed the poem's formal requirements.

Since it appeared, Schiller's superb song to joy has inspired countless compositions—entire collections have been made, even of published versions—but not a single one has been satisfactory. And none will be; that is in the nature of the poem, its theme and its form. It must be treated as a Lied. If a composer tries to seize on what is common to all stanzas, he will have to generalise, and will therefore fail to match the poet's enthusiastic, but clearly defined flights of fancy. If, on the other hand, he concentrates on details, then, because of the great diversity of the material in the various stanzas, his music might just suit some of them, will barely suit others, and will fit the remainder not at all, and might even contradict their meaning.

This critique appeared in the *Leipziger Allgemeine Musikalische Zeitung* of April 1818, and, as can be seen, touches very generally on the whole problem of the strophic song. The critique was written before Beethoven's composition appeared, which naturally eclipsed all other settings. Whether Schubert would even have considered his youthful setting for publication is more than doubtful.

Meanwhile the critics had found a good deal to marvel at in the novelty of Schubert's romantic expressiveness and at the free and uninhibited nature of his settings. The *Leipziger Zeitung* of 24th June 1824:

The composer evidences a noteworthy talent which, with youthful courage, scorns the old well-worn paths and strikes out on new ways which he follows consistently. Schubert does not really write songs [Lieder] and does not want to write them, but rather free vocal compositions [Gesänge] sometimes so free that they could be called caprices or fantasies. The latest poems, if greatly varying in quality, are well chosen, and their translation into music is generally to be praised. The vocal part, mostly declamatory, is, at times, not very singable, frequently unnecessarily difficult, the harmony as a rule is pure. The modulation free, very free, and often more than that.

The Leipzig critic recognised something not generally realised even today. The originator of the German Lied often overstepped with pleasure the bounds of the Lied, in its narrower sense. Sheer beauty of tone, advanced again and again as the sole yardstick of correct Schubert interpretations, can never satisfy the composer's demands.

Nothing human is excluded from Schubert's music, and the very first bars of the magical Rückert song, *Daß sie hier gewesen* (D 775), for example, conjuring up insubstantial soughing breezes with *Tristan*-like sounds, must have horrified his contemporaries. The beauty of this neglected song, written in 1823, will only be revealed to those willing to penetrate beneath its surface. The singer is bidden to avoid sentimentality as well as any slowing-down of the tempi, if the delicate structure of the song is to make its full effect. The key of the song is not revealed in the opening bars. Inexplicable, almost haphazard, chords veil the poet's introductory hints, until at the words 'Daß sie hier gewesen' ('That she was here'), a key-signature of C major brings an answer and, with it, certainty. (*Daß sie hier gewesen* was published, together with other Rückert settings, as opus 59 in 1826.)

Rückert's poetic language, tinged with oriental mysticism, in *Du bist die Ruh* (D 776) determined the restrained nature, the only mood possible, of Schubert's setting. The slow *crescendo* and *decrescendo* ascent of

> Dies Augenzelt,
> Von Deinem Glanz
> Allein erhellt,
> O füll' es ganz!

(Let these eyes, illuminated by Thy glory, be filled to the brim.)

is a far more valuable, and, at the same time, far more difficult vocal exercise than all those found in the text books.

The conclusion to the song is divided up, not according to the *rhyme,* but to the *meaning;* a great climb up to 'erhellt', and then, after a rest, as if exhausted by such efforts, the humble plea, 'O, füll' es ganz'. *Du bist die Ruh* is a model of the strophic song with an 'afterstrain', a concluding refrain. Schubert joins two of the quatrains together to make one line, as it were; the middle rhyme is subsumed. The resultant arching four-bar melody justifies the method in an illuminating way. The piano begins with a two-part line, in the fourth bar it becomes three-part, and in the next one, four-part. The concluding refrain takes up the melody of the opening stanzas and reaches its ecstatic climax by climbing up a veritable ladder of chords. On the repetition, the high G is a *diminuendo*, something often overlooked, because of the general difficulties of execution. However, Schubert is not singing to an audience out over the prompter's box, he is singing rather to the inner soul.

There is no profundity behind the setting of *Lachen und Weinen* (D 777), No. 4 of the same opus 59, but, within its confines, the two moods, 'laughing and weeping', are cleverly distinguished from one another by a humorous simplification of the major–minor polarity, and the declamation is wonderfully fluid. (The last of the Rückert songs, *Greisengesang*, which forms opus 60 with *Dithyrambe*, was discussed on pp. 184–5.)

The Viennese poet, Johann Gabriel Seidl, provided Schubert's next texts. A friend of the composer, Seidl wrote poems, operettas, short stories and Lower Austrian dialect works, but his sentimental verses made no impact outside Austria. Lawyer, schoolmaster, librarian, book-censor, Court treasurer, and government minister, he also wrote for literary periodicals, and composed epic and folk poetry, as well as plays for the Burgtheater in Vienna. He too now joined the ranks of Schubert's opera librettists with *Der kurze Mantel* ('The short coat'), but Schubert never managed to start work on this one. In compensation, he produced the loveliest of the five settings of Seidl's *Der Wanderer an den Mond* (D 870). The tired traveller, who holds an intimate conversation with the moon, envies his travelling companion's fixed abode. The typical strolling gait, only found in Schubert, is enchanting. The piano has to re-produce the appropriate dry notes of the guitar. The dotted minims serve as a warning to the performer not to allow the tempo to drag, although an imperceptible yielding to the rounded major mode at the apostrophe to the moon is permissible. The accompanist should not try to make too much of the interludes, since it is their folk-song character which makes them so moving. Once again, and particularly clearly in this example, we find the most basic, most personal characteristic of Schubert's music, one which is elevated from a mere musical function and given the validity of an utterance —the major–minor polarity. This is the source of all musical tension: the contrast of masculine and feminine, of hardness and softness, of light and shade, of day and night. Schubert was the first composer to breathe musical life into this elementary dramatic principle. It symbolised heaven and earth for him (and heaven could be in the minor mode), and he united them. It is in the transition of one to the other that the essence of Schubert's art lies. During these hardly perceptible moments a metamorphosis occurs, a gliding-over into another realm. There is a spiritual power, a concentrated dramaticism in this transformation which becomes free and unfettered when, for example, the wanderer looks up at the moon at 'Du aber wandelst auf und ab' ('But you wander up and down'); this is certainly much more than a mere transformation.

Schubert came back to earth, however, to write, rather exceptionally, 'chansons' to Seidl's cheeky *Unterscheidung* (D 866 no. 1) and to the suggestive *Die Männer sind mechant* [*sic*] (D 866 no. 3), but, possibly because they lack depth, neither song is very convincing, although they have become favourites of countless sopranos who, if they possess the charm of an Elisabeth Schumann, can naturally make something out of these trifles. All four of these 'Refrain-Lieder', published in 1826, are dedicated to the poet, who also won a State prize for his lyrics to Haydn's Imperial national anthem.

In May 1824, Schubert travelled once again with the Esterházy family to Hungary, during which time he is supposed to have had a romance with the Countess Karoline. All we know of this is a few hints and the dedication to her of the Fantasia in F minor for Piano Duet. The nineteen-year-old girl seems to have known nothing of Schubert's feelings towards her; at any rate, she did not reciprocate them.

Schubert's brother, Ferdinand, to whom Schubert was very attached, wrote to him on 3rd July 1824, in Hungary, that he had given Ludwig Mohn ten songs. Schubert replied on 16th/18th July:

As for the songs given to Mohn, I comfort myself that only a few seemed good to me, as for example, *Wanderers Nachtlied* and *Der entsühnte Orest* (not der entführte); I had to laugh at that mistake. [Ferdinand had written 'entführte' (abducted) instead of 'entsühnte' (absolved). Ed.] Try to get at least these ones back as soon as possible.

Orest auf Tauris (D 548) recalls the enthusiasm with which the youthful Schubert described Vogl's interpretations of Gluck's operatic hero (see p. 22). Nor are we disconcerted that the poem gives us only a fragmentary glimpse of the fate of the unhappy hero—the legend is too well-known. The nobility, richness of colour and economy of Schubert's musical language give a fore-taste of what Schubert might have done with the classical operatic style.

There is a curious anticipation of Wagner in the pendant song *Der entsühnte Orest* (D 699) where the intonation and harmonies of a Wotan are evoked by the words 'Schwert' ('sword') and 'Speer' ('spear'). (Schubert's shy love for Karoline turned in the course of the year into a deep friendship which the aristocratic lady reciprocated.) Bauernfeld was probably near the truth when he wrote:

The conflict between an impetuous love of life and a restless intellectual activity is always exhausting, when there is no balance of forces in the soul. Fortunately for our friend, an ideal love had a mediating, conciliating and balancing effect.

Such an effect is mirrored in the middle stanza of the song *Glaube, Hoffnung und Liebe* (D 955), from a poem by Christoph Kuffner, which Schubert set in an onward-rushing tempo, in contrast to the solemn first and last stanzas. Christoph Kuffner (*c.* 1780–1864) was an official in the Imperial War Office in Vienna, a censor and later a Court secretary. He published short stories, poems, dramas and translations of Plautus. (See also p. 276.)

Apart from the magic of the nineteen-year-old Karoline, Schubert was certainly attracted by the temperament of Baron Schönstein. Even at their meetings in Vienna, at the house of the music-loving Esterházys, they had had vigorous arguments about the merits or demerits of Italianised opera. Although Schubert defended German opera manfully, he always gave Rossini's operas their due meed of praise, as his setting of Friedrich Schlegel's *Der Fluß* (D 693) makes clear. The completely Italianate vocal part could have been taken from an early work of Giuseppe Verdi, who had grown up as an admirer of Rossini. One is conscious again of the little-noticed similarity between this other great melodic composer and Schubert, whom Verdi always admired and to whom he always felt indebted.

The words of the poem explain why the melody is so exalted:

Wie rein Gesang sich windet
Durch wunderbarer Saitenspiele Rauschen,
Er selbst sich wiederfindet,
Wie auch die Weisen tauschen,
Daß neu entzückt die Hörer ewig lauschen.

(Just as pure song threads its way through the wonderful rustling of the strings and finds itself again, however much the melodies change, so that each time the listeners stand entranced . . .)

Schönstein, on the other hand, shared the aristocratic prejudice against German art. Vogl's protégé had an excellent trained voice. Sonnleithner recalls that he 'had a fine noble-sounding tenor-baritone voice, a good voice training, an aesthetic and literary background and emotional warmth'. Where conversation could not bring agreement, Lieder did. Schönstein soon became a lively supporter of the German Lied, better still, of the Schubert Lied. It was the twenty songs of *Die schöne Müllerin*, the first volume of which had been published after a great deal of effort, and which, to the great disappointment of Schubert's friends, had created 'no stir', that converted the prejudiced Baron. From that moment on, the lover of opera, ballet and horses became an apostle of the Schubert-Lied. Schubert's dedication of the *Schöne Müllerin* songs to Schönstein was probably the most justified of all his dedications in his short life.

Schubert had failed three times with his operatic attempts in 1823, yet overnight he succeeded in writing a new chapter in the history of chamber music: the song-cycle, the 'musical *Novelle*'. Again and again, when he and Schönstein performed songs from the cycle after their return from Hungary, audiences were moved to tears by this indescribable experience. Sonnleithner called Schönstein 'one of the best, perhaps *the* best Schubert singer'.

A few days after the twenty-fifth performance of Weber's *Der Freischütz* in Vienna, the appointment of Domenico Barbaja as director of the Viennese Opera heralded the end of German opera productions there; Rossini came with his wife to the city, and the enthusiasm of the Viennese rose to a climax of fashionable euphoria. People wore Rossini hats and Rossini cravats, they ate Rossini dishes and watched Rossini parodies in the popular theatres. *The Barber of Seville* was followed by the *Barber of Sievering* (a suburb of

Vienna) and Johann Nestroy (see p. 261) followed Rossini's famous aria 'Di tanti palpiti' (from *Tancredi*) with his no less famous dialect 'Die Tante dalkete'.

Schubert composed two overtures in the style of Rossini, and some of his Lieder show the Italian's influence. Weber exclaimed in comic rage, 'If these damned fellows manage to make me actually begin to like this rubbish, then the devil could put up with it too!'

According to eye-witnesses, the Viennese sat like 'herrings in a barrel' at every Rossini performance. Schubert, who was also a great admirer of Paganini, conceded that Rossini was a man of 'extraordinary genius'.

On 12th August 1824 the official *Wiener Zeitung* announced the publication of the complete *Schöne Müllerin* cycle. On 2nd February Schwind, in a letter to Schober, had hinted that Schubert had decided to take a nature-cure. He added later (22nd February):

> Schubert is very well, he has done away with his wig and is showing the beginnings of a nice curly head of hair. Once again he has a pile of the loveliest 'Germans' [i.e. German dances. Ed.]. The first volume of the *Müllerlieder* is out.

Sauer & Leidesdorf had indeed published the first volume (nos. 1–4). Nos. 5–9 were announced for the following week, but were not in fact published until 24th March. While in Hungary, Schubert learned from a letter from his father—which indicated a marked improvement in his relations with his family, probably aided by Schubert's diplomatic behaviour towards his young step-mother[1]—that the complete *Schöne Müllerin* cycle had now been published by Sauer & Leidesdorf as opus 28, without Schwind's projected vignettes, however. Schwind answered a letter from Schubert complaining about the delay in the publication of *Die schöne Müllerin,* not directly, but by writing, on 20th August, to Schober, who was acting at a theatre in Breslau:

> He is well and working hard—at a symphony as far as I know. Now and then I have the pleasant opportunity of hearing things by Schubert at a certain Herr Pinderitz's [Pinterics] whom I met at Vogl's house. He is a very good, energetic man, sympathetic and full of old German *objets d'art.*

[1] Schubert's father had married Anna Kleyenböck (1783–1860) in 1813 (Ed.).

Carl Pinterics, a good friend of Beethoven, and a very good amateur pianist, lived in the so-called 'Zuckerbäckerhaus', ('confectioner's house'), where Schubert's friends regularly met. By collecting all the autograph manuscripts which Schubert carelessly left lying around, Pinterics had amassed a considerable Schubert collection, which, on his death, came into the possession of that other 'saviour' of Schubert's works, *Hofrat* Josef Witteczek. We have cause to be grateful to the good *Hofrat*, who even used to take his collection to his office, because he was reluctant to let the songs out of his sight.

On 8th November 1824, Schwind wrote to Schober: 'Schubert is here, healthy and divinely carefree, rejuvenated by joy and pain and a happy life.'

The somewhat depressing monotony of Schubert's stay in Hungary seemed therefore to have been overcome. Worries and doubts still plagued him as a letter to Schober on 21st September reveals: 'What should we do with happiness since unhappiness is the only attraction left to us?', a mood also reflected in the strange song, *Im Abendrot* (D 799) to a poem by the Pommeranian poet Carl Lappe (1773–1843), two of whose many poems found their way to Schubert and will be discussed later (see pp. 235–6).

On 2nd December 1824 Schober wrote to Schubert from Breslau:

My good, ever faithful friend!
   You have never lost your affection for me, you have always loved me for my own sake, just like Schwind, and Kupelwieser will remain faithful, too. And are we not just the ones who made art their lives while the others only talked about it, we were the ones who understood each other's innermost thoughts, as only a German can understand them?

Schubert had complained to his friend in the letter mentioned above: 'Things are going badly for Leidesdorf, he cannot pay and nobody is buying anything, neither my things nor anyone else's, only miserable popular music.'

Schober refers to this:

So things are going badly for Leidesdorf? I'm sorry about that, and that your *Müllerlieder* haven't caused a stir. These dogs have no feelings or ideas of their own and blindly follow the loud noise and opinions of others. If you could only get a few critics to beat their drums for you and keep writing about you in the papers, you would be all right. I know some quite insignificant people who have become famous and popular in this way, so why should it not happen to someone who deserves it so much? Castelli [Ignaz Franz Castelli, 1781–1862] is writing in a few foreign journals. You composed an opera of his [*Die Verschworenen*], he should open *his* mouth. Moritz [von Schwind] sent us the *Müllerlieder*, send me anything else that has appeared. How happy I am that you are completely well again. I will soon be too.

On 12th December 1824 the 'Royal Prussian Premier Court Theatre and Chamber Singer', Anna Milder-Hauptmann, honoured Schubert with a letter, in which she regretted that her desire to meet him during her last guest appearance in Vienna had not been realised. She admitted to being charmed by his songs and enclosed a long Goethe poem 'Verschiedene Empfindungen an einem Platz' ('Several emotions in the same place'), with a view to a possible setting by Schubert. Schubert ignored that, but, on her suggestion that she should show one of his operas to the Berlin *Intendant*, he sent her his *Alfonso und Estrella*—but the hoped-for results failed to materialise. He also dedicated Goethe's *Suleika II* to her.

After a short stay with his family over the New Year period, Schubert took up lodgings with a retailer in the oil trade, Herr Kellner, who lived in the 'Fruhwirthhaus' in the suburb of Alte Wieden. The house was quite close to Moritz von Schwind's and this meant that they saw each other frequently—and they fell in love with the same girl. This was 'Netti' Hönig, the daughter of the Dean of the Faculty of Law at Vienna. On 14th February, Schwind wrote to Schober: 'Schubert is well and after a break is working industriously again. There is a Schubertiad at Enderes' every week [*Hofrat* Karl von Enderes, 1787–1861] that is to say, Vogl sings.'

Many of the Schubertians, who were usually more intoxicated by beauty and art than by wine, made their names in the coming years—the poet philosopher Eduard Freiherr von Feuchtersleben (born 1806), some of whose poems Mendelssohn set to music,

Franz Grillparzer, Niklaus Lenau, and the painters Moritz von Schwind, Leopold Kupelwieser, Josef Danhauser and Ludwig Schnorr von Carolsfeld. Schubert wrote once to his brother Ferdinand that they were all fortunate in being able 'to repel miserable reality through the power of their imaginations'.

On 24th February 1825, Vogl and Schwind had been invited to dinner by Sophie Müller, a pretty, young and talented actress. She was at that time the most famous tragedienne at the Burgtheater in Vienna, but she was also a most accomplished singer; Anselm Hüttenbrenner told her that she 'was the most sensitive interpreter of Schubert's songs after Schönstein'.

On the same evening, at the thirteenth evening concert of the *Gesellschaft der Musikfreunde*, Mayrhofer's *Der zürnenden Diana* (D 707) and *Sehnsucht* (D 516) were performed. *Sehnsucht* gives some proof of the conflict between poet and musician. The first quatrain, with its description of spring and the lark's rejoicing over the passing of winter, is very much to Schubert's taste; the melody and the lark's trills dance along together. But then the poet goes on to lament his failure to realise his dreams in this hostile world, and, in his imagination, he takes wing with the migrating cranes to friendlier climes. Schubert is obviously disconcerted by the sudden abandonment of the joyous exaltation of spring. He does his best to reflect his friend's forlorn melancholy, but the song loses its initial intensity. (How much poorer we should be, however, without the many Mayrhofer-Lieder with their multifarious tones and tints!)

Der zürnenden Diana ('To enraged Diana'), as melodic as *Iphigenia*, is not only the greatest, but possibly also the liveliest of Mayrhofer's 'arias'. The rich passionate eloquence must be judiciously measured out over the long stretches, if the tension is to be maintained to the end. The youth's enthusiastic death at the conclusion is portrayed with all the graduations of a stage demise.

The song, together with Mayrhofer's *Nachtstück*, had just been published and dedicated to Frau Katherina von Laszny (née Buchwieser) (1789–1828), with whom Schwind had fallen in love, and whom Schubert also briefly knew. She seems to have been something of a woman of the world, and Schubert's friends were amazed that a woman who 'had such a reputation in the town' could look so intelligent.

The popular *Nachtstück* (D 672) first sung at her house, is based on an inflated Romantic poem by Mayrhofer. There are unusual polyphonics in the introduction, and Schubert's main melody shows a willingness to feel the same degree of compassion for this rather nebulous 'guten, alten Mann', as with the Harper or the Wanderer. It is rare to find Schubert repeating a melody, complete and unchanged, but he does so here, and the murmuring of the leaves and the rustling of the branches lose none of their magic in the repetition. The old minstrel is introduced on the scene with some deliberation by the piano and he begins to sing his last song, to which everything so far has been only the prologue. By the alteration of a single note, Schubert expressively intensifies the repetition of the word 'erlöst' ('freed'). Suddenly the character of the music changes. The piano accompaniment begins to rock like the 'grünen Bäume' ('green trees') which lull the old man to sleep. This lulling motion is carried through to the end, even though the hymn has long since ceased: 'Der Alte horcht, der Alte schweigt' ('the old man listens, the old man is silent'). The effect is indeed indescribable; it would be futile to attempt to put into words the force of the modulations of the old minstrel's gradual passing-away.

Sophie Müller, who was less generous with her feminine charms than Frau von Laszny, captivated Schubert with her keen brain and her elegance. She recorded in her diary:

Vogl and Schubert came at midday and brought new songs. Vogl sang beautifully. *2 March*: Schubert came after lunch. I sang with him till after 6 o'clock, then I went to the theatre. *3 March*: Schubert brought a new song *Die junge Nonne*. Vogl came later. I sang it with him. It is a lovely composition.

Die junge Nonne (D 828) is the first of three stylistically surprising songs from poems by Jakob Nikolaus Reichsfreiherr von Craigher de Jachelutta (1797–1855), which had just been composed, and which were all far ahead of their time. The piano bass's stormy description of night is reminiscent of Carl Loewe, although the latter does not begin to approach Schubert's artistic power. A dark storm-*motif* is mingled with the tolling of mysterious convent-bells and a vocal theme that progresses in semi-tones and expresses hysteria by means of curious retardations, and which then ends in a religious frenzy, expressed in the whispered 'Halleluja': That is the high drama of *Die junge Nonne*. It is yet another indication of what Schubert might have done with a suitable opera libretto. At the end of the song, the air seems to clear a little, but the music of the weather is still heard, and when the convent bells toll their F's and C's, the *tremoli* in the right hand hint at the arrival of freshening rain. (*Die junge Nonne* was published as opus 43 along with the antipodally serene *Nacht und Träume*.)

On 7th March 1825, Sophie Müller wrote in her diary:

Vogl and Schubert brought new songs of which a scene from Aeschylus [*Fragment aus dem Äschylus*], *Ihr Grab*, *Die Forelle* and *Der Einsame* are excellent.

The *Fragment aus dem Äschylus* (D 450) is taken from the *Eumenides*, the third play of the *Oresteia* Trilogy. Aeschylus (*c.* 525–456 BC), whose *Persae* is probably the first extant contemporary play, took the theme not from a myth, but from an event of recent history. Such a break with the traditions of the Greek theatre heralded a departure from the mystery-play.

Schubert used a new translation by Mayrhofer of the *Eumenides* fragment, and, in 1816, composed two almost identical versions. Once again, Schubert is on 'classical' terrain. Although intended originally for chorus, it appears here as a solo declamation which begins with a weighty recitative already announced by the piano. The word 'versinken' ('sink') plunges downward in the ninth of D flat–C. The piano *tremolo* represents the passage of time, the interval leap E flat–D flat–C leads downward to damnation. At the point where Schubert writes 'im Takt' ('in time'), the *arioso* begins. The scene is brought to life by the staccato quavers of the man's cry for help, the four semiquavers at 'den Banden der Not verstrickt' ('caught in the net of despair'), and by the 'versinkt er' '(he drowns'), which ends the song, not on the tonic, but rather on the inconclusive third.

Ihr Grab (D 736), which Sophie Müller was right to praise as well, is by Richard Roos, a pseudonym for Karl August Engelhardt (1769–1834), a Saxon archivist who later became a secretary in the War Ministry and was a member of the literary circle in Dresden, where he published geographical and historical studies, stories and poems.

Ihr Grab begins with a prelude outside the main key of E flat major. The melody follows the cadence of the frequently repeated phrase 'dort ist ihr Grab' ('there is her grave'). The song illustrates that Schubert, the artist, did *not* long for death, the dark side of life. It is indeed remarkable how seldom the songs that deal with death leave the listener with a feeling of sadness. The central experience of such songs is rather one of consolation and trustful optimism. This is true of songs like *Der Tod und das Mädchen, Am Grabe Anselmos, Totengräbers Heimwehe, Totengräberlied, Auf den Tod einer Nachtigall, Grablied, Die frühen Gräber, Totenopfer, Die Sterbende, Totenkranz für ein Kind, Fahrt zum Hades, Das Grab, Eine Leichen-phantasie, Auf einen Kirchhof, Totengräberweise, Todesmusik, An den Tod,* and *Der Jüngling und der Tod.*

On 8th March 1825 Anna Milder-Hauptmann at last answered Schubert's letter of the preceding year:

Dear Herr Schubert!

I hasten to inform you that I have received your Estrella and the Suleika song with infinite pleasure. The song is divine and moves me each time to tears. It is indescribable. You have imbued it with all possible magic and yearning.

She was unable to give him any further information about his operatic plans, since 'one is accustomed here to the very dramatic grand opera or the French *opéra comique*'.

Although Schubert's hopes that the all-powerful Gasparo Spontini, the Prussian Music Director, might take an interest in his opera, were dashed, this did not prevent him from making renewed plans for a stage work. He was helped in this by Eduard von Bauernfeld (1802–1890), whom he had met in 1822, and who now became a close acquaintance of Schubert's, not least because he was an accomplished pianist. Bauernfeld, also a skilful playwright, worked until 1848 in the Austrian lottery headquarters under Josef von Spaun. Now he offered himself as yet another possible lib-rettist. He recorded in his diary in March 1825:

Spending a good deal of time with Schwind and Schubert. He sang new songs at my house. Recently, we slept at his place. He wants an opera libretto from me and has suggested the *Bezauberte Rose* [The Enchanted Rose]. I said that I was playing with the idea of a *Graf von Gleichen* [Count von Gleichen].

This project never came to anything, for Schubert died before he could finish it.

In May 1825, Wilhelm Rieder finished his now famous Schubert portrait, which, as an etching, was to decorate the title-pages of most Schubert publications in the years to come. Schwind always held Rieder up as a model to Schubert, saying that it would reward him to copy Rieder's success in conquering the Court 'establishment'. He wrote to Schubert on 14th August:

> Rieder is a Professor at the Academy of Engineering with a salary of 600 florins, but there is a rumour that he is about to get married. If you would try for the post of Court Organist in earnest, you could do as well too. Otherwise, you will just have to live respectably, for in view of the absolute and complete poverty of your friends, you will have to satisfy your material and spiritual needs for pheasant and punch in an isolation which will be every bit as desolate as Robinson Crusoe's on a desert island.

But Schubert let most of the opportunities of gaining such a post slip by him. He avoided firm commitments on principle.

Carl Pinterics gave concerts for Schubert at his home, and, by his interest, contributed in no small measure to winning recognition for the works of his unpractical friend. Freiherr von Schönstein worked hard to popularise the Lieder in aristocratic circles.

On 6th June 1825 Diabelli & Compagnie announced the publication of Schubert's settings of the Goethe poems *An Schwager Kronos*, *An Mignon*, and *Ganymed* 'respectfully dedicated to the poet'. This time Schubert did not wait for permission from Weimar; he decided to dedicate the songs without asking. At the beginning of the month, he sent two copies of the beautifully engraved volumes to Goethe, along with an accompanying letter:

> Your Excellency!
> If through the dedication of these compositions of your poems I should succeed in making clear my boundless veneration for Your Excellency and perhaps gain some recognition for my insignificant person, then I should regard the favourable outcome of my wishes as the happiest event of my life. With deepest respect, Your obedient servant, Franz Schubert.

And, indeed, Goethe's journal for 16th June 1825 records: 'Packet from Felix Mendelssohn from Berlin, quartets. Packet from Schubert from Vienna: compositions of my songs'—but no reply was sent to Vienna. Schubert never learned that 'Jean Paul' (Johann Paul Friedrich Richter, 1763–1825) lying on his deathbed in Bayreuth about this time, begged again and again to hear Schubert's songs, above all, 'the wonderful setting of *Erlkönig*'.

ELEVEN

Journey to Upper Austria, 1825

In the summer of 1825 Vogl invited Schubert to accompany him on another long journey. After short stops in Kremsmünster, St Florian near Linz, Steyr and its environs, as well as in Gmunden, they journeyed through the Salzkammergut. Therese Clodi, the daughter of Florian Clodi of Schloss Ebenzweier, wrote enthusiastically on 22nd June: 'I heard Vogl singing and Schubert playing, twice, it is always a divine pleasure to hear the two of them.'

On 19th July 1825, Anton Ottenwalt wrote in a letter to his brother-in-law, Josef von Spaun, in Lemburg, of Schubert's stay with him:

> Schubert looks so strong and well, he is so cheerful, so friendly and open that it is a joy to see. Today he is moving into the room where you used to put up. His trunk is being taken in, a table put up for writing on, and we shall supply him with books etc. I am proud to have this guest of yours, and all the affection and honour that we show him is also meant for you . . .

Spaun had left Linz just before Schubert's arrival, and the latter was greatly disappointed to have missed him. Schubert wrote to Spaun on 21st July:

> Here I am in Linz half-dead with sweat in this disgraceful heat with a whole volume of new songs and you are not here! Aren't you ashamed? . . . I was only 14 days in Steyr, then we (Vogl and I) went to Gmunden where we spent six very full and pleasant weeks. We put up at Traweger's, who possesses a magnificent pianoforte, and, as you know, is a great admirer of my humble self. I lived most pleasantly and informally there.

Schubert was as fortunate as he had been in Steyr. Ferdinand Traweger, a prosperous merchant, lived in a large house in the picturesque village of Gmunden on Lake Traun, and held regular musical evenings. He had long been an admirer of Schubert, and, through Schubert's brother, Karl, who had been painting in the district, Traweger had commissioned vocal quartets and octets in Vienna. Traweger's son, Eduard (who died as recently as 1909) recalled later in his memoirs the enthusiasm engendered by the six weeks' presence of Schubert and Vogl: 'My dear father, who had a great talent for entertaining and for arranging things, was in seventh heaven. He always spoke of Schubert with enthusiasm and was quite attached to him.'

The five-year-old Eduard had to learn by heart, and with the help of a silver coin, the song, 'Guten Morgen, schöne Müllerin' (*Morgengruß* from *Die schöne Müllerin*), arranged by Schubert himself —and would then be told: 'Come on, Eduard, sing "Guten Morgen" and you'll get a nice *Kreuzer*!' Eduard, a regular attender at these performances by Vogl and Schubert, wrote later:

Relatives and friends were often invited to these pleasant affairs. Such compositions, performed in this way, inevitably raised emotions to such a pitch that, when the song was finished, it was not unusual for the gentlemen to embrace each other and let their emotions find their relief in tears.

Traweger's house was not the only centre of music in Gmunden. Schubert wrote to his parents on 25th (28th?) July:

We played a good deal at *Hofrat* von Schiller's, among others, some of my new songs from Walter Scott's *Lady of the Lake*. The hymn to the Blessed Virgin [*Ave Maria*] was particularly well received.

Ferdinand von Schiller was a highly-placed Imperial official in the Salzkammergut to whose *soirées musicales* Gmunden's high society flocked, especially to listen to Vogl and Schubert. Schubert met and fell in love with the seventeen-year-old Anna Wolf, a daily luncheon companion and daughter of the schoolmaster. (Niklaus Lenau fell in love with her later.) Schubert accompanied 'Nanette', a very fine pianist herself, in what was probably the first performance of Ellen's songs from the *Lady of the Lake*.

Sir Walter Scott established the historical novel in Great Britain and had a lasting influence on the genre in Germany too. On the other hand, his ballad translations, above all of Gottfried August Bürger's works, and of Goethe's, did much to introduce German literature to Great Britain. His verse epic *Lady of the Lake* (1819) circulated throughout Europe and appeared as an opera, in Rossini's version, in Vienna as early as 1822.

Lake Traun afforded Schubert an ideal backcloth against which to compose almost all the songs of the cycle, which is a series of cameos in the style of Schwind's vignettes. The songs likewise contain various characters. The three long Ellen songs are solos for the female voice, the laments of Norman and the Earl of Douglas were meant for Vogl's baritone voice. The warrior's boating song (*Bootgesang*, D 835) and the women's lament for Duncan (*Coronach*, D 836) were part-songs for male quartet and female trio respectively.

In *Ellens erster Gesang* (D 837) (Soldier, rest, thy warfare is o'er), the soprano sings an extended lullaby to the resting warrior. The second song, *Ellens zweiter Gesang* (D 838) ('Huntsman, rest! thy chase is done'), in which the romantic horn creates a strange twilit atmosphere, remained as little known as the first. The strophic treatment of *Ellens dritter Gesang* (D 839), the celebrated *Ave Maria*, is a hymn of overwhelming intensity, sung above harp sestolets. The song has not only become part of the standard repertoire of most female singers, but also the victim of countless arrangements for the most varied instruments. It has proved a touchstone of technical perfection, for it needs a superlative breathing technique to sustain the long phrases. The harp accompaniment, much criticised as being too secular, agrees in fact with Scott's intentions, since Ellen is singing to her *own* harp accompaniment.

Probably the most characteristic song of the series is the *Lied des gefangenen Jägers* (Lay of the imprisoned huntsman) (D 843), in polonaise form. The Polish dance-rhythm is accurately translated into 'Scottish', and is, in fact, a not unusual feature of Scottish songs. In the section in the minor mode, masculine grief is hidden beneath the noisy externals. In the major mode section, a transfiguring memory stirs, but is laid to rest again by the epilogue. While, on the one hand, the limited range (one octave) of the vocal part, a very narrow piano range and the complete absence of interesting modulations, do capture the exhaustion and basic meaning of the poem, they militated on the other hand against the song's ever becoming popular.

While in Steyr, on 8th July, Schubert received a letter from his father:

Madame Milder's father brought me this letter for you and let me read the many laudatory remarks contained in the Berlin papers about the evening concert given by his daughter on 9th June of this year, in which your compositions were also highly praised.

Among these reviews there was the following, which was, strangely enough, not forwarded, from the *Berlinische Zeitung* of 11th June:

The evening entertainment given by Madame Milder was well and glitteringly attended and afforded rich enjoyment. We hear of the grandiose voice of this singer, but we prefer her simple, noble sustained singing which she gave us in the two Goethe songs, *Suleika II* and *Erlkönig*; they were presented with true mastery, from the heart to the heart. Franz Schubert in Vienna is an ingenious song-composer who loves modulations . . . even though his compositions transcend the Lied-form, the oriental spirit has been captured in the music nevertheless. The whole idiosyncratic pianoforte accompaniment receives the colouring of the vocal part. The longing of tender love is symbolised accurately by the music. The *Erlkönig* is highly original and treated with tragic earnestness. Night and horror, storm and terror are painted in this nocturnal piece with fearful fantasy.

In the letters which Frau Milder wrote to Schubert, we again see that Schubert was by no means uncritical about the poems which he set. The diva asked Schubert to set Karl Leitner's 'Der Nachtschmetterling'—Schubert had set many of Leitner's poems—and Goethe's 'Verschiedene Empfindungen an einem Platz'. Schubert ignored both suggestions, as he ignored Rochlitz's 'Der erste Ton' and Zedlitz's 'Nächtliche Heerschau', and in 1828, he rejected one of Seidl's poems as well.

Schubert replied to his father's letter on 25th July:

I felt at home at Traweger's, absolutely free. Later, when *Hofrat* von Schiller arrived—he is the monarch of the whole Salzkammergut—we (Vogl and I) dined daily at his home and played a lot of music there, as well as at Traweger's. My new songs, from Walter Scott's *Lady of the Lake,* were especially well received. People were also surprised at my piety expressed in my Hymn to the Blessed Virgin, which, it seems, moved everyone and made them feel devout. I think that that comes because I never force myself to be devout, and except when I am involuntarily overpowered by it, would never compose such hymns or prayers, but, when I do, it is usually the right and true devoutness.

In Steyeregg we visited Countess Weissenwolf, who is a great admirer of my humble self and possesses all my things and sings many of them very prettily. The Walter Scott songs made such a very favourable impression on her that she made it quite clear that their dedication to her would not at all displease her. I am thinking however of a different procedure than the usual (which yields so little profit), with the publication of these songs, since they bear the celebrated name of Scott on their foreheads and could therefore awaken more curiosity, and, if the English text were added, could make me better known in England as well. If only one could do some decent transactions with these —— of publishers—but the State has seen to it that its wise and beneficent laws make the artist remain forever the slave of every miserable shopkeeper.

With respect to Milder's letter, I was delighted with the favourable reception of the *Suleika* song, although I wish I could have seen the review for myself, to see if I could not have learned something from it; for, however favourable the verdict might be, it can also be laughable if the reviewer lacks the necessary intelligence, which is none too rarely the case.

Two days after Schubert's letter to his parents, Anton Ottenwalt wrote to Josef von Spaun about the visit of Schubert and Vogl to his house and their performance of the Scott songs:

Even if I cannot speak equally well of his latest songs by Scott, I also cannot keep silent about them. There are five in particular: *Ave Maria,* Ellen's evening song and prayer for her father in the wilderness where they are hiding. 2. *Warrior's Rest*: An ingratiating lullaby such as Armida might sing to Rinaldo's magic harp. [The references are to characters from Tasso's *Gerusalemme liberata,* a much-used theme for nineteenth-century opera. Ed.]

3. *Huntsman's Rest*. Also a lullaby, simpler and more intense, I feel. The accompaniment: a horn song, I should say like the echo of a hunting-song in a beautiful dream. 4. *The imprisoned hunter*. 'Mein Roß im Stalle so müde sich steht . . .' ['My horse is weary of his stall'] . . . accompaniment—now how can I describe the angry, throbbing, stabbing broken chords? I am almost ashamed that I even thought of writing about them. My dear friend, we kept on wishing that you could hear it! If we could only bring the melodies into your dreams, as they surround us into the sinking hours of the night!—Schubert was so friendly and communicative . . . When he spoke of art, poetry, of his youth, of his friends and other important people, of the relationship of ideals to life . . . etc.—I could not help but marvel again and again at this genius of whom it is said that his artistic achievements are so unconscious, that he himself is barely aware of them and barely understands them and so on. And how simple everything is—I cannot speak of the extent and the wholeness of his convictions— but these were glimpses of a very personal philosophy of life, and the share which his noble friends may have of it detracts not at all from the uniqueness of mind expressed in it.

In September the two friends arrived in Bad Gastein; Schubert was working on a symphony, and two songs of Ladislaus Pyrker, whom they had met here. Before leaving on 4th September, Schubert recorded his name in the guest-of-honour book of the celebrated 'Wildbad' inn as 'abgereist' ('departed').

The Catholic priest and future Archbishop of Venice, Johann Ladislaus Pyrker von Felsö-Eör (1772–1842), maintained throughout his life an interest in social welfare. He established convalescent homes in Karlsruhe and Gastein for soldiers wounded in the wars with France, and also strove to raise the general standards of the teaching profession by founding a teachers' training college. The influences of Klopstock's *Messias* is reflected in his own epic poetry. Schubert had dedicated *Der Wanderer* to him and also set two of his poems. Pyrker wrote once to Schubert, 'I am proud to belong to the same fatherland as you!'

Das Heimweh (D 851) did not appear in print before its publication as a song, and it can be assumed that Pyrker wrote it especially for Schubert. How well the composition recaptures the essence of the songs of the mountaineers is evidenced by the assumption of the Leipzig *Allgemeine Musikalische Zeitung* on 23rd January 1828 that the song was based on a theme from the *Ranz des Vaches*. This so-called *Emmentaler Lied* (Song of the Emmental) bears in fact little resemblance to Schubert's composition. The later opus 79, dedicated to Pyrker, is one of Schubert's cantata-like pieces, but it is far superior to the Zumsteegian bombast of his earlier works. The longing of the young mountaineer, attached to his homeland 'mit kindlicher Lieb'' ('with childish affection') for his mountains, was a popular poetic *motif* of the age (cf. Robert Burns!). Schubert structures the outward sections like a scherzo; the second version (that of the Mandyczewski Edition), through the repetition of the final part, surprisingly and radically extends and develops this scherzo: Particularly in the passage

> Sieht das dunkele Föhrengehölz,
> Die ragende Felswand über ihm,
> Und noch Berg auf Berg in erschütternder
> Hoheit aufgetürmt,
> Und glühend im Rosenschimmer des Abends.

(He sees the dark coppice of firs, the sheer mountain rock above him, and peak upon peak towering on high in frightening majesty, glowing in the roseate hue of the evening.)

Schubert departs from the somewhat old-fashioned musical language of the opening of the song and seizes the listener's attention with a power reminiscent of *An Schwager Kronos*. *Das Heimweh* reflects the overpowering effect that the Austrian landscape had on him.

While Vogl was trying to soothe his arthritic joints in the thermal baths, Schubert was enjoying the mountain air of the glaciers in the nearby Hohen Tauern mountains. The tunes of the cowherds and the peasants enchanted him, and they reappear in his music; even the most sophisticated harmonies cannot completely conceal them.

The other Pyrker song is certainly the most concentrated of all Schubert's religious works: *Die Allmacht*. Both his friends and his family took exception to the unorthodox form in which he expressed his relationship to the transcendental. Schubert found no doubts to plague him in Pyrker's hymn to God in Nature, and he must have welcomed the opportunity to give vent to his deepest emotions. However, there is no contradiction between Schubert's unorthodox beliefs and his setting of texts which hymn the Almighty: 'Groß ist Jehova, der Herr!' (Great is Jehovah the Lord!) transcends romantic *Biedermeier* and religious obscurantism alike. As Schubert put it in a long travel report to his brother Ferdinand on 21st September, the sight of mountains creates the relationship to the Divine. One has to admire the poetic way in which Schubert can express his feelings about Nature in words as well as in music:

So we went on through Gölling, where we came across the first high, impassable mountains, whose frightening ravines are traversed by the Lueg Pass. After we had slowly scrambled up one huge mountain with terrible ones on either side and in front of our noses, as though the world were boarded off, suddenly, on reaching the highest point of the mountain, we were looking down into a fearful ravine and, for the first moment, it threatens to make your heart tremble. After you have recovered from the first shock, you see these enormously high sheer rock-faces which seem to close together some way off, like a *cul-de-sac*, and you look in vain for an exit. Amid these terrifying natural obstacles, man tried to immortalise his still more terrifying bestiality. For it was here that the Bavarians, on the one side, and the Tyrolese on the other side of the [River] Salzach, which roars along its course far, far below, committed that gruesome massacre in which the Tyrolese, concealed in the rock caves, fired down with hellish shouts of joy on the Bavarians, who were striving to gain the pass, and who plunged down mortally wounded into the depths, without ever knowing whither the shots came. People have sought partly to commemorate and partly to expiate these most infamous happenings which continued for several days and weeks, by erecting holy symbols, a chapel on the Bavarian and a red cross on the Tyrolese side. O glorious Christ, for how many shameful deeds must You lend Your image, You who Yourself are the most terrible memorial to human depravity. They erect Your image as if to say: See! Our impious feet have trampled on God's most perfect creation—should it then be difficult to destroy that other noxious insect, Man, with an easy conscience?

The powerful closing double homage of *Die Allmacht* (D 852), which underlines and extends the meaning of the poem, can be more effective than any of the other intensified repetitions in Schubert. He has unerringly blended together the most disparate nuances of expression—pathos, longing, and great dramatic tension. There is good reason for the appeal of this song to powerful voices, but the many lyrical passages prescribed *pianissimo* should not be overlooked. The song falls victim all too frequently to the 'Brünnhilde'-type of voice. Of course it demands a big voice with a wide range, but intensity of expression and meaningful interpretation are much more important. It is not enough to trumpet forth Jehovah's greatness and his revelation through Nature.

The song is no sooner under way than Schubert's charming A flat major turns up on the words 'sternebesäten Himmels' ('star-spangled Heaven'), and the singer must then proclaim the Almighty 'more feelingly' (fühlbarer noch'). The ending, too, looks inward, and when the plea ascends Heavenwards ('empor'), the high note must not ring out too obtrusively, but must grow out of the depth of the emotions and express the hope of 'Huld und Erbarmen' ('grace and mercy'); then the colossal emphasis of the final 'Groß ist Jehova, der Herr' will be all the more convincing. God is not only *seen* here—he is *felt* with all our being.

In the 'travel-report' requested by his brother Ferdinand, Schubert went on to describe Salzburg and, at the same time, the feeling of a musician who was entering a region of creative activity:

And now we come through some magnificent avenues into the town itself. Fortifications of ashlar surround this famous seat of the former Electoral Princes. The town gates with their inscriptions proclaim the vanished might of the clericals. You see only four- or five-storeyed houses along the broad streets; after passing the curiously decorated house of Theophrastus Paracelsus, the bridge leads you over the River Salzach which rushes past, dark and troubled. The town itself made a somewhat gloomy impression on me, for dull weather made the old buildings darker still, and, over it all, the castle which stands on the highest point of the Mönchsberg and sends its ghostly greeting down into every street of the town. Since soon after our arrival it began to rain, which happens very often here, we could not see a great deal, apart from the many palaces and superb churches which we saw as we drove by. Through Herr Pauernfeind, a merchant friend of Herr von Vogl, we were introduced to Count von Platz, the President of the Law Courts, whose family, having already heard our names, welcomed us most warmly. Vogl sang some of my songs, whereupon we were invited for the following evening and requested to show our wares before a very select circle. They were much appreciated by all, particularly the *Ave Maria*, which I mentioned in my first letter. The way in which Vogl sings and I accompany, how we appear at that moment to be one, is something quite new and unheard-of for these people.[1]

There are also touching scenes in the audiences at Linz. Once the concert had to be broken off, 'because after the performance of some sad songs, all the ladies and girls dissolved into tears, and even the men could hardly keep theirs back'.

Spaun refers here to the great novelty of the seven Scott songs in which a new Viennese publisher had shown an interest and had asked Schubert for a 'beginner's'-price. This was the manager, Franz Hüther, of the newly-founded Pennauer Verlag, to which Schubert, before departing for Upper Austria, had given *Suleika II*, *Nacht und Träume* and *Die junge Nonne* as well as the A minor Sonata. According to Lachner, Schubert thought that the 'beginner' referred to himself and refused to give the firm the Scott cycle. This bi-lingual collection of songs, a good commercial proposition, was then published by Artaria.

Die junge Nonne attained its final version on this journey. Above all, Collin's *Nacht und Träume* (D 827) (incomprehensibly attributed in many editions to Schiller) is shown to be one of the most magical of Schubert's *adagio* settings. This is not the only Schubert song which calls for such breath control that the 4/4 rhythm can hardly encompass the slow tempo. These songs are so full of a longing for purity and of devotion that only the controlled rhythm prevents them from spilling over into unbounded emotion. Melody and rhythm together trace a line, which, when followed by the listener, affords a sensation of inner release. Out of the serene, low, accompanying chords, the long-drawn-out vocal line in the second part leads into the 'listening' G major ('die belauschen sie mit Lust')

[1] Curiously enough, Mozart's name is never mentioned.

('they eavesdrop with joy'), and then returns with unreal beauty into the original key of B major, until the music whispers away into nothingness. As it finishes, the singer seems to be kneeling down in prayerful meditation. The first and second parts are separated by the descending third, yet, at the same time, connected by the relationship of B major to G major. The end of the song echoes the end of the first section, giving a sense of cohesion. The only dynamic notation is *pp,* but this does not mean that the singer is not allowed to follow the text by a barely perceptible increase in volume, for example, on the word 'Lust' ('joy'), the joy of eavesdropping on dreams, in the middle section. (Schubert left singers many such possibilities of interpretation.) After the song had been neglected for generations, Johann Messchaert, the baritone, rescued this superb masterpiece from oblivion, a worthy tribute from Schubert to his friend Matthäus von Collin, who had died in 1824.

In the same September of 1825, Schubert read *Lacrimas,* a play by Wilhelm von Schütz (1776–1847), and set two of the interpolated vocal numbers, *Florio* (D 857 no. 1) and *Delphine* (D 857 no. 2). The Peters Edition attributes them both, wrongly, to the elder Schlegel, a mistake made even in the first edition of 1829. *Landrat* von Schütz had retired in 1811 and devoted himself to literary and historical studies, as well as to political journalism, but he really made his name as the publisher of the first German edition of Casanova's works (F. A. Brockhaus, Leipzig, 1822–1828). That he should later become the subject of the doctoral thesis of a certain Joseph Goebbels seems almost grotesque.

Florio, a dancing serenade which almost banishes the sorrowful sentiments of the poem, was followed by *Delphine,* an enormous song, based on a constant flowing piano theme, and universally condemned as unperformable. On the only occasion that I have ever heard it, however, at a recital by Eleanor Steber, a singer who is always looking for neglected material, I had the impression that it offered a big voice extremely interesting possibilities. The most interesting musical structures are in the exhausting of a mood rich in contrasts, in confused distraught states: 'Wie kann mich mit Schmerz so bestreuen die Freude?' ('How can joy bring me such pain?'). Before the preceding seventh can be resolved, the Neapolitan B flat major chord on the word 'Freude' ('joy') is driven in like a wedge, whose own 'Fürsichleuchten' ('shining for itself') puts the 'joy' into sharp focus. The feeling of tonality widens, the cadence is expanded and the tone becomes independent. Yet there are even more daring examples in Schubert's work of a Romanticism projected into our own age.

On 19th October 1825 the publishing firm Artaria & Co. paid Schubert a substantial sum (some 200 florins) for the Scott songs, which were, as promised, dedicated as opus 52 to Countess Sofie von Weißenwolf, née von Brenner (1794–1847). The English text preceded the German; the metre of *Normans Gesang* caused the translator difficulties, however, and it was decided to make a new German version to match the rhythm of the original English. The onrushing, galloping, dotted rhythms of *Normans Gesang* (D 846) make great demands on a pianist's wrists and are a rewarding challenge for the declamatory technique of a singer. The torrent of words is skilfully caught up in this explosive gallop, and the song is over in a flash. It is no wonder that Ottenwalt wrote to Josef von Spaun on 27th July: 'Vogl performs it heavily but magnificently, with a syllable, often a whole word on each note.' (It is likely that the revealing caricature, probably by Schober, was done during this journey; the singer is at the front of the scene; behind him, almost hidden, the shy, retiring pianist and creator of the songs.)

On 3rd October, the last Linz Schubertiad was held at Anton von Spaun's, after which Vogl and Schubert parted company; Vogl was going to Italy with an old friend. Schubert travelled back to Vienna with Josef von Gahy (1793–1864) in a hired coach which took three days for the journey. Schubert was never to see this much-loved countryside again.

TWELVE
Prelude to <u>Die Winterreise</u>, 1826 - 1827

After his return to Vienna Schubert spent many long evenings with his friends but strenuously refused Bauernfeld's and Schwind's offer to move in with them. He did not want to lose his old room in the street 'Auf der Wieden'.

> As to moving in with you [he wrote to Bauernfeld from Steyr on 18th (or 19th) September] it would be very pleasant indeed, but as I already know this sort of bachelor and student life, I shouldn't like to end up sitting on the ground between two stools.

The need to isolate himself within his own four walls, no longer to have to appear so often socially, and to concentrate on his work, had become particularly apparent in February 1825 when Schubert was working on his setting of Schlechta's *Des Sängers Habe* (D 832). The song begins with a defiant gesture, then the singer becomes more and more absorbed in the dreamy music of the zither, here an allegory of the art of composing. But when Schubert was with his friends, he gave no signs of being unsociable. Now that he had received his first satisfactory return from the sale of the new Scott songs, the money was divided, according to Bauernfeld, like this:

> Naturally it was Schubert who played the part of Croesus and swam in silver whenever he had sold a few songs or even a cycle, like the Scott songs for which Artaria paid him 200 florins, a sum with which he was very pleased, and which he wanted to put aside—but, as always, it stopped at the intention. At the beginning he would live and entertain handsomely and give away money right and left—but then it was back to short commons. In short, the tides went in and out.

In a letter (27th November 1825) Ottenwalt wrote to his brother-in-law, Josef von Spaun, he said:

> I have nothing to tell you or us about Schubert. His works reveal the genius who creates the divine, unharmed by the passions of an all-consuming sensuality, and he seems to care deeply about his friends. He is cheerful, and, I hope, also well.

Hofrat Raphael von Kiesewetter invited Schubert frequently to his house. He was vice-president of the *Gesellschaft der Musikfreunde* and a sometime pupil of Salieri, but it was not so much his amateur singing voice which attracted Schubert as his charming daughter, Irene, who was also a fine accompanist. There really does not seem to be any substance in the contemporary rumour of an affair between them; this was perhaps welcomed to fill in the lack of sentimental background to Schubert's life. It seems rather that their relations were as proper as the works dedicated to Irene, a choral work (*Der Tanz*, D 826) and an Italian cantata (D 936). However, the pulsating setting of Ernst Schulze's *An mein Herz* (D 860) might indicate a secret passion. A note of unrequited love speaks out of the little variations of the restless accompaniment to:

> O Herz! sei endlich stille!
> Was schlägst du so unruhvoll?
> Es ist ja des Himmels Wille
> Daß ich sie lassen soll.

(O heart, be still! Why do you beat so restlessly? It is Heaven's will that I should leave her.)

The brief move into the major does nothing to lessen the heart's agitation.

On 6th December 1825, he paid another visit to Sophie Müller, as she noted in her diary:

> Schubert came too and we made music until half-past nine. I very much like the four-handed overture [to *Alfonso und Estrella*] and his latest compositions from W. Scott's *Lady of the Lake*.

On 1st January 1926, Bauernfeld wrote in his diary: 'New Year's Eve at Schober without Schubert, who was ill. . . .'

Although Schubert had recovered from the original neurasthenia, he still suffered from violent headaches and other disorders, whose venereal cause he knew only too well.

During this period Schubert set Goethe's *Lied der Mignon* (Nur wer die Sehnsucht kennt) (D 877 nos. 1 and 4) from *Wilhelm Meister,* for the fifth and sixth times. The duet version (D 877 no. 4) comes closest to the original, since it is sung in *Wilhelm Meister* as 'an irregular duet with the most touching expression', a phrase which should be recommended as the most accurate interpretative guide. The poem may well lose some of its intimacy when sung as a duet, and it is likely that it was written before the novel anyway. Yet the beauty of the music of the duet is far and away superior to that of the solo versions. The poem clearly reflected Schubert's personal experiences.

The last solo version of *Nur wer die Sehnsucht kennt* (D 877 no. 1), touchingly simple in the main section and dramatically intense in the middle one, expresses sadness with great economy of means.

Heiß mich nicht reden (D 877 no. 2) in the minor key is reserved and chastely secretive. At the word 'Geheimnis' ('secret'), the melody moves into the major, pauses there to take a relieving breath, and then returns resignedly to the basic tonality. A swelling melody animates the middle section, and in the major mode of the final stanza 'ein jeder sucht im Arm des Freundes Ruh' ('each one seeks rest in the friend's arms'), Schubert reveals his most intimate emotions. A declamatory pathos then raises the song to a mysterious grandeur. The exhausted tones of longing in the closing words demand a singer who can employ her head tones in the service of the poem without any trace of coquetry. Schubert seems to have felt himself limited by the strophic form, for, although the music looks inward and faithfully follows the words of the poem, the second stanza differs from the first. The third has only tenuous connections with the first with flights into declamation. The 'death-rhythm' haunts the song, hinting at the relationship between love and death.

Mignon's farewell *So laßt mich scheinen* (D 877 no. 3), a strophic song with variations, expresses in childlike music the renunciaton of this earth. There is no trace here of the fear of death. The modulations to the minor seem only transitory, like unhappy memories fleeing before joyous thoughts of the future.

It is characteristic that, this time as well, the Mignon and the

Harper's Songs should be set and not Philine's lighter, gayer 'Singet nicht in Trauertönen'. Schubert comes close to the border-line of light-heartedness—but he never oversteps it. This is where his Romantic contemporaries, like Loewe and Schumann, and his successors, like Wolf, have rounded out the world of Lieder. On his own admission, Schubert did not master these songs on the first occasion, or, at any rate, he found that time had overtaken his settings. Years lie between the earlier and these later versions; one has the impression that he had waited for the right moment to give them validity, to set to music the secret that 'only a god can unlock'.

On 25th January 1826, at Sophie Müller's villa in Hitzing, where he was a regular visitor, Schubert sang songs based on Ernst Schulze's poems. Sophie sight-read such songs as *Die junge Nonne*, *Die Rose*, *Lied der Annot* (*Anne*) *Lyle* (D 830) and *Ellens Gesänge*; they must have lain well for her voice, since Hüttenbrenner reports that she had sung these ones in particular 'most touchingly'.

Sophie Müller died only a year after Schubert. Ernst Schulze (1789–1817), from Celle, had published numerous poems, although he was actually a lecturer in philology at Göttingen. He had taken part in the Wars of Liberation in 1814.

In the spring of 1826, Schubert was so captivated by Schulze's poems that he sat in his room near the Karlskirche and composed nine songs and an ensemble to them. The name of Ernst Schulze was familiar to him since, only the previous year, he had asked Bauernfeld for a libretto based on Schulze's *Die bezauberte Rose* (see pp. 83 and 207), but it was never written. The libretto, which Schubert's doctor, Dr J. Bernhardt, wrote and which Schubert took with him to Hungary in 1824, has never been found. Bauern-feld, who was well aware of the dramatic weaknesses in the play, probably heaved a sigh of relief when Franz von Schober wrote to him in June 1826: 'You've lost the "Enchanted Rose". The Mayor of Teplitz has made an opera out of it.' (The name of this composer was Joseph Maria Wolfram, born 1789, and his opera was still being performed in Germany in this century.)

In general, the Schulze settings are long, not in the sense that Schubert's early cantatas were long, but rather in a kind of relentless exposition of a musical idea over long stretches, without any formal concession to changes in mood.

'Und mit mir wandert meine Qual / Will nimmer von mir

scheiden' (My agony wanders with me and will never leave my side) sings the lonely wanderer in *Im Walde* (D 834), and Schubert turns this comparatively innocuous reflection of the poet into vivid, onward-rushing despair. Just as in *Erstarrung*, in *Winterreise*, the scurrying triplets never cease, and if, in the latter song, flowers are sought as a symbol of warmth, here they are left standing by the roadside—for they cannot bring the hoped-for consolation.

All the Schulze poems come from the *Poetisches Tagebuch* (the Poetic Diary) to be found at the beginning of Volume III of his Collected Works published by Brockhaus.

'Ich wand're über Berg und Tal' has the title *Im Walde hinter Falkenhagen*, under the date 22nd July 1814. These are probably the woods of Seulingen near Göttingen where the poet wandered restlessly over the fields and meadows. And it is, of course, no coincidence that the lines,

> Wo find' ich eine Blüte?
> Wo find' ich grünes Gras?

> (Where can I find a flower, where can I find green grass?)

from *Erstarrung* in the *Winterreise*, offer the key to Schulze's song, since the melody is like a preliminary study for the *Winterreise* song.

The inspiration behind Schulze's poetry was Caecilie Tychsen, a beautiful intelligent girl who, a student of Forkel, played a good deal of Bach's keyboard music and urged Schulze on to the twenty-seven verses of his poem *Sebastian Bachs Apotheose*, to a poem on the 'Musikalische Fantasie' and one to Saint Cecilia. Schulze added to the poem on the 'Musikalische Fantasie':

> It is an attempt to clothe in thoughts and words the various impressions which a rich musical composition makes on our emotions. Of course such an attempt can never be completely successful, because music is too mystical for rational contemplation. The inspiration for it was the Chromatic Fantasia of Sebastian Bach, an artist whom the most perceptive judges recognise to be the greatest harmonist of all time.

It is regrettable that Schubert and Schulze never met. In 1817, shortly after the death of his beloved Caecilie, not quite eighteen, Schulze himself died of tuberculosis. That his poetry reflected Schubert's own personal *Weltanschauung* is shown by the latter's use of these poems to perfect the form of the modified strophic song which was to play so essential a rôle in Schubert's last works.

Shortly before his death Schubert gave the Schott publishing house in Mainz the Schulze songs along with some Goethe, Schiller and Schlegel settings.

In the stormy D minor of *Über Wildemann* (Wildemann is a small township in the Harz Mountains) (D 884), the combination of self-willed *sforzati* and violent broken chords borders on the daemonic. The passage,

> Ich muß vorüber mit wildem Sinn
> Und blicke lieber zum Winter hin.

(I must hurry past in this wild mood, preferring Winter's tempers.)

shows the textual relationship to *Winterreise* as well. Both in musical structure and vocal line, the song anticipates Brahms.

The B flat major of *Um Mitternacht* (D 862) lends the song a deep soulfulness. The lines

> Keine Stimme hör' ich schallen,
> Keinen Schritt auf dunkler Bahn,

(I hear no voice, no step on the darkened paths,)

are a tone-painting of the gentle ecstasy which the leap of a ninth in the vocal line intensifies. The numerous stanzas account for the seeming monotony of this hymn. We are brought closer to the period of Schubert's last great song-cycle with *An mein Herz* (D 860), whose syncopated A minor chords depict a heart in turmoil. This completely unknown jewel may be confidently recommended to any lover of the *Winterreise* who does not yet know it.

Tiefes Leid (D 876) seems to come from the very heart of the *Winterreise* cycle:

> An einem Ort nur find' ich Frieden,
> Das ist der Ort, wo alles ruht.

(I shall find peace in one place only, the place where all are at rest.)

The similarities to *Rückblick* (in the *Winterreise*) extend even to the texts, for example where Schulze speaks of the 'unbeständigen

Welt' ('the fickle world'). Schubert must have had the music to *Tiefes Leid* in mind when he came to the passage 'du Stadt der Unbeständigkeit' (the 'fickle town'), in *Rückblick*.

Der liebliche Stern (D 861) contains rather less pathos and suffering. The passage 'Wohl und Wehe' ('bliss and torment') is divided perhaps too schematically into the major and the minor.

The most graceful of the Schulze settings is *Im Frühling* (D 882), whose gently flowing movement is permeated with the magical atmosphere of romantic nature. Two of Schubert's best-known melodies, continually and expressively varied, personify German Romanticism. The structure is finely delineated, and the principle of the variations emerges mainly from the combination of the accompanying figures, the rhythm and, particularly, the harmony. Schubert combines the six stanzas into three sets 'of pairs, and each of these new divisions contains two related and recurring melodies. The piano prelude's way of introducing the second of the first pair of melodies is particularly attractive, and has been copied in countless drawing-room *chansons*. The music gives us the serenity and joy of a spring morning, rather than the sentimental laments of the poet.

Schulze was indeed fortunate to have Schubert interested in his poems in these years 1825–1826, a time when almost every note that Schubert wrote bore the stamp of genius. In view of the perfect blending of word and music in *Im Frühling*, it is surprising that the dialogue *Blume und Quell* remained unfinished.

Both Schubert and Schulze took a lively interest in the tense political situation of their day and they shared the note of resignation which Schubert found for Schulze's lines for one of the best of his settings for male chorus:

> Gewagt und gewonnen!
> Schrieb mancher aufs Schwert;
> Gewagt und zerronnen!
> Ist mir nur beschert.

(Many a warrior wrote: ventured and victorious! on his sword; Ventured and lost! was my fate.)

A great Schubertiad took place in April 1826, attended by musicians and painters, at which *Totengräbers Heimwehe* (D 842), composed in 1825, from the poem of Jakob Craigher, was first sung in public. Craigher had been a merchant and later became Belgian consul in Austria. He travelled all over the East and composed poems and made translations from English literature. Born in 1797, he was a friend of Friedrich Schlegel, Zacharias Werner and the other Romantics. He died in 1855. (See p. 205.)

All three Craigher settings were written in 1825. *Totengräbers Heimwehe* was to occupy a very special place among German Lieder —but it had to wait until after Schubert's death before it was thought to be commercially viable. Even today, it is difficult to see what made this song—related in its sentiments to Bruckner's symphonies—such a popular favourite. In addition, it is very difficult to identify the singer, that is, Schubert himself, with the woes and wails of the Romantic gravedigger, who was already rather out of fashion, even at that time. The music has nevertheless enormous power, the accented notes in the score bring the gravedigger's shovelling in the darkness (represented in the bass) closer to the indicated and required *rubato*, and this provides the foundation from which the song develops. This restless 4/8 *motif* then changes to the transfigured mysticism of the 'death-rhythm', thus symbolising the union of the gravedigger longing for release from this life, with those to whom release has already been granted.[1]

Joseph Eybler had in 1824 replaced the infirm Antonio Salieri as Principal Music Director to the Court, and after he learned that negotiations with two foreign applicants had fallen through, Schubert resolved to apply for the position of Assistant Music Director. His application, on 7th April 1826, went directly to Emperor Franz II, and listed *inter alia* the following special qualifications:

> Through his vocal and instrumental compositions, his name has received favourable attention, not only in Vienna, but throughout Germany. . . .

[1] Reference might be made here to the incisive structural analyses of this and other Schubert songs given by Hans Joachim Moser in his *Deutsches Lied seit Mozart* ('The German Lied since Mozart'), 2 vols. Berlin, 1937. These could hardly be more comprehensive or more helpful. However, the advice on interpretation which he offers to the student in his *Singakademie* ('Singer's studio') could lead to misunderstandings, which is the reason why in this book such advice or suggestions as to interpretations have largely been avoided. Neither recordings nor the printed word can be a substitute for a course of study tailored to the individual needs of a student under the supervision of a teacher or an accompanist.

6. Finally, he enjoys no position at the moment, and believes that he will be able to reach his ultimate artistic goal only in a secure career. To do complete justice to the most gracious acceptance of this petition will be the most serious endeavours of Your most devoted servant, Franz Schubert.

Schubert's offer to exchange his freedom for a secure official appointment may well have been only half-hearted, for he had already refused the post of Deputy Court Organist which could have easily led to the position for which he was now applying. Why then did he make this new application? There were signs nevertheless that he was adopting a rather more sober and critical attitude to life, for he said to Josef Hüttenbrenner: 'The State must support me, I was born for nothing but composing.'

Schubert waited until January 1827 only to learn that they had appointed Josef Weigl (born in 1766 and already retired) to the post—the Court had to pay him only a small salary and thus saved money—a typically Viennese solution!

Schubert made the laconic comment: 'Since they chose such a deserving man, I will just have to put up with it!'

The next Schulze poem which he set, *Lebensmut* (D 883), probably reflected his mood at this period. The first verse reads:

> O, wie dringt das junge Leben
> Kräftig mir durch Sinn und Herz!
> Alles fühl' ich glüh'n und streben,
> Fühle doppelt Lust und Schmerz.

(O how young life pulses through my mind and heart. I feel everything glowing and striving, feel pain and joy in double measure.)

But the seeming healthy energy which these opening lines suggest is deceptive, for two of the five stanzas are set in the minor. (Schubert supplied most of the titles to Schulze's poems, since the author simply dated his works.)

The last two songs from poems by A. W. Schlegel are really only peripheral products. Only by omitting one or two of the unnecessary repetitions of *Wiedersehen* (D 855), a purely strophic song, can 'der Freude leises Aufgebot' ('the gentle promise of joy to come') be enjoyed. But one just has to put up with the eight boring stanzas of *Abendlied für die Entfernte* (D 856), since Schubert only omitted one verse of Schlegel's tiring meditation. It is an embarrassment to the most sympathetic interpreter. The last verse might have been the attraction for Schubert, for he could have written it himself:

> Mit hohem Trotz im Ungemach
> Trägt es, was ihm beschieden,
> So schlumm'r ich ein, so werd' ich wach,
> In Lust nicht, doch in Frieden.

(With great defiance it bears its fate, and so I slumber and wake again, if not happy, at least at peace.)

The song was published in 1827 as opus 88 no. 1.

But there were not *only* disappointments in Schubert's professional life. Since 1816 a group of poets, journalists, musicians, painters and academics had been meeting almost every evening, at first in an inn 'Zum Blumenstöckl', and later in the 'Pfuntnersche Bierhaus'. The group took its name 'Ludlams-Höhle' ('Ludlam's Cave') from a fairy-tale by the Dane, Adam Oehlenschläger, being performed at the time at the Theater an der Wien.

The humour and the intelligence here belonged to the intellectual élite of Vienna, and, since among its members were several poets whose poems Schubert had set, such as Castelli, Grillparzer, Zedlitz, Rückert, Seidl and Rellstab, not to mention musicians such as Beethoven, Gyrowetz, Moscheles, Weber and Salieri, it was not surprising that Schubert and Bauernfeld also applied for membership. The members produced periodicals in the inn which were read out on certain days of the week and which bore titles like 'Fliegende Blätter für Magen und Herz' ('Fly-sheets for stomach and heart'), 'Der Wächter' ('The Observer') and 'Die Arschwische' ('The Arse-Wiper'). The police became suspicious and smelt a conspiracy. In April 1826, the members had their houses searched, all their writings and the group's meagre funds fell into the hands of the police. After the closure of 'Ludlams-Höhle', it was discovered that there had been a serious mistake. Only a few pornographic cartoons had given the police authorities the slender excuse to accuse the club of being an 'erotic secret society'! Schubert and Bauernfeld saw themselves cheated of the opportunity of profiting from the intellectual, social and possibly even financial advantages accruing from membership of this group.

Schubert neglected himself in the summer of 1826; he idled about and drank heavily, while waiting for Bauernfeld to finish the libretto of the opera *Der Graf von Gleichen*. (On 6th June, the von Hartmann brothers (see p. 183) began keeping their diaries. The entry reads: 'Dashed off to Walding. Sang the loveliest Schubert songs on the way.')

Sophie Müller, who had taken to copying down Schubert songs, noted in her diary for 26th June that the 58-year-old Johann Michael Vogl had married a certain Kunigunde Rosa. The thermal baths in Gastein, and his Italian journey, seem to have rejuvenated the singer, and he amazed his friends with this late marriage. The old bachelor's choice had fallen on the daughter of the Court painter, Rosa. She was no youngster either and can be seen immortalised in Schwind's charming painting of a Schubertiad. The couple spent their honeymoon (without Schubert, of course) in Steyr, and thus Schubert was deprived of his annual musical journey.

Schubert never paid for any of his journeys out of his own pocket. Not wishing to remain in Vienna, he went with Schwind and Schober to Währing, where the latter had rented a cottage, since he had had to give up his own lodgings to a diplomat. In July 1826, Währing was still a village on the outskirts of Vienna. The house, surrounded by lilac and elderberry bushes, seemed itself to symbolise the romantic group of Viennese friends, set, as it was, in the valley of the River Wien on the edge of the town, with courtyard and bower and a wonderful view of the hills by the Danube.

The trio loafed about, did a few exercises in the sun—and worked. When the nights were warm, they slept outdoors. Schubert's new friendship with Bauernfeld had, alas, not led to the hoped-for libretto, but the poet now introduced him to Shakespeare's dramas.

The credit for the popularising of Shakespeare's works in Germany is rightly given to the translators, August Wilhelm Schlegel and the Tiecks, although they did not translate all of his plays into German. With the help of some young literary men (Ferdinand Meyerhofer von Grünbühel and Bauernfeld himself, for example), the indefatigable Josef Trentsentsky (the publisher of Schwind's popular 'Mandlbogen' lithographs of patriotic scenes) had undertaken a 'Wiener Ausgabe' (Vienna Edition) of Shakespeare's works. He commissioned Bauernfeld to translate *Antony and Cleopatra* and *The Two Gentlemen of Verona*. There have been many unsuccessful attempts (including Hans Joachim Moser's) to substitute a more satisfactory text for Bauernfeld's poor translation of the page's song *An Sylvia* (D 891), from *The Two Gentlemen of Verona*. Fortunately, the stilted, wooden text has not detracted from the popularity of Schubert's magical, quite unpretentious, seemingly improvised song. Its effect is achieved by the charming contrast between the emotional *legato* of the song and the *pizzicato* of the accompaniment.

Schubert then set the *Trinklied* (D 888) ('Come thou monarch of the vine'), from *Antony and Cleopatra,* to which the actor Friedrich Reil added a verse for the first edition. This does not appear however in the Collected Edition, and rightly so, since Shakespeare confined himself to six lines. Handel, and Mozart's Osmin, are the progenitors of this song, which is a jovial piece in C major and a perfect choice for an encore. The original English words can be sung to Schubert's melody.

Cymbeline, in Schlegel's translation, is the source for the famous *Ständchen* ('Hark, hark, the lark') (D 889). Bauernfeld's additional verses can be omitted, since brevity can only enhance Schubert's brilliant and charming idea of a guitar-like accompaniment. The exultant high-spirited song, with its joyous accompaniment, has conquered the world, both as a song and in manifold orchestral versions.

Only in these three cases did Schubert respond to the Shakespearean challenge. A curious inhibition may have restrained him from setting, say, the songs of Ophelia or of the fools, which had just been published in the 'Vienna Editions'. (Shortly after Schubert's death, *An Sylvia* was published with three other 1827 songs, as opus 106, dedicated to his charming hostess in Graz, Frau Marie Pachler.) The story that Schubert composed the best-known of the three Shakespeare songs (*An Sylvia*) on the back of a menu in the restaurant 'Zum Biersack' can be taken to be apocryphal.

The tiny but valuable note-book, with its pencil-drawn staves, in which Schubert wrote the Shakespeare songs, contained a fourth song—*Hippolits Lied* (D 890). The authoress, Johanna Schopen-hauer (1766–1838), was the mother of the celebrated philosopher. The poems interpolated into her novel *Gabriele* are not, however (as she admitted later), by her, but by Friedrich von Gerstenbergk. A monotonous piano obbligato accompanies the song of the desolate lover with a charming mordent. The similarity of both content and expression to *Winterreise* is striking.

Bauernfeld apparently introduced Schubert also to the young Viennese translator, Jakob Nikolaus Craigher (see p. 229), from Friaul, and a legal agreement was concluded for Craigher to trans-late English, Spanish, French and Italian poems for Schubert —these to be 'translations faithful to the original'. As in the case of the Scott songs, they were to be published in a bilingual edition, a curiously efficient-sounding venture, which however, came to naught, because Schubert used other translations for his Scott settings.

Nor did Schubert's projected opera based on Ernst Schulze's *Die bezauberte Rose* come to fruition. Schulze had died in 1817, and Schubert immortalised him, too, by the addition of *Auf der Bruck* (D 853) to his other settings; this is one of the best of his many 'riding'-songs, with a tempestuous on-driving accompaniment in octaves, which is technically as difficult as that of *Erlkönig*.

Nor had Schubert better fortune with foreign publishers. He had made contact with the Swiss publisher Nägeli about the publication of some of his piano works, but his demand (on 4th July 1826) for an advance was greeted with stony silence, and he heard no more from that source. This refusal came at a bad time; he had absolutely no money at all and so, on 10th July, he had to write to Bauernfeld:

Dear Bauernfeld!

I just cannot come to Gmunden or anywhere else—I have absolutely no money and I am not at all well either. However I'm not letting it get me down and am cheerful. But try to come to Vienna as soon as possible. Since Duport [see p. 162] wants an opera from me, but does not like any of the libretti I have set to date, it would be marvellous if your libretto were to be accepted. Then there would be at least money, maybe even fame! Schwind is completely in the dumps about Nette [Anna Hönig, Schwind's girl friend]. Vogl has got married ! ! ! Please come as soon as you can.

By the end of the month all the friends were together again; but, apart from the completed opera libretto (*Der Graf von Gleichen*), which Schubert had at last received, no ray of hope was visible on the horizon. Their poverty was oppressive and petty disputes broke out. On 12th August 1826 Schubert tried his luck by writing identical letters to two publishers at the same time—Breitkopf & Härtel, who were still insisting on their policy of 'no advance', and to the Leipzig music publisher, Heinrich Albert Probst.

Esteemed Sir!

In the hope that my name might not be completely unknown to you, I hereby venture to enquire whether you would be willing to accept some of my compositions against a modest honorarium, since I very much wish to become as well known as possible in Germany. You can make your selection from songs with pianoforte accompaniment, string quartets, pianoforte sonatas, four-handed pieces etc. etc. I have also written an Octet for two violins, viola, violoncello, double-bass, clarinet, bassoon and horn [In F, D 803]. In any event, regarding it as an honour to have entered into correspondence with you, I remain, in the hope of an early reply, respectfully, your Franz Schubert.

Herr Probst replied on 26th August:

... I am very willing to do what I can towards spreading your artistic reputation. Yet I must frankly confess that our public does not as yet sufficiently understand the unique, indeed often brilliant, yet at times also somewhat curious course of your artistic creations. I ask you therefore to bear this in mind when forwarding your manuscripts. Selected songs ...

Yet, despite all his efforts, Schubert's situation altered little. He presented his 'Gastein Symphony' (D 849) to the *Gesellschaft der Musikfreunde* and received an honorarium of 100 florins ('without reference to your gift') towards 'further artistic stimulation'.

In October, Bauernfeld recorded: 'The opera libretto banned by the censor. Schubert wants to compose it nonetheless.'

On 23rd October, the tenor Ludwig Tietze (or Titze) (1789–1850), at an evening entertainment of the *Musikfreunde*, sang *Der Einsame* (D 800) by Carl Lappe (1779–1843). Lappe, a schoolmaster and later a farmer, was Pomerania's most distinguished poet.

The two Schubert settings rescued from oblivion the name of this former pupil of Kosegarten who later became a hermit.

Schubert makes *Der Einsame* a song of praise to 'true contentment'; a *Biedermeier* figure, played as if by the bassoon, precedes the voice. Under descending semiquavers in the piano, the bass line gives the impression of fire-tongs poking at the falling embers, while, towards the end, the cricket chirps to the same musical material. But, hand in hand with the feeling of genial comfort, goes hidden pain and longing; Schubert emphasises with good reason the words 'bin ich nicht ganz allein' ('I am not completely on my own'), and invests these innocuous lines with his own general attitude to life. The high G's on the final page appeared only in Diabelli's edition of 1826. They are not in the version first published on 12th March 1825 as a supplement to the *Wiener Zeitschrift für Kunst, etc. Der Einsame* was 'rediscovered' by the Berlin operatic singer, Alexander Heinemann.

The other Lappe setting, *Im Abendrot* (D 799), is the expression of a devotion which is humbly and piercingly aware of the transitoriness of human happiness. A glance at the simple A flat major arpeggios and the tonic-dominant bass gives at best only a superficial idea of the art and craftsmanship needed to create such beauty. In some mysterious way, emotions themselves are given shape, while the religious spirit underlying the music is that of a child of nature, whose gods are the stars, the mountains, the seasons and the flowers. The feeling of enraptured silence in the presence of such natural phenomena as expressed here by the gentle sighs which accompany the setting of the sun dominates Schubert's purely religious songs.

Antonie Adamberger (born 1790), a popular Burgtheater actress, famed for her cultivated acting, sang Schubert songs as well. Shortly before her retirement from the stage, she introduced Bauernfeld as a member of the Schubert circle to Grillparzer. Although she herself was never a close friend of Schubert, she sang the Harper's Song *Wer nie sein Brot mit Tränen aß* and *Ave Maria* in October 1826 to a group which included Grillparzer. Grillparzer, returning from a visit to Goethe, met the group in the Abbey of St Florian.

The Schubertiads continued to be held. Franz von Hartmann, an attentive observer, has left us a picture of them in his diary. On 8th December he wrote:

At 8.30 I went to Spaun's (who had returned to Vienna after almost five years away) where at first I found only the two brothers and Fritz [his brother]. Then Schubert came and played a wonderful, but very melancholy composition. Eventually Schwind, Bauernfeld, Enderes and Schober. Then Schubert and Schwind sang the most marvellous Schubert songs.

The piano work was the Fantasia in G major dedicated to Spaun. The same evening they heard *Das Zügenglöcklein* (D 871), to a poem of Johann Gabriel Seidl and dedicated to Joseph Witteczek. This charming song in Ländler style was rescued by Karl Erb (see p. 310). It was moving to hear the already ageing tenor voice the apprehensive questions on hearing the tolling of the cemetery bells.

> Aber ist's ein Müder,
> Den verwaist die Brüder,
> Dem ein treues Tier
> Einzig ließ den Glauben
> An die Welt nicht rauben,
> Ruf' ihn, Gott, zu Dir!

(But if he is tired, has lost his brother, and his belief was saved by one faithful beast, then call him, Lord, to you!)

Schubert's supplication is prophetic:

> Ist's der Frohen einer,
> Der die Freuden reiner
> Lieb' und Freundschaft teilt,
> Gönn' ihm noch die Wonnen
> Unter dieser Sonnen
> Wo er gerne weilt!—

(If he is one of the happy ones who shares the joys of love and friendship, then grant him these pleasures in this world where he wants to live.)

In 1826, ten further Seidl settings followed the first one, *Der Wanderer an den Mond*.

It is to be hoped that *Am Fenster* (D 878), at present only known to a small band of devoted Schubertians, will soon become more popular. With concentration and intense emotion, Schubert touchingly translates the poet's beautiful verses into music, particularly that memory

> Als ich in mir allein mich sah,
> Und Keiner mich verstand.

(When I saw only myself in myself and no one understood me.)

The triplets in *Sehnsucht* (D 879) express the yearning to be out and about, because the lover, confined to his house by the wintry weather, can only fly in his thoughts to his beloved. The chill of *Winterreise* permeates the song, which only takes on a true shape towards the end:

> Wie mild mich's wieder grad durchglüht
> Sieh' nur, das ist ja schon ein Lied!
> Wenn mich mein Los vom Liebchen warf,
> Dann fühl' ich, daß ich singen darf.

(Now I am all aglow again! And just look here's a song after all! When Fate parted me from my beloved, I was able to sing.)

There is a personal utterance, and also 'work in progress', in this song—a preliminary study for *Erstarrung* in *Winterreise*.

Seidl's four 'Refrain-Lieder' (D 866 nos. 1–4) are something quite different (see p. 198). When they were published in 1826 as opus 95, the publisher, Thaddaeus Weigl, advertised them as a new and welcome move on Schubert's part to write more folklike music. Indeed, the two songs for female voice, *Die Unterscheidung* (no. 1) and *Die Männer sind mechant* (no. 3), are in comic couplet vein, where the girl is unable to assure the boy of her faithfulness and yet wants him all for herself, or where she is expressing her anger at her fickle lover. In *Bei dir allein* (no. 2), the male voice can go into raptures without musical or vocal restraints.

Finally, *Irdisches Glück* (no. 4) shows us how Schubert might have inserted songs into a musical play as Ferdinand Raimund did. It is a mystery why the romantic music of the first of these four songs, and the cheeky march-like melody of the last, are not better known.

On 15th December 1826 Schubert's friends celebrated Spaun's homecoming with a Schubertiad. Franz von Hartmann reported:

I went to Spaun's where a big, big Schubertiad was held. On entering, I was rudely greeted by Fritz, and very impudently by

Haas [Karl Haas, a medical student, and friend of Schubert].
The gathering was enormous. The Arneths, the Witteczeks,
the Kurzrocks, the Pompe couple, Witteczek's mother-in-law,
the wife of Dr Watteroth, Betty Wanderer, the painter Kupelwieser and his wife [Johanna Lutz, just married], Grillparzer,
Schober, Schwind, Mayrhofer and his landlord, Huber, Derfell,
Bauernfeld, Gahy, who played four-handed music beautifully
with Schubert, Vogl who sang almost 30 songs, Baron Schlechta,
and other Court officials and secretaries were there.

Mayrhofer, the recluse, had kept faith with Schubert, and Franz
von Schober had written six poems for him. It is also possible that
Schlechta's humorous trifle *Fischerweise* (D 881), composed that year,
was on Vogl's programme for that evening. The song was written
in the March and appeared in 1828 as opus 96. The naïvety of the
carefree fisherman is wittily characterised by the piano's half-bar
rhythms which also mark the flowing tempo. The poem, by the
friend of Schubert's youth, Baron Schlechta, reflects an untroubled
gaiety, and inspired Schubert to the declamatory witty caesura in
the final stanza which follows the text without disturbing the flow
of the music, by pointing ironically at the 'Hirtin' ('shepherdess'),
and then making up the time lost by speaking the words 'schlaue
Wicht' ('sly lass') almost with a laugh. Schubert omitted one of
Schlechta's stanzas which did not fit into the contrasting a–b–a–b
pattern of the music.

Schubert's vocal line is not always self-contained. As in Schlechta's
Totengräberweise (D 869), it is often so interwoven with the figures
and harmonies of the 'accompaniment' that the unity of the conception is immediately made visible. The voice is then not independent, but is entirely reliant on the harmonies. Perhaps this
harmonic richness compensates for the rather monotonous rhythmical structure of this funeral march-like composition.

The Schubertiad described above by Hartmann is the one
depicted later from memory by Moritz von Schwind in his famous
sepia drawing of 1868 ('Schubert-Abend bei Ritter von Spaun'). In
order to present a typical Schubertiad, the then sixty-four-year-old
Schwind made some adjustments by excluding many of Schubert's
friends, who were still alive and present at the gathering, and
including some who could not have been present, such as Karoline

Esterházy, or the poet Senn, whom Schwind did not even know. Spaun noted in his diary that Vogl on this occasion had sung 'not without some dandyisms', and that he had tried to compensate for his failing voice by gesticulations. Schwind is said to have made derogatory remarks to the singer about this.

Vogl also performed at this Schubertiad the *Romanze des Richard Löwenherz* (D 907) from Scott's 'The Crusader's Return' ('high deeds achieved of knightly fame'), in which the dotted rhythms of the two simulated fanfares in the accompaniment convey a sense of irresistible vitality. However, the song would have lent itself better to an instrumental treatment, since Schubert cannot avoid monotony over the eight pages of the music.

In January 1827, Schubert wrote his only setting of poems by Ignaz Franz Castelli (1781–1862), the librettist of his opera *Der häusliche Krieg*. This charming Viennese writer's *Memoiren meines Lebens* give a delightful picture of his age. He is also said to have composed a pornographic satire on Schiller's *Lied von der Glocke* (1799) ('The Song of the Bell'). *Das Echo* (D 868) is, however, a peasant girl's innocent confession to her mother.

Castelli belongs to that group of Viennese writers of comedies who loved to set broad comedy against a background of fantasy. This is also the ambience of Schubert's *Singspiel Die Verschworenen* ('The Conspirators') based on Aristophanes's *Lysistrata*, which Schubert began in 1823 and which, because the censor considered the title to be 'political', had to be renamed *Der häusliche Krieg* ('The Domestic War'), still however not being performed until 1861.

One month before Beethoven's death, in February 1827, Schubert came across new poems by Wilhelm Müller. He found them in the Leipzig almanach *Urania* of 1823, together with Müller's *Ländliche Lieder* ('Rural Songs'), Rückert's *Liebesfrühling* ('Love's Spring'), and twelve sonnets by Count von Platen, a poet highly esteemed by the Schubert circle. Schubert's inner rapport with Müller had already been revealed in the *Schöne Müllerin* cycle—Müller's simple, genuine emotions, encompassed in a seemingly artless poetic framework and allowing a composer unlimited freedom of expression, were the ideal *point de départ* for a musical setting. Schubert probably ignored Müller's ironical or revolutionary undertones intentionally, as for example in *Einsamkeit* (no. 12) when Müller writes of the silence over European cemeteries:

Ach, daß die Luft so ruhig,
Ach, daß die Welt so licht!
Als noch die Stürme tobten,
War ich so elend nicht.

(Oh, the air is so still and the world so bright! When the storms
were still raging, I was never as miserable as I am now.)

Spaun, in his memoirs (1858), has described the excitement with
which Schubert tackled these twelve poems which were completed
within a matter of weeks:

Schubert had been gloomy for some time and seemed to be un-
well. When I asked him what was wrong, he only said, You will
soon hear and understand.

The traces of this intense activity are plain to see in the autograph manuscripts. Mayrhofer who, after Spaun's return, had
rejoined the friends, wrote in his recollections (1829):

The poet's irony based on despair attracted Schubert, and he
expressed it penetratingly. I was painfully moved.

The literary man's ear must have played him false, for this
'irony' is only hinted at in Schubert's music. Heine, discussing this
aspect of Romanticism, which he himself had helped to underline
with consummate clarity, said that it was 'the only way still open for
the honest writer, and the ironic is the most moving manifestation
of this honesty'.

But then came an event which shook the whole world of music
and pushed all thoughts of work aside. On 29th March 1827,
Bauernfeld wrote in his diary:

Beethoven died on the 26th, 56 years old. Today was his funeral.
I went with Schubert. Anschütz [Heinrich Anschütz, born 1785,
a famous actor at the Burgtheater] read a funeral oration by
Grillparzer at the Währing Cemetery.

A newspaper reported that Schubert was one of the thirty-eight
torchbearers who accompanied the coffin. So Schubert stood at
Beethoven's grave and must have heard Grillparzer's words:

There lives still—and long may he live!—the master of the
German language [Goethe]. But the last master of the musical
Lied, the divine mouth of music . . . has ceased to live.

But what did Grillparzer, what did Vienna, what did the world really know of Franz Schubert? Hartmann's diary entry of 29th March records:

I went to the Schloß Eisenstadt where I stayed till 1 am with Schober, Schubert and Schwind. Naturally, we spoke only of Beethoven, of his works, and of the well-deserved respects paid to his memory.

Schubert, in his almost fearful reverence, had raised Beethoven to god-like heights. The master's isolation, caused by his deafness and consequent rudeness, probably contributed to Schubert's feeling of shyness. His idolisation of Beethoven went so far as to throw a shadow over this modest composer, from which he could never escape as long as he lived. And the time granted to him was, after all, so pitifully short.

If the broad stream of Schubert's joyous music gives him equal status with Beethoven, how might not Schubert's genius have marked his century, if a longer life had been given to him?

Beethoven's, with Goethe's, was the decisive influence on Franz Schubert. Beethoven's courageous expression of powerful musical ideas, his incomparable determination, in the face of sufferings, to force these first inspirations into a final musical mould, his life-long fighting spirit—everything that Schubert admired in him—may well have been detrimental to Schubert—temperamentally so different.

The doubts of his youth: 'I believe that something could become of me, but who can do anything after Beethoven?' were still present; he sensed that Beethoven was both an end and a beginning. In addition, he was living in the same town as his idol, who had been worshipped by his followers in the years since the Congress of Vienna. Schubert's own gentle spirit, his unprepossessing appearance, his shyness, his delicate and dreamy nature, compelled him to invest Beethoven with those characteristics which he himself seemed to lack. The young schoolmaster did not therefore seek the 'Titan's' friendship; he did not meet Beethoven on his one and only visit, but left him a set of variations dedicated to him.

On his deathbed, however, Beethoven did see some of Schubert's songs, for in February, Anton Schindler, Beethoven's devoted help-mate, had laid a packet of Schubert's songs on his counterpane, some already published, others manuscript copies made by Schindler himself. We can agree with the remark which Beethoven is said to have made, even though it may be an invention of Schindler's: 'Truly, this Schubert is possessed of the divine spark!'

In a newspaper article, and again in his biography of Beethoven, Schindler, who, it must be said, has always been mistrusted as a none-too-reliable reference source, reported how Beethoven's interest was evidenced by his remarks about the number, length and variety of the songs. He is reported to have said: 'Had I had that poem, I should have set it to music, too!'

This does not mean necessarily, of course, that he approved of Schubert's version. The manuscript copies made by Schindler have been preserved, and Maurice Brown, in his *Schubert*, records that they 'are in the possession of Otto Taussig of Malmö'. He also draws attention to the fact that 'the prelude of four bars in early editions of the song *Augenlied* was genuine Schubert and not, as Mandyczewski considered, an addition of the publishers. *Augenlied*, as copied by Schindler, is so ornate compared with the published song that it is almost certainly an embellished version by Vogl.'

The relations between the men and the artists, Franz Schubert and Ludwig van Beethoven, are as obscure and unexplained as they were shortly after their deaths. It is difficult to fight one's way through the jungle of hypotheses which grew up out of this mystery. The secondhand accounts, at best acceptable as written evidence, seem to cloud rather than clarify the issue. Perhaps it was even the jealous hangers-on who crowded round the two giants (and who incidentally represented many strata of society), who killed their interest in each other? Beethoven's pupils, admirers and patrons were to be found in the nobility and aristocracy of *Vormärz* Vienna.[1] Schubert's friends, the artists, the officials, or aristocrats who had renounced their titles, represented the new bourgeoisie who could not wait for 1848. In any case, none of those who wrote memoirs dealt with the Schubert–Beethoven relationship. A remark of Beethoven's nephew, Karl, in the former's conversation-books for August 1823, *is* authentic: 'Schubert is highly praised; but he [Mosel] says that he is in hiding.' This could have been due either

[1] *Vormärz* ('pre-March'), a word used to characterise the extreme reactionary groups in Austria prior to the 1848 Revolution. (Ed.)

to Schubert's shyness, or to his need for privacy because of his disease.

Yet some happy times were still in store for him.

From Weimar, where he had been visiting Goethe, came Johann Nepomuk Hummel, conductor at the Court of the Grand Duke Karl August of Weimar, a man whom Beethoven admired as a composer and a friend, to stay at Madame Laszny's. Vogl and Schubert performed some songs to his great enjoyment, and Hummel, a brilliant improviser at the piano, was moved to respond with a much-applauded fantasy on the very impressive song *Der blinde Knabe* (D 833). In 1825 Schubert had made two settings of the poem by Craigher based on the English poem *The Blind Boy* by Colly Cibber (1671–1757). Schubert's setting raises the tone of a rather nasty poem which seeks to evoke a cheap tear of sympathy. Its rhythmic structure is dominated by a somnambulistic, groping figure whose wide interval-span under the natural flow of the melody exactly catches the feeling of melancholy and uncertainty.

Hummel's sixteen-year-old pupil, Ferdinand Hiller, had also come to Vienna to meet Beethoven. He describes in his memoirs how impressed he was by Schubert:

I heard the songs of Franz Schubert for the first time. An old friend of my Master's, the once famous actress Buchwieser [the maiden name of Frau Laszny], at that time wife of a rich Hungarian magnate, invited Hummel and me a few times to her house. The charming lady still bore traces of her former beauty, but was in extremely poor health, scarcely able to move; her husband received the guests with friendly warmth. The rooms in which we sat were imposing and brilliant and breathed a deep, genuine, aristocratic calm. No one else was invited with us except Schubert, the favourite and protégé of our hostess, and his singer Vogl. A short while after we had left the luncheon table, Schubert sat down at the piano with Vogl at his side, we made ourselves comfortable in the large drawing-room, wherever we pleased, and a unique recital began. One song followed the other—the donors were tireless, the receivers were tireless. Schubert had little technique, Vogl had little voice, but both had so much life and feeling, were so absorbed in their delivery, that it would have been impossible to perform these wonderful compositions with greater clarity or with greater sincerity. We thought neither of the piano playing, nor of the song, it was as though the music had no need of any material sound, as though the melodies were revealing themselves like visions to ethereal ears. I cannot speak of my emotions or my enthusiasm—but my master who after all had almost half a century of music behind him, was so deeply moved that tears were trickling down his cheeks.

It is not surprising to read that the performers had technical difficulties, for they were interpreting *Schiffers Scheidelied* (D 910), from a poem by Schober, which had been composed in February. The ceaseless *tremoli* of lashing waves and roaring wind, and, above all the clangour, the seaman declaiming his untimely departure from his girl, demand the greatest technical control, so as to maintain such tension. The song is lacking somewhat in development, for which the slight changes in the minor melody, repeated five times, and in the major melody, repeated four times, hardly compensate, even though the honesty and intensity of the composition are far beyond that of any contemporary music. Once again, we find a stanza which seems to express Schubert's own feelings:

O laß mich im Bewußtsein steuern,
Daß ich allein auf Erden bin,
Dann beugt sich vor'm Ungeheuern,
Vor'm Ungehörten nicht mein Sinn.
Ich treibe mit dem Entsetzen Spiel,
Und stehe plötzlich vielleicht am Ziel.

(Oh let me sail away in the awareness that I am alone on this earth, then I shall not bow down before monsters or unheard-of dangers. I shall jest with horror and will suddenly find myself at my destination!)

And, at the conclusion, Schubert cries characteristically: 'Entsagung ist leichter als Verlust!' ('Renunciation is easier to bear than loss!')

At the beginning of 1827, Schubert wrote a setting of a well-known poem by Schober, *Jägers Liebeslied* (D 909), which is also in the old student song book, though set there to another melody. Schubert's version gives the song a magical soaring quality. The prelude and interludes, where the piano imitates the distant sound of horns, are particularly effective.

On 23rd April 1827 a gathering was held in the house of the Witteczeks, in gratitude for which Schubert dedicated to his old friend his three settings of Seidl poems, *Im Freien, Das Zügenglöcklein* and *Der Wanderer an den Mond*. (Tobias Haslinger published them in May 1827 as opus 8.)

The nocturnal mood of *Im Freien* (D 880) is beautifully captured by a delicate melody which is duplicated in the technically very difficult rippling piano accompaniment. It belongs to the group of songs whose accompanying *motif* is carried through the composition. Although of a 'heavenly length', as Schumann said about Schubert's symphonic movements, it belongs to the best of Schubert.

After a long interval, Schubert brought himself to write another dedication in an autograph book, when on 24th April 1827 he dedicated *An die Musik* to Albert Sowinsky, the Viennese piano virtuoso. From May to the beginning of June, Schober and Schubert were in Dornbach, a village to the west of Vienna where they took a room in the inn, the 'Kaiserin von Österreich' ('Empress of Austria'). They were amidst the hills of the Vienna Woods—where better to write *Das Lied im Grünen* (D 917)? The poem was by Friedrich Reil (1773–1843), who had been an actor at the Burgtheater since 1801, and later became an equerry at the court of Emperor Franz I of Austria, and published dramas, other literary works and some translations. *Das Lied im Grünen* offers a clear proof of Schubert's love for the broken triad, so characteristic of his style, floating away as if borne on gentle waves. Indeed, here the piano makes quite clear that it is a song about a brook whose ceaseless rippling hides many enchanting melodies. What the voice has to say, is stated freely, like a breathless improvisation—and the song must be sung accordingly. This song in simple rondo form is usually sung in the shorter version of the Friedländer edition, and it may well be true that Schubert decided not to have all the verses sung. But the sections which, it has been suggested, were added by another writer, or by the publisher, do not really make the song too long, and contain so much of relevance to Schubert's life that few can fail to be captivated by it, despite its length. (After Schubert's death, his desolate friends gave the song the sentimental title *Traueropfer dem Verklärten* ('A mourning sacrifice to him who is transfigured'.) It was published in 1829 with two earlier songs, as opus 115.)

Moritz von Schwind left Vienna on 7th August 1827 to study in Munich with Peter Cornelius, the painter, and uncle of the composer of the same name. Bauernfeld recorded on 31st August: 'Gap in our circle of friends. What will become of us all? Will we keep together?'

But new faces did keep appearing. A departmental head in the Austrian Foreign Ministry, Johann Vesque von Püttlingen (born 1803), was a song-composer known throughout Europe under his pseudonym of J. Hoven. A former pupil of composition with Leidesdorf, Moscheles, Worzischek and Sechter, he then came to Vogl for voice training. In only a few years, however, his name was forgotten. He became acquainted with Schubert, and, in the summer of 1827, when they visited Vogl, the latest songs were sung to him, mint-fresh. Vogl gave his pupil commentaries to the songs and spoke about the interpretation and performance of German songs generally, stressing the importance of clear enunciation in particular. His famous words were: 'If you have nothing to say to me, then you have nothing to sing to me.' (Vesque von Püttlingen dedicated his opus 10 settings of Sposetti poems to Vogl.)

It was probably on such an occasion that the two songs from poems by Friedrich von Rochlitz (1769–1842), written in January 1827, were performed for the first time. *Alinde* (D 904), the story of an almost abortive rendezvous, is based on a not very good idea of a not very convincing poet, who as a short-sighted critic and long-serving publisher of the Leipzig periodical *Allgemeine Musikalische Zeitung* was respected by Beethoven and had therefore hoped to write his biography, a hope that did not materialise. By making changes in the text, Schubert matched the music to the existing stanzas with a simple, charming effect, the barcarolle rhythm being a little reminiscent of *Das Fischermädchen*.

Rochlitz's *An die Laute* (D 905), which received late recognition, is delicate and charming; its *Viennoiserie* is always appealing, to audience and performer alike. These songs, composed as early as 1816, were published as opus 81 in May 1827, along with *Zur guten Nacht* (D 903) for baritone solo and male voices, likewise to a poem by Rochlitz.

On 2nd September, Schubert and his friend Johann Baptist

Jenger (1792–1856) were invited to Graz by Frau Marie Pachler, a patroness of music, who had married Dr Karl Pachler, a lawyer and brewer. Pachler's secret hobby was really the direction of the theatrical activities in Graz, but their home had become the centre of its musical life.

Schubert, as an honorary member of the *Musikfreunde* of Graz (see p. 169), was to be honoured by a concert to be held 'by double wax candle illumination', and at which he himself was to perform. Frau Pachler's good friend, Julius Schneller, the history teacher at the Graz Lyceum, arranged the visit of Schubert and Jenger, with whom he was very friendly. His admiration for Schubert and his songs can be seen in the poem which he wrote later while in Germany, 'An Franz Schubert vom Rheinstrome' ('To Franz Schubert from the River Rhine'). The poem ends with a near-quotation from *Der Wanderer*: 'Dort, wo du, Harfner, bist—dort ist das Glück' ('There where you are, harper—there is happiness').

Anyone coming from Vienna used to stay with the Pachlers, as Sophie Müller and Heinrich Anschütz often did. Even when she was young, Marie Pachler was considered the finest pianist in the town. Beethoven thought highly of her and left this description of her piano-playing:

> I have never found anyone who could perform my works as well as you can, the great pianists not excepted, they only have the mechanics and affection. You are the true guardian of my brain-children.

It is no wonder then that Schubert enjoyed his stay and thanked Frau Pachler cordially for the invitation. The programme of the concert in Graz's Ständetheater contained a late programme change in deference to the honoured guest—a solo song, *Normans Gesang*, a male voice quartet and a quartet for female chorus.

Two days later the Pachlers arranged a three-day coach excursion to an estate at Wildbach near Deutsch-Landsberg, some twenty miles away. Here another surprise awaited Schubert. Maria Masegg, a twenty-four-year-old local girl, sang some of his songs, accompanied by her music teacher, much to his satisfaction. Schubert repaid the compliment by improvising countless Ländler, German dances, *galoppes*, and Ecossaises. But the best Schubertiads were held in the Pachlers' house, where, in the absence of Vogl or

Schönstein, Schubert himself sang and occasionally played four-handed music with Jenger.

While in Graz, Schubert set *Eine altschottische Ballade* (D 923), for two voices and piano, from the well-known text of Herder's *Stimmen der Völker in Liedern* (see p. 24), translated from the English of Bishop Percy. Apparently Frau Pachler had given Schubert the poem in Carl Loewe's setting which Schlesinger had published three years previously in Berlin, for all of Loewe's textual changes reappear in Schubert's version. Ballads in imitation of Percy's *Reliques of Ancient English Poetry* (1765) were all the rage in literary circles in Germany, since Herder had begun the movement with the intention of linking the *Sturm und Drang* movement with medieval German literature. Among his translations of Percy was *Edward*, which Schubert set as *Eine altschottische Ballade*. One ought to obey Schubert's instructions that the song should be sung alternately by a male and female voice. Dialogue replaces narration. Seven stanzas are set to a two-part simple folk song-like melody which resists all interpretation. Schubert, it was plain, had not abandoned the simplest strophic form. The reason for his using this form as late as 1827 lay in the natural narrative character of the ballad. The singer is given an unhewn block of melody, as it were, and he has then to shape and highlight it.

The 'Auszug aus einem Briefwechsel über Ossian und die Lieder alter Völker' ('Extracts from correspondence on Ossian and the songs of ancient peoples') where the 'ancient Scottish ballad' first appeared, was published in 1773 in *Von deutscher Art und Kunst*, the fruits of Herder's conversations with Goethe. Herder's examples of folk-poetry are: Scottish ballads, Nordic myths, Latvian, English and German folk songs.

Shakespeare had given Herder the taste for this ballad, which he called 'really gruesome'. The instructions that the original Scottish was to be accompanied by a 'touching country air' justify Schubert's setting.

Frau Pachler recommended another poem to Schubert: Karoline Louise von Klencke's *Heimliches Lieben* (D 922). The piece flows along rather too exuberantly and, because of the poem, may have become rather long. We should not be too surprised at the exuberance of the poem since, as has already been said, Baroness Klencke was the mother of Helmine von Chézy, the authoress of the libretti of *Euryanthe* and *Rosamunde*. Reichardt had also set the poem in 1780 and had enthused about its authoress: 'By a woman. Whom I sought for a long time to thank her with all my soul for this wonderful Sapphic song.'

Schubert tries to moderate the rococo style by altering the beginning of the poem. Reichardt has: 'Myrtill, wenn Deine Lippen mich berühren' ('Myrtill, when your lips touch mine'); but, as a result, Schubert's cantilena sobs and sighs with an Italianate romantic sweetness, which is just not Schubert, but more Carl Loewe (in, say, his *Gruft der Liebenden*). Further, there is no genuine Schubertian emotion here, everything remains *biedermeierlich*, as the good ladies of Graz might perhaps have played their music; except that, in this music, there is a touch of genius, which might have proved to Frau Pachler that even a musical dessert can be made into a work of art, and, in addition, be extremely flattering to the voice. It is incomprehensible that the song has still not been discovered by singers.

After his return to Vienna, Schubert wrote a letter of thanks to his hosts on 27th September:

Your Graces!

I am beginning to discover how happy I was in Graz and I can't quite get accustomed to Vienna; it is of course rather big, but, on the other hand, it is devoid of warmth, sincerity, genuine ideas, sensible words and, particularly, of intelligent actions. There is so much confusing chatter here that you never know whether you are clever or stupid, and you seldom or never attain inner happiness. 'Tis of course possible that I am myself to blame for that, for I am slow to warm up.

The letter is very much part of the major–minor contrast which marked his stay in Graz. After some preliminary notes in the February, the first settings of the *Winterreise* songs were written there, and he continued work on them after his return. The active tempo of his work did not diminish in intensity, but his physical movements did. He seldom went out, even when he should have attended performances of his own works. He was not even present when his *Ständchen* ('Zögernd leise') (D 920), by Grillparzer, received its first performance on 25th March 1828 by Anna Fröhlich's pupils, even though it was sung in honour of Leopold Sonnleithner's fiancée and the soloist was Pepi Fröhlich. As long as they did not constantly badger him, he loved going 'picnicking' with his friends; Fritz von Hartmann records in his diary for 14th February 1827:

Picnic. A Herr Kandler played a great deal on the piano and also sang some Schubert songs,

and on 4th March 1827:

We went to Schober's because Schubert had invited us to hear his latest compositions. All were assembled, but Schubert did not turn up. At last Schwind agreed to sing some of the earlier songs which delighted us. At half past 9 we all went to the 'Schloß Eisenstadt' [the same inn where they had met after Beethoven's death] where Schubert soon arrived and conquered all our hearts with his simplicity, although he had disappointed our expectations with his laziness.

Towards the end of 1827—the exact date of the work is not known—Schubert composed the Fantasia in C major for pianoforte and violin with variations on the Rückert song *Sei mir gegrüßt*. Along with *Frühlingsglaube* (D 686), and the less important *Hänflings Liebeswerbung* (D 552) (a Ländler to words by the librettist of *Der Freischütz*, Friedrich Kind), it was dedicated as opus 20 in 1823 to Justina von Bruchmann, the mother of Schubert's friend from the *Konvikt* days, Franz von Bruchmann.

Sei mir gegrüßt (D 741), a *point de départ* for a series of technically brilliant instrumental works, was the first of the group of highly successful Rückert settings. After a hymnic intensification of thoughts of love, the devotional outpouring is moderated to that yearning modesty which faithfully reflects Schubert's own personality.

Rückert (1788–1866), the orientalist whose poems occupied Schubert for only a few years, but who was later to have a more considerable influence on Schumann, Loewe and Gustav Mahler, again uses here the ghazal, or Persian love-poem form. After a very beautiful prelude, the feeling of inwardness is gradually intensified to a dithyramb which replaces the initial serenade-like music, and the melody pounds forward in longing, as did Verdi's melodies later. A sentimental interpretation can, of course, reduce this wonderful song to banality (which also happened to Verdi's music). Inwardness and nobility are needed to accord the song its true status; after the passionate *fortissimo* of the conclusion, the longing fades away in a *pianissimo*—which is expressly marked.

Schubert had made many alterations to his piano accompaniments, either to suit the technical abilities of the accompanists—or because a piano was not available. Thus, after the original edition for piano, many, many songs appeared with guitar accompaniments, which were not necessarily written by, but usually approved by Schubert. In the case of *Sei mir gegrüßt*, Walther Dürr in the *Neue Schubert-Ausgabe* (New Schubert Edition) mentions a harp accompaniment. Ludwig Josef Cramolini (1805–1884), the singer and stage-manager, wrote in his diary:

> It was in the early 20's. Capus von Pichelstein came to me one morning and brought me Schubert's divine song *Sei mir gegrüßt* from Rückert's *Östliche Rosen* and begged me to sing it a few days later at a *Serenade*. . . .
>
> He wanted to accompany me on the harp which he played excellently. I expressed my willingness and we studied the song under Franz Schubert's direction in my room. . . .

After the performance, the entry goes on, Schubert embraced him and said:

> No one can sing that song as you do, you have moved us all to tears.

Schubert also found time to keep old promises. Faust Pachler, Frau Pachler's seven-year-old son, had taken a great liking to Schubert. On 12th October 1827 Schubert wrote the following on a manuscript which he sent to the boy's mother:

> Enclosed I send your Grace the four-handed piece for little Faust. [The pianoforte duet *Kindermarsch* in G major. Ed.] I fear I will not earn his praises, for I really do not feel that I am made for this sort of composition. I trust that Your Grace is in better health than I, since my old headaches have started up again.

He also dedicated to Frau Marie Pachler the song *Das Weinen*

(D 926) in which one might trace Schubert's feelings on the re-
currence of the symptoms of his old disease:

> Gar tröstlich kommt geronnen
> Der Tränen heil'ger Quell,
> Recht wie ein Heilungsbronnen
> So bitter, heiß und hell.
> Darum, du Brust voll Wunden,
> Voll Gram und stiller Pein,
> Und willst du bald gesunden,
> So tauche da hinein.

(The holy spring of tears starts up again like a fountain of
salvation, so bitter, so hot, so fair. So, cover thyself in them, thou
breast full of wounds, full of anguish and silent grief, if thou
wouldst get well.)

The poet, Karl Gottfried von Leitner, who was highly thought
of by the Pachlers, was called the 'Austrian Uhland'.[1] Schubert now
set eight of his poems, almost one after the other. Konradin Kreutzer
(born 1780), and Schubert's old friend Lachner, also set Leitner's
poems to music.

Das Weinen, which extols the curative power of tears, had a
chorale-like flowing melody whose accompaniment resembles the
perfervid polyphonic form of those to *An die Freunde* and *Vom
Mitleiden Mariä.*

Vor meiner Wiege (D 927) came next. Richard Capell could not
have studied the song very closely to be able to write: 'Schubert's
music for *Vor meiner Wiege* flowed in a moment of no great control'[2]; he was perhaps blinded by the admittedly absurd text. The
three-part song brings five stanzas together; the two outer sections
are in the minor, the inner section in the major mode. A profound
earnestness, lightened only now and then by a smile, speaks to us
out of this music. In the final stanza, surely one of Schubert's
loveliest, the required swelling of the tone on the high note of

---

[1] Johann Ludwig Uhland (1787–1862) of Tübingen was a poet of radical
views and a member of the Frankfurt Parliament of 1848. He is now best
remembered for the poem, 'Ich hatt' einen Kameraden' ('I had a comrade').
(Ed.)

[2] In his book *Schubert's Songs* (Macmillan 1928, rev. 1957) p. 245. In the revised
edition, Martin Cooper mentions that Capell admitted later that he had under-
rated *Vor meiner Wiege* (Ed.).

'tiefe Ruh' ' ('Deep peace') makes the *mezza voce* extremely difficult to achieve. Even if the words of the poem stray beyond the permitted bounds of sentimentality, Schubert's setting does not. When the mother sings of 'roses and angels', for example, we hear a melody which only a Schubert could invent.

Schubert's first Leitner setting was the 1823 song *Drang in die Ferne* (D 770). The seed planted here came to fruition in Chopin's 24 Preludes:

> Ach! von Gewölk und Flut
> Hat auch mein wildes Blut
> Heimlich geerbt den Drang,
> Stürmet die Welt entlang!

(My wild blood has secretly inherited its passion from the clouds and the oceans and so it storms through the world!)

There is an undercurrent of longing here which made Schubert, the son of Bohemian parents, something of a 'secret wanderer', even though he felt very attached to his beloved Vienna. And Leitner also supplied these words:

> Sorgt nicht, durch welches Land
> Einsam mein Weg sich wand,
> Monden- und Sternenschein
> Leuchtet auch dort hinein.

(Fear not, wherever my lonely way leads, the moon and the stars will shine on me there, too.)

With these words Schubert sought to answer the worried questionings of his friends who were beginning to feel excluded from his inner life. The delicacy with which pain and joy are united in music is uniquely Schubertian. (*Drang in die Ferne* appeared in the *Wiener Zeitschrift für Kunst etc*. in 1823 and was published as opus 71 in 1827.)

In order to publish them as opus 106 with a dedication to Marie Pachler, Schubert put the Leitner songs and the two other Graz songs, *Heimliches Lieben* and *Eine altschottische Ballade*, together. The music was engraved by the Lithographic Institute of Vienna, although, at the last moment, *An Sylvia* was substituted for the ballad. Jenger wrote to Frau Pachler about the group of songs and promised to bring them to Graz himself. This he failed to do,

Schubert did not send her a copy either, so that in the end she had to buy them for herself.[1]

The same November Schubert set some more of the Leitner poems from the collection given him by Frau Pachler.

Der Wallensteiner Lanzknecht (D 931), *Der Kreuzzug* (D 932), and *Des Fischers Liebesglück* (D 933), were the first three.

Der Wallensteiner Lanzknecht [or *Landsknecht*] *beim Trunk* is the strophic song *par excellence*. Schubert makes an eight-line stanza out of two four-line stanzas, which is then sung three times. Originally, however, there were only five short stanzas—so Schubert repeated the fifth in the third stanza, in order to make a sixth, satirising by this dramaturgical trick the soldier's love of the bottle. The soldier's demand that the wine be poured into his helmet is made all the more effective by the repetition. The archaic sound of the music, a rare device in Schubert, is not the only means of characterising the mood of a seventeenth-century military camp; the 6/8 rhythm, moving between G minor and B flat major, gives an impression of corpulence, and there is a rough poetic quality in the soldier's story of his Swedish foe who dies in the dust, and of the spiked helmet which protected him and now serves as a drinking cup.

Fischers Liebesglück (D 933), far too rarely heard, captures its muted loveliness by means of its syncopations. The ascending, almost yodelling octaves indicate a new meaning each time, most touchingly in the final

> Enthoben
> Der Erde, schon oben,
> Schon drüben zu sein.

(To be above, beyond this earth.)

Schubert compresses a whole range of events, from the lover's first glimmerings of hope to its final fulfilment, into the musically

---

[1] During alterations to the building housing the music collection in the Széchényi National Library in Budapest in 1969, a manuscript volume was found which was clearly that used by the Lithographic Institute of Vienna for its edition of these songs. According to an article in the 1969 October edition of the *Österreichischen Musikzeitschrift* by I. Kecskemeti, Franz von Schober took the manuscript to Hungary when he went there in 1839 to act as social secretary and agent to some titled families and, incidentally, also for a time as private secretary to Franz Liszt.

compact barcarolle. He seemed to be concerned only with the sounds and colours of Nature into which the fisherman's contours are allowed to merge.

On 7th November 1827 *Hofrat* Johann Friedrich Rochlitz wrote a long letter to Schubert, who had long admired the poet of *Klaglied* (see p. 19). Despite this, however, the Leipzig author's letter displayed a singular ignorance about the composer. He did not in fact say anything in his letter about earlier offers of help, but, having heard from Tobias Haslinger, the publisher, that Schubert was thinking of setting another, the fourth of his poems, asked him to consider his opus *Der erste Ton*, since he had not been happy with Carl Maria von Weber's treatment of the text. He had also sought to interest Beethoven in it—but without success.

Schubert received as detailed a set of instructions as can ever have been issued for writing a work, which was to be half-sung, half-declaimed, and to an orchestral accompaniment. Schubert's answer in the same month speaks for itself:

> I have given careful consideration to your suggestion with reference to your poem: 'Der erste Ton', and agree that your suggested treatment of it could be very effective. But since in that way it would be more a melodrama than an oratorio or a cantata, and since the former (perhaps rightly), is no longer popular, I must frankly confess that a poem which could be treated as an oratorio would be preferable, not only because a performer who can declaim like Anschütz is not always available, but also because it is my dearest wish to create a pure work of music, with no extraneous element other than the sublime idea of a great poem set completely to music.

It looks as if he had been searching for a new form. The strong inspiration which according to Hüttenbrenner, Spaun or Kathi Fröhlich, Schubert received from Handel's oratorios might well have made his yardstick in his search for a text on the grand scale. His application, shortly after this, to study counterpoint with Simon Sechter may also have some connection with this plan.

On New Year's Day 1828 Eduard von Bauernfeld read one of his poems to friends who had come to the house in which Schubert and Schober were living. It contained this darkly prophetic stanza:

Der Zauber der Rede, der Quell der Gesänge,
Auch er vertrocknet, so göttlich er ist;
Nicht rauschen die Lieder, wie sonst, im Gedränge,
Denn auch dem Sänger ward seine Frist:—
Die Quelle eilt zum Meere wieder,
Der Liedersänger zum Quell der Lieder.

(The magic of speech, the source of songs, it too dries up, divine as it is. The songs no longer pour forth in a flood, for the singer's time has run out too. The river flows back to the ocean; the singer of songs to the source of the songs.)

Did Bauernfeld suspect that, within a short year, Schubert would live on for his friends only in his songs?

THIRTEEN
Die Winterreise, 1828

It was probably his work on *Die Winterreise* which was the main reason for Schubert's not attending the still popular Schubertiads; Marie von Pratobevera noted on 10th January 1828:

> Schubert did not turn up, but, in his place, Tietze sang so many of his songs so movingly and soulfully, that his absence was not so painfully missed.

Mayrhofer, in his memoirs, confused cause and effect:

> The choice of the *Winterreise* proved how much more serious the composer had become. Seriously ill for a long time—Winter had set in for him.

Spaun describes how Schubert's friends reacted to the astonishingly new creation:

> Schubert had been in a gloomy mood for some time and seemed unwell. When I asked him what was wrong, he would only say, 'Now, you will all soon hear and understand.' One day he said to me: 'Come to Schober's today. I shall sing you a cycle of frightening songs. I am curious to see what you will all say to them. They have taken more out of me than was ever the case with other songs.' He then sang us the whole *Winterreise* with great emotion. We were taken aback at the dark mood of these songs, and Schober said that he had only liked one song, *Der Lindenbaum*. To that Schubert only said: 'I like these songs better than all the others and you will like them too.' And he was right; we were soon enthusiastic about the impression made by these melancholy songs which Vogl sang in a masterly way.

Schubert must have written *Die Winterreise* (D 911) under an extraordinary physical strain. Yet the work involved probably offered him some little relief from the severe headaches which were the evidence of his continuing physical suffering. The intensity of the uninterrupted flow of music of this year is positively frightening. Spaun's assumption that the strain of composing *Winterreise* partly caused Schubert's premature death is refuted by Schubert himself, for, immediately after finishing the song-cycle, he wrote the E flat piano trio, a work full of a glowing *joie de vivre*, then a second series of Impromptus, and, in between them, new Leitner songs and Italian songs for Luigi Lablache, the much-admired bass from Barbaja's operatic company. Lablache showed his respect for Schubert by holding frequent recitals of his German Lieder. Among the new Metastasio settings were the pretty cavatina *L'incanto degli occhi* (D 902 no. 1), the dramatic aria *Il traditor deluso* (D 902 no. 2) and the *aria buffa* in Rossini-style, *Il modo di prender moglie* (D 902 no. 3). Three wonderful bass studies, three completely untypical, technically skilled works, which stand outside the Schubertian canon.

The very first rehearsal of the new cycle had left no doubts that the *Winterreise* was in stark contrast to the general run of sentimentally complacent Lieder of the age. Schubert was therefore understandably reluctant to part with the songs before they had attained their definitive form; certainly none of his other songs underwent so much revision and re-touching as did those of the *Winterreise*. His illness and his financial straits, however, made a parting from them an inevitability. He asked Lachner to take the first group of songs, including *Der Lindenbaum* (no. 5) to Haslinger, the publisher, with strict instructions to bring back some ready cash for them, with which he might pay for his medicine and his soups. Lachner wrote later:

> The publisher considered the situation and paid—one florin per song.

The previous year Schubert had said to Bauernfeld:

> I can already see you as a *Hofrat* and a famous writer of comedies. But me? What will become of this poor musician? I shall probably be like Goethe's Harper in my old age, begging for bread from door to door.

The tragically ironic self-portrait in Müller's *Der Leiermann* (no. 24) is relevant to that remark:

Drüben hinter'm Dorfe
Steht ein Leiermann,
Und mit starren Fingern
Dreht er, was er kann.

Barfuß auf dem Eise
Wankt er hin und her;
Und sein kleiner Teller
Bleibt ihm immer leer.

Keiner mag ihn hören,
Keiner sieht ihn an;
Und die Hunde knurren
Um den alten Mann.

Und er läßt es gehen
Alles, wie es will,
Dreht, und seine Leier
Steht ihm nimmer still.

Wunderlicher Alter!
Soll ich mit dir gehen?
Willst zu meinen Liedern
Deine Leier drehen?

(Over there behind the village stands the organ-grinder and he turns his organ-handle with frozen fingers. He shuffles barefoot on the ice and his little plate remains empty. No one wants to listen to him, no one looks at him and the dogs growl round his feet. But he lets it all go past him and goes on turning the handle. Strange old man! Shall I go with you? Will you play your organ for my songs?)

Müller's own material position cannot be compared with Schubert's poverty. Nevertheless, Müller's ironic poem goes a good deal farther than Schubert by presenting the poet as a receiver of alms from a society hostile to the arts. It is curiously moving to compare Müller, the poet and librarian in Dessau, free from material worries and politically *engagé*, with Schubert, the musician, who, poor as a churchmouse, nevertheless sings of the sufferings of all mankind.

On 14th January 1828, four days after Ludwig Tietze (or Titze, born 1797) had sung the first song *Gute Nacht* at an evening concert of the *Gesellschaft der Musikfreunde*, Tobias Haslinger announced the publication of the first twelve songs of the *Winterreise*. Tietze, an amateur singer and Court official and a frequent performer in vocal quartets at these gatherings, would probably have put many a professional singer of today to shame. Tietze and Josef Barth both had excellent tenor voices; the latter was extremely proud that the String Quartet in D minor 'Der Tod und das Mädchen' was first played at his house in 1826, even before the performance at Lachner's.

In the first five months of 1827 alone, Tietze gave six evening recitals of Schubert-Lieder accompanied by the composer. (A curious sidelight might be added here. The celebrated Viennese comic playwright, Johann Nestroy, used to sing the baritone parts in Schubert's vocal quartets, although he left after two years to write full-time for the theatre.)

The manuscript of the first half of the *Winterreise* gives February 1827 as the date of the end of the composition. That date refers to the day on which Schubert wrote the final version of *Gute Nacht* (no. 1). Once again, this is a song in the 'wandering'-rhythm, like the first song of the *Schöne Müllerin* cycle—but what a contrast! There is barely a hint here of what has gone before; we are actually at the end of the plot. Why is the young man leaving? He was in love with a girl, and believed that she loved him. Along came a richer suitor, whom the girl preferred, and now all is over. Life has lost its meaning; he longs for the end. The piano prelude is marked 'Mäßig, in gehender Bewegung' ('Moderato, in a walking movement') but it is only rarely observed that the 'walking movement' is orientated round the minims. Schubert emphasised the downward turn in the lover's fortunes by stressing the recurring up-beat in the treble at the beginning of each verse. The modulation to F major shows how different it all was once. 'Das Mädchen sprach von Liebe' ('The girl spoke of love'); the repetition here in B flat major takes on an ironic colouring, but the bitterness dissolves into tears at the piano's lament in E–F–E and A–B flat–A. The unexpected transition from the minor into the major mode causes the change of mood in the last stanza. Things seem less desperate—but Schubert is not finished yet. By reverting to the acerbity of the original minor mode during the postlude, he rules out any possibility of self-indulgence or sentimental self-pity. There is no sentimental slush here—only the naked truth. The absence of false illusions which the piano postlude transfers to the next sombre station on the journey should serve the singer as a warning to avoid the lachrymose interpretation sometimes offered. This will be all the easier for those who observe the discrepancies which arise between the cycle's painful tonalities and its occasional bitter ironies.

Schubert had read the first twelve poems in *Urania*, a literary almanach published in Leipzig in 1823. One can measure from the enthusiasm with which he tackled the project how well these poems suited his particular creative needs at that moment. In the late summer of 1827, *after* having completed the first group of twelve songs, Schubert found Müller's complete cycle in the *Gedichten aus den hinterlassenen Papieren eines reisenden Waldhornisten* ('Poems from the posthumous papers of a travelling horn-player'), as the second part of the collection of poems. The second group of twelve was not a continuation of the first group; the poems were scattered throughout the collection, with certain alterations in the order. (Müller dedicated his poems to the 'master of German song', Carl Maria von Weber, as a token of his friendship and admiration'. Weber died in 1827 before Schubert had finished his cycle.)

Since Schubert set the poems just as they came and added them to the original group which he had already set, it might be imagined that he had intentionally altered Müller's own order. But this could be claimed only of the lyrics of individual poems; most, if not all of Schubert's revisions, should be respected. As far as the placing of the songs within the cycle is concerned, then other points of view must be considered. For example, Hans Joachim Moser and Günther Baum have from time to time tried to reconstruct Müller's own sequence in concert recitals, but then the key-sequences—which, incidentally, should be retained as far as possible, even in transpositions—and Schubert's dramatic structure are rendered meaningless.

If Müller's order were followed, the Schubert Edition numbers would become: 1–5, 13, 6–8, 14–21, 9–10, 23, 11–12, 22, 24. Likewise with the text: most of Schubert's alterations, even when they are due to memory lapses, are so bound up with the music that the original text could hardly be restored. Possible exceptions to that remark might be: In no. 4 *Erstarrung*, 'Mein Herz ist wie *erfroren*' ('My heart is frozen') instead of 'erstorben' ('dead'); In no. 9

Irrlicht, 'Unsere Freuden, unsere *Wehen*' ('Our joys, our sorrows') instead of 'unsere Leiden' (our sufferings'), and in no. 20 *Der Wegweiser*, 'Weiser stehen auf den *Straßen*' ('Signposts stand on the streets') instead of 'auf den Wegen' ('on the roads').

The two complete manuscripts of the cycle have survived. The first was so full of corrections and additions as to render it illegible. Therefore, when Schubert was lying ill in bed, it was decided to prepare another copy which he himself corrected, though not without making further radical changes, particularly in *Die Wetterfahne* (no. 2). This corrected copy disappeared for many years, and, as a result, the editors who followed Haslinger, Max Friedländer (1884), Eusebius Mandyczewski (1894) and Erwin Schaeffer (1938) worked from the first surviving manuscript and drew attention to what they took to be errors, but which were, in fact, Schubert's own emendations for the first edition.

It is interesting to note that the melody of *Täuschung* (no. 19) is very similar to that of Schubert's settings of a poem by Schober, *Troilas Leid*, at the beginning of Act II of *Alfonso und Estrella*. Naturally enough, Schubert recalled his earlier interpretation of similar ideas. *Täuschung* exemplifies the irregular use of three-beat phrases. The restless vagaries of the seductive, imaginary light are depicted, while, at the end of each line, the piano seems to parody the singer's words.

Die Winterreise symbolises the intensity, empathy and maturity of technique of all Schubert's later works. What had been clearly promised at the beginning is now revealed in a much more dominating participation of the intellect in the act of composition, especially in those sections which were through-composed. *Die Wetterfahne* and *Irrlicht* offer something new and entirely original. The weather-vane on the roof of the girl's house seems to mock the fugitive wanderer and becomes a symbol of fickleness. The restlessness which marks the whole song is best expressed by the unwritten, not clearly indicated *rubato*, and a too hasty tempo (the marking is 'zeimlich geschwind'—'fairly quickly') could ruin the effect. The provocative novelty of such inventive ideas—or of those in songs like *Die Krähe* (no. 15)—makes Schubert's premature death appear all the more tragic. His descriptions of spiritual and natural landscapes are more intense and more daemonic than those of any of his contemporaries; the sombre image of *Die Krähe* ('The Crow'), for example, awaiting the death of the wanderer who 'suffers patiently' his oncoming insanity. One would have to go back to an Altdorfer, a Rembrandt or a Goya, to find images of comparable intensity, although Schubert shuns conscientiously all realistic 'tone-painting'. 'But then,' wrote the Viennese critic, Witeschnik, 'where did Schubert *not* create the earth anew through music?'

Wilhelm Müller died in the same year (1827) in which Schubert set his poems to music. A year later Schubert, now lying on his own deathbed, corrected the proofs. But it can hardly be maintained that these songs were written by a man 'entering on the winter of his life' at the age of thirty, when the same musician was able to write so many works in the years 1827 and 1828 full of sparkling ebullience and the presence of Spring. There is just no simple explanation for the phenomenon *Die Winterreise*—we must accept that Schubert came across the poems, that they were written by the author of the *Schöne Müllerin*, that they, too, told of a heart in travail, but in a different seasonal mood, and that here it is a man, and not a youth who is despairing of life. Do we really need to look for external motivation? After all, are not the laments of Hagar, of the young nun, of Gretchen and the boundless despair of the Harper—all works of Schubert's youth—still ringing in our ears? Depression alone cannot account for Schubert's sickly appearance, commented on by his friends; such creative agony encompassed, after all, discoveries and innovations beyond the realm of possibility. Even when all the accompanying circumstances of his disease and his depression are taken into account, there remains Schubert's superhuman joy in the way his work was going, in the unexpected reunion with a partner whose verses had already set him alight once before, and in the countless musical inspirations offered by these poems. There was no reason here for omitting a poem, all twenty-four were set to music, however much the unrelieved gloom of his mood might have militated against it. Although Schubert himself once said that, for him, there was no really happy music, he had never before attempted such a chain of variations on the theme of grief.

In the *Schöne Müllerin*, there are, after all, variations of mood, lighter interludes. Nor is the 'hero' the sole character; we are given glimpses of his beloved, her father and the young miller-lad's rival. Here, however, from the very beginning, all relations with others have been severed; not only do we never meet the cause of his anguish, she is never even mentioned.

If the main character remains a shadowy figure, natural phenomena intrude all the more persistently. The wintry landscape, its snowstorms, frozen streams, bare lime trees and the fugitive victim of inhospitality and cold, combine to form an unceasing lament. Schubert loved to listen to the sounds of nature; his music echoes a gentle, almost inaudible rustling. Fierce storms, whispering woods and plants, the singing meadows, all are translated into music. Not only in *Der Lindenbaum* (no. 5) are plants endowed with a musical language. The unpretentiousness and simplicity of Müller's poems are matched by the simplicity of Schubert's musical texture. His sole interest is in the depth of feeling, not in psychological overrefinements. Regret and renunciation are his themes. Dreams are the lover's torture. The battle with his emotions is long and despairing. Sixteen of the poems are in minor keys, the agony is unending before insanity breaks in. Schubert's simplicity is proven by the succession of emotional states. Which of our latter-day composers could have avoided so consistently any hint of sentimentality, on the one hand, and a super-refined characterisation in favour of 'pure music', on the other? Schubert did not even allow himself the luxury of repeating musical *motifs*, thereby avoiding the danger of a too selfish intrusion into the poetry. There is no sentimental connection between the events described, we must face quite unprepared the overwhelming shock of each new manifestation of despair.

With his song-cycles, Schubert introduced into the genre 'Lied' the concept of that higher unity which he had hitherto confined to the larger instrumental works. He also expanded the external dimensions of this intimate genre. Again, these cycles are important for what they reflect of their creator's personality. It is certainly no longer a platitude to claim that, in them, we see Schubert whole, for there are traits here which are either not to be found, or are not so clearly delineated, in his other works. And there are likewise signs here of an almost hysterical sensibility, which borders at times on the pathological. In *Der Wegweiser, Der Leiermann, Im Dorfe* (no. 17), Schubert reaches out to the farthest limits of the visionary, to realms no less mystical than those of E. T. A. Hoffmann, Novalis or the Swabian poet Justinus Kerner. Consider, for example, the frequent extended trills in *Im Dorfe* with which Schubert says more than one has the right to expect from what is normally only an embellishment. That semiquaver trill expresses a profound psychological disturbance, as well as the realistic noise of a dog barking. The basic concept, the contrast between domestic bliss and the lonely wanderer's death-wish, is hinted at symbolically. In contrast to the realistic babbling and chattering *leitmotifs* of the *Schöne Müllerin* songs, the 'wandering' *motif* in the first song of the *Winterreise, Gute Nacht*, is only hinted at in the other songs of the cycle. The connections between the songs are internalised, they have become psychological.

The unified style of interpretation demanded of the singer of the *Winterreise*, as well as of the *Schöne Müllerin*, is more easily achieved in the former than in the latter, although the emotional variations are still a matter of personal expression. The singer of *Die Winterreise* must seek to vary his interpretation, for a continuous flow of lovely tone spread over twenty-four songs would lead to monotony.

The musical construction of *Der Leiermann*, the last station on the journey of sorrow, makes it one of Schubert's most original creations. The scene is depicted in two equal stanzas, the very short third stanza puts the question to which no answer is given. The *motif* in the right hand of the piano and the bagpipe-like fifths in the left hand (this is the older form of the lyre, hung round the neck and supported by a wooden strut)—the monotonous declamation of the voice—the characterisation is almost perfect. The musical triviality of the old man, who is no longer aware of his miserable situation, anticipates Gustav Mahler. And yet—the realism remains musically formal. Schubert never breaks the musical framework of the whole cycle.

Der Leiermann is not only the emotional nadir of the cycle—this song is the culmination of everything that Schubert ever wrote, for there is no escape from this agony—where there is in *Der /Doppelgänger*, for example. Life has little more to offer in these lines. The effect on the listener is paralysing.

This brings us to a question much discussed in years past: Should one perform *Die Winterreise* in public at all? Should one offer such an intimate diary of a human soul to an audience whose interests are so varied? Since these days, it has been proved that the views of that section of the audience which expects only a refined, aesthetic entertainment from a *Liederabend* cannot be allowed to prevail. The singer must have no fears about the chilling effect which these songs can have, given the correct interpretation; he must make no concessions to Austrian charm or maudlin sentimentality, and must be prepared to be criticised for his attitude. If these songs only please us, or stir us or frighten us, then we are a long, long way from fully understanding Schubert's personal statement.

Die Winterreise demands much more than the purely lyrical approach—it runs the whole gamut of emotions, up to, and including drama. Michael Vogl, its first interpreter, and those who followed him, have made the cycle a baritone preserve, and it is therefore all the more to be welcomed that, in recent times, a few tenors, such as Julius Patzak and Peter Pears, have sung it in the original keys. The latter's recording has the added attraction of allowing us to hear the first version.

The following excerpts from a review in the *Theaterzeitung*, which appeared as early as 29th March 1828, on the occasion of the publication of the first half of the cycle, shows sound critical judgement on the part of the reviewer:

Winterreise by Wilhelm Müller, set to music for voice with pianoforte accompaniment by Franz Schubert, op. 89, no. 1. Property of the publisher Tobias Haslinger, Music Publisher in the building of the Savings Bank, Am Graben, Vienna. To recommend a successful work is the most pleasing task that a lover of the arts can undertake. We therefore speak with great pleasure of the present work whose publication does honour to the poet, the composer and the publisher. Schubert has displayed his genius in his interpretation of the poet. He has truly appreciated the emotions expressed in these poems and reproduced them in music which none can sing or hear without being deeply moved. Schubert's spirit soars so boldly that he carries along all who approach him and we are borne through the immeasurable depths of the human heart into worlds beyond, where the promise of the infinite opens up longingly in the radiance of the setting sun, but where also the gentle confining hand of the present joins with the fearful bliss of an inexpressible premonition to define the boundaries of human existence. Herein lies the very essence of the Romanticism of German culture and in such a genuine union of external and internal harmonies lies the main achievement of both the poet who speaks and the poet who sings. Since this paper is not concerned with theory, this is not the place to discuss the technical beauties but rather to point out how this beautiful and noble work can be most deeply and completely enjoyed, an urgent need in our time, since it has become almost a mania to give one's self up solely to material impressions in music.

FOURTEEN

Schwanengesang and Premature Death

Schubert's works were not favourably received everywhere, however. On 16th January 1828 the tenor Karl Adam Bader, accompanied by Felix Mendelssohn-Bartholdy, had sung the *Erlkönig* (always a certain success) in Leipzig. The *Leipziger Zeitung* did not accept the greatness of the Schubert work,

> which in the reviewer's opinion matches neither Reichardt's nor Zelter's setting, although it is over-endowed with modulations and eccentricities and was sung by Herr Bader to the accomplished and powerful pianoforte accompaniment of the young Mendelssohn.[1]

How far Schubert's music surpassed that accepted by his contemporaries may be evidenced from the following review of the songs published by Haslinger in the *Leipziger Zeitung* for 23rd January 1828:

> Schubert is an able composer and he usually succeeds in finding the most important emotional and therefore musical element in whatever he reads. His accompaniment is however rarely just an accompaniment, he embellishes the melody, often displays originality of invention and execution, sound knowledge of harmony, and the results of industry. On the other hand, he often goes beyond the limits of the genre, at times substantially so. For the sake of piquant novelty, he is given to an excess of notes in the pianoforte accompaniment, simultaneously or after one another.

[1] Strangely enough, Mendelssohn, a great favourite of Goethe, had little time for the Reichardt and Zelter versions so admired by Goethe, and found Schubert's the only one worthy of public performance.

Among the songs mentioned in this review was *Im Freien* (D 880) by J. G. Seidl, dedicated to Joseph Witteczek. When one examines the repeated octaves in the accompaniment (anticipating Schumann), one can understand the reviewer's astonishment.

To the annoyance of his Viennese publishers, Schubert had given two of his songs to the Graz publisher, Josef Andreas Kienreich, whom he had met that previous summer, and whose name he promptly forgot again. On 18th January 1828 he wrote to Anselm Hüttenbrenner, with whom he was on friendly terms again, and whose influence he hoped would be used to help his brother Carl obtain an art-master's post in Graz. He also asked him:

> Have you done anything new? *A propos*, when are the two songs going to be published by Greiner, or whatever his name is? What is all this then? Get on with it!!

Among a number of solo songs offered to B. Schott's Sons of Mainz is the melodically and harmonically enchanting song to a poem by Leitner, *Der Winterabend* (D 938), whose beauty was first revealed to many by the moving interpretation of the ageing tenor, Karl Erb. Despite the uninterrupted stream of semiquavers which run through the seven-page-long composition, Schubert manages to intensify the serene evening mood so as to gain a most personal involvement in the poet's sighs. Critics like Capell who complain that 'the mood needed more defining' have probably not really taken the trouble to listen to the song properly.[1] A cursory glance at the row of seemingly similar notes will not do here

Schott had written to Schubert on 9th February:

> . . . We are now in a position to beg you to send a few of your works to our firm. Pianoforte works or songs for one or several voices, with or without piano accompaniment, will always be welcomed. You may name your fee, which we shall pay you via H. Franck & Cie in Vienna. We must also point out to you that we own an establishment in Paris where we shall also publicise your compositions. . . .

On the same day by an amazing coincidence, there also came a letter from Probst in Leipzig with further offers. Schubert answered Schott on 21st February 1828:

[1] Capell, R., *Schubert's Songs*, p. 246.

Sir! I felt very honoured by your letter of February 8th [sic] and enter with pleasure into close relations with such a well-established publisher able to make my works better known abroad.

Among the works he offered were the following: '(f) Songs for solo voice with piano accompaniment, poems by Schiller, Göthe [sic], Klopstock, etc., etc., and Seidl, Schober, Leitner, Schulze, etc., etc.' Schott's Sons requested Schubert to send all the works mentioned with the exception of string quartets and solo songs. However, in the end the protracted negotiations fell through since Schubert was tired of accepting the paltry fees offered for his works.

After a long interval came the last big Schubertiad on 28th January 1828, in honour of Josef von Spaun, who was to leave Vienna after his wedding. Franz von Hartmann wrote in his diary on that day:

All were beside themselves with joy at the celebrations. Bocklet [Karl Maria von Bocklet, 1801–1881, a pianist. Ed.] kissed the composer's hand and opined that the Viennese did not know what a treasure they possessed in Schubert.

Reading-circles devoted to contemporary literature now took the place of the Schubertiads, Goethe's *Faust*, Kleist's stage-works and *Novellen*, Tieck's *Novellen* and Heine's *Buch der Lieder* (Book of Songs), being among the works read. The latter work was the source of Schubert's inspiration for his final testimony in *Schwanengesang*. Schubert knew the much-discussed Romantic writers' works intimately, and it is therefore all the more surprising that he never set one of the folk-songs in the collection made by Achim von Arnim and Clemens Brentano, *Des Knaben Wunderhorn*. They would seem to have been particularly suited to his genius.

Schubert, after much prevarication and complicated preparations, agreed to present the first and only concert of his own works on the first anniversary of Beethoven's death on 26th March 1828. Kupelwieser had been trying to plan this concert since 1825, and Bauernfeld had at last in 1827 persuaded Schubert to agree to hold it.

Your name is on everyone's lips and each of your songs is an event. You have written the most glorious string quartets and trios, not to mention the symphonies. Your friends are delighted with them but no music firm will buy them at the moment, and the public has no idea of the grace and beauty which repose in these works. So take a chance, conquer your idleness, give a concert, only of your things, of course. Vogl will support you with pleasure, Bocklet, Böhm [a violinist] and Linke [a cellist] will consider it an honour to put their talents at the disposal of a master like you. The public will fight for tickets and, even if you don't become a Croesus straightaway, a single evening would suffice to keep you for a whole year. You could repeat such an event annually, and, if your new works cause a sensation, as I do not doubt they will, then you can drive your Diabellis, Artarias and Haslingers and their niggardly fees up into the sky! A concert then, listen to my advice, a concert!

Schubert was reluctant to ask the *Gesellschaft der Musikfreunde* for their hall and he did not conceal his reluctance from Bauernfeld: 'If only I did not have to ask these people!' When the request was granted, the event had to be postponed from 21st March to 26th March, but the success was then all the greater.

The Viennese press completely ignored the concert. Not until 12th June was there a mention of it in the *Dresdner Abendzeitung*, and the *Berliner Allgemeine Musikalische Zeitung* gave this reserved reaction on 2nd July:

. . . Franz Schubert, who presented a private concert devoted exclusively to his own works, mostly songs; a genre with which he has had some considerable success. The numerous friends and patrons present did not fail to applaud each piece enthusiastically and asked for many to be repeated.

Franz von Hartmann reported in his diary for 26th March:

With Louis [Hartmann's brother] and Erik [Karl Erik von der Burg] to Schubert's concert. I shall never forget how wonderful that was. To the 'Schnecke', where we celebrated until 12 o'clock.

Bauernfeld's diary for the end of March reads:

Schubert's concert was on the 26th. Enormous enthusiam. The hall was packed to the doors, each piece was applauded to the skies, the composer called forward countless times. The concert brought a clear profit of almost 800 florins.

It must be said, however, that the concert was a limited and rather qualified success. What one might call the 'musical world' took no note of the event, and its consequences were slight and unrewarding. Schubert was still not recognised, he was thought of as a romantic 'Lieder-compositeur' whose sphere of influence was small, as was usually the case with this type of musician. He would never reach the composers' Mount Olympus. The guest appearance in Vienna of Paganini a few days later explains how relative one must regard the success of Schubert's concert in a hall for three hundred people. Paganini played in the Great Hall, and an audience composed of all classes clamoured for entrance. The takings were correspondingly larger. Schubert spent his earnings straightaway, took Bauernfeld to the Paganini concert, bought himself, at last, his own piano to replace the eternally rented one, and began to pay off some debts. In a few weeks, however, he was back to where he had started.

The programme on the invitation cards reads:

Invitation to the Private Concert which Franz Schubert will have the honour to give on March 26th, at 7 o'clock in the evening in the rooms of the Austrian *Musikverein*, Unter der Tuchlauben No 558. The programme will be:

1. First movement of a new String Quartet [in G op. 161] played by Herren Böhm, Holz, Weiß and Linke.
2. (a) *Der Kreuzzug* by Leitner.
   (b) *Die Sterne* by the same.
   (c) *Der Wanderer an den Mond* by Seidl.
   (d) *Fragment aus dem Äschylus*, songs with pianoforte accompaniment, performed by Herr Vogl (retd), Imperial Court Opera Singer.

Leitner's *Die Sterne* (D 939), like *Der Winterabend*, paints in music what it is almost impossible to say in words about the night-sky. The undulating rhythm is maintained throughout, but the modulations at the end of each stanza closely follow the meaning. The third line of each stanza modulates each time out of the basic key of E flat major, in the first stanza to C major, in the second to C flat, in the third to G major, and finally back into the original key. Schubert addresses the stars without any false sentiment, and the continuous motion captures their flickering and twinkling. The modulations sound like involuntary improvisations on the piano, and yet seem to develop logically out of each other. Leitner's *Kreuzzug* (D 932), now so popular, is so simply constructed that it could well be taken for a pilgrim's song. It was a moving stroke of genius to have the monk's words in the last stanza sung in unison with the accompaniment in the bass, while the right hand takes over the melody, as though the watcher were trying to join in the crusader's song.

The programme went on:

3. *Ständchen* by Grillparzer, Soprano solo and chorus. Performed by Frl. Josephine Fröhlich and the female pupils of the Conservatoire.
4. New Trio for the pianoforte, violin and the violoncello [in E flat op. 100] performed by Herren von Bocklet, Böhm and Linke.
5. *Auf dem Strome* by Rellstab. Song with horn and pianoforte accompaniment. Performed by Herren Tietze and Lewy (junior).
6. *Die Mondnacht* by L. Pyrker. Song with pianoforte accompaniment. Performed by Herr Vogl. [This is probably a printing error for *Die Allmacht*. I could not discover a *Mondnacht* by Pyrker.]
7. *Schlachtgesang* by Klopstock. Double chorus for male voices.

All the pieces of music are compositions of the concert giver. Tickets at 3 florins are available in the premises of Herren Haslinger, Diabelli and Leidesdorf.

The scena *Auf dem Strom(e)* (D 943) had been specially composed for the concert, and if it is true that the younger Lewy brother (Josef) Rudolf Lewy-Hoffmann, played the French horn, and not, as Professor Deutsch claims to have discovered[1] a provisional cello accompaniment, then this is the inventor of the valve horn. In *Auf dem Strom(e)*, the sole counterpart to *Der Hirt auf dem Felsen*, the horn supports the tenor voice most impressively. The piece was made popular by Louis Savart who, as a horn virtuoso-cum-concert singer, mastered both parts, and once even performed a version which enabled him to sing and play alternately.

On 28th April 1828, Schubert wrote *Herbst* (D 945) into the album

[1] *Thematic Catalogue*, p. 461.

of Heinrich Panofka (1807–1887), a musician and singing teacher from Silesia with whom the poet Hoffmann von Fallersleben had searched Vienna in the hope of meeting Schubert in the early part of 1827. The dedication, 'Zur frdl. Erinnerung Franz Schubert' (In kind remembrance Franz Schubert), preceded the poem by Ludwig Rellstab (1799–1860) who, coming from a musical family, became at an early age one of the leading Berlin music critics on the *Vossische Zeitung*. This argumentative and industrious man, whose extremely patriotic attitude in artistic matters brought him many a prison sentence, wrote novels and dramas, as well as the libretto to Meyerbeer's play in honour of Prussia, *Ein Feldlager in Schlesien*. He had no great importance as a literary figure, although his connection with Schubert has made his name immortal. Of the ten poems set by Schubert, one composition remained unfinished.

The main feature of *Herbst* is its remarkable similarity to Brahms's *Herbstgefühl* both in the *tremolandi* thirds and the presentation of the melody in the bass of the prelude, and in the related textual content, all proof of the respect shown by Schubert's successor and the later co-editor of the *Gesamtausgabe*.

Once again, Schubert's accompaniment is an independent musical statement which proclaims the sovereignty of nature. The piano is frequently contrasted with the vocal line, so that we have a counterpoint which, if not strictly theoretical, nevertheless has its own inner logic. The sorrowing autumnal season is rendered by the musical transparency, the recollection of experiences, even the smell, all created by Schubert's sympathetic and sensitive genius. The summer moods met with in, say, Beethoven's 'Pastoral Symphony' are rare in Schubert's work. (The first version of *Herbst* has been lost, but when the volumes devoted to Lieder in the *Gesamtausgabe* were near completion, the 1828 copy was discovered in Panofka's album and published in 1895 in the final volume of Lieder.) It is a mystery why Herr Panofka's pupils failed to rescue this little masterpiece from oblivion, but it was probably due to the same casualness as that evinced by Princess Kinsky, who believed that this insignificant little Schubert man, who never cared about money anyway, could be fobbed off with alms, so long as he was allowed to make music. At the very grand *soirée musicale* of 7th July 1828, Schubert (the concert-host) accompanied Baron von Schönstein in his own songs, and received from this great lady, the widow of Beethoven's patron, a gracious letter thanking him for dedicating the songs of opus 96 to her—and some small change in the envelope.

In August, Schubert finished a vocal ensemble *Glaube, Hoffnung und Liebe* (D 954) for chorus and wind instruments, the music for which, in 6/8 time, was written for the consecration of the new church bell in the Holy Trinity Church in Alsergrund.

The friends now met only rarely because of Schubert's worsening health. The Court doctor, Dr Rinna, advised Schubert to part company with Franz von Schober, who was also in poor health. Schubert therefore took up lodgings with his brother Ferdinand in a newly-completed house in the Firmiansgasse, No. 694, in the Vienna suburb of Neue Wieden. The sick man was certainly nearer the countryside, but the house was still damp and unsuitable for a person in Schubert's condition. Yet he kept on writing letters, as can be seen from this note to Johann Baptist Jenger of 25th September:

> I have already sent the second part of *Die Winterreise* to Haslinger. I won't be going to Graz this year, since both my money and the weather are quite unfavourable. However, I gladly accept the invitation to Dr Menz's [a doctor who lived with Jenger. Ed.] as I always enjoy hearing Baron Schönstein sing.

Franz Lachner maintained later in his memoirs that Schubert received one florin for six of the twelve songs, but this is nowhere near the truth. The second part of the cycle is dated October 1827, but this can only refer to the date of the composition of *Die Post*, the first song of the series. It is therefore perfectly possible that the last songs were written at the same time as, or even later than, the Heine settings. The second part of *Die Winterreise* appeared on 30th December 1828 after Schubert's death. Along with the final piano works for two and four hands came a group of superb songs, including the seven Rellstab settings from the *Schwanengesang*. Rellstab had offered his poems, copied out in a beautiful copperplate, to Beethoven, but the master had died without being able to consider them, and Rellstab thought that he had lost all chance of having them set to music. When Haslinger published Schubert's last thirteen songs after his death, however, Rellstab was astounded to find his missing poems among them. He described how his manuscripts were returned to him by Anton Schindler from Beethoven's estate:

A few had pencil marks on them, in Beethoven's own hand; those were the ones which he liked best and which he then passed on to Schubert to be set, because he was himself too ill. These are now among Schubert's best-known songs. I received the manuscripts with some emotion since they had travelled a very strange route before they came back to me—but they had fructified Art on the way.

Whether Beethoven did in fact tell Schindler, his secretary, to pass the poems on to Schubert, or whether the secretary had acted on his own initiative cannot now be established. It is certain however that Schubert wanted to publish the seven songs as part of his next song-cycle. An eighth, wonderfully powerful song with the title *Lebensmut* (D 937) was to be the opening song, but this remained a fragment. The Heine songs too, with a few additional ones, were planned to form an independent cycle. Haslinger put the two un-completed groups together without examining them, added the beautiful *Taubenpost* at the end—it really has no connection with the others—so that, as a result, *Schwanengesang* is a collection of disparate songs. Spaun records that it was Schubert's intention to dedicate the collection 'to his friends'. It was a business arrangement between Schubert's brother Ferdinand and Haslinger after Schubert's death which led to the grouping of the songs and their publication, without an opus number, in April 1829 (D 957, nos. 1–14).

The first of the Rellstab songs is the charming *Liebesbotschaft* (no. 1) which is lightly carried along on an even undulating rhythm. For the last time, we can hear the murmuring of the Schubertian brook, and the pianist must not deprive the song of the pleasant, unhurried reflection of the happy lover, for the three melodies, the first of which is heard again at the end, flow along almost as if spoken inwardly. Schubert inserts one-bar echoes after the first four lines but, so as to avoid monotony, he sensitively omits them from the second stanza and then reintroduces them all the more effectively at the end. A sketch exists for a quite different version of the same poem in 9/8 and 4/4 time. The initial oppres-siveness of *Kriegers Ahnung* (no. 2) is followed by a yearning lyricism, but the dominant emotion throughout is melancholy, and it has the last word in this emotional chaos. Once again, we have the final example of a Schubertian Lied-form, the small operatic *scena* of the type of *arioso* passages he used to write when young. Here too, as in the earlier works, the at times merely external connection with the text, in the gentle A flat major section, for example, deprives the song of any sustained sense of conviction. Because of the song's great range and its continually changing emotions, the baritone voice, for which the song was intended, should not be tempted to continual bursts of explosiveness. In spite of the many high F's of the original C minor key, this is a song for a true bass-baritone and the text reminds us of Schubert's early friendship with Körner.

Repeated hesitations interrupt the mood of the four-bar passages of *Frühlingssehnsucht* (no. 3). Schubert crowns the mood of surging passion with an energetic final cadence. The concert singer might well omit the repetitions of the second and fourth verses so as not to lessen the effect of the uncertain question. This is an example of the strict strophic song, here with slight variations in the minor, being written even in Schubert's final years. The mood and the use of the left-hand in the piano suggest a close relationship to *Liebesbotschaft*.

The popular *Ständchen* (no. 4) probably needs no commentary. The sensuousness of this plaint in the minor mode becomes more passionate in the third stanza; the whole song is framed in mandolin music. The charm of the song has guaranteed its universal popularity, not always to the advantage of the performance. Here again a sensuous lyricism must not be confused with a continuous *forte*. Yet this work, too, was written in a vale of tears. A characteristic Schubert ploy is his expressive use of the caesura—a much more ambiguous device in music than in the spoken word. Whenever the echo of the vocal cadence appears in the piano, one seems to be able to hear the serenader holding his breath as he strains to listen.

Aufenthalt (no. 5) exemplifies Schubert's tendency in his later works to combine completely unrelated tonalities in chords, as here at the climax 'starrender Fels' ('high on the crags'). This is one of the tempestuous songs, something that must be stressed, since the marking 'nicht zu geschwind' ('not too quickly') tends to make singers let the tempo drag to the detriment of the music. Nor does the swelling conclusion, to be sung freely, permit any real *ritenuto*.

Schubert's dynamic directions carefully avoid any premature release of the *fff*'s on the last page.

In *In der Ferne* (no. 6) the move into the major mode hints at soughing winds, lapping waves, all the sympathetic phenomena of nature comforting the homesick exile. The underlying poetic idea could have come from the *Winterreise*: Woe to the disappointed lover who leaves his homeland in a fit of temper. Schubert endows this dark song with an imposing breadth, a gentleness in the major mode section, and an intensification and great sweep in the final section.

The last of Schubert's 'riding'-songs is *Abschied* (no. 7). He turns the rather self-conscious simplicity of the poem into a graceful naturalness, the horse trots gently along, which gives just the right tempo. The cries of 'Ade!' ('Farewell!') are differently coloured at each repetition while the mood darkens at the end. Schubert set the six stanzas to alternating but similar melodies in E flat and A flat major, until the last, quite different melody halts the song in the far-distant key of C flat. Schubert delighted in letting a mood fade away, and here, too, the horse's hoofbeats seem to echo away into the distance at the end.

On 2nd October 1828 Schubert made an urgent request to Schott and Probst to publish the works that they had accepted from him. He wrote to Probst:

> Sir! I have been asking myself when the trio [Piano Trio in E flat, op. 100, published in full 1886. Ed.] will finally appear? Have you not yet decided the opus number? It is No. 100. I await its appearance with longing. Among other things, I have composed three sonatas for pianoforte [The three last sonatas, No. 13 in C minor, No. 14 in A major and No. 15 in B flat major, published by Diabelli in 1838. Ed.] which I should like to dedicate to Hummel. I have also set several songs by Heine from Hamburg which were extraordinarily well-liked here [The six Lieder now in the *Schwanengesang*. Ed.] and finally a quintet for two violins, one viola and two violoncellos [The String Quintet in C op. 163 was not published till 1853 by C. A. Spina. Ed.]. I have played the sonatas in several places to great applause, but the quintet is to be rehearsed shortly. If any of these compositions seem to be suitable for you, please let me know. Respectfully yours Frz. Schubert.

On 12th January the Schubertian circle had held their first readings of Heine's poems. The 'Reiseideen' ('Travel Thoughts') were discussed, and there was more or less unanimity, wrote Franz von Hartmann, that they contained 'much that was pleasant, a good deal of wit and many wrong-headed views'. Schubert took the newly-published 'Buch der Lieder' ('Book of Songs') away with him with the intention of setting six of the poems to begin with. The boldness of these six creations matches the novelty of Heine's cynical style, which mocks the Goethe epigones. Their first performance—most enthusiastically received—seems to have taken place at a *soirée musicale* at Dr Ignaz Menz's house. Schubert himself supplied the titles to Heine's untitled poems. We can see from these songs that his spirit was still lively and unbroken by his illness. His approach to the texts and his manner of setting them may not have changed, but how new every detail is, how different the degree of intensity and the indications of aesthetic awareness. When listening to these miraculous compositions, one must have mixed feelings of astonishment and regret at the artistic breakthrough which they represent. No other prematurely deceased artist ever produced such startling innovations in the last months of his life.

The symphonic opening theme of *Der Atlas* (no. 8), staggering along and groaning under its burden, has a tragic grandeur. The repetition of the first stanza introduces a triumphant cry of self-laceration into this pain-stricken song. The defiance, the tension of the recitatives, the echo of pride in the middle section and the negative triumph of the conclusion combine to give an impression of a gambler about to make his last throw. The minor mode represents loneliness, a ghostly unison in *Ihr Bild* (no. 9), but this changes immediately into the major when the picture of the beloved is brought to life. The initial B flat minor section is followed by the smiling G flat major. When the lover realises, however, that he has lost the girl for ever, the opening melody returns, not just repeated, but intensified, to confirm the sad fact. The writing could hardly be more economical; there is not a superfluous note in this restrained lover's lament.

Those who maintain that Schubert failed to capture Heine's irony in *Das Fischermädchen* (no. 10) cannot have read the music carefully. The barcarolle form could hardly be used more simply to catch the delicate sultriness of the poem. And what about the nonchalant seventh slurs at the end of each stanza, which really do not take themselves at all seriously? Just when we are expecting to come to the end of the melody line, Schubert takes the voice up in a sort of caressing gesture. One of the three quatrains slips abruptly from A flat major to C flat major and this, along with the word-repetitions which do not occur in the poem, lends a touch of impertinence to the setting.

These were followed by three of Schubert's greatest master-pieces. *Die Stadt* (no. 11) is a representation of the dark side of Nature. The monotonous wave-figure is pursued by two beating chords as though the boatman were sinking his oars into the water 'mit traurigem Takte' ('with a sad beat'). The picture of melancholy is without parallel in music. The *ostinato motif* and the accusatory ending are closely related to the *Winterreise*. In the middle section, the *motif* of the piano prelude is repeated in the postlude and the song ends on the loneliest of all single notes. *Am Meer* (no. 12) displays a superb control of freely formed stanzas that blends lyricism and recitatives and introduces dramatic *tremoli* as well. The pure vocal line, so difficult to sing in the *adagio,* has contributed substantially to the folk-like character of the song. Although the ending dies away, the turn on 'Tränen' ('tears') has that sort of irony which some critics claim to be absent from the Heine songs. *Der Doppelgänger* (no. 13) treads a path not without hazards for Schubert's successors. The singing voice alone assumes the dramatic function of speech, while both melody and rhythm are sacrificed to 'atmosphere' and the description of the conflict situation. Only Schubert's genius could put the amusical technique of the *Sprechgesang* completely at the service of the music. His successors, who followed him along this path, have not fully succeeded in avoiding the many pitfalls. Despite the three climactic moments in the song, the unity of the whole is preserved: the voice and accompaniment moving parallel in unison vividly depict the identical movements of the man and his shadow. Like *Der Atlas, Der Doppelgänger* is an outsider standing on the periphery of events. Neither song is completely *durchkomponiert*, they develop rather out of the text. They held enormous importance for the development of dramatic singing, particularly as far as Wagner was concerned. It is rather surprising that no one has pointed out the close connection between Wagner and Schubert, since only a superficial study would claim that they had nothing in common. Fourteen years of resignation preceded this dramatic outburst at the end of Schubert's life, and he seems to have rid himself of a lifelong yearning with this one cry. Yet his confession ends in the major; it does not wallow in self-pity. The theme of the *Agnus Dei*, from the Mass in E flat of a few months earlier, is the basis of the song, a clear proof of the enigmatical connections between unrequited love and a struggle with God.

Der Doppelgänger is built up on a series of four-bar phrases reminiscent of the classical *passacaglia*. The echo-repetition after 'wohnte mein Schatz' ('my love dwelt') seems to be a mere Schubertian formal mannerism, but it never fails to be deeply moving; there is always something heartfelt and gentle in such repetitions of parts of the melody.

In the final song of the volume (which, as we have said, was added later), *Die Taubenpost* (no. 14), one senses the spiritual pivot of Schubert's musical testimony:

> Sie heißt—die Sehnsucht!
> Kennt ihr sie? Die Botin treuen Sinns.

(She is called Longing! Do you know her, this messenger of faithfulness?)

Although it belongs in content and meaning to neither the Heine nor the Rellstab group, *Die Taubenpost* (by Seidl) is nevertheless first-class Schubert. The syncopated accompaniment depicts the impatient beating of the yearning heart. The vocal line and the piano share many of the phrases. We feel that Schubert has returned to the style of the *Schöne Müllerin* songs, which only further proves how innovative and transforming an effect Heine's language had on him compared with that of the conventional Seidl poem. At the same time, it meant two feet on the ground again, a return of that longing to which Schubert was never afraid to give voice, even when it pained him. The scarcely perceptible alteration in the repetition: 'Kennt ihr sie?' ('Do you know her?') marks the inner development that is taking place. The loss of illusions is manifested, at first casually, on two identical notes, simply harmonised, and then later by the descent from E flat to D, and in the darker harmonies. Now and then the composition resists declamation in obeying an inner necessity. There is no sense of finality here; hope, and the anticipation of experiences yet to come, speak to us out of this music. But *we* know that thoughts of the future, and of their realisation, were vain hopes.

Shortly before these last songs were written, Schubert wrote *Der Hirt auf dem Felsen* (D 965) based on Wilhelm Müller's poem 'Der Berghirt' ('The Mountain Shepherd'), in his mind the voice of Anna Milder-Hauptmann who, three years previously, had sung his *Suleika* so successfully, and who had taken *Erlkönig* with her on her concert tours. She was the quintessential opera singer, the first Leonore in *Fidelio*, a shattering Medea and a superb Iphigenia. Beethoven worshipped her, Napoleon was said to have been in love with her. Her versatility astounds us today, for what Leonore would dare to attempt the coloraturas of *Der Hirt auf dem Felsen*? With this song, Schubert hoped to win her over to taking a rôle in the prospective production of his opera, *Der Graf von Gleichen*; but he did not live long enough either to complete the opera, or to hear the first performance of this song with clarinet obbligato. After Schubert's death, Ferdinand Schubert gave the manuscript to Vogl, who then handed it over to the soprano. It may sound surprising that Schubert took more than three years to fulfil Milder's wish for a bravura concert piece. Nor did the announcement of her concert tour hurry him on. Probably not even this tempting offer could deflect him from his path, which led in the direction of German lyrical Lieder rather than that of brilliant Italianate virtuoso pieces.

The Schubert songs that Anna Milder had performed in Berlin were the formally bold songs, *durchkomponiert* and with structured *motifs*, in which the accompaniment was of equal stature, and in which voice and instrument blended into a unity. The traditional strophic song with a modest accompaniment could certainly not complain of neglect in the Prussian capital. One has only to think of the names which helped it to flower here: Johann Peter Schulz, Carl Friedrich Zelter, Johann Friedrich Reichardt, Ludwig Berger, Bernhard Klein and the young Mendelssohn. In hesitating so long, Schubert seemed to have been well aware of the innovative nature of his creations. Perhaps the song would never have been written at all had he not hoped that Frau Milder would accept the rôle in his opera. In this song *scena*, he combines brilliance and the 'suitable passages' requested by Frau Milder, with naturalness. He also meets the singer's wish for alternating moods. He even decided on a, for him, rare alteration of the text which he had found among Müller's *Ländliche Lieder* ('Rural Songs'). Wilhelmine von Chézy rewrote the middle section. When Vogl finally handed the song over to Frau Milder she could not thank Schubert, for he was dead by the time she performed it in Riga for the first time in 1830. The shepherd greets Spring on his flute which, for the sake of the pastoral effect, becomes a clarinet in the song. What was to be a virtuoso piece becomes a deeply moving work of art, which has only come into its own in the last forty years, through interpreters like Elisabeth Schumann, Lotte Schöne, Adele Kern, Erna Berger, Rita Streich and Elly Ameling. (The copy used by Frau Milder-Hauptmann for the first performance was made by Ferdinand Schubert after his brother's death.)

An attempt to repeat Schubert's successful concert in Hungary unfortunately failed. Schindler had left Vienna after Beethoven's death and settled in Budapest where he managed to present Lachner's first opera, *Die Bürgschaft*, based on the same Schiller ballad which Schubert had set in 1815. Schindler's invitation (of 11th October 1828) to the première included a tempting inducement to stage a similar concert to the one in Vienna, but to no avail. Schubert had experienced attacks of giddiness and haemorrhages and any travelling was out of the question. We quote the following from Schindler's none-too-tactful letter of 11th October:

Since and whereas your name has a good reputation here, we propose the following enterprise to you, namely: that you decide to give a private concert at which mainly your songs will be performed. This promises to be a great success, and since we already know that your timidity and easy-going ways will keep you from participating in the venture yourself, I am informing you that you will find people here only too willing to give you a helping hand, no matter how heavy you are. Yet you must contribute something yourself, namely, you must obtain five or six letters from aristocratic houses in Vienna to the same here. Lachner is thinking for example of Count Esterházy and I think, for example, that you should say a word to your solid friend Pinterics who will certainly get you some of his princes . . . So go to it! Let us not have any long arguments and no airs please.

You will have the very best support available. There is a young amateur singer here who sings your songs well, very well, in a very beautiful tenor voice, he is here, also the gentlemen from the theatre, so all you have to do is to plump your fat self down in a chair and accompany what is to be sung.

Schubert felt too weak to answer. The contaminated drinking-water and the lack of sanitary facilities in Ferdinand's new house were already showing their catastrophic consequences. It is difficult to appreciate the hopelessness he felt, particularly as the Viennese public remained completely indifferent to, and took scarcely any notice of him, so that this Hungarian concert would really have meant a step forward. When typhoid fever attacked him, he had nothing to fight the infection with but a useless body without any powers of resistance.

With Spaun acting as intermediary, Schubert had sent his 23rd Psalm (D 449) to the Frauen-Cäcilien-Verein in Lemberg. The conductor of the choir, Franz Xaver Wolfgang Mozart, Mozart's second son, sent Spaun back to the composer with an address of thanks which pleased Schubert greatly. Spaun wrote later in his memoirs:

He told me: 'Copy out the Grillparzer *Ständchen* and send it to the ladies in Lemberg'. I did this and took the copy to Schubert for him to look through. I found him ill in bed, though his condition did not seem too grave. He corrected my copy in bed and was pleased to see me, saying: 'I have everything I want only I feel so exhausted, I think I shall fall through the bed.'

In the last days of his life, Schubert was frequently delirious, during which times he sang continuously. In his conscious moments he did not rest, but corrected the proofs of the second part of *Winterreise* which Haslinger had sent him before publication. The fight with death was waged by an already weakened body consumed by a restlessness of spirit and by a creativity beyond all human understanding. 'Nervous fever' was the name given to the typhoid fever which was a frequent cause of death in Vienna at that time and was caused by inadequate sanitation. Schubert died on 19th November 1828, having been lovingly cared for by his step-sister, Josefa, and his brother Ferdinand.

FIFTEEN

Post Mortem

On 22nd November Schubert, according to his wishes, was buried near Beethoven, after his brother Ferdinand had paid the extra costs of having the body moved to the district cemetery of Währing. At the request of the Schubert family, Schober wrote new words to the song *Pax Vobiscum* (D 551), which were sung at the consecration of the body in the church of St Josef, in the suburb of Margareten. The official account of Schubert's estate read:

His estate according to the testimony of his father and brother consists solely of the following:

3 cloth evening-dress coats, 3 frockcoats, 10 pairs of trousers, 9 waistcoats	*37fl.*
1 hat, 5 pairs of shoes, 2 pairs of boots	*2fl.*
4 shirts, 9 scarves and handkerchiefs, 13 pairs of socks, 1 sheet, 2 coverlets	*8fl.*
1 mattress, 1 pillow, 1 blanket	*6fl.*

Apart from some old music books, estimated at 10 florins, no other belongings of the deceased have been found.

The music books mentioned were indeed only used music paper, his father and Schober having taken possession of the manuscripts. Ferdinand and the rest of the family hastened to settle all the many outstanding debts, although they could only manage this in instalments. Among the manuscripts were works of the last, but also many of the earlier years.

The friends and admirers who stood round the open grave well knew what they had lost, yet not even they, who knew but a few songs, some chamber works, the four-handed piano and dance pieces, could imagine the true dimensions of Schubert's musical legacy. Many, too many, of the over 600 songs are still unknown, even today. In the nineteenth century, only a few were made known to the general musical public and many of those only in simplified arrangements, such as Friedrich Silcher's strophic setting of *Der Lindenbaum* for male chorus. A 'divine melody' still made the greatest impact, but one is astonished at the lack of readiness and desire in these years to get to know more about the less easily understood qualities of the 'unknown' Schubert, that is, of five-sixths of his total output of songs.

In order to clear Franz's debts, Ferdinand sold the last three piano sonatas and the so-called *Schwanengesang* ('Swan Song') minus the *Taubenpost*, to Tobias Haslinger. The publication of the songs was announced for the beginning of 1829. Ferdinand received 300 florins, about £30 in today's currency, as an advance payment and about £20 in the same month from Czerny. By July, about £135 had been gathered in.

Schubert's friends could not understand that he had gone so quickly. The familiar picture of a man long marked by death, working feverishly under such a burden, bears little relation to the facts. Nor is Grillparzer's inscription for the Schubert memorial a judgement based on ignorance, as has been said. On the contrary, Schubert's friends chose this from five others because it best expressed their feelings about a prematurely terminated creative life:

'Music buried here a rich treasure but many more beautiful hopes.' (Die Tonkunst begrub hier einen reichen Besitz, aber noch viel schönere Hoffnungen.)

Of the four inscriptions which the cautious Grillparzer submitted to Schubert's friends the first again stressed the dominant presence of the songs in the minds of men: 'Wanderer! Hast du Schuberts Lieder gehört? Unter diesem Steine liegt er. (Hier liegt, der sie sang.)' (Wanderer! have you heard Schubert's songs? He lies under this stone. (Here lies the man who sang them.)) The fourth version is beautifully and accurately worded, again with reference to the songs: 'Er hiess die Dichtung tönen und reden die Musik. Nicht Frau und nicht Magd, als Schwestern umarmen sich die beiden über Schuberts Grab.' (He bade poetry sing and music speak. Neither is a mistress, neither a servant, the two embrace as sisters over Schubert's grave.)

The third version, the one destined for posterity, went with that ghastly memorial from the late nineteenth century which was erected in Vienna's Central Cemetery after the second exhumation.

It is possible that Grillparzer's parting words might be more readily appreciated in the knowledge that, only a few days before his death, Schubert had applied to Simon Sechter, the future teacher of Anton Bruckner, to take classes in counterpoint. This is the action of a maestro whose conscience has driven him to husband his rich talents, since he has suddenly become aware that he is only on the threshold of his life's work. Seen in this light, Grillparzer's inscription is not so lacking in understanding.

In order to raise money for a memorial fund, Schubert's friends decided to present a concert similar to the first one held in March 1828. They engaged Anna Fröhlich and the latest Schubert interpreter, Franz Schoberlechner, already a frequent performer at the soirées of the *Gesellschaft der Musikfreunde*. (These latter continued incidentally under seven 'directors', and always came back to Schubert's songs and male-voice quartets. These were popular, too, in domestic music-circles in Vienna, among music-lovers in Salzburg, Linz or Graz, and also in the seminaries along the Danube.)

Seidl's *Wiegenlied* (D 867) was published with three other songs as opus 105 on the day of Schubert's funeral. Schubert repeats the lovely tune five times, as if half-asleep. In case the listeners *do* doze off, however, it is advisable to shorten it somewhat.

The other lullaby from these last weeks, *Der Vater mit dem Kind* (D 906), is by Schubert's friend Bauernfeld, who continued to write frothy comedies in the French style which had almost 1,200 performances at the Burgtheater. Both these lullabies seem to be written and sung by parents—thus, at the end of his life, Schubert returns with these gentle songs to his first attempts at writing songs—the lullaby he wrote for his little sister.

At the time of Schubert's death, only a few of his compositions were published; none of his nine symphonies, no operas, only two of the piano sonatas, one of the fourteen string quartets, a total of 200 of the more than 600 songs. Yet it would be wrong to claim that he was neglected. His opp. 1–100 were published before his death, and which young composer, then or since, can claim that *all* of his works have reached publication? With the best will in the world (and granted that that was not always forthcoming), the market could probably not have taken much more Schubert. His industry and productivity would have driven twenty publishers to the brink of despair. The songs published to date were, after all, not the 'commercially popular' ones, but, strangely enough, the great, profound, deeply emotional ones like *Gretchen am Spinnrade*, *Gruppe aus dem Tartarus* or the Harper's Songs from *Wilhelm Meister*.

1828 saw the publication of three groups of songs: the first part of *Die Winterreise* as opus 89, three songs of Walter Scott as opus 85–86 and three Goethe settings (*Der Musensohn, Auf dem See* and *Geistes-Gruß*) as opus 92. Some individual works were privately engraved in the summer. Few of the works which now appeared corresponded to Schubert's own grouping. He had perhaps planned opus 108 (with *Über Wildemann*) and the second part of *Die Winterreise*. There were a few negotiations with publishers still proceeding, and Ferdinand made tremendous efforts to place other works with publishers during the next thirty years. For the time being, the works of Schubert's last days remained in Ferdinand's house. The copies of *Der Tod und das Mädchen* and *Der zürnenden Diana* were in Graz. Albert Stadler possessed *Der Kampf, Thekla, Der Strom* and *Das Grab*; Spaun, the 'musical letter' *Epistel* and the four Italian Canzonettas. A few songs were in Hungary, at Karoline von Esterházy's. Other autographs were in the possession of Joseph von Gahy, Witteczek, Schober, Streinsberg and the Freiherr von Stiebar, many were lost, many again came into the possession of national and state libraries.

In 1830 little was heard of the name of Franz Schubert. A memorial had been erected, piles of manuscripts were heaped on Diabelli's shelves, others lay in the chest which Ferdinand had had made for their safe storage. Chopin came to Vienna in 1830, but no Schubert work was heard, and one seeks in vain in the memoirs of a musician like Carl Czerny for the name of Schubert. For the equivalent of about £500 ($1,000), Diabelli acquired a portion of the manuscripts held by Ferdinand, among them the balance of the solo songs which were published throughout the nineteenth century. Many remain unpublished to this day, among them five completed songs which, one assumes, will be incorporated in the new Collected Edition being prepared by Bärenreiter: *Jägers Abendlied* (by Goethe, 1815), *Mailied* (Hölty, 1816), *Am ersten Maimorgen* (Claudius, 1816), a song without a title and without words from 1817 and *Lebensmut* (Leitner, 1828).

On 18th November 1830 Heinrich Heine ('that Heine from

Hamburg', as Schubert had called him in a letter to his publishers), who was almost the same age as Schubert, wrote to Eduard Marxsen in Vienna. Marxsen, Brahms's future teacher, was studying composition with Ignaz Xaver Seyfried and piano with Karl Maria von Bocklet. Discussing various settings of his poems, Heine mentions Bernhard Klein and 'Schubart' from Vienna. 'I like Klein's compositions very much. I am told that shortly before his death, Schubart also wrote very good music to my songs which unfortunately I have not heard yet.' We have no record of any later comment on Schubert's settings of Heine's poems.

In Robert Schumann's diary for 1828 there are repeated and admiring comments on Schubert. He even wrote a long letter to him but, for some unknown reason, never despatched it. Later he expressed his admiration for Schubert thus:

'He has music for the most sensitive emotions, thoughts, even for events and conditions of life. Schubert's music is as varied as the thousand shapes of mankind's thoughts and aspirations.'

Schumann did not only don Schubert's mantle as a composer after 1840, by raising the Lied to new heights and giving it a contemporary vitality, he was also one of the few to be interested in the future of the musical treasure-trove which he found almost by chance in Ferdinand's house. No one else had even looked at the piles of manuscripts which Schumann proceeded to have catalogued. The first performance of the 'Great' C major Symphony under Mendelssohn's bâton in Leipzig on 21st March 1839, and the discovery of countless songs were among the results of the young man's labours. Only reluctantly was the interest of publishers outside Vienna awakened.

Michael Vogl, now over sixty, never tired of singing the songs which he had helped make famous. Spaun relates in his memoirs: 'Our sad loss did not prevent us from enjoying his creations for long, it rather stimulated us to enjoy them more. Vogl and Schönstein, accompanied by [Emanuel] Mikschik and Jenger sang the wonderful songs at my house or at that of my hospitable friend, Witteczek, and they evoked growing enthusiam.'

Vogl sang *Erlkönig* as late as 1834 at a public concert, and just a few days before his death in 1843 he sang the *Winterreise* to a small group of friends. Spaun remembered the evening at *Hofrat* Enderes':

'. . . the whole company was most deeply moved. It was his swan-song. Few who enjoyed that performance by Vogl are still alive, but these few will never forget the impression—they have never heard anything like it since.'

Hofrat von Mosel, in his study *Die Tonkunst in Wien in den letzten fünf Dezennien* ('Music in Vienna in the last five decades') wrote about Vogl's death:

'. . . . which is all the more to be regretted since, despite my urgent and repeated entreaties, I never succeeded in getting him to write a text-book on the art of declamatory and dramatic singing which no one would have been as qualified to write as he.'

Vogl would certainly have frowned, and Schubert would just as certainly have laughed, had they known that, in 1835, a baritone of the Paris Opéra would introduce *Der Wanderer* into France as 'The Wandering Jew', although this *gaffe* did nothing to detract from the song's popularity in France.

In the early part of 1838 an event of some importance for the Schubert-Lied took place in Vienna. Franz Liszt gave the first performances of his piano-transcriptions of Lieder. Since then, these arrangements have generally been howled down and condemned as sacrilege. On the other hand, it must be understood that Schubert's art, brought in this way for the first time to the attention of a wider public, could not have been rendered a greater service. Audiences were stunned by the electrifying effect of Liszt's playing of these songs. The critic of Breitkopf & Härtel's *Musikzeitung* reported to Leipzig that, in these works, Liszt 'makes the piano sing as none before him'. Liszt made these transcriptions in Paris, Geneva and Nohant, and continued to polish them on his travels. His first performances were of *Lob der Tränen* and *Horch, horch die Lerch'*. Liszt retains all the characteristics of the song without unnecessary additions or alterations. His instinct for stylistic peculiarities made his treatment of Schubert's Lieder quite different from his transcriptions of Italian salon arias or operatic melodies. Only occasionally does he attempt to replace the missing words with a dash of that nineteenth century 'tone-painting' which sounds so old-fashioned today. Liszt's frequent habit of transposing the vocal line to the left hand of the piano, as if the baritone were singing the first verse, and then only later surrounding it with figurations, can become a disturbing mannerism. Yet, despite all the liberties he took, and all the brilliance of his pianistic technique, Liszt nevertheless did not employ his usual extravagantly ornate virtuoso effects in these transcriptions, but rather placed them at the service of art. He said once of Schubert: 'In the short compass of a song, he makes us witness to brief but mortal conflicts,' which proves that he had a clear awareness of the true significance of these creations.

That same spring (1838) Haslinger published the first group of Liszt transcriptions under the old-fashioned title (later removed) of *Hommage aux Dames de Vienne* (Homage to the Ladies of Vienna):

1. Ständchen	2. Lob der Tränen
3. Die Post	4. Die Rose

Diabelli published the next, larger collection: *Sei mir gegrüßt, Auf dem Wasser zu singen, Du bist die Ruh', Erlkönig, Meeresstille, Die junge Nonne, Frühlingsglaube, Gretchen am Spinnrade, Ständchen, Rastlose Liebe, Der Wanderer, Ave Maria*. Then followed, at irregular intervals, these songs published by Schuberth, Schlesinger, Spina, Diabelli and Haslinger: *Litanei, Himmelsfunken, Die Gestirne, Hymne, Lebewohl, Des Mädchens Klage, Das Sterbeglöcklein (Zügenglöcklein* is meant), *Trockene Blumen, Ungeduld, Die Forelle, Das Wandern, Der Müller am Bach, Der Jäger, Die böse Farbe, Wohin, Die Stadt, Das Fischermädchen, Aufenthalt, Am Meer, Abschied, In der Ferne, Ständchen, Ihr Bild, Frühlingssehnsucht, Liebesbotschaft, Der Atlas, Der Doppelgänger, Die Taubenpost, Kriegers Ahnung, Gute Nacht, Die Nebensonnen, Mut, Die Post, Erstarrung, Wasserflut, Der Lindenbaum, Der Leiermann, Täuschung, Das Wirtshaus, Der stürmische Morgen, Im Dorfe.*

These transcriptions offer us the rare opportunity of studying a great artist's view and interpretation of fifty-four Schubert songs. To these must be added the orchestral transcriptions: *Die junge Nonne, Gretchen am Spinnrade, Lied der Mignon, Erlkönig*. At the end of 1870 in Budapest, Liszt arranged *Die Allmacht* for tenor, orchestra and male chorus. Even if no account were taken of the transcriptions of orchestral works, it can be seen how much Liszt championed Schubert's cause. When he called Schubert 'le musicien le plus poète que jamais', he showed a discrimination rare in an age in which the study of style counted for little.

In 1864, the *Schöne Müllerin* was published for the second time in its original form. This naturally revived the controversy about

Vogl's alterations, the so-called 'embellishments'. The original versions were first published by Sauer & Leidesdorf in 1824. In 1829, *after* Schubert's death that is, Diabelli published an edition with the ornamentations then in general use. There were also changes in harmony, melody, ties and dynamics such as had already been made in the other Schubert songs. The 'editors' are not named, but one can safely assume that the publisher and the singer were jointly responsible. Friedländer has proved beyond all doubt that Vogl was responsible for the 'improvements' in the *Schöne Müllerin* songs. Diabelli's new edition continued to be published until into the 1880's, and Spina's 1864 edition of the original version stirred up the controversy only temporarily. After the establishment of a 'clean' Schubert edition, Max Friedländer published Vogl's alterations in a supplementary volume, erring there, however, in ascribing the singer's 'corrections' to his predilection for the Italian school of singing. Vogl's actual ornamentations were kept within quite reasonable bounds—shortage of breath and vocal limitations were the much more frequent cause of alterations. Above all, however, he wanted to emphasis the *drama* of the song—which reminds us of the strange remark he made to Schubert at their first meeting: 'You are not enough of a charlatan.' These alterations were certainly not arbitrary decisions on Vogl's part, but rather a remembrance of improvisations agreed with Schubert before certain performances, which, however, could only relate to himself and could have no general validity. There is a passage in a letter to Stadler of 1831 which may reveal something of Vogl's attitude here:

> Nearly everyone enjoys singing this or that note. Usually one also puts other suitable words under the notes written for the voice; that is because few musicians really treat music as a language which like German, French, Italian wants to say and express just this or that: but I should like to know who could write other words under Schubert's *Erlkönig*, *Gretchen am Spinnrade*, *An Anselmos Grabe*, *Müllerlieder*, *Winterreise*, etc., etc.

The growing popularity of Schubert's music brought with it a sad phenomenon: Schubert was frequently cast as the hero of stage- and later film-scenarios. The first example was Hans Max Freiherr von Päumann's 1864 'Original *Liederspiel* [lit. song-play. Ed.] in one act, with music, based on Schubert's compositions, by

Franz von Suppé.' What do we find? A dramatisation of the *Schöne Müllerin* songs with *Ungeduld* as the show number, written here, of course, for Karoline Esterházy. The miller-lad gets the girl and the wicked hunter must resign himself to it. Schubert, as the Fairy Godmother, comes onto the stage and asks the master miller to bless the happy pair. The composer who brings happiness to all is praised by the assembled company and can throw himself into the arms of his Esterházy fiancée, bellowing 'Dein ist mein Herz und soll es ewig bleiben' ('Thine is my heart and it will be so for ever'). This trash was not only not rejected, it was actually printed in 1879. In 1897, for the centenary of Schubert's birth, two 'Festspiele' (festival plays) made their appearance. Gustav Burchhard introduced the melancholy artist, resigned to death, to his tearful audience, not forgetting to have the Erlking's daughters appear in a vision to the febrile Schubert, and attempt to abduct him into the land of the spirits. But at the very last moment this catastrophe is averted, the staunch hero clings to 'the glorious Virgin' and breathes his last to the strains of *Ave Maria*. Heinrich Zöllner called his play *Eine Schubertiade,* although it has absolutely no connection with these gatherings, but is rather (or naturally!) about a sentimental love-affair with a countess.

In spring 1865, some of the songs were to be sold to help members of the far-flung Schubert clan out of financial difficulties. Franz Theodor Schubert had founded a family, some of whose descendants are alive today. Köhler's *Stammtafel der Familie Schubert* (Genealogy of the Schubert Family), in Vienna's city library, stretches into the twenties of the present century and lists more than two hundred names. Franz's second-oldest brother, Ferdinand Lukas, contributed greatly to the spread of the Schubert name. When headmaster of the Normal-Hauptschule, St Anna, he married twice, to Anna Schülle and Theresia Spezierer, and was blessed with twenty-eight progeny, of whom no fewer than eighteen survived into adulthood. He died in 1859, and his widow found herself financially embarrassed. Johann Herbeck, who was enthusiastically supporting the erection of a Schubert memorial, arranged a concert by his orchestra, the Vienna Philharmonic, in spring 1865 to raise money for the memorial fund. In addition to performances of the great C major Symphony and two Entr'actes from *Rosamunde*, Karoline Bettelheim sang *Memnon, Gruppe aus dem Tartarus, Am*

Grabe Anselmos and *Geheimes*. Ferdinand's widow received a comparatively substantial sum from the proceeds, which, however, was not a permanent solution to the Schubert family's financial problems.

In 1867, Johannes Brahms, resident for some time now in Vienna and a life-long, sympathetic admirer of Schubert, began to campaign for a new edition of the works. He helped with the revisions and was one of the first who sought to publish the *Schöne Müllerin* songs in the original version, that is, without the now fashionable disfigurements. Although his publisher, Rieter-Biedermann, did not accept his suggestions, Brahms nevertheless prepared the ground for their later realisation. He also campaigned for a revision of Schubert's forgotten opera *Fierrabras*, but a librettist who could save this charming music has never yet been found. The following passage from a letter by Brahms to Reiter testifies to the pleasure his work on Schubert gave him:

> Altogether I owe my most satisfying hours to the unpublished works of Schubert, a great number of which I have in manuscript form here at home. Yet, however enjoyable and pleasurable it is to look at them, everything else connected with them is so sad. Another whole pile of unpublished things was sold recently at an unbelievably low price; fortunately they were acquired by the *Gesellschaft der Musikfreunde*. How many things are scattered here and there in the houses of private individuals, who either guard their treasures like dragons, or let them carelessly disappear.

And in another letter to Schubring in 1863 he wrote:

> My love affair with Schubert is a very serious matter, precisely because it is not a passing fancy. Where else is there a genius like his, soaring so boldly and certainly up to the heavens, where we see the few giants sitting enthroned? He seems to me to be like a young god playing with Jupiter's thunder and handling it a little bit singularly now and then. But he plays in regions, and at a height, which others cannot scale for long.

In 1862 Brahms composed orchestral versions of a few Schubert songs, among them *Im Abendrot* and *Der Einsame* for his friend, the eminent baritone, Julius Stockhausen, who then took the unpublished material to England, where it was lost. Otto Erich

Deutsch discovered *Geheimnis*, *An Schwager Kronos* and *Memnon* in 1936 in the library of Windsor Castle, and published the scores, enriched by a version for chorus and large orchestra of *Gruppe aus dem Tartarus*, which Brahms had fashioned for Stockhausen, who did not have this song in his repertoire. It does credit to Brahms that he asserted that of all the Schubert songs there was not one 'from which our generation could not learn something'.

The famous singer and choral conductor, Julius Stockhausen, (1826–1906) had sung *Die schöne Müllerin* in 1854 in Vienna for the first time as a complete cycle and, on that occasion, he earned about three times what Schubert himself received for the work. The impending commercialisation of concert-going had begun. The singer's scores in the Stockhausen archives in Frankfurt am Main show that in almost all cases he preferred Müller's original text to Schubert's minor alterations.

'Ein Schubert-Abend bei Ritter von Spaun' (A Schubert evening at the Spaun house), the sepia drawing by Moritz von Schwind, so attractive to every Schubertian, was completed in 1868 at Lake Starnberg and came into the possession of the city of Vienna in 1906. Schwind had painted musical themes all his life. The *Magic Flute* frescoes in the Loggia, and the composer's *lunettes* in the foyer of the Vienna Opera, were his last works. Seven years after Schubert's death, he was planning to decorate a 'Schubert Room', in which each wall would be dedicated to one of the most important of Schubert's authors. Later he conceived a 'Schubert Apotheosis' for the third wall of a music room, in which Mozart was to be glorified by a Magic-Flute picture, and Beethoven by Schwind's 'Symphonie', in which Schubert can also be vaguely detected. Finally, he painted the 'Schubert-Abend' which was to show 'my very good friend Schubert at the piano with an audience . . . old Vogl singing and all our friends of that time, men and women, gathered round.' The sketch in oils of somewhat later date is one of the few pictures which testify to Schwind's mastery of that medium, too.

In 1883, Max Friedländer discovered a treasure among the bequeathed papers of Karl Schubert—a draft in pencil of the *Credo* of the A flat major Mass. The same papers also contained the first version of *Die gefangenen Sänger* (A. W. von Schlegel) (D 712) with the date January 1821. The sketch lay under the pile of manuscripts which came to Schubert's brother Ferdinand after Schubert's death and were passed on to Ferdinand's son Karl. (The duet fragment *Linde Lüfte wehen*, not catalogued in Deutsch, was also found.) Schlegel's caged birds naturally symbolise the suppression of artistic freedom, but there is little trace of that theme in Schubert's lovely 6/8 melody. The first idea could really only last for one page, and, to fill out the remaining five stanzas, Schubert links a whole chain of ideas together, which nevertheless result in a musically satisfying whole. Songs like this one would have remained hidden in libraries and archives throughout the world had not scholars taken such pains to gather all this material together, catalogue it in editions which agreed with the findings of contemporary scholarship, and present it to the music-loving public.

The interpretation and understanding of music depends to a large extent on the authentication and identification of its sources and their publication. This scholarly activity is not limited to the publication of single works, but also sets itself the task of preparing a comprehensive survey of the composer's whole *œuvre*. Thus it became necessary to compile *Gesamtausgaben* (Collected Editions), memorial series, work catalogues, publishers' catalogues and musical encyclopaedias. Special mention must be made here of Tobias Haslinger's proposed Collected Edition of Beethoven's works in the early years of the nineteenth century, which was based on handwritten copies, but which was unfortunately never completed. The first truly complete editions were not produced by publishers, but by societies founded specifically for this purpose. After Bach, Handel, Beethoven and Mozart, it was Schubert's turn in 1884–1897. Among those who sponsored the new edition were the leading musical scholars of the day: Chrysander, Spitta, Becker, Sandbecker, Mandyczewski, Seiffert and many more, the most prominent of whom was Johannes Brahms. Eusebius Mandyczewski (1857–1929) who has often been mentioned as the editor of the section on Lieder of Breitkopf & Härtel's Schubert *Gesamtausgabe*, owed his romantic first name to the admiration of his father, a Greek Orthodox priest, for a saint. In the light of the significance which Robert Schumann attached to the name, it seemed most appropriate for a musician, who combined comprehensive knowledge with enthusiasm. When Hanslick retired from the Chair of Music at the University of Vienna in 1895, Mandyczewski was considered as his successor. The modest archivist wrote to Brahms:

I have one serious concern about the University matter; that my knowledge is not sufficient for the moment. For under Spitta's marvellous influence, musicological research has made such progress and is so far-reaching as one could not have suspected twenty-five years ago, and so much more knowledge is now demanded today of one who occupies a chair like Hanslick's than before him.

Nevertheless, Mandyczewski taught for more than thirty years, up until his death, at the Vienna Conservatoire. In addition to this work and his activities as publisher, he also acted as choral director of the Vienna Academy of Singing, and later as conductor of his own female choir, for which he composed a series of works.

In preparing his critical edition of Schubert's songs he used autographs, original editions—that is, those which Schubert himself had supervised and supplied with opus numbers—then the earliest editions of songs not published by Schubert himself, and finally, copies made during Schubert's lifetime and by his closest friends. Here, the copies made and collected by Schubert's friends Stadler and Witteczeck proved the most valuable. Stadler's collection, written in a beautiful, practised hand, began in 1815 and finished with three collected volumes in 1817. Joseph Witteczek probably did not begin his collection until somewhat later.

A debt is owed to the American Musicological Society which, jointly with the Music Library Association, reprinted this Collected Edition in 1964, thus making it available to a wider audience. While this reprint was still in preparation, the world of music learned of the planned 'New Schubert Edition' to be published by Bärenreiter; fortunately, however, the Americans went ahead without thoughts of rivalry and thus the demands of the moment are satisfied, at least until the conclusion of the later project.

By the end of the nineteenth century, the creative influence of the Schubert Lied could be seen everywhere. In 1883, the twenty-three-year-old Gustav Mahler began work on his *Lieder eines fahrenden Gesellen*, in the last of which the melody 'Auf der Straße steht ein Lindenbaum' ('In the street stands a lime tree') is so close to Schubert that only the most wilful critic would deny its inner relationship to the *Winterreise*. (It is interesting that Mahler and the other great Austrian successor to Schubert, Anton Bruckner, have both been accused of 'heavenly length'.)

In 1886, Peters published Max Friedländer's praiseworthy edition of Schubert's songs. However, one cannot refrain from mentioning that the lack of system in arranging the songs and in the presentation of the scores was bound to lead to many errors in interpretation. In addition, only three of the volumes appeared in transposition for lower voices, which is one of the reasons why all too many of the songs from the 'volumes at the back' remained in the twilight of oblivion, for the transposed editions have always sold best. However, a selection, compiled many years ago by Eduard Behm, made some additional songs available to singers, and those of Friedrich Martienszen and Wolfgang Rosenthal also helped to introduce unfamiliar songs. Friedländer's edition omitted whole groups of songs which were included in the later *Gesamtausgabe,* but he did include a revised version of Goethe's *Liebe schwärmt auf allen Wegen* (D 239, no. 6) which, in expression, is related to the little songs of 1815, but which was originally part of the music to the *Singspiel, Claudine von Villa Bella.* Shortly after 1900 two more theatrical works appeared, one of which by Johann Raudnitz bore the title *Horch, horch die Lerch'*! This 'biography in one act' has Schubert wavering between two women—Therese and Karoline! Karl Costa wrote a popular play called simply *Franz Schubert,* but he made no attempt at biography. The most famous and most fateful product of this sort set out on its triumphant progress during the first World War and always found enthusiastic champions—who claimed that this was the most effective public relations exercise for Schubert's cause. Fortunately, we have become very sensitive to this kind of 'conversion job' and react accordingly. We no longer need to accept Moments-Musicaux-with-words-attached or a Schubert steeped in *Kitsch,* such as the librettists Willner and Reichardt and the music-arranger Berthé brewed up, freely based on the character in Rudolf Hans Bartsch's novel. The flood of Schubert films has also begun to ebb (though not all that long ago), and their task of making the world happy has been given up.

It was due to the efforts of the *Wiener Schubertbund* just before the turn of the century that many unknown masterpieces were given public performances. For example, *Der Hirt auf dem Felsen*: apart from one performance in the 1860's, reported by Hanslick, and which seemed to call forth little response, this song was rediscovered at a 1902 Schubertiad of the *Schubertbund,* when it was performed by Marie Seyff-Katzmayr and the clarinettist, Andreas Dietsch. Since then, the song has become more or less part of the standard concert repertoire.

Schubert's image became even clearer, not only through interpretations of his music, but also because music researchers were clearing away the jungle of hypotheses and falsifications in the presentation of the composer. The Austrian scholar Professor Otto Erich Deutsch made a fundamental and exemplary contribution here; his *Schubert: A Documentary Biography* (trans. Eric Blom)[1] presented readers with so much unknown and previously lost material that we saw how, for the public of 1818–1828, Schubert was hardly the shrinking violet of the descriptions published after his death. The reason for that might well lie in the total silence which surrounded Schubert, until Schumann and Liszt began to campaign for him.

Rarely has one scholar been able to make such an exhaustive collection of material on one of his favourite subjects as did Deutsch. It is shameful that his *Schubert: Thematic Catalogue of all his works in chronological order*, published by Dent in 1951, is still not available in German. The indefatigable Deutsch had to emigrate from Austria to England in 1939. In Cambridge he continued his researches into Schubert and published his findings between 1939 and 1951. Although Deutsch returned to Vienna, his major reference works have still not appeared in German. When will a German publishing house espouse the cause of a scholar who is the equal of a Kinsky or a Köchel?

Deutsch died in 1967 and Schubert scholarship lost its most important pioneer figure. His early *Schubert-Brevier* (1905) was typical of the biography developed by him in other similar works, notably on Schubert and Mozart. The selfless way in which he shared his biographical knowledge and the results of his research with all his colleagues and friends, among them the latest Schubert biographer, M. J. E. Brown, was exemplary. Many British and Austrian libraries are indebted to him for gifts of valuable first editions and bibliographical rarities, many of them bearing on

[1] See also Deutsch, *Schubert: Memoirs by his Friends* (trans. Ley and Nowell).

Schubert's song *œuvre*. Fortunately, at least Deutsch's Schubert documentation has appeared in German, as part of the Collected Edition of the International *Schubert-Gesellschaft*, which appointed Deutsch its Honorary President.

The winter of 1968–1969 saw the latest significant step in Schubert scholarship, when Christa Landon discovered Schubert manuscripts and copies of a few works previously unknown to researchers in the archives of the Vienna *Männergesang-Verein* (Male Choral Society). Of particular interest to me among the very diverse finds was a copy of extracts of handwritten Schubert manuscripts, for they contained two songs believed lost, *Vollendung* and *Die Erde*. (They are listed as one song under D 989 in Deutsch's catalogue.) Dietrich Berke established that the author of *Die Erde* was Friedrich Matthisson; he even found the copy of the poem which Schubert probably used. The *Lesebuch für Mädchen von 10–15 Jahren* (Reader for Girls from 10–15 Years) and the *Lesebuch für Jüngling von 15–20 Jahren* (Reader for boys from 15–20), Vienna 1811–1812, were found to be the source of the poems, and they contained stanzas which Schubert omitted. A copy from the estate of Kreissle von Hellborn, Schubert's first biographer (1865) has *Vollendung* complete, while the last seven bars of *Die Erde* are missing. In a pile of manuscripts by unidentified composers in the archives of the *Gesellschaft der Musikfreunde*, Christa Landon found the two pieces with the title *Lieder für eine Singstimme mit Begleitung des Pianoforte betitelt I. Vollendung: II. Die Erde* (Songs for solo voice with pianoforte accompaniment entitled I. Vollendung II. Die Erde), along with a pencilled note by the archivist: '*unknown*'. This is a copy from the middle of the nineteenth century. Mrs Landon, basing her findings on hints given by Kreissle, dates the songs September or October 1817 although the style and the form suggests rather the Matthisson songs of 1814.

Mrs Landon is also involved in the publication of the section on Lieder in the new Bärenreiter *Gesamtausgabe*, which was begun in 1969 under the joint editorship of herself, Walther Dürr and Arnold Feil. The sequence of songs does not follow a strict chronological order, such as Mandyczewski sought to achieve on the findings available at the turn of the century. The editors have grouped together, firstly, those songs published in Schubert's lifetime, some of which he himself put in sequence, and they have then followed the chronological order established in Deutsch's *Thematic Catalogue*, whereby the variants, or the musically independent versions, are grouped with the earliest version. This allows an interesting view of Schubert's own ordering of his compositions and his groupings for publication. An example of this is the first Goethe volume which was assembled entirely on the principle of internal importance. If, later on, simultaneity became the guiding principle for determining the sequence, one can still recognise laws of inner connections.

This new ordering is not my only reason for regret that I was not able to consult the new edition when making my latest recordings of the Schubert songs.[1] The far-reaching reconstruction of Schubert's idiosyncratic notations, especially in the piano parts, allows an interpretation vastly at variance with those hitherto accepted. Schubert blends the two piano voices to a unity in such a way that, by the addition of an 'eleventh' line, the musical lines ascend and descend beyond the five-line *staves*. Above all, however, there have been so many arbitrary decisions made in the posthumous editions in the matter of ties that their elimination casts a new light on those melismata in the voice where Schubert, in stressing a particular emotion, specifically added one himself. One must eagerly anticipate the completion of this enormous project.

[1] Schubert: *Lieder: Volume I*, DGG 643547–643558: *Volume II*, DGG 2561013–2561025: *Volume III*, DGG 2561235–2561238.

SIXTEEN

Some Interpreters

The twentieth century which has brought so many striking changes in so many fields of art, which has nipped so many lazy practices in the bud, and which, above all, has developed the desire for accurate interpretations, has also greatly advanced the growing interest in Schubert. The works of the great Viennese master were eventually performed on every concert-platform of the musical world—as their content, their musical language and their purity deserved—only after Schubert's death. Anna Milder-Hauptmann and Wilhelmine Schröder-Devrient continued to excite audiences with their Lieder concerts. The names of the professional singers who now and then sang Schubert's songs have not come down to us; many of those who devoted themselves to the pleasant task of singing Schubert were amateurs: the Fröhlich sisters, for example, Karl von Schönstein, August von Gymnich and Karl Umlauff, or that Herr Tietze with the beautiful tenor voice who was kindly hailed by the critics as 'Herr Dilettant'. Tietze sang the soprano solo (in the tenor register, of course) at the first performance of the cantata *Mirjams Siegesgesang* (D 942) in 1829. The singers all did what they could for Schubert, either in domestic circles or in semi-public concerts, but although their enthusiasm knew no bounds, their influence was inevitably comparatively limited. Not every good intention had artistic merit, but some names ought to be mentioned which prove the exceptions to the rule.

Anton Haizinger (1796–1869), a pupil of Salieri, is an important figure in the history of the Schubert-Lied. His beautiful tenor voice gained the enthusiastic recognition of Carl Maria von Weber when he appeared as the first Adolar in *Euryanthe* (in 1823). He sang the tenor part in that memorable première of Beethoven's Ninth Symphony on 7th May 1824. His son of the same name, a lieutenant-general in the Imperial Austrian Army, inherited his father's

Schubertian style and became an even more successful singer. On Haizinger's death in 1893, Eduard Hanslick wrote an obituary in which he paid tribute to Haizinger's expressive tenor voice in songs like *Der Zwerg, Die Allmacht* or *Kriegers Ahnung*.

One of the first foreign champions of the Schubert-Lied was Adolphe Nourrit (1802–1839). As with Haizinger and Staudigl, the paternal talents were inherited by the son, who, here again, emulated the father. When Louis Nourrit retired from the Paris Opéra, Adolphe, his father's image both in looks and voice, followed in his footsteps, and was for twelve years the darling of the French public, singing all the great French baritone rôles and teaching at the Conservatoire as well. When a rival singer was engaged at the Opéra, this nervous, depressive artist asked to be released from his contract and embarked on ill-managed tours abroad. Enthusiastic receptions in the South of France, Belgium and Italy could not stave off his depressions, however, and, in 1839 just after a triumphant appearance in *Norma* in Naples, he threw himself out of a window. A gifted composer as well, Nourrit did a great deal to popularise Schubert's Lieder in France.

The German–Bohemian singer Eugen Gura (1842–1906) was a popular concert artist, especially in Loewe-ballads or Schubert-Lieder, such as *Greisengesang*. The Wagnerian singer, Ferdinand Jäger, was not only the prophet of Hugo Wolf, but also an enthusiastic Schubertian. Julius Stockhausen introduced Schubert's great song-cycles to the concert halls, as did the 'Swedish nightingale' Jenny Lind, who would sing the male Schubert songs with as little compunction as many lady singers after her. Fortunately such 'breeches-rôles' are no longer fashionable on the concert-hall platform. After making his name in oratorio and as a concert artist, Stockhausen, a fine baritone, became the teacher of generations of singers. His particular *forte* was the performance of complete song-cycles, where he always managed to put his technique at the service of the meaning of the work. This many-sided man was also well-known as a conductor; from 1862–1867, he directed the Philharmonic concerts and the Academy of Music in Hamburg. He was especially fond of Beethoven's *An die ferne Geliebte*, Schumann's *Dichterliebe* and Brahms's *Die schöne Magelone*, which is dedicated to him. He scored a great success with Schubert songs as early as 1854 in Vienna, and sang his beloved *Schöne Müllerin* for the first time complete, with Joseph Dachs, in 1857 and again, accompanied by Brahms, in Hamburg in 1861. Stockhausen's fame did not rest on a particularly powerful voice—Brahms's treatment of the vocal line in *Die schöne Magelone* speaks volumes here—but rather on his interpretative gifts, his artistic sensitivity, and his subtle technique, which he had partly learned from his father-like friend, Manuel Garcia. Hanslick wrote this about his *Schöne Müllerin* and Schubert-recital in 1854 in Vienna:

> It is difficult to decide in which of the songs this artist's soft, intimate style was most winning. The most impressive song was probably *Der Müller und der Bach* and the delicate 'Ich frage keine Blume' [Hanslick found the title *Der Neugierige* 'very inappropriate'. D. F-D.] In the field of the ballad, Herr Stockhausen sang the strangely eerie tragedy of Schubert's *Zwerg* with a restraint peculiarly applicable to this overwhelmingly beautiful composition.

And so the history of music can record the remarkable fact that Julius Stockhausen, once coloratura baritone at the Paris Opéra, became the quintessential German Lieder singer. He remained attached to Schubert's work to the end of his long life, making the *Schöne Müllerin* songs, in particular, popular throughout Germany, Austria and Switzerland, as well as in Britain and Russia (where Anton Rubinstein was his accompanist once in St Petersburg). In his retirement in Frankfurt, he handed on his love for, and understanding of, Schubert-Lieder to hundreds of singers.

Until his tragic end in a Viennese asylum, the bass of the Kärntnertortheater, Joseph Staudigl (1807–1861), was the apostle of *Der Wanderer*. His artistic talents were inherited by his son. The Viennese baritone Johann Nepomuk Beck (1827–1907) also put his highly dramatic voice at the service of the Schubert-Lied. Julius Stockhausen had first conceived the idea of a *Liederabend*, which meant originally *Schubert-Liederabend*. A sort of successor to Stockhausen's *Schöne Müllerin* interpretations were the Schubertiads of the Viennese Court opera tenor, Gustav Walter (1834–1910). Held in the Bösendorfersaal, these were enormously popular, although critics have attacked his rather sickly-sweet and exaggerated interpretation of songs like *Sei mir gegrüßt*. Stockhausen's pupil Karl Scheidemantel (1859–1923), Amfortas in the Bayreuth *Parsifal* of 1886, used

his powerful voice to effect in the bigger Schubert songs, in contrast to Raimund von zur Muehlen (1854–1931), a Baltic baron with
much more modest vocal means, who devoted himself eventually
entirely to the concert platform, and who, after an extremely successful career, gathered around him in East Prussia and England a great
horde of devoted pupils, who came from far and near. I myself felt
something of the fanaticism with which zur Muehlen fought for
truth of expression, from my own teachers, who had been through
his school, and who themselves were versatile Schubert interpreters: the oratorio tenor Georg A. Walter and the bass-baritone
Hermann Weissenborn.

The first Bayreuth Wotan, Franz Betz (1835–1900), sang Schubert
only infrequently and his interpretations were reputedly rather dry.
Nor was Alexander Heinemann, the Berlin Court opera singer,
heard very often in Schubert songs, but he could transfer his
mighty voice with astounding agility from the *forte* of *Die Allmacht*
into the *piano* of *Nacht und Träume*. Theodor Reichmann (1849–
1903), Bayreuth's first Amfortas, is said to have put his rivals in the
shade with his Schubert performances, when he could spare time
from the opera stage, where he was worshipped as Heiling,
Vampir, Tell, the Flying Dutchman or Hans Sachs. According to
witnesses still alive, the intensity of his interpretations of *Doppelgänger* or *Erlkönig* was unforgettable, even if he introduced such
unsanctioned mannerisms as the eerie exaggerated echo on the final
'war tot' ('was dead') of *Erlkönig*, an abomination still indulged in
occasionally nowadays, as, for example, in Lotte Lehmann's recording of the song. Pupils of the baritone Johannes Messchaert
(1857–1922) speak of his profoundly eloquent and fluid interpretations, particularly of Bach. He quite clearly probed more deeply
than any of those already mentioned into the special demands posed
by Schubert, and his programme-building, in particular, was an
example to many later singers. *An die Musik, Nacht und Träume,
Meeresstille*—these were models of his artistry. His bottom register
was particularly sonorous, so that he could be very convincing in
the final notes of *Der Wanderer* and *Der Tod und das Mädchen*. Like
his teacher, Stockhausen, this Dutch singer championed the seldom-
heard Schubert songs. Some Schubert interpretations of the tenor
Felix Senius (1868–1913), a frequent partner to Messchaert in performances of the Bach Passions, have been preserved on records.

In 1912 Viktor Heim revived the custom of holding Schubertiads. They were opened by a performance of *Die schöne Müllerin* in the Hölderichs-Mühle near Mödling in Vienna, which has, however, only legendary connections with the cycle. Otto Erich Deutsch gave the introductory address. *Winterreise*, *Schwanengesang* and countless other songs were heard at subsequent programmes. Like Heim, Hans Duhan (born 1890) devoted himself particularly to the cycles, being most successful in the more melancholy songs. Although famous in Mozartian operatic rôles, he also enjoyed singing the rare songs such as *Memnon, Heliopolis* or *Grenzen der Menschheit*, and he was the first to produce complete recorded versions of the song cycles.

The soft bass voice of Richard Mayr (1877–1935) was heard to best advantage in the darker songs. *Fahrt zum Hades, Greisengesang* and *Gruppe aus dem Tartarus* all took on a special magic in his intimate interpretation. His recording of *Grenzen der Menschheit*, however, can give little idea of how he really sounded. Leo Slezak (1873–1946), whose powerful voice made him better remembered as a *Heldentenor* than as a Lieder singer, did in fact make early recordings of excerpts from the *Schöne Müllerin* and *Winterreise*, and through all the sobbing and the sighing and the distortions of tempi, so distasteful to us today, one can sense his loving understanding of Schubert. In addition, the ease with which Slezak could coax the tiniest *piani* out of his mighty voice was astonishing. The velvety-smooth bass-baritone voice of Josef von Manowardas (1890–1942), who became a diplomat and philosopher, was also very impressive in Schubert songs.

The individuality of Paul Bender (1875–1947), the bass from the Munich Opera and the Metropolitan in New York, can be heard on his few surviving recordings. He mastered the dark masculinity of *Prometheus, Der Zwerg, An Schwager Kronos* and *Grenzen der Menschheit* as effectively as the playfulness of *Alinde* or *Geheimnis*. The rather dry voice of the reciter and actor Ludwig Wüllner (1858–1938) certainly made some of his musical 'interpretations' problematical, yet I myself was able to experience how moving and graceful the voiceless interpretation of a song like *Im Grünen* could be, when my father took me to a concert given by his friend Wüllner.

Outside German-speaking countries, the American David Bispham (1857–1921), first well-known as an operatic baritone, and then America's greatest oratorio singer, commands attention as a stylish singer of Schubert. After a varied career in music-hall, operetta, opera and oratorio, the British tenor John Coates (1865–1941) devoted himself intensively to the Schubert-Lied after 1914. Although he lost the heroic ring in his voice in later years, this did not prevent his giving *Liederabende* on the BBC when he was well over seventy—*and* introducing the programmes himself. Karl Erb is a parallel case in Germany.

One can turn from boxing to Lieder-singing too, as the Australian Peter Dawson (1882–1961) has proved. He began recording as early as 1904 and he eventually recorded over 3,000 titles, of which the majority were Lieder. He seldom appeared on the stage, and then only in minor rôles. Nor must we forget Sir George Henschel (1850–1934), a spiritual brother to Julius Stockhausen. Born in Breslau, he studied composition in Leipzig and Berlin, became a conductor and a concert-singer much praised by Brahms, who frequently accompanied him in recitals. He then became the first conductor of the Boston Symphony Orchestra before finally settling in London after 1884. His post as the conductor of the London Symphony Orchestra did not prevent his appearing in oratorios and giving Lieder recitals, where he generally accompanied himself, a practice followed earlier by Carl Loewe and later by Richard Bitterauf, the recently deceased *Heldenbariton*. George Henschel, knighted in 1914, was also a prolific composer. He preserved his voice well into old age, so that he was making recordings as late as 1928, which are now, however, rare collector's items.

Of the countless singers of the pre-World War I era, let me just mention Paul Knüpfer, Edward Lloyd, Franz Naval and Julius von Raatz-Brockmann. From this list of male singers, it will be clear how much more Schubert has to offer the male than the female voice, whereas there has never been any dearth of female singers of Schumann and Brahms. Yet there is enough that is essentially feminine in Schubert-Lieder to have sufficed to make other composers immortal. In fact, one is surprised at the limited Schubert repertoire of most female singers, since, after all, there are many songs reserved to them alone: the *Gretchenlieder*, *Suleika* I and II, Mignon's songs, those from Scott's *Lady of the Lake*, *Die junge Nonne*, *Berthas Lied in der Nacht*, Goethe's *Die Liebende schreibt*, the flower songs, the lullabies, two *chansons* of Seidl, *Des Mädchens*

Klage, and all the miniatures which could just as well be sung by women. But, of course, there have been superb female singers of Schubert as well, even in the days when opera singers only rarely gave Lieder recitals. The highly dramatic Marie Wilt, for example, whose interpretations were said to have the softest of colourings. (Born in 1833, she committed suicide in 1891.) The great, dramatic voice of Marianne Brandt from Vienna, effective in both the mezzo-soprano and soprano registers, was particularly suited to Wagnerian rôles, although she devoted herself later to Lieder. The career of the British contralto Clara Butt reminds one of that of her fellow-countrywoman, Kathleen Ferrier. Clara Butt's Lieder-singing conquered the world on her 1913 tour, and she was made a Dame in 1920. Her teacher, Etelka Gerster in Berlin, was likewise the teacher of the later world-famous Dutch singer, Julia Culp, who died as recently as 1970. One of the greatest interpreters of the Lied, Julia Culp began her career in Germany. As a Jew, she had to take refuge from the Gestapo during the German occupation of Amsterdam. Her skilful phrasing and subtle textual interpretation can still be admired on some of her records.

Discovered, trained and usually accompanied by Arthur Nikisch, Elena Gerhardt (1883–1961) very soon became a celebrated Schubert singer, having given up an operatic career in favour of Lieder. From 1903, the year of her first *Liederabend* in Leipzig, to her last recordings in 1953, she captivated her audiences by her refined interpretations and her inspired singing.

The Romanian contralto, Lula Mysz-Gmeiner, who studied under a succession of brilliant interpreters—Gustav Walter, Emilie Herzog, Etelka Gerster and Lilli Lehmann—should be mentioned here; she became a close collaborator of Raimund von zur Muehlen who, after 1911, helped her greatly on her successful career. Later, as professor at the Berlin Music Academy, she passed on her knowledge to countless pupils, among them the tenor Peter Anders, who married her daughter. Unfortunately, her only recordings are of lightweight Schubert songs, to which her dark-timbred voice does not really do justice.

It seems that the panorama of Schubert singers between the wars was greatly extended, an impression naturally supported by the large number of gramophone records preserved. On the periphery, rather, was the velvety voice of the American Negro, Marian

Anderson, who must be credited with opening up the world of the art-song to Negro singers.

From 1925 on, after her return from a tutoring post in Montevideo, until 1960, when she took up the post of professor at the Music Academy in Hamburg, Erna Berger charmed audiences with an extensive repertoire, which included unfamiliar songs, too. She revived many long-neglected Schubert songs, and some of these can be heard, not only on her records, but also on the German radio tape-recordings which she made with Sebastian Peschko.

The Parisian Pierre Bernac, accompanied by Francis Poulenc, did not confine himself exclusively to French works, but employed his high baritone to good effect in Schubert-Lieder too.

Karl Erb, a municipal clerk in Ravensburg, was self-taught, and, from 1907–1930, sang mainly *Heldentenor* rôles, until an accident forced him to concentrate on concert work, where he sang Bach's Evangelists as well as Schubert-Lieder. Even after he had turned seventy, he continued to sing in public and make records, whose richness of expression is something to marvel at.

In 1934, the contralto Lore Fischer gave her first recitals, accompanied on her extensive tours usually by her husband Rudolf Nel or by the composer Hermann Reutter.

Karl Hammes, a young baritone, was killed in World War II after only six years of what would have been a highly successful career.

The tenor Roland Hayes, the first world-famous Negro singer, displayed a sureness of style and a richness of nuance which made him much more than the most distinguished interpreter of Negro spirituals. After twenty years of the most exhausting study, he discovered Sir George Henschel for himself as a teacher, and sang for another thirty-five years, his Schubert style provoking great enthusiasm all over the world.

Hans Hotter's rising star led him to Schubert at the very outset of his career as a *Heldenbariton*. His powerful yet gentle voice, capable of the most astounding *pianissimo* colourings, helped revive many long-neglected Schubert songs. After 1945 too, together with Michael Raucheisen and Gerald Moore, he made many important recordings.

Equally at home in opera, Gerhard Hüsch, with his pianist Hans Udo Müller, dedicated himself in a uniquely penetrating way to the Schubert song-cycles. His recordings are now respected throughout the world as documents of their time, since we can now make a comparative assessment of their singular quality.

Herbert Janssen, the star of the New York Metropolitan Opera, was one of the fine Lieder interpreters of his generation, while the recordings of Alexander Kipnis, the Ukranian bass, display a far more 'theatrical' talent; Kipnis could act with his deep, heavy voice and yet still provide a 'modern' subjectivity in his interpretations.

Lotte Lehmann, a famous interpreter of Strauss operatic rôles, had a fresh and natural approach to the Schubert-Lied which occupied mainly the last six years of her professional life. Since her retirement she has been passing on her immense knowledge to pupils who come from all over the world to her home in Santa Barbara, California. She has also written books giving her views on the interpretations of Lieder, though it must be added that these views have not gone unchallenged.

The interpretations of the North German contralto Emmi Leisner proved an invaluable contribution to the development of the art of singing. She stressed the importance of being faithful to the work of art, and of the clearest possible interpretation of the poem. Her glorious dark voice was heard for only eight years in opera, and then she let music-lovers the world over enjoy her extensive repertoire, which included the Schubert songs for male voices. She was introduced to many of the Schubert rarities by the leading German accompanist of those days, Michael Raucheisen. He did the same for Tiana Lemnitz, the lyric soprano of the Berlin State Opera, whose sensitive treatment of Schober's flower-ballads (*Viola* and *Vergissmeinnicht*) is fortunately preserved on record, whereas none of Frau Leisner's Schubert performances have come down to us.

Lotte Leonard, the Hamburg soprano, gave typical twentieth-century interpretations of Lieder-singing before fleeing from Germany to France and then to America. The intensely emotional singing of the soprano Maria Müller, one of the mainstays of Bayreuth, could be a shattering experience for those who heard any of her infrequent Lieder recitals. Sigrid Hoffmann, who took her name from her composer-husband, Onegin, has left us recordings of Lieder which display a beautiful *bel canto* or, rather, beautiful sounds placed alongside one another. This makes it difficult for the listener to judge fairly her reputation for powerful and intensely expressive interpretations. Reports and ear-witnesses testify, how-ever, to the unique quality of her Lieder singing.

Schubert singing is also deeply indebted to the French baritone, Charles Panzera. He has an assured place in music-history, not only because Gabriel Fauré dedicated his song-cycle *L'horizon chimérique* to him, but also because he championed the Schubert-Lied (and the works of countless young composers) in France. One should mention his, the only, recording of *Erlkönig* with Hector Berlioz's orchestral accompaniment. The Austrian tenor, Julius Patzak, was a pupil of Mandyczewski and Franz Schmidt and an immensely gifted musician, who, apart from his unforgettable Palestrina in Pfitzner's opera of that name, was well-known as a Bach Evan-gelist, a Mozartian *bel canto* singer and a Schubert singer of a unique kind. Naturalness and spontaneity were his hallmarks.

A particular intensity of declamation, on the other hand, was the hallmark of the popular Munich baritone Heinrich Rehkemper, who also had a firm following outside Germany. His recordings with Michael Raucheisen reveal a vitality which counter-balances the rather heavy voice. His career was cut short by illness, as was that of the contralto Martha Rohs, who sang Lieder as convincingly as opera.

Measured by such performances, the Schubert style of the Russian bass Feodor Chaliapin, preserved for an astonished pos-terity in two recorded examples, can only be regarded as a curiosity. Even in those most emotional and, musically, most liberal days at the turn of the century, such exaggerations were normally avoided. The baritone voice of Theodor Scheidl, who was also an opera singer, had a more inward resonance. A similar heart-warming quality is found in the voice of the Silesian singer Hermann Schey, who emigrated to Holland, and who, by limiting himself to con-cert-singing, has managed to preserve his voice from the beginning of his career in 1922 to the present day.

The Danish singer Aksel Schiøtz made his début in 1938. Brain surgery in 1955 forced him to change his voice from tenor to bari-tone, and I was deeply impressed by the results of his courageous determination when I heard him accompanied by Gerald Moore. His enormous general knowledge and his work as a teacher led him to write a very interesting book on the interpretation of Lieder. The most popular Schubert singer in Germany in the '30s was probably Heinrich Schlusnus, who had a seductively beautiful voice. Nevertheless, the uncertainties in intonation and musical inaccuracies of which he was not infrequently guilty would make it difficult for him to satisfy present-day standards. His accompanists, Franz Rupp and Sebastian Peschko, were responsible for the rehabilitation of many Lieder.

Gerald Moore: to be fair to this King of Accompanists, a special chapter would have to be devoted to him, but that would go beyond the limits set for my book. It is in keeping with his pre-eminence that he is probably the only pianist in the world who has played *every* Schubert-Lied. His feeling for rhythm is perhaps the major feature of his work, and no Schubert interpretation can do without that. But he is also a master of the art of *legato*-playing and this, along with his empathetic understanding of the poem, make him an almost ideal partner in solving even the most complicated technical problems posed by Schubert. One soloist among the many who also accompanied singers should be mentioned here: Artur Schnabel, a fascinating accompanist in Schubert. The few extant recordings of him and his wife, Theresa Behr-Schnabel, a pupil of Stockhausen and Etelka Gerster, testify to the intensity of his accompanying, which also allows one to overlook the occasional vocal weaknesses of the contralto.

Among the first of the singers who sang Schubert in the modern, textually accurate manner was Karl Schmitt-Walter, the baritone of the German Opera in Berlin. No one who heard it can ever forget his *Winterreise* with Ferdinand Leitner at the piano. (At that time, Leitner was still an accompanist.) Friedrich Schorr, that incomparable Hans Sachs, usually chose seldom-heard songs for his rare excursions to the concert platform, but he enriched the art of song as much as his Austrian colleague, the coloratura soprano, Lotte Schöne, whose bell-like voice is preserved on many highly successful records. With a not dissimilar voice, but with an incomparably more refined diction and emotional content, Elisabeth Schumann, from Thuringia, accompanied either by her husband, Karl Alwin, or by Gerald Moore, made her *Liederabende* the star attraction of the concert season in all the world's capitals.

His incredible popularity as an operetta singer has overshadowed Richard Tauber's fame as an opera and Lieder singer. Even today, his sure intonation and his musicality make his early recordings quite distinguished, e.g. the selections from the *Winterreise* [made by HMV for the 1928 Schubert centenary. Ed.]. However, his contribution to the success of the record run of *Lilac Time* cannot evoke a similar enthusiasm.

After the reawakening from the catastrophe of World War II, the variety of possible Schubert interpretations and individual styles of performance has been still further extended. Even to name all of those who have interpreted Schubert on the concert platform would be impossible, but, beside my own efforts, I should like to mention here the most distinguished performers, whose recordings are now so freely and substantially available that any interested listener is in a position to form his or her own judgement.

Elly Ameling, Peter Anders, Victoria de los Angeles, Walter Berry, Kim Borg, Grace Bumbry, Anton Dermota, Mattiwilda Dobbs, Helen Donath, Kieth Engen, Kathleen Ferrier, Nicolai Gedda, Agnes Giebel, Josef Greindl, Elisabeth Grümmer, Horst Günter, Ernst Haefliger, Waldemar Kmentt, Werner Krenn, Erika Köth, Anneliese Kupper, Richard Lewis, Walther Ludwig, Jessye Norman, Peter Pears, Hermann Prey, Leontyne Price, Heinz Rehfuss, Anneliese Rothenberger, Elisabeth Schwarzkopf, Irmgard Seefried, Martial Singher, Gerard Souzay, Eleanor Steber, Rita Streich, Eberhard Wächter, William Warfield, Lawrence Winters, Fritz Wunderlich. So many names, so many temperaments, so many musical associations! They bring to mind Karl Straub's remark: 'The whole truth is always with us, but we recognise only that part of the truth, which, according to our temperament, is accepted by and absorbed into our own understanding.' Built into the subjective nature of a singer's conception of a song—and that is largely conditioned by the character of the singer's voice—and the ability to build up therefrom a whole world on a basic idea, is the magic of transforming dead notes on paper into a life of sound. Through their individual realisation of a Schubert-Lied, all the singers named above have wrought this transformation.

SEVENTEEN

Final Thoughts

One must assume that future generations will continue to be drawn to Schubert, which of course presupposes the presence of adequate interpreters. It is not enough to have recordings available which preserve the moment, the quality of the individual singer, but not the ever-new and living interpretation. The readiness of audiences to listen to Schubert's works will have to be kept alive, if not intensified, through knowledge and sympathy. Modern methods of communication offer the most favourable opportunities for this, even if the structure of our concert-going activities were to be radically altered. If we are to be condemned to live with the unmusical rubbish that a predominantly materialistic society and its alienated individuals seem to deserve, then it could become more and more essential that we look out for these signposts which show the way to Schubert and the other great composers.

These point precisely to those places that the world is seeking after two destructive wars. They do not represent the so-called 'sane world' (*heile Welt*), but rather the lost objectives of all art. It may sound absurd to say that the hope of stimulating increased intellectual interest among musicians and listeners may well rest with such purely commercial ventures as are represented by certain collected editions of authors and composers. In the case of Schubert, however, we must think of such helpmates, if we are ever going to discover his true legacy, and one would wish young singers would take more interest than hitherto in the neglected Lieder, to enlarge the scope of their programmes and to experiment with new ideas, a sort of dramaturgy of the *Liederabend*. This in turn will liberate audiences from their conventional demand for what is familiar.

Let me mention here just a few of the ideas that are always being discussed among musicians: we want to introduce a transitional stage in order to win over a wider concert audience. After all the cacophony, we want to find our way back to peace and quiet. Even in the pop-mentality of the moment, we want to rediscover a little yearning, we want to rediscover the lost unity of melody, the melodic 'non-decadence' that Nietzsche was seeking. Even amid the distortion of our age, we want to be able to find that joy which can keep the spirit of art alive and which enables it to transform itself again and again.

Such a programme of theses may sound less pretentious if we are made aware that the rejection of Romanticism, declared obsolete by later nineteenth-century thinkers, has since been replaced by a recognition of its central position in the history of music. The defiant reaction of, firstly, 'new classicism', then 'new objectivity' and other literary adventures were taken *ad absurdum*, for they only helped to reawaken a nostalgia for the past century. The destruction of the musical substance and the excitation to new heights of ugliness led to disappointment and rigidity. Will we ever be able to communicate with each other again? Will we ever rediscover musical structures which can be listened to, played and therefore understood?

Schubert, above all others, makes one realise again and again how essential melody is to the art of musical invention. Will musical theorists ever pluck up enough courage to admit the impossibility of making music *without* melody?

Many questions indeed—and they were posed in the full awareness that the Wheel of Art can never be turned back. Perhaps, in this era of creative stagnation, which is trying to find new meanings mainly by restructuring old forms, the Lied can salvage something for the future, which might help us to gather the shattered pieces together again.

Granted, there are only certain moments, even in the music of Schubert, who is all love, which do not demand concentrated attention. But when the musical qualities of unknown songs are revealed, our historical awareness comes into play and we do justice to the works. Even though the nineteenth century as a whole has not remained a *terra incognita* in Hermann Abert's sense of the term, this is unfortunately not the case with the Schubert-Lied. We remember, and we study, so many peripheral composers and their works—the second major composer of the century must make do with being understood, at the most, by specialists.

To change this situation was the intention of this modest contribution. Of course, the pre-eminent position once enjoyed by vocal music on the concert platform can never be recaptured. On the other hand, the absolute dominance of instrumental music continued into our age has distorted one's impression of our musical heritage. And that even in the case of Schubert, whose song *œuvre*, because of its enormous volume, still accounts for a comparatively high number of items in programmes of Lieder. One thing is certain: If in the future there are to be listeners with a sensitivity for art—and always assuming that we are talking about communication between interpreters and audiences at the highest level—then the musical setting of a poem by a master's hand will always remain an incomparable experience.

SELECT BIBLIOGRAPHY

ABRAHAMS, Gerald (ed.): *Schubert: A Symposium*. London 1947.

BIEHLE, Herbert: *Schuberts Lieder als Gesangsproblem*. Langensalza 1929.

BROWN, Maurice J. E.: *Schubert. A Critical Biography*. London 1958.

——*Essays on Schubert*. London 1966.

BÜCKEN, Ernst: *Das deutsche Lied. Probleme und Gestalten*. Hamburg 1939.

CAPELL, Richard: *Schubert's Songs*. 2nd rev. ed., London 1957.

DAHMS, Walter: *Schubert*. Leipzig 1912.

DE CURZON, Henri: *Les Lieder de Franz Schubert*. Paris 1899.

DEUTSCH, Otto Erich: *Die Originalausgaben von Schuberts Goetheliedern. Ein musikbibliographischer Versuch*. Vienna 1926.

——*Franz Schubert. Die Dokumente seines Lebens und Schaffens*. 3 vols. Munich and Leipzig 1913–1914.

——*Schubert. A Documentary Biography* (translated Eric Blom). London 1946; New York 1947 as *A Schubert Reader*.

——*Schubert: Memoirs by his Friends* (trans. Rosamund Ley and John Nowell), London, 1958.

——*Schubert. Thematic Catalogue of his Works*. London 1951.

EINSTEIN, Alfred: *Schubert* (translated David Ascoli). London 1951.

FEIL, Arnold: *Franz Schubert*. Stuttgart 1975.

FRIEDLÄNDER, Max: *Franz Schubert. Skizze seines Lebens und Wirkens*. Leipzig 1928.

GAL, Hans: *Franz Schubert oder die Melodie*. Frankfurt 1970, English edn. 1974.

GALLET, Maurice: *Schubert et le Lied*. Paris 1907.

GEORGIADES, Thrasybulos: *Schubert: Musik und Lyrik*. Göttingen 1967.

GOLDSCHMIDT, Harry: *Franz Schubert. Ein Lebensbild*. Berlin 1954.

HOECKER, Karla: *Wege zu Schubert*. Regensburg 1940.

HUTCHINGS, Arthur: *Schubert*. 4th ed., London 1973.

JELINEK, Walter: *Schubert und die poetische Lyrik seiner Klavierlieder*. Vienna 1939.

KOLB, Annette: *Franz Schubert. Sein Leben*. Erlenbach/Zürich 1947.

KREISSLE VON HELLBORN, Heinrich: *Franz Schubert*. Vienna 1865.

LAFITE, Carl: *Das Schubertlied und seine Sänger*. Vienna 1928.

LIESS, Andreas: *Johann Michael Vogl*. Graz/Cologne 1954.

MIES, Paul: *Schubert, der Meister des Liedes*. Bern 1928.

MOORE, Gerald: *The Schubert Song Cycles*. London 1975.

MOSER, Hans Joachim: *Das deutsche Lied seit Mozart*. 2 vols. Berlin 1937.

PAUMGARTNER, Bernhard: *Franz Schubert*. Zürich 1943–1947.

VON DER PFORDTEN, Hermann: *Franz Schubert und das deutsche Lied*. Leipzig 1916.

PORTER, Ernest G.: *Schubert's Song Technique*. London 1961.

REED, John: *The Final Years*. London 1972.

REHBERG, Walter and Paula: *Franz Schubert. Leben und Werk*. Zürich 1946.

ROSENWALD, Hans Hermann: *Geschichte des deutschen Liedes zwischen Schubert und Schumann*. Berlin 1930.

SCHNAPPER, Edith: *Die Gesänge des jungen Schubert vor dem Durchbruch des romantischen Liedprinzips*. Bern 1937.

SCHUBERT, Franz: *Werke*. Serie 20: Lieder und Gesänge. 10 vols. Leipzig 1894–1895.

——*Neue Ausgabe sämtlicher Werke*. (8 series in 60 vols. Bärenreiter, 1964– Lieder: Series 4, Vol. 6, 1969– .)

——*Lieder*. Published by Max Friedländer, 7 vols. Leipzig 1871–1887.

SCHULZ, Helmut: *Johann Vesque von Püttlingen*. Regensburg 1930.

SCHWARMATH, Erdmute: *Musikalischer Bau und Sprachvertonung in Schuberts Liedern*. Tutzing, W. Germany 1969.

VON SPAUN, Josef: *Erinnerungen an Schubert*. Berlin 1936.

STEFAN, Paul: *Franz Schubert*. Vienna 1928. Rev. ed. 1947.

STUDER-WEINGARTNER, Carmen: *Franz Schubert. Sein Leben und sein Werk*. Olten, Switzerland 1947.

VETTER, Walther: *Der Klassiker Schubert*. 2 vols. Leipzig 1953.

WERLÉ, Heinrich: *Franz Schubert in seinen Briefen und Aufzeichnungen*. 4th ed., Leipzig 1955.

Indexes

SONG TITLES

The dates given here accord with those established by
Maurice J. E. Brown

Abendbilder 1819 (Silbert) 119
Abendlied 1815 (Stolberg) 68
Abendlied 1816 (Claudius) 86–7
Abendlied der Fürstin 1816 (Mayrhofer) 77
Abendlied für die Entfernte 1825 (A. W. Schlegel) 231
Abendröte 1823 (Fr. Schlegel) 124
Abendstern 1824 (Mayrhofer) 193–4
Abschied (nach einer Wallfahrtsarie) 1816 (Mayrhofer) 76–7
Abschied, from 'Schwanengesang' 1828 (Rellstab) 279, 292
Abschied von der Erde, Melodrama (Pratobevera) 110
Abschied von einem Freunde 1817 (Schubert) 104–5
Adelaide 1814 (Matthisson) 29, 30, 68, 165
Adelwold und Emma 1815 (Bertrand) 40
Alinde 1827 (Rochlitz) 247, 307
Allein nachdenklich 1818 (Petrarch) 114–15
Als ich sie erröten sah 1815 (Ehrlich) 54
Alte Liebe rostet nie 1816 (Mayrhofer) 77
Amalia 1815 (Schiller) 41, 68–9
Am Bach im Frühling 1816 (Schober) 84
Am Erlafsee 1817 (Mayrhofer) 26
Am ersten Maimorgen 1816 (Claudius) 136, 289
Am Feierabend, from 'Die schöne Müllerin' 1823 (Müller) 178
Am Fenster 1826 (Seidl) 237–8
Am Flusse 1815 and 1822 (Goethe) 53, 161, 167–8
Am Grabe Anselmos 1816 (Claudius) 86, 207, 293, 294–5
Am Meer, from 'Schwanengesang' 1828 (Heine) 7, 169, 281, 292
Amphiaraos 1815 (Körner) 25
Am See 1814 (Mayrhofer) 31–2
Am See 1823 (Bruchmann) 159
An Chloen 1816 (Uz) 72
An den Frühling 1815 (Schiller) 41
Andenken 1814 (Matthisson) 30
An den Mond 1815 and 1816 (Goethe) 44, 45, 52–3, 62
An den Mond 1815 and 1816 (Hölty) 58–9, 60
An den Mond in einer Herbstnacht 1818 (Schreiber) 112–13
An den Tod 1817 (Schubart) 106, 107–8, 207
An die Apfelbäume 1815 (Hölty) 59
An die Entfernte 1822 (Goethe) 161–2
An die Freude 1815 (Schiller) 194
An die Freunde 1819 (Mayrhofer) 120–1, 253
An die Laute 1827 (Rochlitz) 247
An die Leier 1822 (Bruchmann) 186–7
An die Musik 1817 (Schober) 76, 83, 246, 306
An die Nachtigall 1816 (Claudius) 87
An die Natur 1816 (Stolberg) 68
An die untergehende Sonne 1816 (Kosegarten) 57, 74
An eine Quelle 1817 (Claudius) 87
An Emma 1814 (Schiller) 28

An Laura 1814 (Matthisson) 30
An mein Clavier 1816 (Schubart) 108
An mein Herz 1825 (Schulze) 223, 227
An Mignon 1815 (Goethe) 61, 208
An Rosa, I und II 1815 (Kosegarten) 56
An Schwager Kronos 1816 (Goethe) 4, 63–4, 101, 150, 208, 216, 296, 307
An Sie 1815 (Klopstock) 46
An Sylvia ('Was ist Sylvia?') 1826 (Shakespeare) 233, 254
Antigone und Oedip 1817 (Mayrhofer) 96
Apollo, lebet noch dein hold Verlangen 1818 (Petrarch) 114
Auf dem See 1817 (Goethe) 89, 289
Auf dem Strome 1828 (Rellstab) 274
Auf dem Wasser zu singen 1823 (Stolberg) 188–9, 292
Auf den Tod einer Nachtigall 1816 (Hölty) 59, 207
Auf der Bruck 1825 (Schulze) 234
Auf der Donau 1817 (Mayrhofer) 97, 98
Auf der Riesenkoppe 1818 (Körner) 26
Auf einen Kirchhof 1815 and 1820 (Schlechta) 74, 207
Aufenthalt, from 'Schwanengesang' 1828 (Rellstab) 278–9, 292
Auflösung 1824 (Mayrhofer) 192
Augenlied 1817 (Mayrhofer) 94–5, 243

Bei dem Grabe meines Vaters 1816 (Claudius) 126
Bei dir allein 1826 (Seidl) 238
Berthas Lied in der Nacht 1819 (Grillparzer) 117, 308
Blanka 1818 (Fr. Schlegel) 124
Blondel zu Marien 1818 (anon) 113
Blume und Quell 1826 (Schulze) 228
Bundeslied 1815 (Goethe) 44, 62

Danksagung an den Bach, from 'Die schöne Müllerin' 1823 (Müller) 178
Daphne am Bach 1816 (Stolberg) 68
Das Abendrot 1818 (Schreiber) 112
Das Bild 1815 (anon.) 37
Das Echo 1827 (Castelli) 240
Das Fischermädchen, from 'Schwanengesang' 1828 (Heine) 247, 280, 292
Das Geheimnis 1815 and 1823 (Schiller) 41, 189
Das gestörte Glück 1815 (Körner) 26
Das Grab 1816 (Salis) 65, 207, 289
Das große Halleluja 1816 (Klopstock) 126
Das Heimweh 1825 (Pyrker) 215–16
Das Lied im Grünen 1827 (Reil) 246–7
Das Lied vom Reifen 1817 (Claudius) 103
Das Mädchen 1819 (Fr. Schlegel) 122
Das Mädchen aus der Fremde 1814 (Schiller) 34
Das Mädchen von Inistore 1815 (Ossian, trans. Harold) 56
Das Marienbild 1818 (Schreiber) 112, 126